The Spanish Republic and Civil War

JULIÁN CASANOVA
Translated by Martin Douch

CAMBRIDGE
UNIVERSITY PRESS

CAMBRIDGE UNIVERSITY PRESS
Cambridge, New York, Melbourne, Madrid, Cape Town, Singapore,
São Paulo, Delhi, Dubai, Tokyo, Mexico City

Cambridge University Press
The Edinburgh Building, Cambridge CB2 8RU, UK

Published in the United States of America by Cambridge University Press, New York

www.cambridge.org
Information on this title: www.cambridge.org/9780521737807

© Cambridge University Press 2010

Originally published in Spanish as *Historia de España, vol. VIII:
República y guerra civil* by Crítica 2007 © Crítica 2007

First published in English by Cambridge University Press 2010 as
The Spanish Republic and Civil War © Julián Casanova 2010
English Translation © Julián Casanova 2010

Printed in the United Kingdom at the University Press, Cambridge

A catalogue record for this publication is available from the British Library

Library of Congress Cataloging in Publication data
Casanova, Julián.
    [República y guerra civil. English]
    The Spanish Republic and Civil War / Julián Casanova ; translated
by Martin Douch.
        p.   cm.
    "Originally published in Spanish as Historia de España,
vol. VIII: República y guerra civil by Crítica, 2007."
    Includes bibliographical references and index.
    ISBN 978-0-521-49388-8 – ISBN 978-0-521-73780-7 (pbk.)
    1. Spain – History – Republic, 1931–1939.   2. Spain – Politics
and government – 1931–1939.   3. Social conflict – Spain – History – 20th
century.   4. Spain – History – Civil War, 1936–1939 – Causes.
    5. Spain – History – Civil War, 1936–1939.   I. Title.
    DP254.C32713   2010
    946.081–dc22   2010021901

ISBN 978-0-521-49388-8 Hardback
ISBN 978-0-521-73780-7 Paperback

Contents

Maps

Chronology

| 1875–1923 | Constitutional monarchy |
| 1923: 13 September | *Pronunciamiento* by Primo de Rivera. |

1930

28 January	Overthrow of Primo de Rivera.
17 August	Meeting of republican leaders in San Sebastián. They agree to form a revolutionary committee.
10 October	The *Partido Socialista* joins the revolutionary committee.
12 December	An unsuccessful uprising in Jaca. Captains Galán and García Hernández are shot.

1931

| 12 April | Municipal elections. Republican victory. |

THE REPUBLIC

14 April	Proclamation of the Republic and exile of the King.
7 May	Pastoral letter by Cardinal Segura lauding the Monarchy.
10–11 May	Burning of monasteries and convents.
May–June	Decrees on secular education, social and employment reforms.
3 June	Announcement of elections for the Constituent Cortes.
16 June	Azaña issues the first set of decrees regarding the reform of the army.
28 June	Elections for the Constituent Cortes.

14 July	Opening of the Cortes; closure of the General Military Academy in Zaragoza. Its director was Francisco Franco.
9–14 October	Debate on Article 26 of the Constitution, regarding religious orders; resignation of Niceto Alcalá Zamora, head of the provisional government of the Republic; Manuel Azaña, Prime Minister.
December	Founding of the JONS.
9 December	Passing of the Constitution, the first republican Constitution in Spain's history. Niceto Alcalá Zamora is elected President of the Republic.
31 December	Assassination of Civil Guards in Castilblanco.

1932

January	Dissolution of the Company of Jesus; implementation of the divorce law; secularisation of cemeteries.
5 January	The Civil Guard kills eleven people during a demonstration in Arnedo (La Rioja).
20–27 January	Rising in the Llobregat coalfield; general strikes called by the CNT.
10 August	Revolt by General Sanjurjo against the Republic.
September	Statute of Catalonia and Agrarian Reform Acts.

1933

January	Anarchist revolt in Casas Viejas (Cádiz).
1 March	Founding of *Renovación Española*, an ultra-right monarchist group.
17 May	Religious Confessions and Congregations Act.
4–5 September	Defeat of the government in elections to the Guarantees Tribunal. Alcalá Zamora dismisses Manuel Azaña.
9 October	Dissolution of the Constituent Cortes.
29 October	José Antonio Primo de Rivera founds the *Falange Española* party in Madrid.
19 November	Centre right wins the elections; Alejandro Lerroux, Prime Minister.
8–11 December	Anarchist risings in Catalonia and Aragon.

1934

February	The *Falange* merges with the JONS.
5–11 June	Strike by agricultural workers in Andalusia and Extremadura.
1 October	Lerroux governs with three CEDA ministers, the grass-roots organisation of the Catholic right.
6 October	Rising in Catalonia and Asturias; state of war declared; the Foreign Legion and Moorish troops sent to Asturias.

1935

7 May	Gil Robles, leader of the CEDA, Minister of War.
29 October	Lerroux forced to resign following the *estraperlo* corruption scandal; short-lived centrist governments.

1936

7 January	Dissolution of the Cortes.
15 January	Electoral pact and platform of the *Frente Popular*, under the leadership of republicans and socialists.
16 February	Elections won by the *Frente Popular*.
19 February	Azaña government; amnesty of political prisoners.
13 March	Failed Falangist attempt to assassinate Jiménez de Asúa, one of the fathers of the Constitution.
15 March	The *Falange* declared illegal; arrest of José Antonio Primo de Rivera.
7 April	The Cortes dismisses Alcalá Zamora as President of the Republic.
10 May	Azaña, President of the Republic.
12 May	The republican Casares Quiroga becomes Prime Minister after the post was refused by the socialist, Indalecio Prieto.
12 July	Assassination of the Assault Guard, Castillo and, a day later, Calvo Sotelo, leader of *Renovación Española*.
17–20 July	*Pronunciamiento* in Morocco and the Peninsula.

CIVIL WAR

20 July	The republican José Giral forms a government; the government appeals to France; Franco sends emissaries to Italy and Germany.
27 July	Seville under control of the rebels; reinforcements flown in from Morocco.
28–30 July	Italian and German aircraft arrive in Morocco and Seville; outdated French aircraft go to Madrid.
8 August	Closing of the French border; unilateral declaration of non-intervention.
24 August	Italy, Germany and Portugal accept non-intervention 'in principle'.
4 September	The socialist Largo Caballero leads a government with republicans, socialists and Communists.
7 September	Aguirre forms the Basque government, supporting the Republic.
9 September	First meeting of the Non-Intervention Committee in London.
27 September	Government of the *Generalitat* of Catalonia, with *Esquerra*, the PSUC and the POUM; anarchist participation.
28 September	The rebels seize Toledo.
1 October	The republican Cortes passes the Basque Statute; in the other camp, Franco is designated *Generalísimo* and supreme head of the military rebels.
6 October	The Soviets declare that they will feel no more bound by non-intervention than Germany, Italy and Portugal do.
24 October	First Russian tanks in action; Russian officers arrive in Madrid; German and Italian aircraft bomb the capital.
4 November	The anarchists, in a historic move, join Largo Caballero's government.
6 November	Worried that the Nationalists will take Madrid, the republican government transfers to Valencia.
8 November	General attack against Madrid; arrival of the International Brigades.

| 18 November | Attack on Madrid suspended; Germany and Italy recognise Franco's government in Burgos. |
| 20 November | José Antonio Primo de Rivera, leader of the Fascist FE JONS, is executed in Alicante. |

1937

10 February	The Nationalists take Málaga.
6–15 February	Battle of the Jarama.
8–18 March	Battle of Guadalajara.
19 April	Franco orders the merging of the *Falange* and Carlists, giving rise to the single party, FET-JONS.
26 April	Bombing of Guernica.
3–8 May	Barricades and political fighting, with several hundreds of deaths, in Barcelona.
17 May	Dismissal of Largo Caballero; a new government under the socialist Juan Negrín.
16 June	Arrest of POUM leaders, accused of provoking the events of May in Barcelona; disappearance of its leader, Andreu Nin.
19 June	The Nationalists take Bilbao.
1 July	Collective letter by the Spanish bishops supporting the civil war as a religious crusade.
7–26 July	Battle of Brunete.
24 August–15 September	Battles of Belchite and Quinto.
26 August	The Nationalists take Santander.
19 October	The Nationalists seize Gijón.
31 October	The Negrín government transfers to Barcelona.

| 14 December | The beginning of the Teruel offensive, which the republicans take – the only provincial capital they were able to seize during the war. |

1938

22 February	The Nationalists recapture Teruel.
9 March	Beginning of the Nationalist offensive in Aragon.
5 April	Reshuffle in Negrín's government; Prieto resigns as Minister of Defence.
15 April	The Nationalists arrive at the Mediterranean.
24 July	Start of the Battle of the Ebro.
15 November	Retreat from the Ebro; farewell parade to the International Brigades.
23 December	Nationalist offensive in Catalonia.

1939

15 January	The Nationalists seize Tarragona.
26 January	Occupation of Barcelona.
4 February	Occupation of Gerona and mass withdrawal to the French border; the Nationalists end their occupation of Catalonia.
13 February	Nationalist Political Responsibilities Act, the principal repressive law of Franco's dictatorship.
27 February	France and the United Kingdom recognise the Burgos government; Azaña resigns.
7–11 March	Communist revolt in Madrid against Negrín's government, which hastens the end of the Republic.
28 March	The Nationalists enter Madrid.
1 April	Total surrender of the republican army. Official end of the Civil War.

Introduction

Until the beginning of the Second Republic, Spanish society seemed to have managed to avoid the problems and troubles that had beset most other European countries since 1914. Spain had not taken part in the First World War, and therefore had not undergone the upheaval that this war had caused, with the fall of empires and their subjects, the demobilising of millions of ex-combatants and massive debt caused by the vast spending on the war effort.

The Spanish Monarchy was overthrown not by a war, but by its inability to provide the Spanish with a smooth transition from an oligarchic and cacique-style regime to one of reform and democracy. The fall of Primo de Rivera's dictatorship on 28 January 1930, in power from September 1923, led to a process of political radicalisation and an upswing in republicanism. This surge brought together old conservatives who had decided to abandon the King, lifelong republicans, new republicans, socialists who felt the need to influence the movement from the inside, and prominent intellectuals. Together they made a commitment to prepare the uprising against the Monarchy and to implement the Republic.

The insurrectional approach, with its long history of setting the military against politicians, failed in Jaca in December 1930. Just four months later, the local elections of 12 April were turned into a plebiscite between Monarchy and republicanism. It was soon clear that the republicans had won in most of the provincial capitals. Admiral Juan Bautista Aznar's government resigned, Alfonso XIII abdicated, and a good many cities and towns proclaimed the Republic on 14 April 1931.

By the end of that year, with Niceto Alcalá Zamora as President of the Republic and Manuel Azaña as Prime Minister, Spain was a parliamentary constitutional Republic. The first two years of the Republic were given over to the organisation of the army, the separation of Church and State, and the implementation of comprehensive radical measures with regard to land distribution, workers' wages, employment protection and public education. Never before had Spain experienced such an intense, rapid period of change and class conflict, democratic advances or social conquests.

But at the same time, republican legislation was responsible for bringing into the open some of the tensions that had been germinating during the previous two decades, with industrialisation, urban growth and class conflicts. This opened up a breach between various clashing cultural worlds, between practising Catholics and hard-line anticlericalists, bosses and workers, Church and State, order and revolution.

As a result of these clashes, the Republic had vast problems in consolidating itself and had to confront firm challenges from above and below. It went through two years of relative stability, followed by another two years of political uncertainty and a final few months of disturbance and insurrection. The first firm challenges, which were the most visible as they usually ended up as confrontations with the police, came from below, first as social protests and later as insurrections from anarchists and socialists. However, the coup de grâce, the challenge that finally overthrew the Republic with the force of arms, came from above and from within – that is to say, the military command and the powerful ruling classes that had never tolerated it.

The division of the army and police forces thwarted the victory of the military rebellion, as well as the achievement of their main objective: the rapid seizure of power. But by undermining the republican government's power to keep order, this coup d'état was transformed into open violence such as had never been seen before, by the groups that supported it and those that opposed it. It was July 1936 and thus began the civil war.

There were several distinct conflicts during this war. Firstly, a military conflict was initiated when the coup d'état buried political solutions, to replace them with arms. It was also a class war, between differing conceptions of social order; a war of religion, between Catholicism and anticlericalism; a war revolving around the idea of *patria* and nation; and a war of ideas, beliefs that were at the time at loggerheads on the international stage. It was a war that was impossible to reduce to a conflict between Communism and Fascism, or between Fascism and democracy. In short, the Spanish Civil War was a melting-pot of universal battles between bosses and workers,

Church and State, obscurantism and modernisation, settled in an international context that had been thrown out of balance by crises of democracies and the onslaught of Communism and Fascism.

The destruction of the opponent became the primary objective. The policy of extermination initiated by the military rebels was fervently supported by conservative sectors, landowners, the bourgeoisie, property owners and 'respectable people', who rejected once and for all the defence of their order via the law. Wherever the military coup was unsuccessful, it was time for the long-awaited revolution and the final judgement for the wealthy bosses. With no rules or government, with no mechanisms for forcing people to comply with laws, revenge and class hatred spread with a devastating force to wipe out the old order.

The Spanish Civil War has gone down in history, and in the memory that remains of it, for the way it dehumanised its adversaries and for the horrific violence that it generated. Symbolised by the *sacas*, *paseos* and mass killings, it served the two sides in their struggle to eliminate their respective enemies, whether natural or unforeseen. While carrying out this extermination, the rebels were also given the inestimable blessing of the Catholic Church from the very beginning. The clergy and sacred objects, however, were the prime target of popular rage, by those who took part in defeating the military rebels and who played leading roles in the 'popular terror' that took place in the summer of 1936. Thus, Catholic religion and anticlericalism were passionately included in the battle involving basic themes related to the organisation of society and the State that was being unleashed in Spanish territory.

The international situation at the end of the 1930s was hardly conducive to peace, and this played a decisive role in the duration, progress and final result of the Spanish Civil War, a conflict that was clearly internal in its origin. International support for both sides was vital for fighting and continuing the war during the early months. As the war progressed, non-interventionism, imbalances in the material resources of the two sides, the participation of Nazi Germany and Fascist Italy and, in most cases, the non-involvement of the western democracies were, together with disunity in the republican camp and unity among the Francoists, decisive factors in tipping the balance towards the final victory of the military rebels.

Spain began the 1930s with a Republic and finished the decade immersed in a right-wing authoritarian dictatorship. It only took three years of war for Spanish society to undergo a wave of violence and an unprecedented disdain for the lives of others. Despite all that has been said about the violence that preceded the civil war, in an attempt to justify its outbreak, it is clear that the coup d'état of July 1936 marked a watershed in twentieth-century Spanish history. Furthermore, for at least two decades after the end of the civil war in 1939, there was no positive reconstruction such as had occurred in other countries in western Europe after 1945.

The climate of order, *patria* and religion overrode that of democracy, the Republic and revolution. In this respect, there was not much difference between Spain and other European countries. In 1920, all but two (Bolshevik Russia and Hungary, under the right-wing dictator, Horthy) of the twenty-eight States in Europe could be described as democracies or as having restricted parliamentary systems. By the beginning of 1939, more than half of them, including Spain, had succumbed to dictators with absolute powers. Seven of the democracies that were left were dismantled between 1939 and 1940, after being invaded by the German army and incorporated into the new Nazi order, with France, Holland and Belgium being the most significant examples. By the end of 1940, only six democracies remained intact: the United Kingdom, Ireland, Iceland, Sweden, Finland and Switzerland.

But this should never be used as an excuse, a convenient argument for offloading the responsibilities of broad sectors of the Spanish population – the better-educated groups, the owner classes, the political and union leaders, the military and the Church – who did little to conform to the rules and respect the law or the election results, or to defend the freedoms of expression and association, or civil rights.

Thus there is no simple answer as to why the climate of euphoria and hope in 1931 was transformed into the cruel, all-destructive war of 1936. The Republic lasted for eight years, five in peace and three at war, and interpreting them still arouses passionate opinions rather than historical debate.

What I offer in this book is a history of the Republic and the Civil War, based on my own research and the large output of the best specialist historians of the period. I have examined the most significant events, drawn up an account with the main players in this fiesta that ended in tragedy, and have attempted to provide answers, without compromising the historian's constant quest for accuracy and truth, to some of the basic questions that a good many Spaniards have asked in the seventy years that have passed since the civil war. My personal view, the representation that I offer of those years of tumult, also appears explicitly at different stages of the account. The book's structure, the organisation of the chapters and their titles, are a component of this view. It is not a detached view, or one from somebody who has been commissioned to write a book. Neither can it be a dispassionate consideration, because I have spent over twenty years researching and revealing the darkest and most convoluted part of this past. It is left to the reader to judge whether this history contributes to a better understanding of these events.

PART I

Republic

1 | The winds of change

'The elections held last Sunday clearly show me that I do not have the love of my people today', wrote King Alfonso XIII in a farewell note to the Spanish people, before leaving the Royal Palace on the night of Tuesday 14 April 1931.

According to Miguel Maura, 'the Monarchy had committed suicide', so he, the son of Antonio Maura, former leader of the monarchist conservatives, had decided 'to join' the Republic almost a year before it was proclaimed, as he stated in an address in the *Ateneo* (literary society) in San Sebastián on 20 February 1930. Maura was joined by other distinguished monarchists who realised that it was better to defend 'legitimate conservative principles' within the Republic, rather than leaving 'the way clear' for the leftist parties and workers' organisations.[1] Nineteen-thirty was a year of noteworthy resignations of politicians who had hitherto been loyal to the Crown. José Sánchez Guerra, the former leader of the *Partido Conservador*, took this step in February, a few days after Miguel Maura. Niceto Alcalá Zamora, a liberal minister under Alfonso XIII, did so in April. In little more than a year – the period that spanned the fall of the military dictatorship of Miguel Primo de Rivera, which had seized power in September 1923, and the abdication of the King – hostility towards the Monarchy spread unchecked through the medium of meetings and demonstrations throughout Spain.

The death throes of the Monarchy

The first signs of the suicide of the Monarchy began to be seen in the last three years of Primo de Rivera's dictatorship, when his refusal to

---

[1] Miguel Maura, *Así cayó Alfonso XIII. De una dictadura a otra*, Ariel, Barcelona, 1966, p. 48.

return power to parliament, and the King's inability to force him to do so, reinforced people's perception that they were one and the same, and gave way to a period of plots and *pronunciamientos* to overthrow the dictatorship by military means. They did not succeed, but Primo de Rivera was put into a difficult position, with his credibility shattered. On 26 January 1930, he asked his Captains-General to express their confidence in him. As no one offered it, he resigned two days later.

The same day, 28 January 1930, Alfonso XIII asked General Dámaso Berenguer, head of his Military Household, to form a government, which was to include certain aristocrats who had the King's confidence and former politicians of the cacique system. Attempts to organise the political system, returning to the situation prior to the coup d'état of September 1923, failed because the dictatorship had destroyed the two parties on which the Restoration regime had been based for fifty years, the liberal and conservative parties, and had left Spain without a Constitution. That left the caciques and their network of clients and political friends in the rural world, but this, by 1930, was not enough to maintain order and constitutional normality.

Indeed, many things had changed in Spanish society during the first three decades of the twentieth century. The repatriation of capital after the colonial defeats of 1898 and Spain's neutrality in the First World War had prepared the way for the spectacular growth of the 1920s. This growth was mainly concentrated in areas that had already had an industrial infrastructure in the last quarter of the nineteenth century. The first of these was Barcelona and its area of influence, which experienced notable financial activity and greater industrial diversification, and where, despite the continued dominance of the textile sector, major new companies in the chemicals and metal sectors were being founded.

Much more marked and precipitate in the early decades of the twentieth century was the industrialisation of Bilbao and the Nervión estuary. As Vicente Blasco Ibáñez noted in *El intruso*, 'a forest of chimneys' sprang up there, with 'multicoloured smoke' that radically changed the landscape.[2] It was Spain's second most important industrialised area, more diversified than Catalonia, with insurance

---

[2] Vicente Blasco Ibáñez (1867–1928), writer, journalist and republican politician, published *El intruso*, an account of the social conflicts in Vizcaya, in 1904 (there is a recent edition in the Biblioteca Nueva, Madrid, 2000).

companies, chemical works, power stations, banks, machinery manufacture and, above all, steel companies.

The repatriation of capital, the effects of the Great War and the
building boom of the twenties had also left their mark in other cities
such as Madrid, Valencia, Seville and Zaragoza. These were industries of modest proportions – small workshops, never large factories,
mostly dependent on agriculture and building – but they changed the
face of these cities and enlarged their urban space.

All these cities doubled in population between 1900 and 1930.
Barcelona and Madrid, with over half a million inhabitants each in
1900, reached a million three decades later. Bilbao went from 83,000
to 162,000; Zaragoza from 100,000 to 174,000. Admittedly, these
populations are not particularly significant if we compare them to the
2.7 million in Paris in 1900, or the number of European cities, from
Birmingham to Moscow, including Berlin and Milan, whose populations were higher than Madrid's or Barcelona's in 1930. But the
demographic panorama was undergoing a notable change. The total
population of Spain, which was 18.6 million at the beginning of the
century, reached almost 24 million in 1930, due mainly to a sharp fall
in the death rate. Up to 1914, this demographic pressure had given rise
to a high rate of emigration, but from the First World War onwards, it
was Spanish cities that experienced mass immigration.

The surge of industry and the growth of the population transformed
the old-fashioned medieval cityscape that many Spanish cities still maintained at the end of the nineteenth century. Imbalances in this growth
were reflected in the social division of the cities. The new suburbs, built
to control chaotic growth in the inner cities, were where the middle
and business classes, traders, industrialists and well-to-do professional
people were concentrated. On the outskirts, around the factories, were
the working-class slums, and it was in these very districts and run-
down areas that diseases and epidemics originated. This was because
this urban growth also spawned speculation and get-rich-quick building schemes, with no thought for social justice or shared interests.

This urban explosion, and its accompanying social disparities, also
saw the germination of the seeds of republicanism, anarchism and
socialism, seeds that had been sown in the last third of the nineteenth
century. They germinated in response to the solid dominant social
block, which was made up of the heirs of the old privileged classes,
the aristocracy and the Catholic Church, as well as the rural and

Basque and Catalan industrial oligarchy. From this block came most of those who governed in the corrupt pseudo-parliamentary system that had held sway in Spain between 1875 and 1923, the system that had excluded, either through restricted suffrage or electoral fraud, what began to be called 'the *pueblo*', the urban proletariat, craftsmen, small industrialists and traders, and the middle classes, which many people termed 'the bourgeoisie', but who in fact earned their living from their professions, independently of the capitalist business concerns. Many of these professionals became republicans in the final years of Primo de Rivera's dictatorship.

The fall of the dictatorship effectively caused a sudden process of politicisation and a surge in republicanism, which had hitherto been weak, incapable as it was of breaking the stranglehold of the caciques and of suggesting real alternatives. Various republican sectors had already joined to form a Republican Alliance in 1926, which took its lead from Alejandro Lerroux's old *Partido Radical* and from a new group, *Acción Republicana*, led by Manuel Azaña, which had broken with Melquíades Álvarez's reformists in 1923. The extreme left wing of this new republican initiative was occupied by the *Partido Republicano Radical Socialista*, founded at the end of 1929 by two *Alianza Republicana* dissidents, Marcelino Domingo and Álvaro de Albornoz. The right was catered for by the *Derecha Liberal Republicana*, founded in July 1930 by Niceto Alcalá Zamora and Miguel Maura, the most legitimate representatives of the monarchist sector that embraced the republican cause following the fall of Primo de Rivera's dictatorship.

In just a few months, the old form of republicanism, made up of small discussion groups, transformed into a movement of various political parties, with recognised leaders and new social foundations. Among these names were conservatives and Catholics, such as Maura and Alcalá Zamora, passionate defenders of anticlericalism, such as Álvaro de Albornoz, as well as nationalists in *Esquerra Republicana de Catalunya*, such as Francesc Macià and Lluís Companys, or the Galician *Organización Republicana Gallega Autónoma*, led by Santiago Casares Quiroga. Together, despite their noticeable differences in ideology and principles, they formed a comprehensive republican coalition, which came into being on 17 August 1930 in San Sebastián.

From what was known as the San Sebastián pact emerged the revolutionary committee that made a commitment to channel the demands for autonomy by the Catalans, to prepare an uprising against the Monarchy and to proclaim a Republic. The meeting in San Sebastián was attended by the socialist Indalecio Prieto, 'on his own behalf', without representing anyone, since the dominant feeling in the *Partido Socialista Obrero Español* (PSOE) and in the *Unión General de Trabajadores* (UGT) was one of complete lack of confidence in any chance of taking joint action in league with the republicans.

The republicans insisted that the proposed revolution needed the socialists, although Julián Besteiro's dissent and the numerous doubts expressed by Francisco Largo Caballero delayed any commitment by the PSOE and UGT until October 1930. Several conversations and meetings were needed between the republicans (represented by Alcalá Zamora and Azaña) and the socialists (with Largo Caballero, Besteiro and Fernando de los Ríos) to solve the dilemma facing the socialists and the UGT syndicalists: either stand back or join in the call for a Republic. An essential factor at that point was the attitude of Largo Caballero, who ended up convinced that the socialists had to help the republicans 'to have an influence' from within 'on the orientation of the revolution', and thus enable a peaceful and gradual move towards socialism. As Santos Juliá has pointed out, the same arguments that Largo Caballero used to commit the UGT to participating in the corporatist system of Primo de Rivera's dictatorship served him in the autumn of 1930 'to [persuade them to] follow the path leading to the Republic'.[3]

The decision was taken at the meeting of the executive committee of the *Partido Socialista* on 20 October of that year; it was decided, by eight votes to six, to accept the three posts the republicans had offered them on the revolutionary committee and to 'call a general strike wherever there were committed elements so that, as soon as they found themselves on the streets, they would be helped by the people who would spur them on'. The three socialists designated to enter the future provisional government of the Republic were Francisco Largo Caballero, Indalecio Prieto and Fernando de los Ríos.

While these meetings and preparations were going on, the *Confederación Nacional del Trabajo* (CNT), the other big syndicalist

---

[3] The best synthesis on the positions of the socialists at this time may be found in Santos Juliá, *Los socialistas en la política española, 1879–1982*, Taurus, Madrid, 1996, pp. 147–53, which is the source of the information provided here.

organisation that had become established during the final years of the Restoration, emerged from the silence and repression imposed on it by Primo de Rivera's dictatorship, and its leaders – except for the odd name, such as Ángel Pestaña or Joan Peiró – showed very little interest in the Republic, a 'political entity' that, for the moment, had nothing to do with the 'revolution that will transform all political and economic values', which they, as anarchists and revolutionary syndicalists, claimed to support. So wrote Valeriano Orobón Fernández, a CNT delegate at the AIT (the initials of the Spanish name for the International Workers' Association), in a letter from Berlin on 2 July 1930 to Eusebio Carbó, an anarchist of the old school. 'The liberal constitutional breeze blowing through Spain at the moment', wrote Orobón, would not be enough: 'We shall need a hurricane'.[4]

In fact, what was blowing through Spain at that time was more a gale than a breeze, and much of the responsibility for the stirring up of the atmosphere and morale of the Spanish was borne by the intellectuals. During that year, 1930, distinguished writers and university professors 'defined themselves', as their contemporaries put it, to express their rejection of the Monarchy and support for the Republic. This unrest began just a few days after the fall of the dictator, with the return from exile of Miguel de Unamuno, who was acclaimed by crowds at every stage of his journey from Irún to Madrid, and it ended with the famous article by the philosopher José Ortega y Gasset, published in *El Sol* on 15 November 1930. 'The Berenguer error', as the article was entitled, gave the lie to the idea that everything would return to normal after seven years of dictatorship, as if nothing had happened. The Monarchy was now beyond hope of salvation. '*Delenda est monarchia*', concluded Ortega, in a phrase that summed up the anti-monarchist feeling that was rife among politicians, intellectuals and the common people at that time.

These speeches by politicians and intellectuals, demonstrations and mass republican meetings, such as the one held in the bullring in Madrid on 29 September, with Azaña, Alcalá Zamora and Lerroux as the main speakers, all ultimately led, as Miguel Maura said later, to a 'tragic outcome for the king': leading politicians and ex-ministers

---

[4] I have summarised the anarchist positions in the months prior to the proclamation of the Republic in Julián Casanova, *Anarchism, the Republic and Civil War in Spain: 1931–1939*, Routledge, London, 2004, pp. 3–5.

deserted 'the legal framework of the Monarchy, some turning openly republican and others moving for the Cortes to be called without the king, so that the decision as to what to do next would be made there'.[5]

But before any future Cortes could resolve such a momentous matter, republicans and socialists together put into practice the insurrectional option, an option that had had wide acceptance in contemporary Spanish society. Once again, the plan was for a military insurrection, organised by a revolutionary committee and backed up in the streets by a general strike called by the workers' organisations. Also involved in the plan were certain anarcho-syndicalists, who for several years had been in contact with radical sectors of the army, and the less hardline leaders of the CNT, who pledged their support for the insurrection with a general strike. Such was the plan that failed in Jaca, in the province of Huesca, on 12 December 1930.

Captain Fermín Galán, born in Cádiz in 1899 to a military family, arrived in Jaca at the beginning of June, four months after he had been released from the Montjuich military prison, having been granted an amnesty after serving his sentence for actively taking part in the *Sanjuanada*, the military plot that had tried to overthrow Primo de Rivera in 1926. He already had firm links with Catalan anarchists, who had visited him in prison, and in Jaca he came into contact with other officers who were prepared to take part in an insurrection against the Monarchy, particularly Captain Ángel García Hernández, born in Álava in 1900, who, like Galán, had served in the *Tercio* (infantry regiment) of Africa. From there he extended his network of contacts to include syndicalists in Zaragoza, as well as Ramón Acín, an anarchist, painter and sculptor, and lecturer in drawing at the Huesca Teacher Training College, and he travelled to Madrid to talk to the revolutionary committee, a meeting that was reported by Marcelino Domingo. If we are to believe this radical-socialist leader, Galán was willing to take part 'if action were taken swiftly'. He and Lerroux tried to convince Galán that 'unless a tight control is kept on all elements, the revolution, with more options and requirements than ever, will once again fail'.[6]

[5] Maura, *Así cayó Alfonso XIII*, pp. 59–60.
[6] The information on the insurrection comes from José María Azpíroz and Fernando Elboj, *La sublevación de Jaca*, Guara Editorial, Zaragoza, 1985.

But Galán did not wait until 15 December, the date that most sources say had been set by the revolutionary committee for the uprising. At five o'clock in the morning of 12 December 1930, a group of officers called out the troops in Jaca, arrested the military governor and his staff and seized the telephone exchange, post office and station, after killing, in an exchange of fire, a Civil Guard sergeant and two carabineros who opposed them. At eleven that same morning, they proclaimed the Republic in the town hall, 'on behalf of the Revolutionary Provisional Government'. From Jaca they sent two columns to Huesca. Officers of the 5th Military Region, based in Zaragoza, put down the uprising. They arrested García Hernández and, in the general chaos, Galán surrendered. As a back-up to the insurrection, the CNT and UGT had called a strike, which received limited support in Zaragoza and Huesca, as well as in certain locations in the Five Towns, the district where socialism was most firmly entrenched in Aragon.

On Sunday 14 December, a summary court martial sentenced Captains Galán and García Hernández to death, and they were shot immediately afterwards. Even before its birth, the Republic already had its first martyrs, and King Alfonso XIII was held responsible for failing to grant them a pardon. 'The Monarchy committed an outrage in executing Galán and García Hernández, an outrage which in no small way led to its destruction', wrote Manuel Azaña.[7]

The uprising set for 15 December also failed, in spite of the fact that General Gonzalo Queipo de Llano and Major Ramón Franco managed to capture the Cuatro Vientos aerodrome for a few hours, from whence they fled to Portugal when they discovered that troops loyal to Berenguer's government were approaching, and that no one had gone on strike in Madrid. The socialists did not go on strike because they did not think that the officers would go through with the uprising, and the committed officers hesitated because they thought they lacked the vital back-up of the strike and demonstrations in the streets. Meanwhile, most of the members of the revolutionary committee had been arrested. In the end, it was not insurrection that would bring about the Republic.

---

[7] Manuel Azaña, *Diarios 1932–1933 (los 'Cuadernos robados')*, Crítica, Barcelona, 1997, p. 45.

Nor did the return to constitutional normality proposed by General Dámaso Berenguer's government produce concrete results. Firstly, it decided to hold elections in the autumn, convinced that republican advances in the cities would be counterbalanced by the strong conservative support and by vote-rigging in the rural areas. Next, following the failure of the Jaca uprising, it announced that elections would be held on 1 March, with the unanimous rejection of Sánchez Guerra's constitutionalists, republicans and socialists, who wanted nothing to do with a return to the 1876 Constitution, and they called for elections to the Constituent Cortes. Berenguer stood alone, abandoned even by members of his government with strong loyalty to the King, such as the Count of Romanones, and he resigned on 13 February 1931. Alfonso XIII, after an unsuccessful attempt to persuade the liberal Santiago Alba, living in exile in Paris because of his disagreements with the dictatorship, asked Sánchez Guerra to form a government, and he went to the Modelo prison to meet members of the revolutionary committee to ask them to take part in the new government. 'We refuse to have anything to do with the Monarchy', replied Miguel Maura, the most conservative of all those who were there.[8]

With no hope of any agreement, a government was finally formed, on 17 February, by Admiral Juan Bautista Aznar, another government loyal to the Monarchy, with the Count of Romanones keeping a close eye on the Admiral's every move. He only had time to call municipal elections for 12 April; the provincial and general elections would have to be held in May and June, because two months later this government and the Monarchy had ceased to exist.

The calling of elections caught the traditional parties of the conservative and liberal right in complete disarray, and the extreme right, those faithful to the deposed dictator, in the process of re-arming and powerless to mobilise their counter-revolutionary forces, although they did try to with the formation in July 1930 of the *Unión Monárquica Nacional*, a pale imitation of the *Unión Patriótica de la Dictadura*; among the members of this party were certain ex-ministers, such as the Count of Guadalhorce and José Calvo Sotelo, the intellectual,

[8] A good summary of the final months of the Monarchy, the source of the information provided here, is in Miguel Martorell, 'El Rey en su desconcierto. Alfonso XIII, los viejos políticos y el ocaso de la monarquía', in Javier Moreno Luzón (ed.), *Alfonso XIII. Un político en el trono*, Marcial Pons, Madrid, 2003, pp. 375–402.

Ramiro de Maeztu, and the ex-dictator's son, José Antonio Primo de Rivera. Their old politics were in their death throes, and the new authoritarianism had yet to find a niche. As José María Gil Robles wrote later, those 'select groups' that used to attend monarchist meetings or acclaim the Queen were now 'merely a small minority as opposed to the vast masses hostile to the regime, made up mainly of rightists that supported revolution'.[9]

For the republicans, both those of long standing and new adherents, their moment had come. On 10 February 1931, one of the last intellectuals to 'define himself', José Ortega y Gasset, together with two other prestigious intellectuals, Gregorio Marañón and Ramón Pérez de Ayala, signed the foundational manifesto of the *Agrupación al Servicio de la República*, which asked 'all Spanish intellectuals' to contribute to the victory of the Republic 'in elections conducted under the maximum guarantees of civic integrity'.

The moment had also come for street politics, propaganda, meetings and calls for action to support the Republic. On 20 March, at the height of the election campaign, the imprisoned revolutionary committee faced a court martial, an event that was transformed into a major manifestation of republican avowal, another triumph for this combination of republicans and socialists who now had power in their reach. Having recovered their freedom, the members of this revolutionary committee, future members of the republican provisional government, concentrated all their efforts on transforming this election day, 12 April, into a plebiscite between the Monarchy and the Republic.

And that is how it turned out. Up to the very end, the monarchists thought they were going to win, confident of their ability to manipulate the mechanism of government, which is why they showed their 'consternation' and 'surprise' when they learnt very soon of the republicans' victory in forty-one of the fifty provincial capitals. Only Juan de la Cierva proposed resorting to arms to prevent the rout of the Monarchy. But the other ministers, headed by Romanones, acknowledged defeat. Aznar resigned on the night of 13 April. The following day, many municipalities proclaimed the Republic. Alcalá Zamora called for the King to leave the country. He did so from Cartagena, and when he arrived in Paris he declared that the Republic was 'a

---

[9] José María Gil Robles, *No fue posible la paz*, Ariel, Barcelona, 1968, p. 32.

storm that will soon blow over'.[10] It was to take longer to blow over than Alfonso XIII thought, or indeed wished. This Republic was to experience over five years of peace, until a military uprising and a war destroyed it by force of arms.

Republican dawn

The Republic was welcomed by celebrations in the streets, a great deal of rhetoric and a holiday atmosphere that combined revolutionary hopes with a desire for reform. Crowds thronged the streets, singing the 'Himno de Riego' (the republican anthem) and 'La Marseillaise'. Workers, students and professional people all joined in. The middle class 'opted for the Republic' because of the 'disorientation of conservative elements', wrote José María Gil Robles a few years later. And the scene was repeated in every town and city, as was borne out by the press, photographs of the time and the large number of accounts by contemporaries who wished to testify to the great change that had something of a magical quality about it, having arrived peacefully and bloodlessly; however, certain authors, including Enric Ucelay da Cal and Stanley G. Payne, attributed it to a 'street plebiscite', popular pressure orchestrated by the republicans and their worker allies, who occupied 'town halls and other political premises everywhere before the official handover of power'.[11]

The Republic was received with joy by some and misery by others. The Catholic Church, for one, was not at all happy with the arrival of the Republic. Juan Crespo, then a student in a Church college in Salamanca, told Ronald Fraser how the headmaster delivered a sermon that day on the tragedy that was looming: 'He criticised the ingratitude of the Spanish towards the king, praised the service the monarchy had given the country, and reminded us of the example of the Catholic Monarchs, who had united the nation. At the end, he was almost in tears, and so were we'.[12]

---

[10] Quoted in Eduardo González Calleja, 'El ex rey', in Moreno Luzón (ed.), *Alfonso XIII*, p. 406.

[11] Gil Robles, *No fue posible la paz*, p. 32; Enric Ucelay da Cal, 'Buscando el levantamiento plebiscitario: insurreccionalismo y elecciones', in Santos Juliá (ed.), 'Política en la Segunda República', *Ayer*, 20 (1995), pp. 63–4.

[12] Ronald Fraser, *The Blood of Spain: Experience of the Civil War*, Viking, London, 1979.

Indeed, it was with grief, prayers and pessimism that most Catholics, clergy and bishops reacted to this Republic that was being celebrated in the streets by the people. And their reaction was logical. Also logical was the confusion and bewilderment of the landed gentry and the large number of titled industrialists and financiers. 'The power bloc' was the name given by Manuel Tuñón de Lara to this convergence of the old and new nobility. Spain in 1930 had some 1,900 titled people. The problem was not their number, but the influence they wielded and the type of background – far from democratic or 'bourgeois' – in which they had been born and raised. They had suddenly lost the King, their faithful protector, whom many of them had abandoned. 'They made us a gift of power', commented Miguel Maura. 'All we did was carefully, lovingly and peacefully take Spain into our hands, a Spain that they had left in mid-stream'.[13]

And as well as leaving her 'in mid-stream', they had left her without money, with a State in crisis and a paltry budget. Between 1 April and 30 June, 917 million pesetas was withdrawn from bank accounts, an amount equivalent to 15 per cent of total deposits. Loans granted by the private banks fell by the same percentage. The share index fell sharply between 1931 and 1933. The issue of shares in the Madrid Stock Market plummeted. The Republic, as the indicators show, was not welcomed by a certain sector of the money masters, and they were not prepared to see how these indicators would develop either.

The background and habits of this oligarchy were very familiar to the proletariat that served it, land workers who lived in the areas of the large estates in Andalusia, Extremadura and La Mancha. They had no land or basic living resources, and from the outset these agricultural day-workers were highly confident that the Republic would abolish excessive class privileges, mobilised as they were by socialists and anarchists under the banner of share-outs and collectivisation.

The socialists, and we include here the affiliates of the UGT, had seen massive growth in the final years of the dictatorship, and there were over 300,000 of them by the time the Republic was proclaimed. Their leaders decided that this mass of affiliates and the working classes they

---

[13] Some of the basic hypotheses of the extensive output of Manuel Tuñón de Lara on the 1930s are summarised in *Tres claves de la Segunda República. La cuestión agraria, los aparatos del Estado, Frente Popular*, Alianza Editorial, Madrid, 1985; Maura, *Así cayó Alfonso XIII*, pp.147–72.

represented should be incorporated into the new regime, even though not everyone supported the Republic for the same reasons. Indalecio Prieto, the leader of the Basque socialists and representative of one of the three tendencies in Spanish socialism at that time, thought that the Republic needed to be democratic, liberal and parliamentarian, and that for this to come about the socialists needed to build a coalition government with the republicans. Such a coalition was also defended by Francisco Largo Caballero, the leader of the workers' sector, because he felt this would be the best way of strengthening the UGT, achieving more power for the organised working class and progressing towards socialism. Julián Besteiro, on the other hand, with the support of other UGT leaders, wanted to keep the party and the syndical organisation apart from alliances with the republicans and governmental responsibilities. His posture was overruled, and for the first time in Spain's history, the socialists formed part of the government of the nation. For Largo Caballero, the Republic was a means, and for Prieto, an end, and both came together in the establishment of democracy. When they left the government in 1933, these two differing conceptions were translated into deep discrepancies.

Thus it is probably true to say that for broad sectors of the organised labour movement, supporting the Republic did not mean supporting a liberal, parliamentary democracy, such as those that had been established after the First World War in certain countries of western Europe. This was certainly true for the workers' sector of socialism, and more so for the CNT, the revolutionary syndicalist organisation that competed with the UGT to defend the interests of urban workers and agricultural day-labourers. At first, the anarchists joined in the festive atmosphere, the 'air of expectation and boundless enthusiasm' that the Republic brought with it.[14] The Republic opened a great many doors to this revolutionary syndicalism that had been crippled ten years earlier by gun-wielding anarchists and bosses, and silenced by Primo de Rivera's dictatorship. It enabled it once more to come out into the open and implement all the resources it used to employ that were the trademark of the anarchists: propaganda, demonstrations, rallies and incitement to revolutionary action.

[14] Valeriano Orobón Fernández, *La CNT y la Revolución*, address given in the Madrid Athenaeum on 6 April 1932, published in *El libertario*, Madrid, 1932.

Of this Republic, 'originating from the people', preferable to a 'monarchy by the grace of God' and made possible by a good number of CNT votes, many things were asked, but above all freedom. Indeed, the CNT, aware that governments would probably not make any changes to the class-based social structure, at least hoped for a package of freedoms that would enable it to provide better organisation for the unions and transform the proclamation of the Republic into 'a revolution that will essentially change all political and economic values'.[15] But instead of doing this from within the government, which was Largo Caballero's dream for socialism, the anarchists would employ their trademark methods: direct action and taking the struggle to the streets.

Although they were anti-parliament and pro-revolution, they debated long and hard as to whether they should oppose the republican regime from the outset, just one more manifestation of the feelings that impregnated the atmosphere in Spain at the time of the King's abdication. Galo Díez, one of the movement's most respected leaders, was in no doubt, and he said as much to his comrades at the Extraordinary Congress of the CNT held in Madrid two months later. There was a need to talk to the people not only of their revolutionary dreams, but also of 'their wishes, their needs, their misfortunes and their rights'. Compared to Primo de Rivera's dictatorship, the Republic offered much more and, therefore, it was not wise to 'sacrifice what little we have by chasing something much more unattainable'. Most Spaniards, thought this syndicalist, were 'like children with new shoes' with their Republic, and under the circumstances, it was better not to get caught up in 'the movement of reaction'.[16]

'Reaction', at that moment, was not apparent. The last monarchist government no longer represented anyone; nor did the officers mobilise the troops to confront the masses of people demonstrating in the streets in cities all over the country. Those who did take action were the members of the revolutionary committee, the ones who were most hopeful that this new democratic and liberal State would become the instrument of social change. Without waiting for the transfer of power, they formed, following the outcome of the election and in response

---

[15] *Boletín de la CNT*, 5 (February–April 1932) and 16 (April–June 1933).
[16] *Memoria del Congreso Extraordinario de la CNT celebrado en Madrid los días 11 al 16 de junio de 1931*, Cosmos, Barcelona, 1931, pp. 191–2.

to public pressure, the provisional government of the Republic. It was the evening of 14 April, a few hours after the Republic had been proclaimed in other locations (the first to do so having been the city council in Eibar), and Francesc Macià had proclaimed in Barcelona the Catalan Republic within the Federal Spanish State. Niceto Alcalá Zamora went out onto the balcony of the Interior Ministry, and in a message broadcast by radio, officially proclaimed the Republic. At a meeting the same night, the provisional government drew up its own Legal Statute that would define its situation until the Constituent Cortes was called.

The government was headed by Alcalá Zamora, an ex-monarchist, Catholic and man of order, whose role was essential in ensuring the necessary support of the more moderate republicans for the new regime. Another conservative latecomer to the republican cause was Miguel Maura, the Interior Minister, whose idea of authority soon came into conflict with that of other republican ministers and politicians. More to the centre was Alejandro Lerroux, the old *Emperador del Paralelo*, born in 1864, thirteen years before Alcalá Zamora and sixteen before Manuel Azaña, who was the leader of the main republican party, the *Partido Radical*; however, he was given a minor post as Minister of State, and was therefore kept separate from major decisions by some of his own colleagues – or enemies if we are to believe the various testimonies they left behind – as they did not trust him or his party for its long history of corrupt practices. The other *Partido Radical* minister, Diego Martínez Barrio, a masonic Grand Master, a Seville city councillor in the first decade of the century and a resolute plotter against Primo de Rivera's dictatorship, was put in charge of Communications. Catalan nationalism was represented in the government by Lluís Nicolau d'Olwer, the founder in 1922 of *Acció Catalana*, and leader of the recently created *Partit Catalanista Republicá*, a tiny party compared to *Esquerra Republicana*, the runaway winner of the municipal elections in Catalonia. Nicolau d'Olwer became the Second Republic's first Minister of Economic Affairs.

Leftist republicans were represented by Manuel Azaña, a former member of Melquíades Álvarez's *Partido Reformista*, and spokesman for *Alianza Republicana*, who was appointed Minister of War. Santiago Casares Quiroga, a lawyer and leader of the *Organización Republicana Gallega Autónoma*, was appointed Minister for the Navy. Development and Education were given to the two *Partido*

Radical Socialista ministers, Álvaro de Albornoz and Marcelino Domingo. Finally, there were three socialist ministers in the first government of the Republic: Fernando de los Ríos, a professor at the University of Granada and veteran PSOE militant, became Minister of Justice; Indalecio Prieto was given Finance; and Francisco Largo Caballero became Minister of Labour.

Four of the ministers were from Andalusia, three from Madrid, two from Asturias (although Prieto had lived in Bilbao most of his life), one from Galicia and two from Catalonia. Eight of them were university graduates, Marcelino Domingo was a teacher and the three others without academic qualifications, Martínez Barrio, Prieto and Largo Caballero, were successful self-made men. They represented the professional middle classes, the petite bourgeoisie and the militant working class or socialist sympathisers. None of them, except Alcalá Zamora, had held a high political post under the Monarchy, although they were by no means young untried amateurs: most of them were in their fifties and had spent a long time in the political struggle, at the head of republican parties and socialist organisations. Nor, despite what has often been said, was it a government of intellectuals. Except for Azaña, in the government as leader of a republican party, none of the intellectuals who had done so much to goad the Monarchy with their speeches and writings in 1930 were given ministries: neither Unamuno, nor Ortega, nor Pérez de Ayala, nor Marañón. Indeed, they very soon disappeared from public life, or were even rejected by the republican regime.

What this government did in the early weeks, with popular jubilation still in the air, was to legislate by decree. Indeed, it is hard to imagine a government with more plans for political and social reform. Before the inauguration of the Constituent Cortes, the provisional government implemented a Military Reform Act, drawn up by Manuel Azaña, and a series of basic decrees issued by Francisco Largo Caballero, the Minister of Labour, whose aim was to radically modify labour relations. Such a reformist programme embodied the government's faith in progress, and a political and social transformation that would sweep away the cacique system and the power of the military and ecclesiastical institutions.

What happened, however, was that the Republic could not neutralise these power structures with such a long history in Spain, and this is where some of its major problems were to arise. The republican government's first serious encounter was with the Catholic Church, although this institution desisted from direct confrontation at the beginning. One of the reasons for this was that on 24 April, with the Republic barely proclaimed, the papal nuncio, Federico Tedeschini, wrote to the Spanish bishops on behalf of the Secretary of State at the Vatican, Cardinal Eugenio Pacelli, the future Pope Pius XII, recommending them 'to respect the constituted powers and obey them so that order may be maintained, and for the common good'.[17]

Around that time, the Vatican was much more prudent and diplomatic than the Spanish ecclesiastical hierarchy, with its internal letters and circulars. 'We have now entered the vortex of the storm', wrote Isidro Gomá, then bishop of Tarazona, to Cardinal Francesc Vidal i Barraquer of Tarragona on 15 April 1931, the day after the proclamation of the Republic. 'I am thoroughly pessimistic', continued Gomá: 'I cannot begin to fathom the monstrosity that has been perpetrated. History has had many examples, but none such as this. God save the house and peace be to Israel'.[18]

The 'monstrosity' was simply the fact that the overwhelming victory of the republican candidates in the big cities in the municipal elections had shown that the King, as he himself said, no longer enjoyed 'the love' of his people. Meanwhile, saving the house, order and property became a genuine obsession for Catholics. On 12 April, the day of the elections, their main mouthpiece, *El Debate*, asked the faithful to vote for those who respected 'the great institutions that sustain today's society: the Church, the family and property'. And on 17 April, Cardinal Pedro Segura, then archbishop of Toledo, in a 'confidential and secret' circular, recommended his 'brother bishops' to wait and 'pray constantly'. 'With family misfortunes, the links binding brothers grow stronger, and this is what I feel should be happening to us now'.

In spite of his recommendation, however, the Primate of the Spanish Church (a post to which he was elevated in 1927, during Primo de Rivera's dictatorship at the age of forty-seven) did not wait long. A fundamentalist and bitter enemy of republicanism, he published on 1 May a pastoral letter warmly praising the dethroned Alfonso XIII,

---

[17] *Arxiu Vidal i Barraquer. Església i Estat durant la Segona República Espanyola 1931–1936*, Publications de l'Abadia de Montserrat, Barcelona, 1971, p. 24.
[18] Ibid., p. 19.

'who, throughout his reign, has kept the old tradition of faith and piety of his ancestors'.

Following this untimely outburst (in that it went against the advice issued by the Secretary of State for the Vatican), Cardinal Segura was engaged in a struggle with the republican authorities that ended in open conflict. Segura left Spain, but a month later, on 11 June, the frontier police informed Miguel Maura, the Interior Minister, that the Cardinal had re-entered the country via Roncesvalles. Maura knew that he was in Pastrana, in the parish priest's house, and he ordered his expulsion, an event recorded by the famous photograph that was to be found in all Spanish Catholic homes, with the Cardinal leaving the Pauline Convent in Guadalajara surrounded by police and civil guards. It was presented as unmistakeable evidence of the 'persecution' of the Church, which moreover was brought to public notice at a time when Spain was still feeling the impact of the incendiary events of the previous month.

Apart from the bizarre Segura saga, which lasted until 30 September 1931, when, under pressure from the Vatican, he renounced the Toledo see, it was the sudden explosion of anticlerical rage on 11 May that marked the mood of many Catholics. This was not so much for the magnitude of the event – highly localised and with very few people involved – as for the way it was recalled afterwards in books and the Catholic memory, as the event that changed 'the course of the Republic'.

On Sunday 10 May, a group of young right-wingers, assembled in a flat in the Calle Alcalá in Madrid to inaugurate the Independent Monarchist Circle, placed a gramophone playing the *Marcha Real* near the window, just when a good many people were returning from the Retiro park. Some of those who heard it became outraged, and they made their way to the headquarters of the monarchist newspaper, *ABC*, whose owner, Juan Ignacio Luca de Tena, they held responsible for the provocation, and then to the Interior Ministry. Two people were killed as a result of confrontations with the Civil Guard.

The following day, the protests escalated into the burning of churches, religious schools and convents, but Maura was unable to obtain authorisation from his cabinet colleagues to deploy the Civil Guard against the fires. On 12 May, the unrest spread to other localities in the Levante, and particularly to Málaga, where the bishop's palace was burnt. According to the telegrams that the civil governors sent to the Interior Minister, panic-stricken monks and nuns fled from their convents in certain towns in Teruel, Valencia and Logroño. By 15 May, when it was all over, around a hundred buildings had been subjected to arson.

Naturally, this disproportionate action of burning churches was a surprising reaction to an apparently insignificant incident involving some young monarchists. It was not the first time in Spain's history – nor would it be the last – that arson was used against religious symbols and sacred property. But the burning of convents was barely repeated during the Republic, except for the revolutionary events of October 1934 in Asturias, and the previous time it had occurred, the so-called Tragic Week of July 1909 in Barcelona, was under the Monarchy, and that was of far greater magnitude than the fires of 1931.

This time, there was no popular uprising, and it was minority groups, republicans and left-wingers with anarchist tendencies who were involved, although even that is not clear. The main significance of these events is that they occurred barely a month after the proclamation of the Republic and that they were imprinted in the collective memory of many Catholics as the first attack against the Church by a secular and anticlerical Republic, a dress rehearsal for the catastrophe that was on the horizon. The consequences were 'disastrous' for the Republic, wrote Niceto Alcalá Zamora in his memoirs later: 'they created enemies that it previously did not have; they damaged its firm foundations; they tarnished its credibility that up to then had been open and unlimited'. A somewhat similar view was expressed by Cardinal Francesc Vidal y Barraquer in the protest note he sent to the leader of the provisional government on 17 May: 'events of this type ... diminish the confidence that the tactful action of the government in many of its early decisions had inspired in a great many Catholics'.[19]

Elections and the Constitution

Apart from these early conflicts, which, as we shall see, were soon joined by the most radical sector of anarcho-syndicalism, the

---

[19] Niceto Alcalá Zamora, *Memorias*, Planeta, Barcelona, 1977, p. 185; letter from Cardinal Francesc Vidal y Barraquer to Alcalá Zamora in *Arxiu Vidal i Barraquer*, pp. 41–2.

provisional government's main concern was to call a general election and provide the Republic with a Constitution. Elections with universal suffrage, representative governments that answered to parliament, and compliance with the law and the Constitution were the distinguishing features of the democratic systems that were emerging or being consolidated at that time in the main countries of western and central Europe. And this is what the republicans and socialists who governed Spain tried to introduce during the early years of the Second Republic, to a large extent successfully.

The general election to the Constituent Cortes was held on 28 June. According to the election writ, which modified the 1907 Electoral Act, there would be a single chamber, instead of the two that made up the monarchist parliament. The voting age was lowered from twenty-five to twenty-three, and suffrage was restricted to males, although females could now stand for election, with the decision on female suffrage to be taken during the future legislature. To thwart any of the traditional fraudulent cacique-type practices, the first-past-the-post system was to be replaced by open lists, with constituencies by province. Provincial capitals with over 100,000 inhabitants were to have their own district, including their judicial district, and in Madrid and Barcelona the district would take in their municipality only. Seat distribution would be by a majority system, although with the application of a corrective factor that would permit voters to pick only 80 per cent of the deputies for their constituency, with the rest coming from minority lists. There would be one deputy for every 50,000 inhabitants, plus a further deputy for every 30,000 inhabitants after that, which would make up a Cortes of 470 deputies; and the automatic designation of unopposed candidates, as stipulated in the famous Arcticle 29 of the 1907 Electoral Act, was invalidated.

This electoral system favoured the major parties and coalitions, so that there would be governments with substantial parliamentary support, but it also enabled small parties on the fringes of the political scene to obtain, by entering these coalitions, a larger parliamentary representation than their electoral results gave them. This system favoured the coalition of socialists and republicans in 1931, was detrimental to them in November 1933 when they went to the country divided (as opposed to the right, who had reorganised and were united), and contributed to the polarisation of the Cortes that was elected in February 1936. But above all, it was a system that, by doing away with the small districts, attacked the roots of the cacique system and introduced free, legitimate elections for the first time in Spain's history.

The electoral campaign found the right still in disarray and lacking a firm policy, with some of its leaders having fled to other countries in case they were brought to trial for their actions during the dictatorship. Ángel Herrera, the editor of the Catholic daily, *El Debate*, and other members of the *Asociación Católica Nacional de Propagandistas* who had accepted the Republic as 'the only scenario possible', created *Acción Nacional*, whose primary objective was to promote a firm grass-roots policy, act within the bounds of the Republic, following the creed of 'the accidentality of forms of government', and defend the interests of order and the Church in the Cortes. Given the papal blessing and supported by a large number of bishops, this was the beginning of the Catholic grass-roots movement that burst with unexpected vigour onto the political stage two years later. But in June 1931, still in its embryonic phase, *Acción Nacional* could only field thirty-nine candidates in sixteen constituencies.

The victory of the republican–socialist coalition was overwhelming. Between the first and second ballots, envisaged by the election writ of 8 May 1931 for those constituencies where no candidate obtained 20 per cent of the votes, the Cortes voted in by the first of the Republic's elections was made up of nineteen parties or groups, six of which had fewer than five elected representatives. The principal modification to the electoral map was the fact that the *Partido Socialista*, which had never had more than seven deputies under the Monarchy, now had 115, and was the majority political force, with its votes coming mainly from the large estates areas of the south. The second biggest group was Alejandro Lerroux's radicals, with ninety-four deputies, a very important result that enabled the *Partido Radical* to occupy the republican centre, especially because the conservatives, led by Alcalá Zamora and Miguel Maura, the provisional government's Prime Minister and Interior Minister respectively, obtained only twenty-two seats. The fifty-nine *Partido Radical-Socialista* and thirty *Acción Republicana* deputies also showed the notable strength of the republican left, reinforced by the domination of *Esquerra Republicana* in Catalonia, which obtained thirty-five of the forty-nine seats contested there, and the sixteen deputies provided by the *Federación Republicana Gallega*.

The non-republican right-wing organisations obtained barely fifty seats and their results were only favourable in the Basque Country and Navarre, where sixteen of the twenty-four seats were won by the alliance of Carlists, Basque nationalists and independent Catholics. Even so, although few in number, there were some distinguished names among the right-wing deputies, with members of rich land-owning and industrial families, such as José Luis de Oriol, Julio de Urquijo, the Count of Romanones and Juan March. The common interests between landowners, order and religion were perfectly embodied by the agrarian deputies of *Acción Nacional* and by the Carlists and fundamentalists. The Count of Rodezno, a grandee of Spain, owned large properties in La Rioja and an estate in Cáceres. José María Lamamié de Clairac was one of the most powerful landowners of Salamanca, as was Francisco Estévanez of Burgos, both being spokesmen for cereal growers' interests in Castilla.

All the deputies, bar twenty-eight, were entering the Cortes for the first time. There were many intellectuals, journalists, teachers and lawyers, as well as members of the working class. And for the first time in history, there were three women: the republicans Clara Campoamor and Victoria Kent and the socialist Margarita Nelken. The republican vote had come mainly from the Mediterranean provinces, Aragon, Andalusia, Extremadura, La Mancha and Madrid. The old monarchist and Catholic right maintained its influence in Castilla, Galicia, Navarre and the Basque Country. At the opening session of the Constituent Cortes on 14 July 1931, the anniversary of the storming of the Bastille, Alcalá Zamora declared that 'today marks a high spot, a summit, a pinnacle in the history of Spain'. A few days later, the Cortes, with the socialist Julián Besteiro as Speaker, gave a vote of confidence to the provisional government, thereby making it the first official government of the Republic.

There was no sign in that Parliament of any radicalisation or polarisation of Spanish political life. There was no solid extreme right, let alone a Fascist party, while the Communist Party, at the time vehemently opposed to the 'bourgeois Republic', had obtained very poor results and no seats. Two essential ingredients of the process of radicalisation on the European stage, Fascism and Communism, were missing in Spain, although there was a powerful anarcho-syndicalist movement outside this Constituent Cortes, an institution that was viewed by its most extreme sector as 'a bourgeois mechanism whose purpose is to consolidate the regime of constant exploitation'. It was the only established force that clearly had no place in the system at that time. What was important was that the main party of the left was in the government and that a large proportion of the deputies of the Constituent Cortes (more than half of them) represented intellectuals, the middle class, professionals and tradesmen. One-quarter of the radical parliamentary group, as Nigel Townson has pointed out, came from the world of business, while of the leftist republican deputies, only 1 per cent came from this sector.[20]

What set this parliament apart from those of other republics that emerged from the break-up of empires following the First World War was that most of the deputies belonged to the coalition of parties that formed the government. Only around fifty seemed willing to defend the interests of traditional order and the Catholic Church. This did not reflect the views of large sectors of Spanish society, who had strong economic, social and cultural power, but they were not in the Cortes and were not going to be able to have an influence on the drafting of the Constitution. This was because the Republic arrived not as the result of the success of a republican movement with deep social roots, but because of a popular mobilisation against the Monarchy, which reaped its rewards just when the Monarchy was losing social and institutional support.

But this did not necessarily mean that the foundations of the Republic and democracy were shaky from the start. The results of the June 1931 elections showed that a large proportion of the Spanish had placed their hopes in the Republic. And they showed it via the exercise of popular sovereignty, in elections with only a 30 per cent abstention rate, in a vote of confidence for a Constituent Cortes and a parliamentary government. Everything that happened later, the strengths and weaknesses of the system, its successes and failures, up to the coup d'état of July 1936, have their historical explanations, and no predestined fatal outcome was to be found in the origins of this democratic Republic.

One of the fundamental tasks of this Constituent Cortes was to draw up and pass the first republican Constitution in Spain's history,

---

[20] Nigel Townson, *La República que no pudo ser. La política de centro en España (1931–1936)*, Taurus, Madrid, 2002, p. 83. (Original English edition: *The Crisis of Democracy in Spain: Centrist Politics under the Second Republic (1931–1936)*, Sussex Academic Press, 2001.)

and this is what it devoted its energies to during the first few months. Before the elections, the provisional government had commissioned a draft Constitution from a legal committee presided over by the lawyer Ángel Ossorio y Gallardo, a conservative politician under the Monarchy, 'a monarchist without a king' in 1930, and 'a monarchist without a king in the service of the Republic' after the proclamation. The text of the draft, which reflected the idea of a Republic of order held by Alcalá Zamora and the deputies of the *Derecha Liberal Republicana*, which became the *Partido Republicano Progresista* after August 1931, failed to win the unanimous support of the leftist republicans and was rejected by the socialists.

The government then commissioned a new draft Constitution from a parliamentary committee presided over by the socialist Luis Jiménez de Asúa, with the radical, Emiliano Iglesias, as vice-chairman, and Alfonso García de Valdecasas, of the *Agrupación al Servicio de la República*, as secretary. Within barely twenty days, they submitted the new draft, which was debated in the Cortes between 28 August and 1 December, in long evening sessions that often went on until dawn.

The Constitution resulting from this long debate defined Spain, in Article 1, as 'a democratic Republic of workers of all types, structured around freedom and justice. All its authority comes from the people. The Republic constitutes an integrated State, compatible with the autonomy of its Municipalities and Regions'. This Constitution also declared the non-confessional nature of the State, the ending of State financing of the clergy, introduced civil marriage and divorce and banned teaching activities for those in holy orders. Article 36, following heated debates, granted the vote to women, something that was being done in the democratic parliaments of the most enlightened countries during the interwar years. It was a proposal defended by the *Partido Radical* deputy, Clara Campoamor, in spite of the fact that a good many leftist republicans, including the socialist-radical Victoria Kent, feared that women would be influenced by the clergy to give their vote to right-wing organisations. With socialist support, despite the misgivings of Indalecio Prieto, the article was passed by 160 votes to 121. In short, it was a democratic, secular Constitution that confirmed the supremacy of legislative power.

The most serious crisis in the debate on the Constitution was provoked by the 'matter of religion', which left in its wake disturbances, quarrels, insults and angry declarations by the fundamentalists and the most incendiary and anticlerical elements of the left alike. José María Lamamié de Clairac threatened to oppose the Republic, because the Constitution, 'nourished by a spirit of sectarianism does not exist for us'. The lawyer and journalist Ángel Samblancat wanted to see the 'humanisation' of priests via marriage.[21] And many 'Catholic women' began to send telegrams from all over Spain to the Interior Minister, Miguel Maura, asking him to defend the 'matter of religion' in Parliament.[22]

Final approval was given to Azaña's proposal made in his famous speech of 13 October, which moderated the original plan by restricting the constitutional precept of the dissolution of religious orders to the Jesuits only, and ratified the ban on teaching activities for those in holy orders. The text, which was put to the vote in the early hours of 14 October, was passed by 178 votes to 59; 233 deputies were not in the Chamber at that moment, many of them because they did not want to commit themselves to a viewpoint in such a complex matter. Lerroux, for example, stayed away from almost all these discussions, and left it in the hands of the party's spokesman, Rafael Guerra del Río.

The agrarian and Basque-Navarran deputies walked out of the Cortes after Article 26 of the Constitution (the 'matter of religion') was passed, and they published a manifesto declaring that 'the Constitution that is going to be passed cannot be ours' and that they would employ all their efforts in 'mobilising public opinion against it'. Alcalá Zamora and Miguel Maura, the Prime Minister and the Interior Minister, who had voted against it, resigned. The person who came out of all this best, Manuel Azaña, was proposed as the new Prime Minister. He took possession of the office on 15 October and introduced just one change: a new member of his party, José Giral, came in as Minister for the Navy, to replace Casares Quiroga, who in turn took over the Interior Ministry in place of Miguel Maura.

After more than three months of debate, the Cortes finally passed the Constitution on 9 December 1931, with 368 votes in favour, which were later to be joined by a further 17 votes from absent deputies, and none against, as the representatives of the right-wing organisations had stayed away from the Chamber for the vote. Thus

[21] *Diario de las Sesiones de las Cortes*, 13 October 1931.
[22] National History Archives, series A, dossier 6.

the Constitution was born with the opposition and rejection of the non-republican right, which made up its mind, from that moment, to revise it or, in the case of its most extremist elements, to abolish it. Gil Robles, who at that time was already one of the most notable defenders of the 'accidental nature of forms of government', of hoisting the flag of order and religion in Parliament, and who did not agree with Catholic deputies abandoning it, as they had done after Article 26 was passed, declared that this Constitution 'in terms of public liberties is tyrannical; in terms of religion it is persecutory and in terms of ownership it is shamefully Bolshevik-leaning'.[23]

Now that the Constitution had been passed, it was time to elect the President of the Republic. He was to be elected not by direct universal suffrage, as had been envisaged at first, following the pattern in other European republics, but by the Cortes. The government had agreed that the man for the job was Niceto Alcalá Zamora, in an attempt to bring back into the fold the conservative sector that had expressed its opposition to the articles regarding religion. It was also agreed that the Cortes would not be dissolved until certain fundamental laws envisaged in the Constitution had been passed.

Alcalá Zamora called on Manuel Azaña to form a government. Azaña's intention was that all the political forces that had been in the government since the proclamation of the Republic should continue to be represented, in a similar proportion. Lerroux refused to carry on in the government with the socialists. Azaña would have to make a choice: either the socialists or the *Partido Radical*. And he opted for the socialists; 'sending the socialists into opposition would turn the Cortes into a madhouse', he wrote in his diary on 13 December, convinced as he was that introducing representatives of the working classes into the government of the nation was an indispensable condition for stabilising the Republic and democracy, as had been the case in other European countries after the First World War.[24] At that time, the crucial issue in all these democracies was the search for a 'stabilising coalition' that would be able to incorporate the most democratic

---

[23] Quoted in Mercedes Cabrera, 'Proclamación de la República, Constitución y reformas', in Santos Juliá (ed.), *Historia de España de Menéndez Pidal. República y guerra civil*, 42 vols., Espasa Calpe, Madrid, 2004, vol. XL, pp. 20–30.

[24] Manuel Azaña, *Memorias políticas y de guerra*, 4 vols., Crítica, Barcelona, 1981, vol. I, p. 335.

sectors of the middle classes and the more moderate fringe of the workers' movement to defend constitutional order.

The broad republican–socialist coalition that had governed in the early months of the Republic split in December 1931. Even so, the alliance between leftist republicans, some 150 deputies, and the socialists, with 115, ensured the existence of a government, bearing in mind that the 94 deputies who went over to the opposition belonged to a historical republican party, Lerroux's *Partido Radical*, and the monarchist or Catholic opposition was very weak at that time. The course of events, as we shall see, made it impossible for this 'stabilising coalition' to become consolidated, but the new government was formed, with Azaña as Prime Minister – a post he was to hold for almost two years, quite a feat considering the subsequent history of the Republic – and as Minister of War. Casares Quiroga and José Giral continued as Interior Minister and Minister for the Navy respectively. The radical-socialists Álvaro de Albornoz and Marcelino Domingo were given Justice, and Agriculture, Industry and Trade, respectively. Largo Caballero stayed on as Minister of Labour, and the other two socialists, Prieto and Fernando de los Ríos, were to take on the new Ministry of Public Works and Education. For the first time, two independents joined the government, the Catalan Jaime Carner and Luis de Zulueta, who were given Finance and Foreign Affairs, respectively.

Niceto Alcalá Zamora was President of the Republic and Manuel Azaña was Prime Minister. Spain was a parliamentary constitutional Republic. And it had managed all this in the seven months since the fall, the 'suicide', of the Monarchy. In view of the fact that this Republic, barely five years later, was defending itself in a civil war triggered by a coup d'état, all sorts of speculations may be made as to how far this Constitution and its administrators were responsible for the final drama. All the European republics that emerged in the 1920s and 1930s, except for Ireland, but including Germany, Austria, Czechoslovakia, Hungary, Poland, Portugal and Greece, ended up threatened by reactionary forces and overthrown by Fascist or authoritarian regimes. And in all cases, not only Spain, the necessary criterion for the consolidation and stabilisation of democracy was that a large majority of the population would accept, or at least tolerate, these new regimes that had been introduced so swiftly and with hardly any bloodshed.

The Second Republic went through two years of relative stability, followed by another two years of political uncertainty and a final few months of disturbance and insurrection. It was forced to face firm challenges and threats from above and below. The first firm challenges, which were the most visible as they usually ended up as confrontations with the forces of order, came from below, first as social protests and later as insurrections from anarchists and socialists. However, the coup de grâce, the challenge that finally overthrew the Republic by force of arms, came from above and from within – that is to say, the military command and the powerful ruling classes that had never tolerated it. And that is what is recounted in the first part of this book.

2 | *The constraints of democracy*

The political change of April 1931 arrived charged with hope and promise. It heralded the end of a corrupt and decadent past, and many people were hoping for a radical change of direction. No aspect of political or social life was excluded from the scope of reforms undertaken by the provisional government or those led by Manuel Azaña between October 1931 and September 1933. Over two years of feverish legislative activity were given over to the reorganisation of the army, the separation of Church and State, and the implementation of comprehensive radical measures with regard to land-ownership, workers' wages, employment protection and public education.

With republicans and socialists in the government, messages of hope and fear were soon to be heard all over Spain, with pressure from the higher and lower echelons of society to block the revolution that was under way or to eliminate all traces of the past monarchy. The labouring classes, with their organisations, protests and mobilisations, appeared on the public scene, in the streets, in Parliament and in the institutions, as a powerful force that could no longer be excluded from the political system. The old ruling classes, property owners and conventional society, displaced from power by the new republican regime, reacted energetically and resoundingly to the reforms. This mixture of great hopes, reforms, conflicts and resistance was what marked the Republic during its first two years. Never before had Spain experienced such an intense period of change and conflict, democratic advances or social conquests.

Reforms

The reform and reorganisation of the army was implemented by Manuel Azaña barely a week after he had been sworn in as the Minister for War in the provisional government. The army that the Republic inherited in 1931 had a history that abounded with interventions in politics, occupied a privileged position within the State and society, lacked modern armaments and was top-heavy with officers, many more than were necessary. Excluding the security forces, which were also militarised, the armed forces had 21,000 officers to lead 118,000 troops. And if we leave aside the troops stationed in Africa, one-third of the total, which included 4,000 Foreign Legionnaires and almost 9,500 Moroccan *Regulares*, the degree of organisation and preparation of the various units was somewhat lacking.

Azaña wanted an army that was more modern and more effective, as well as more republican, subject to constitutional political order. His first decree, on 22 April 1931, forced officers to make a promise of loyalty to the Republic, which most of them did, using the formula: 'I promise on my honour to serve the Republic well and faithfully, to obey its laws and defend it with arms.' Three days later, another decree, which aimed to tackle the most pressing issue, the overabundance of officers, allowed regular officers to opt for voluntary retirement while maintaining their salary. A total of 84 generals and 8,650 other officers took up this offer. With this measure, Azaña obtained a drastic reduction in the hierarchy, which brought about the reorganisation of the various units and improved promotion prospects, but historians agree that, politically, it was a doubtful measure that did not help to make the army more republican, because a large part of the most liberal sector of officers left active service at that time.

Another of the objectives of this reform, the reorganisation of the army, began with various decrees at the end of May and beginning of June 1931, which reduced the number of divisions from sixteen to eight; the corps of army chaplains was dissolved; command of the Corps of Carabineros, in charge of border policing, was transferred to the Ministry of Finance (*Hacienda*); the regional military headquarters (*capitanías generales*) were abolished, as was the rank of lieutenant general; and the Central High Command, abolished in 1925 by Primo de Rivera, was restored under the command of General Manuel Goded. Four of the seven military academies were closed, including the one in Zaragoza, established in 1927 under the command of General Francisco Franco.

The policy of postings and promotions was complex and controversial too. Although a great many officers were in favour of maintaining the criterion of length of service, there was a minority, closely connected with the army of Africa, who preferred 'merits of war' as a criterion. A decree of 4 May stipulated that postings should be decided by length of service, and left the appointment and promotion of generals in the hands of the Ministry of War. All promotions carried out under the Primo de Rivera dictatorship were to be reviewed, which introduced a major dose of anxiety among several hundred officers, who were afraid of being demoted from the ranks they had obtained.

The reform, which maintained the unfair, undemocratic 'quota' system, whereby military service was excused on payment of a sum of money, was vehemently opposed by a section of the officers, by conservative political media and by the military journals, *La Correspondencia Militar* and *Ejército y Armada*. Manuel Azaña was accused of having stated his intention to 'crush' the army. In fact, what he said in the speech alluded to by the military and right-wing media, delivered in Valencia on 7 June 1931, when referring to municipal control by the caciques, was that 'if ever I get to take part in this type of affair, I will crush and eradicate this organisation with the same energy and resolution, without losing control, that I have put into getting rid of other elements no less threatening for the Republic.' He did not specifically mention the army, but it did not matter. Azaña had become the bête noire of a significant sector of the military, many of whom were to take part in the coup in July 1936.

Although Azaña's first decree on 17 April abolished the 1906 Jurisdictions Act, which gave military tribunals the power to try civilians accused of crimes against the army or the *patria*, and another decree on 11 May reduced military jurisdiction in civilian crimes, the republican–socialist governments of the first two years still granted the army major powers with regard to public order and strict control over society.

Naturally, this public order aspect was no small matter for concern, as events bore out constantly over the years. Public order had become an obsession for the authorities, both political and military. And it was a well-founded obsession, but it quickly undermined the prestige of the republican regime. The fledgling regime provided itself with a Legal Statute, which gave the provisional government 'full powers', a situation that was maintained until the Defence of the Republic Act of 21 October 1931, and extended by means of the Public Order Act of July 1933.

In the medium term, the handing over of public order to the army meant major problems for the Republic; it had never addressed, or was unable to tackle, a serious reform of this sector of the administration. As Manuel Ballbé pointed out some years ago, 'the republican governments were unable to adapt the administration of public order to the principles of a democratic regime.' The republican governments used the same mechanisms of repression as those of the Monarchy, and did not break 'the direct relationship between the militarisation of public order and the politicisation of military sectors'.[1] Military power maintained its presence at the head of a good number of departments in the Administration, including the Police, the Civil and Assault Guards and the General Security Directorate. Sanjurjo, Mola, Cabanellas, Muñoz Grandes, Queipo de Llano and Franco, leading players in the July 1936 coup d'état, were good examples of this connection during the Second Republic. They all played major roles in the police administration and maintenance of public order.

Establishing the pre-eminence of civil power also called for the broad secularisation of society, and this brought the Republic into conflict with the Catholic Church, a mighty bureaucracy that, like the army, exercised a strong influence on Spanish society. The implementation of a series of secularising decrees and laws unleashed an acrimonious, emotionally charged struggle over religious symbols. The 'Royal March', which, during the time of the Monarchy, was always played at mass when the host was being consecrated, became one of the distinguishing marks of reaction, a provocation, as was the case with processions. The removal of crucifixes from schools met with vehement disapproval in many towns and villages in the north of Spain. There were also strong protests over the secularisation of cemeteries, which came into force on 30 January 1932, and the Divorce Act, passed on 2 February the same year.

As far as religion was concerned, there was little room for understanding. Manuel Azaña, who was appointed to head the government as a result of his famous speech on Article 26 of the Constitution, delivered in the Cortes on 13 October 1931, repeatedly insisted that the 'constitutional mandate' should be complied with 'in all its

---

[1] Manuel Ballbé, *Orden público y militarismo en la España constitucional (1812–1983)*, Alianza Editorial, Madrid, 1985, in which he devotes a chapter to this important topic, pp. 317–96.

requirements.' And compliance with Article 26 called for declaring Church property as belonging to the State, and barring religious orders from taking part in industrial and trading activities, and in teaching.

This Religious Confessions and Congregations Act, passed by the Cortes on 17 May 1933, caused much more of a storm than Azaña had foreseen, and stirred the Catholic Church into action. The bishops, who since April of that year had been led by the fundamentalist Isidro Gomá, reacted with a 'Bishops' Declaration', in which they regretted the 'harsh attack on the divine rights of the Church', and reaffirmed the superior, inalienable right of the Church to set up and run educational establishments, while rejecting 'non-Catholic, neutral or mixed schools'. On 3 June, the day after the Act had been endorsed by the President of the Republic, Alcalá Zamora, the Vatican issued an encyclical of Pius XI, *Dilectissima nobis*, devoted exclusively to this Act, which attacked the 'inalienable rights of the Church'. The Catholic press joined in the general outcry. Enrique Herrera Oria, the brother of Ángel Herrera and chairman of the *Federación de Amigos de la Enseñanza* (Federation of Friends of Education), classed the scenario created by the Act as being 'cultural civil war'.[2]

But no 'cultural civil war' broke out at that time, because before the deadline expired for the closing of religious educational establishments, set for 31 December 1933, the left lost the elections and the new *Partido Radical* government suspended the implementation of the Religious Confessions and Congregations Act. But this plan to halt the teaching activities of the Church forced the coalition government of republicans and socialists to initiate an urgent school-building programme, which was actually one of the pillars of the secular Republic: state schools, the reduction of illiteracy and the spreading of popular culture.

The Catholic Church had nearly 5,000 educational establishments with some 352,000 pupils, and 300 secondary education establishments, with over 20,000 students. While there were over 30,000 state primary schools, there were nearly a million children who received no education at all, the result of decades of government neglect as regards

[2] The arguments appearing here on religion and the confrontation between the Catholic Church and the Second Republic are developed in my book *La Iglesia de Franco*, Crítica, Barcelona, 2005, pp. 23–46.

education. The socialist Director-General of Primary Education, Rodolfo Llopis, estimated that in order to offset the closing of Church schools and provide education for all, over 27,000 schools would need to be built, at a rate of 5,000 new schools per year. Although over 10,000 new teaching positions were set up, the lack of resources in many city and town councils, which were responsible for building these schools, meant that this ambitious commitment could not be met. Even so, over 10,000 schools were built during the Republic; the budgetary allocation for education increased substantially between 1931 and 1934, and a great many studies have highlighted the Republic's success in this field.

In a bid to reduce illiteracy, which affected almost 50 per cent of those over 10 years of age, and many more females than males, the *Misiones Pedagógicas* were set up in 1931 'to bring the breath of progress to the people, with preference for those living in rural locations'. Its Board was presided over by Manuel Bartolomé Cossío, who had succeeded Francisco Giner de los Ríos as head of the *Institución Libre de Enseñanza* (Free Institution of Education), and the Board's members included the poets Manuel Machado and Pedro Salinas. One of its aims was to introduce the cinema and theatre to rural Spain, and it was helped in this by, among others, Federico García Lorca's *La Barraca* theatre company, which, with its classical repertoire, was active up to spring 1936.

The proclamation of the Republic also opened the debate over the shaping of the State and territorial organisation. As opposed to the federalist idea, which had placed such a burden on the short life of the First Republic in 1873, the 1931 Constitution introduced the term 'integral State', made up of 'municipalities combined into provinces and of regions under a system of autonomy'.

Catalonia was the first region to begin this process, following the provisional government's restoration of the *Generalitat* by decree on 21 April 1931. Jaume Carner was appointed to head the commission that was to present the draft Statute of Autonomy, which it did on 20 June. What was known as the Statute of Núria was approved by a referendum on 2 August, but subsequent debate in the Cortes delayed its final approval until 9 September 1932, by 314 votes to 24. The Statute proclaimed Catalonia an 'autonomous region within the Spanish State', gave the Catalan government major powers with regard to public order, social services, the economy and culture, and established Catalan and Castilian Spanish as joint official languages within its territory.

The Statute of Autonomy for Euskadi (the Basque Country) had also been strongly mooted since the advent of the Republic, although it was not passed until 1 October 1936, over two months into the civil war. The delay was due to the split in the Basque nationalist movement, which had failed to attend the meeting of the San Sebastián Pact, the existence of different autonomy plans and head-on opposition to Basque autonomy from the Navarran right and Carlism. Furthermore, religion, the distinguishing feature of these organisations, was used to block any potential understanding between the moderate nationalism of the Basque Nationalist Party and the autonomy plans drawn up by the socialists.

By the end of the republican period, only Catalonia had a Statute of Autonomy. It took five years for Basque autonomy to be passed, and autonomy plans for other regions, such as Galicia, had yet to reach the Cortes when a sector of the army decided to put an end to the Republic by force of arms. There was no time for any more statutes of autonomy and, except for Catalonia, neither was there any in-depth discussion about the development of autonomy under the terms of the Constitution.

Socialist participation in the governments of the first two years of the Republic made its presence felt in the labour legislation prepared by Francisco Largo Caballero in the Ministry of Labour. It was aimed at improving the quality of life and working conditions of workers and farm labourers, as well as reinforcing the UGT's position in the negotiation and monitoring of labour contracts. The principal measure of this new legal framework was the *Ley de Jurados Mixtos* (the Law of Joint Arbitration Committees), first in agriculture and then in industry, which extended the powers of the old committees during the dictatorship of Primo de Rivera. The job of these joint committees of employers and workers, presided over by a representative from the Ministry, was to approve labour contracts and to monitor their observance.

This labour corporatism was also backed up by the *Ley de Contratos de Trabajo* (Employment Contracts Act) of 21 November 1931, which regulated collective agreements, stipulated the conditions for the rescission of contracts and protected the right to strike. Of particular importance in the rural sphere were the municipal districts decree of 28 April, whereby local farm-hands were to be employed before bringing in labourers from outside, the decree of 8 May which imposed the compulsory cropping of certain sections of large estates, in order to counter recurrent neglect by absentee landlords, and the authorisation for collective settlements, of 19 May, which allowed agricultural worker syndicates to occupy abandoned estates. The list of reforms was completed by the implementation of various social benefits, including the compulsory worker retirement benefit, and maternity and workplace accident benefits.

With this legislation, a good many city and rural labourers saw their salaries improve and they acquired power and respect in the eyes of the employers. The UGT saw unprecedented growth, particularly the *Federación Nacional de Trabajadores de la Tierra* (National Agricultural Labourers' Federation), but these new State-backed concessions brought it into confrontation with the anarcho-syndicalists. The CNT felt that this government consolidation of worker corporatism gave unfair advantage to the UGT, basically in the control of employment, a scarce commodity in those times, and it began an open dispute to gain, by other means, the monopoly on labour negotiation, through direct action rather than through participation in the joint arbitration committees; and while at first it used warnings and threats, these later turned into coercion and violence.

However, the real improvement in agricultural workers' conditions were to arrive with the much-heralded agrarian reform, the most keenly awaited of all reforms. Spain had certainly progressed along the road to modernisation during the first three decades of the twentieth century. Primary sector employment, 57.3 per cent of the working population in 1920, had fallen to 45.5 per cent in 1930; in the secondary sector, it had risen from 21.9 per cent to 26.5 per cent; and in the services sector, it had risen from 21 per cent to 28 per cent. But at the beginning of the Republic, agriculture still accounted for half of Spain's economic output, and, as Edward Malefakis, author of still the best study on agrarian reform, wrote, control of the land meant control of the main source of national wealth, and this determined the social position of the majority of the population. It has often been said, and is worth repeating here, that in 1931, in spite of her industrial development and urban growth, Spain was still basically an agricultural country.[3]

---

[3] Edward Malefakis, *Reforma agraria y revolución campesina en la España del siglo XX*, Ariel, Barcelona, 1976.

There was no easy solution for what was known as the land problem in Spain for various reasons. The first reason was the complexity of the ownership structure: a predominance of extremes, with very few mid-size properties and marked regional differences, with a great many smallholdings in the north and mainly large estates in the south. The second reason was that although reformist politicians had been advocating some sort of agrarian reform since the end of the eighteenth century, almost nothing had been done by the beginning of the Republic. Repression, rather than reform, had always been the weapon used by the State against peasant protests. The final reason was that, as Malefakis pointed out, politically there was no way of distributing land without running up against strong opposition. The largest properties were not in the hands of the Church, foreign owners or the aristocracy, which would have facilitated matters, as it had done in other countries that undertook agrarian reform in the contemporary era. In Spain, land had to be taken from middle-class owners who, broadly speaking, were fully integrated into the structure of the nation, and who could not take any further pressure without the risk of calling into question many of the basic principles of this political structure. This was why any agrarian reform, however moderate, would have been seen by the owners as a revolution of compulsory seizures. And this was also why land became one of the fundamental pivots of conflict during the Republic and ended up being a substantial component of political violence on the two sides that fought the civil war.

Disagreements in the governing coalition, parliament's blocking of the right and organised lobbying by the landowners delayed the passing of the Act, the drafting of which was fraught with problems. On 21 May 1931, the socialist Fernando de los Ríos, Minister of Justice in the provisional government, appointed an Agrarian Technical Commission to draw up the first draft of the Republic's agrarian reform; the Commission was chaired by the jurist Felipe Sánchez Román, and among the members were experts well versed in rural matters, such as the economist Antonio Flores de Lemús, the notary Juan Díaz del Moral and the agronomist Pascual Carrión. The Commission proposed urgent 'temporary settlement' for between 60,000 and 75,000 landless families per year on large properties of more than 10 hectares of irrigated land or 300 hectares of unirrigated land in the provinces of Andalusia, Extremadura, Toledo and Ciudad Real. There was to be no change of legal ownership because the land would remain in the hands of its owners, and the reform, to be financed by a tax on the big estate owners, would last until the basic needs of all landless families had been covered, some fifteen years.

The socialists thought that this was extremely moderate, as there were no compulsory purchases or changes of ownership, while the big landowners organised themselves and put pressure on President Alcalá Zamora, a landowner like themselves, to prevent this measure from being implemented. A ministerial commission was then set up, chaired by Alcalá Zamora, which presented its project before the Cortes on 25 August 1931. The reform was to concentrate on lands belonging to the aristocracy and absentee landlords, with compulsory purchases, but with extremely high compensation payments that rendered it unworkable; in addition, there was no agreement concerning the scope of the reform or the way to raise money to finance it.

At the end of March 1932, a new plan was brought before the Cortes, drawn up by the team led by the Minister of Agriculture, Marcelino Domingo, which withdrew the tax on large estates and the offensive against the property of the aristocracy, with confiscations only in the case of land-ownership considered to be illegitimate, properties seized by the aristocracy in the nineteenth century. The discussions went on through part of the spring and the whole of the summer, with constant obstruction from the agrarian minority. The representative for Salamanca, Cándido Casanueva, a leading figure in this campaign to block the reform, spoke out against it in over twenty separate sessions of the Cortes.

Everything changed after the failure of the coup d'état led by General Sanjurjo on 10 August of that year. Azaña and his government saw a rise in their popularity, a good many representatives closed ranks in favour of the Republic and, on 9 September, the Act was finally passed, together with the Statute of Catalonia, by 318 votes to 19. There were 120 abstentions, including José Ortega y Gasset and Juan Díaz del Moral.

The Agrarian Reform Act envisaged just four types of land that could be compulsorily purchased: aristocratic estates, land that had been neglected, land that had been systematically leased, and any land located in irrigation zones that had not been planted in irrigable crops. A few days later, a body was set up to oversee the reform, the *Instituto de Reforma Agraria* (IRA; the Institute of Agrarian

Reform), with a budget of 50 million pesetas, just half the amount assigned to the Civil Guard.

The actual scope of the reform was extremely limited. Malefakis summed it up well when he wrote: 'Two and a half years after the proclamation of the Republic, only 45,000 hectares of land had changed hands, benefiting some 6,000 or 7,000 peasants'.[4] In spite of his statements about the urgency of agrarian reform, Manuel Azaña took no part in the drafting of the project presented by his government, nor in the debates in the Cortes, and he never gave this matter, or the situation of the landless peasants in the south, the attention that he devoted to other matters that concerned him. This lack of interest in agrarian reform, which extended to almost all the left-wing republicans, including the Minister of Agriculture, Marcelino Domingo, hindered the implementation of the September 1932 Act. There was apprehension over the resistance of the owners and a genuine social transformation in rural areas.

As was the case with other reformist Acts drawn up by the coalition government of republicans and socialists, the Agrarian Reform Act was moderate in practice but threatening in principle. Those who felt threatened by it very soon organised themselves to fight it. Earlier in August 1931, the big landowners had founded the *Asociación Nacional de Propietarios de Fincas Rústicas* (National Rural Estate Owners' Association) to defend the 'legitimate right of ownership'. In addition, the confusion and fear caused by a law that was threatening, because of clauses dealing with *ruedos* (lands on the edge of a town) and 'systematic renting', with more expropriations from smaller than from big landowners, were exploited by militant Catholicism to spur many of these 'very poor owners', predominant in the north of Spain, into turning against the Republic.

The Republic came to Spain in the midst of an unprecedented international economic crisis, and although, as experts have pointed out, economic factors played no part in the tragic denouement, they did make things difficult for the government and the implementation of reforms. Among the day-labourers, possibly the sector of the population with the highest hopes that this regime would eliminate excessive class privileges, these hopes began to be dashed when it became clear how slowly agrarian reform was progressing, that unemployment was

[4] Ibid., p. 325.

rife and resources had failed and when some of the most radical outbreaks of rural protest were met with harsh reprisals from the armed
forces. In those early years, there were serious public order problems, a good many protests, revolutionary skirmishes and anarchist
insurrections.

Protests

The first episodes of bloodshed occurred in Pasajes and Seville. At the
end of May 1931, a group of striking fishermen from Pasajes, in the
province of Guipúzcoa, started out on a march to San Sebastián; their
progress was blocked by the Civil Guard, who opened fire, killing
eight and wounding over fifty demonstrators. In Seville, after several
weeks of strikes and disturbances, four prisoners were killed in the
early hours of 23 July in the Parque de María Luisa. According to
Manuel Azaña, then the Minister of War, the event 'appeared to be an
application of the *ley de fugas*', the law which legitimised the shooting of detainees trying to escape. In the words of Miguel Maura, the
Interior Minister, 'at dawn, while prisoners were being moved from
Seville to Cádiz, and some of them were being transferred to another
truck in the middle of the Parque de María Luisa, they tried to escape
and the army, under the command of a young lieutenant, opened fire
and killed four of them'.[5]

As early as that summer, as Azaña noted in his diary, 'because of
the strikes being called everywhere by the *Confederación Nacional
de Trabajo*', the government decided 'to impose an urgent and severe
remedy'. Maura set out the general features of a decree, 'a legal instrument of repression', which was to become the Defence of the Republic
Act, and Largo Caballero, who was prepared to reduce the power of
the CNT at any price, stated that 'he would go further, because of the
danger faced by the Republic from the trade union movement'.[6]

Maura and Azaña, who had different ideas about authority and the
way to tackle unrest, did agree about one thing: the unpopularity of
the Civil Guard among the working classes, especially the peasants,

---

[5] Manuel Azaña, *Memorias políticas y de guerra*, 4 vols., Crítica, Barcelona,
   1981, vol. I, p. 55; Miguel Maura, *Así cayó Alfonso XIII. De una dictadura a
   otra*, Ariel, Barcelona, 1966, p. 285.
[6] Azaña, *Memorias políticas y de guerra*, vol. I, p. 48, annotation on 21 July
   1931.

who hated them, although, Azaña went on to say, there were others who adored them 'as the only upholders of social order'. As he explained: 'The Civil Guard has always been harsh, and what's worse, irresponsible'. And it was a situation that did not seem to improve in the early days of the Republic, 'because many are the mayors and local councillors who used to be the victims and quarry of the Civil Guard, which does not get on well with the new authorities'.

Events in various places on 11 and 12 May, with the burning of convents, confirmed for Miguel Maura 'the impossibility of dealing with public disturbances in cities with the Civil Guard', whose Mauser rifles, 'with their long range and slow loading ... made it hard for them to adapt to street fighting'. In any intervention 'it was inevitable that there was a high number of casualties, given their weaponry and their prescribed mode of procedure'. And so a new corps of armed police with a daunting name was born, the Assault Guard, under the command of the then Lieutenant Colonel Agustín Muñoz Grandes, who, according to Maura, 'created from scratch a perfect corps of trained, uniformed troops, who were hand-picked and had impeccable discipline'. They wore dark-blue uniforms and were armed with pistols and truncheons instead of rifles.

With the coming of the Republic, those who had hitherto had no power found new opportunities to become involved in politics, to influence the authorities, thanks to the regime change and the weakened state in which those who had up to then occupied positions of power now found themselves. With the loss of control in the city councils, the increase of socialist influence through the implementation of the joint committees in agriculture and the new legal framework set up by the Ministry of Labour to run labour relations, the owners' resistance to republican legislation greatly intensified. This hostility could be seen to be particularly acrimonious in areas with large estates and a rural proletariat, where social struggles seemed to be most intense. With the employers failing to comply with the basic regulations governing agricultural labour and republican social legislation in general, the gates were opened for a rash of protests from the peasants during the first two years of the Republic. In fact, what they were asking for in these conflicts was not social revolution, confiscations from the rich or land collectivisation – something that could be found in the most radical pamphlets – but better salaries, employment rights and access to land use.

'Situation untenable' were words often repeated in telegrams sent by mayors and civil governors to the Interior Minister, asking for funds for public works and to help the unemployed: '400 unemployed; all Council funds spent, begging in the streets; situation untenable; send funds soonest', wrote the mayor of Casariche, in the province of Seville, to the Interior Minister in a telegram that back in 1931 was a blueprint for many others from various towns and villages in Andalusia and Extremadura. And constantly underlying these messages was an attempt to show what would happen if, as was often the case, the money failed to appear: robberies, attacks on country estates and farms, a 'real danger for the maintenance of public order'.[7]

All this forced the civil governors to maintain a fine balance between pressure from the mayors and people in the provinces, and the higher authority in Madrid. The idea that the solution would come from above was widespread in the early days of the Republic, a time of optimism still, judging by the number of petitions from all over Spain to the authorities to provide relief for problems ranging from hunger to natural disasters and to distribute a little justice and charity. This was a hangover from a paternalistic era which had still not entirely disappeared, but it also shows how the unemployed and their families were neglected in a society in which there was no unemployment insurance whatsoever. It is true to say that, apart from the executive order of 28 May 1931, whereby loans were made by the *Instituto Nacional de Previsión* (National Benefit Institute) 'to solve the unemployment situation', there was no progress at all during the term of the coalition government.

Potential solutions that had been commonly used in the past were now no longer available. There was no money to finance public works, and even those who could provide employment refused to hire union members, who were often forced to leave the union as a condition for being hired. These were threatening messages that, while they might not have met strong resistance, had the twofold effect of getting rid of 'enlightened workers' and of lowering previously agreed wages. Meanwhile, all any civil governor could do was to record the event, come up with a potential 'peaceful' solution, impose it if necessary and, when all else failed, maintain order.

[7] All the quotes taken from telegram exchanges between the civil governors of the various provinces and the Interior Ministry are housed in the National Historical Archive, Madrid.

'Deploy the Civil Guard' was another of the most common petitions made by local authorities, civil governors and employers to the Interior Minister. There was nothing surprising about such requests. All it took was for a strike to be called by a section of a trade union and the local mayor would ask the civil governor to intervene, and he in turn would ask the minister to authorise him to deploy the Civil Guard. At other times, it would be some employer who would contact the minister directly to ask for armed assistance at harvest time, 'with lodging provided and any extra expenses paid for'.

The fact that employers and the local councils had to meet any costs arising from the deployment of the Civil Guard, whenever this was asked for, is highly indicative of the lack of resources and usually poor financial management suffered by the State, and of the structural problems of her law enforcement units, who were badly paid, poorly equipped and, like the rest of the administration in general, somewhat ineffective. The Civil Guard was further affected by the dispersion of its forces. Whenever there was an outbreak of unrest and they had to go to other locations, typically from the provinces to the major cities, their villages of origin were left 'unprotected' and panic would spread among the authorities affected by the threat that 'extremist elements', taking advantage of the situation, would demonstrate against 'order and property'.

Hopes for a radical change in class relationships in the rural sphere were soon dashed. That, at any rate, was how it was perceived by many peasant groups, who, while never ceasing to appeal for protection from the government, showed their discontent in confrontations fraught with illusions and potential demands, with the dream of social revolution tantalisingly round the corner. The legislation implemented by the government was possibly right for the time and, but for the much-discussed agricultural reform that was yet to materialise, a good number of day-labourers and tenants benefited from the early winds of change. But unemployment was getting out of hand and the government had no resources to alleviate the situation. Many landowners were already beginning to express openly their strong hostility towards the 'torment' of the Republic, and the forces of order were incapable of policing it without the use of arms.

Hardly any blood was shed in these disturbances until what one might call the fatal week that ran from Thursday 31 December 1931 to Tuesday 5 January 1932. There was nothing at the end of the year to suggest what was to come, nor was the Republic experiencing any particular tension. The Constitution had been passed on 9 December in the Cortes by a large majority, Alcalá Zamora was elected President a day later, and on 15 December Azaña formed a government.

It all began in Castilblanco, a village in the north-west of the province of Badajoz, in the jurisdiction of Herrera del Duque. The Federation of Land Workers in this province called a general strike for 30 and 31 December, to protest against the Governor and the colonel commanding the Civil Guard, whom the Federation accused of supporting the landlords and caciques in their opposition against the social legislation that had recently been implemented. The strike was generally peaceful, with just the odd confrontation between the Civil Guard and land-workers, and on the second day, when the demonstrators were returning home, the mayor, or else a landlord, according to other sources, asked the Civil Guard to disperse them. There were clashes, and one worker was shot dead by the Civil Guard. The peasants, beset with rage and hatred, that hatred which Azaña had mentioned in his diary, turned on the four guards and slaughtered them with stakes, rocks and knives.

Enraged, undisciplined and faced with the passive attitude of certain government authorities, the Civil Guard worked off steam for a few days with deadly reprisals. The most outrageous incidents, apart from those in Zalamea de la Serena, where they killed two workers and wounded a further three, occurred a long way from Castilblanco and areas with large estates, in locations where the unions and employers were in conflict over matters that were typical of times of low employment. In Épila, in the province of Zaragoza, the workers of the sugar factory, apparently at the instigation of the CNT and with the opposition of the UGT, proposed that with any new hiring, priority should be given to those on this district's census. On Saturday 2 January, with the factory on strike, the agricultural workers stayed away from work and some businesses remained closed. On the Sunday, some 500 people assembled in the town square. The Civil Guard tried to clear the square, and opened fire, killing two day-labourers and wounding several others. The following day, in Jeresa, a village in the district of La Safor in the province of Valencia, an assembly of peasants who were in conflict with their employers over the latter's refusal to accept proposed working conditions, hurled insults and rocks at the mounted Civil Guard. There was a sabre charge and gunfire, resulting in four deaths and thirteen people wounded, two of them women.

And then there was Arnedo. The events in this town in La Rioja, with a population of just over 5,000, the hub of a shoemaking cottage industry, gave rise to an 'outcry' against the Civil Guard for its bloodbath in the Plaza de la República: six men and five women dead; eleven women and nineteen men wounded, five of whom were unable to work again; and a Civil Guard with a light bullet wound. All ages were represented: among the dead were a seventy-year-old woman and a child of four, whose mother was also killed; the wounded included men and women of over sixty and a five-year-old child whose leg had to be amputated. With such a casualty list, it was no wonder that the 'outcry', as Azaña called it, was 'deafening'.

The resource material we have at our disposal is plentiful, varied and reliable, leaving little room for ambiguity. Almost a year before this incident, a dispute arose in the shoemaking firm belonging to the Muro family, when the owner's son fired an employee who subsequently received the support of his colleagues, and they in turn were fired as well. There followed a long period of negotiation, in which the Civil Governor took part, but they were not reinstated, so the workers went on strike on 5 January, with the UGT leaders and strike committee inviting 'all enlightened citizens' to join with the 'downtrodden workers ... to request our and our children's daily bread, which these heartless bosses want to snatch away from us'.

That same day, the Civil Governor, Ildefonso Vidal, arrived to chair a meeting in the town hall with the mayor, various councillors, the commanding officer of the local Civil Guard garrison and some employers who agreed to take on the workers sacked by Muro. The demonstrating workers arrived at the town square, with women and children at the front, to be met by a formation of the Civil Guard with one sergeant, four corporals and twenty troopers under the command of Lieutenant Juan Corcuera y Piedrahita. Without any warning or advisory shots in the air, 'fire was opened unexpectedly and devastatingly', and only ceased 'on the order of the commanding officer when he came out of the town hall'. There had been no 'collective aggression or collective resistance' and the panic-stricken crowd fled the square. According to the conclusions in the inquiry led by the Civil Governor of Vizcaya, 'the Lieutenant commanding the troop should not have broken up the demonstration ... because in the town hall were his superiors, the Civil Governor and the commanding officer, who had given him no order to do so'.

The preliminary investigations by a military judge and by a second judge in further indictments found no case against any of the inhabitants, although there are conflicting versions as to whether the bullet that wounded the civil guard came from a handgun belonging to one of the demonstrators or, as the doctor who treated the injured declared, from a Mauser. The military judgment, handed down in Burgos on 30 January 1934, cleared the lieutenant 'of the crime of murder and inflicting injuries through criminal negligence, because there is insufficient proof that he did commit such a crime, and the same ruling applies to charges brought against the Civil Guard unit under his orders'.[8]

Azaña telephoned General Sanjurjo to notify him that he was being relieved of his post as Director of the Civil Guard. In the conversation that the Prime Minister recorded in his diaries, there is no mention of what Sanjurjo thought of atrocities such as those committed by his subordinates in Arnedo, but the general was in no doubt as to who was to blame. Many socialist town councils were peopled with 'riff-raff', 'undesirables' who 'incite disorder, intimidate employers, cause damage to property and feel bound to clash with the Civil Guard'. Socialists, said the general to Azaña, should not be in the government 'because their presence encourages those who favour excess'.[9] Such was the atmosphere of disorder that he believed existed, that a few months later he led the first military uprising against the republican regime.

The dead were duly buried, Sanjurjo was transferred to become Director of the Carabineros, Miguel Cabanellas was appointed Director of the Civil Guard, and the Arnedo incident faded into the background, dwarfed by other tragic events, particularly those in Casas Viejas exactly one year later. The Civil Guard felt it was being unfairly vilified, and the memory of Castilblanco might have explained their sudden, bloody response. But it was this very response that continued feeding the reality and myth of a State that was failing

---

[8] Extensive information and analysis of these conflicts can be found in Julián Casanova, *Anarchism, the Republic and Civil War in Spain: 1931–1939*, Routledge, London, 2004, pp. 24–6. The best study on Arnedo is by Carlos Gil, *La República en la plaza: los sucesos de Arnedo de 1932*, Instituto de Estudios Riojanos, Logroño, 2002.

[9] Azaña, *Memorias políticas y de guerra*, vol. I, p. 365, annotation on 6 January 1932.

to control, even with military and governmental authorities in place, its machinery of repression, and it did not seem capable of enforcing its new legislation either.

The features of conflicts in the cities during the republican–socialist coalition government were different to those pertaining in the rural world. The most notable of these is the fact that the struggle for control of available jobs, the distribution of trade union influence – which, at a time of crisis, when the unions became employment exchanges, was linked to the previous feature – and confrontation over the corporate structure were the basic connecting threads of anarchist agitation, strikes and bitter clashes between the two branches of trade unionism that were entrenched in the working classes. The government-backed UGT, by legislating and using the machinery of the State, began to exert ever more influence in the sphere of labour relations. The CNT saw this as interference that severely limited its sphere of influence and opted for direct action, without State intermediaries, with the streets as the setting for its struggle and confrontation with the State, and its most radical sector began to preach revolution through disturbances and revolt. This clash unleashed accusations and insults and placed a large sector of the organised working class at odds with the Republic.

The CNT's ability to stir up antagonism against the joint committees soon became evident in cities such as Barcelona, Seville and Zaragoza, where there was a predominance of anarcho-syndicalists. Not surprisingly, Barcelona was the most contested forum in this struggle, with a rapidly reorganised and expanding CNT, and the UGT willing to exploit the situation to make inroads in an area that had hitherto proved hard to penetrate. From the early days of the Republic, industrialists and UGT unions had denounced outrages, insults and 'brutal coercion' by the CNT, whose unions refused to register their members on the social electoral roll set up to elect representatives to the joint committees.

With his customary precision, Manuel Azaña noted on various occasions the importance of this 'civil war' between the two trade union factions, 'probably the harshest political reality in Spain at this time': 'The CNT unions', he noted on 26 September 1931, 'are refusing to comply with social legislation in Catalonia. They do not accept the arbitration committees or Department of Labour inspections. We have had a fair amount of problems in the Cabinet over this matter, and Largo Caballero has fought hard ... to bring the undisciplined unionists under the authority of the departments of the Ministry of Labour'. On 7 May 1932, following a meeting with Largo and Fernando de los Ríos, the Prime Minister expressed it even more clearly: 'The socialists are determined to maintain control of social matters in Catalonia, or rather (because at the moment they do not have this control) in ensuring, through ministerial bodies, their defence against their dire enemies, the syndicalists of the CNT'.[10]

The response to the CNT was soon to be evident on the very stage that many of its militants had chosen for their struggle: the streets. Between May and July 1931, the CNT called various strikes which, in some cases, were joined by the Communists; they led to a good many casualties – for example, in Pasajes and Seville – and dashed many of the hopes of more moderate syndicalists. The 'civil war' between the two trade union organisations escalated in the general strike called by the Asturias Miners' Union in June, and the gap between them opened even wider in the nationwide telephone operators' strike called by the anarchist unions at the beginning of July. This strike was not supported by the other three unions in the company, and Maura opposed direct negotiation by the strikers with the company. Clashes with the forces of order resulted in several casualties, while many people were arrested and others dismissed.

The CNT, with its struggle against State intervention in disputes between employees and workers, contributed to the failure of the 'conciliation' procedure, the essence of the corporate system, but received very few benefits in return. Since the Republic did not, or could not, offer the workers the favourable results they expected, the most radical views very soon began to be heard among the large number of rural and urban unemployed. The internal struggle lead to a schism, with thousands of militants in the most industrialised areas, where the organisation was most firmly entrenched, leaving the CNT, including some of its most outstanding leaders, such as Juan Peiró and Ángel Pestaña.

The hard core of the anarchist movement used killing and repression as a springboard for mobilisation against the Republic and the leaders of the CNT at that time. The term 'government by violence' (*el crimen, método de gobierno*) began to appear in the anarchist

---

[10] *Memorias políticas y de guerra*, vol. I, p. 465.

media following the events in Pasajes and Seville. And it was from January 1932 onwards that this talk of the spilling of 'proletarian blood' finally became rooted in the anarchist media. Protest escalated into revolt. There were three attempts at armed insurrection in two years, incited by anarchist militants, supported to some degree by workers and peasants. The first two were directed against the republican–socialist coalition government. The third, the one with the most casualties, which we shall look at later, occurred a few days after Larroux's radicals and the right won the elections.

Revolts: Death in Casas Viejas

On 19 January 1932, miners from the mining camp of San Cornelio, in Fígols, came out on strike; they disarmed the *somatén* (local civilian defence force) and the conflict spread to other areas of the Alto Llobregat and Cardoner. This was a wildcat strike and thus bore no relation to subsequent uprisings in 1933, which were planned and organised by leading members of the CNT and the Federación Anarquista Ibérica (FAI). The harsh conditions in the mines, with long hours and unsafe pits, the frustrated hopes that the arrival of the Republic would change this situation, and the struggle for the right of assembly, which was not recognised, even in the new political climate, all fuelled a major focus of discontent that was unleashed on the morning of 19 January 1932. At first, it was a simple strike, aimed at improving these conditions, although the more politically aware declared the arrival of libertarian Communism. Convinced that they would only succeed if they managed to arm themselves and thus block the response of the mine owners, they disarmed the *somatén* and began to patrol the streets.

The resistance spread to neighbouring towns the next day. In Berga, Sallent, Cardona, Balserany, Navarcles and Súria, the mines and other businesses were closed. In Manresa, picketing workers blocked access to factories and workshops. The cutting of telephone communications and the replacement of republican flags with black and red banners in certain town halls in the region suggested that this was something more than mere industrial action over working conditions. On that same day, a delegate of the regional committee of the CNT arrived in Fígols. Along with the revolutionary committee set up by the striking miners and other anarchist groups, he announced throughout the region that 'libertarian communism had arrived'.

On 21 January, the Prime Minister, Manuel Azaña, addressed the Cortes. No one was authorised to 'rise up' against the Republic. 'I am not frightened of strikes … because that is a right recognised in law'. But in the face of 'excesses', the military had the obligation to intervene. Effectively, on 22 January, the first military reinforcements arrived in Manresa from Zaragoza, Lérida, Gerona and Barbastro. By 23 January they had occupied all the towns in the area except Fígols. They arrived there the next day and found that the miners had blown up the explosives store and fled to the mountains. Order was restored on 25 January. The miners were dismissed. Local people who had opposed the conflict collaborated in the repression.

The miners' hopes had been dashed. The subversion of order in the mines soon came to an end. There was no looting, nor abolition of private property, nor deaths. However, the National Committee of the CNT, spurred on by the desire to 'call the revolutionary strike', which certain union leaders in Barcelona were demanding, agreed at a meeting on 23 January, when the miners' uprising was already drawing to a close, 'to call a strike in all of Spain, accepting all the consequences'. Only a few towns in Valencia and Aragon responded. In the town of Alcorisa, in the province of Teruel, activists placed two bombs in the barracks of the Civil Guard, and not far from there, in Castel de Cabra, its barely 500 inhabitants experienced for one day what the Governor of the province of Zaragoza, Carlos Montilla, called 'the proclamation of the Soviet Republic'. According to the newspapers at that time, on 25 January, 'the rebels took over the town hall, destroyed the tax register and all the documents in the archive of the municipal secretariat'. Troops from Barcelona and Zaragoza undertook the suppression of the rebellion. By 27 January, it was all over.[11]

Order was accompanied by several dozen arrests and the closing down of all CNT premises in the affected districts. But the impact of this persecution gained disproportionate coverage, thanks to the notorious and controversial affair of the deportations. On 22 January,

---

[11] The insurrections and the various postures of the anarchist movement with regard to them are explored in Casanova, *Anarchism, the Republic and Civil War in Spain*, pp. 64–83.

several anarchist militants had been arrested in Barcelona, including the Ascaso brothers, Francisco and Domingo, Buenaventura Durruti and Tomás Cano Ruiz. Along with other CNT activists, they were transferred the next day to the merchant ship *Buenos Aires*, which was anchored in the port. The news that they were going to be deported, a sentence that was covered under the terms of Article 2 of the Defence of the Republic Act, unleashed the fury of the libertarian media. By 26 January, there were already over 200 prisoners on the ship. On 28 January, about a hundred of them began a hunger strike and, a few days later, issued a communiqué denouncing their helpless situation. The ship finally set sail from the port of Barcelona on 10 February, with 104 prisoners on board. After picking up more prisoners in Cádiz, the *Buenos Aires* called in at the Canary Islands and Fernando Poo, before arriving at Villa Cisneros on 3 April. Some of the prisoners became seriously ill (one fatally), and others were released during the journey. By the time the affair had concluded and the last deportees had returned to Spain in September, the leading lights of the CNT and the FAI had placed themselves at the forefront of opposition to the government of the Republic.

Some months later, the CNT, which by then had been abandoned by tens of thousands of militants, returned to the fray. This time there were preparations, but they were so secret and flawed that hardly anyone had any inkling of them. In a plenary session of regional delegates of the CNT, held in Madrid on 1 December 1932, the National Committee of the Railway Industry, a minority rail-workers' union, had asked for support and financing to call a general strike to obtain wage increases. However, the rail-workers backed down because over half of their unions forecast a 'spectacular failure'. This restraint was a source of great annoyance to the Regional Defence Committee of Catalonia, which, guided by Joan García Oliver, was ready to put into practice his famous 'revolutionary gymnastics', an 'oscillating insurrectional action' that would prevent the consolidation of the 'bourgeois Republic'. The Committee chose 8 January 1933, at 8 pm, as the moment.

Needless to say, it was a fiasco, although strikes and incidents with explosives did once again reach certain towns in Aragon and Valencia. The army and police forces took up strategic positions in towns where disturbances were predicted. The union leaders were arrested and the blame and reproaches multiplied. Just when it seemed it had all blown over, news of disturbances in the province of Cádiz began to arrive, where anarchist groups and local defence committees were threatening order in the capital, Jerez de la Frontera, Alcalá de los Gazules, Paterna de la Rivera, San Fernando, Chiclana, Los Barrios and Sanlúcar.

That same day, 10 January, Captain Manuel Rojas Feijespán received the order to transfer from Madrid to Jerez, with his company of assault guards, and put an end to the anarchist rebellion. They spent the night on the train. When they arrived in Jerez, they found that the telephone lines had been cut in Casas Viejas, a town with barely 2,000 inhabitants, 19 kilometres from Medina Sidonia. Groups of peasants affiliated to the CNT took up positions in the town at dawn on 11 January, and, following the preparatory instructions issued by anarchists in the district of Jerez, they surrounded the Civil Guard barracks, armed with a few pistols and shotguns. Inside were three guards and a sergeant. After an exchange of fire, the sergeant and one of the guards were seriously wounded. The sergeant died the next day; the guard, a few days after that.

At two o'clock that same afternoon, twelve Civil Guards, under the command of Sergeant Anarte, arrived at Casas Viejas. They freed the two guards still in the barracks and occupied the town. Fearful of reprisals, many of the peasants fled. The rest locked themselves in their homes. A few hours later, four more Civil Guards and twelve Assault Guards, under the command of Lieutenant Fernández Artal, joined those who had previously controlled the situation. With the help of the two Civil Guards who knew the town's inhabitants, the Lieutenant began the search for the rebels. They seized two of them and beat them until they mentioned the family of Francisco Cruz Gutiérrez, 'Seisdedos' (Six Fingers), a 72-year-old charcoal burner who sometimes attended CNT meetings, but who had not taken part in the disturbances. But two of his sons and his son-in-law had done so, and following the siege of the barracks, they had taken refuge in Seisdedos' house, a flimsy shack of mud and stones.

The Lieutenant ordered the door to be forced. Those inside opened fire and one of the Assault Guards was killed. At ten o'clock that night, reinforcements arrived, with grenades, rifles and a machine gun. They began the attack with little success. A few hours later, they were joined by Captain Rojas, with forty Assault Guards, under orders from Arturo Menéndez, the Director-General of Security, to transfer from Jerez to Casas Viejas to put down the insurrection and to 'open fire without mercy on everyone who shot at the troops'.

Rojas ordered the shack to be set on fire. By then, some of the occupants had already been killed by rifle and machine-gun fire. Two were riddled with bullets when they ran out to escape the flames. María Silva Cruz, 'La Libertaria', Seisdedos' granddaughter, saved her life because she was carrying a child in her arms. Eight dead was the final tally; six of them were burnt inside the shack, including Seisdedos, two of his sons, his son-in-law and his daughter-in-law. The insurrection in Casas Viejas was over. It was the morning of 12 January 1933.

Rojas sent a telegram to the Director-General of Security: 'Two dead. Rest of revolutionaries trapped in flames'. He also informed him that he was continuing with the search for the leaders of the movement. He sent three patrols to search the houses, accompanied by the two Civil Guards from the Casas Viejas barracks. No sooner had they started, when they killed a 75-year-old man who shouted, 'Don't shoot! I'm not an anarchist!' They arrested a further twelve, of whom only one had taken part in the disturbances. They were dragged in handcuffs to Seisdedos' shack. Captain Rojas, who had been drinking brandy in the bar, began shooting, followed by other guards. They killed all twelve. A little later, they left the town. The massacre was over. Nineteen men, two women and a child were killed. Three guards suffered the same fate. The truth about the incident took time to be made public, because the early versions had all of the peasants killed in the attack on Seisdedos' shack, but the Second Republic now had its tragedy.[12]

Dozens of peasants were arrested and tortured. The prisoners blamed Seisdedos and those who had been killed, in order to save their skins. The government, in an attempt to ride out the attacks against it, from left and right, over the excessive cruelty it had used to put down the uprising, washed its hands of all responsibility. 'There is no evidence of any government blame here', claimed Azaña in a speech to the Cortes on 2 February that year.

[12] The account is based on the excellent description of this insurrection by Jerome R. Mintz, *The Anarchists of Casas Viejas*, University of Chicago Press, 1982, pp. 189–255.

As far as we can see, what happened in Casas Viejas was inevitable. There was a rising in Casas Viejas, under the banner that has turned the heads of the uneducated and the unemployed of the Spanish working class, the banner of libertarian communism; and a few dozen men raised this banner of libertarian communism, armed themselves, attacked the Civil Guard and killed some of them. What was the government supposed to do?

Faced with 'an armed uprising against society and the State', he had no choice, he said several times to the members, even if there was the risk of some agent committing certain excesses 'in the pursuit of his duty'. At any event, he said later in the Cortes on 2 March, the origins of these rebellions against the State, the Republic and social order were not to be found in the government's social policy: 'Did we, this government or any government, sow the seeds of anarchism in Spain? Was it us who founded the FAI? Have we given support, in any way, to the machinations of the agitators who are spreading the slogan of libertarian communism throughout the towns and villages?'[13]

Although certain newspapers, such as *ABC*, initially applauded the punishment meted out to the revolutionaries, the opposition to the government from both the radicals and the right grew steadily from that moment on. Eduardo Guzmán, who visited Casas Viejas along with Ramón J. Sender, seriously questioned the official version in the pages of *La Tierra*. The CNT, which gained nothing from the incident but more martyrs for the cause, made ground in its campaign against 'dictatorial policies and trouble-making politicians'. It did not matter that it was being persecuted, they argued in their media, because 'in prison, in silence, the voice of the revolution is heard by free spirits'.

History was repeating itself: following an insurrection, the CNT would organise demonstrations to protest against the repression. The rest of the year was spent protesting about the growing number of prisoners in the gaols and in feverish preparation for the revolution which, for the moment, would shape up to be another aborted insurrection a few months later.

The origin of all the tragic incidents that accompanied these anarchist insurrections was confrontation with the forces of law and order. There were no atrocities or acts of vengeance against the clergy, nor

[13] Manuel Azaña's speeches in *Obras completas*, 7 vols., Oasis, México, 1966–68, vol. II, pp. 334–6, 597.

was there any violence against employers or symbols of economic exploitation, to name just some of the elements that the anarchists did target in the revolution that followed the coup d'état in July 1936. Nevertheless, the fact that violence was not used in this respect does nothing to mollify the nature of this method of coercion against established authority. What was behind it was, essentially, a rejection of the system of representation and the belief that force was the only way to abolish class privilege and its accompanying abuse of power.

It is hard to dispute the idea that the preparation and putting into practice of these insurrections was the work of anarchist groups inspired by cataclysmic dreams. There were not, nor could there be, many rural or urban workers behind this supposed revolution. Those who made decisions on the suitability of the insurrectional movement failed to show the same ability to organise it. This was because, among other reasons, there was not much to organise. While a strike, a conflict over poor living conditions, non-compliance with working practices or a protest against repression was one thing, armed insurrection was an entirely different matter. An action totally detached from the usual labour practice based on trade unionism, which after all was where the CNT's strength lay, could not be supported by moderate unionists, who were removed from the leadership for refusing to condone confrontation with the authority of the Republic, as they considered it to be a mistaken and suicidal tactic.

CNT opposition deprived the Republic of a fundamental social cornerstone. But although anarchist radicalism helped to spread the culture of confrontation, it was not the only, nor even the most powerful, movement to frustrate the consolidation of the Republic and its reformist project. The dominant groups who had been removed from political institutions with the arrival of the Republic were not slow to react. In less than two years, Catholicism took root as a mass political movement, with the support of hundreds of thousands of small and medium-sized rural landowners, and launched a destabilising offensive that only concluded when it had met its objective of overthrowing the reforms and removing the threat of revolution. Now is the time to examine in some detail the nature and manifestations of this reaction.

3 | *Order and religion*

Religion was a basic component of many of the conflicts that had spread throughout Europe in the period between the two world wars. The Russian revolution and the fear of Communism taking root elsewhere gave rise to a conservative mass reaction that in some countries, such as Germany, Austria, Italy and Poland, took the form, even before the appearance of Fascism, of a popular Catholic movement. The antagonism between the Catholic Church and the political left acquired fresh vigour. However, nowhere was the struggle between the Catholic Church and the various socialist projects, between clericalism and anticlericalism, so intense as in Spanish society in the 1930s. The conflict had deep historical roots, but the coming of the Republic and its attempts to modernise society and politics by debilitating the power of the clergy revealed it in all its harsh reality. The result was the birth of the first mass right-wing party in the history of Spain, a party that played a major role in the hounding and overthrow of the Republic.

Religion, 'the seed of discord'

In the years prior to the proclamation of the Republic, the Catholic Church, under the protective mantle of Primo de Rivera's dictatorship, envisaged no serious changes in store for its privileged position. In spite of the disentailments of Church property and the liberal revolutions of the nineteenth century, the confessional state had remained intact. Catholicism saw itself as the historical religion of the Spanish. As custodian of the highest virtues and a perfect society, in close harmony with the State, the Church was secure, because at the height of the twentieth century, Spain represented the epitome of a society with a single religion, a religion directed and followed by people, bishops, religious orders and laymen, who considered that the thorough preservation of social order was not renounceable in view of the close relationship between order and religion in Spain's history.

However, against this constant power and presence of the Church, a counter-tradition of criticism, hostility and opposition had emerged. Anticlericalism, already in evidence in the nineteenth century, with intellectuals and liberal politicians prepared to reduce the power of the clergy in the State and in society, entered the twentieth century in a new, more radical phase, to be joined by militant workers. And thus it emerged, beginning with Barcelona and followed by other Spanish cities, a network of athenaeums, newspapers, lay schools and other manifestations of a popular culture, basically anti-oligarchical and anticlerical, in which republicanism and organised labourism – anarchist or socialist – joined forces.

The Church resisted with vigour these impetuous onslaughts of modernisation and secularisation. It built up a solid rampart against those who were in disagreement with its opinions. In a confessional State, in which Church and political power were so closely united, there was nothing to fear from mass apostasy. At least, that is what it thought. And it would go on thinking this as long as it held the monopoly on education, as long as its charitable works received the moral and financial blessing of respectable society – in short, as long as Catholics played a leading role in the early stages of social projects.

But industrialisation, urban growth and the escalation of class conflicts substantially changed this situation during the first three decades of the twentieth century. Some writers on Catholic affairs, concerned by the consequences of these changes, noted that the urban poor displayed a deep distrust of Catholicism, as it was always on the side of the rich and the employers, and the Church was considered to be a class enemy.

On the eve of the Republic, so these writers say, the urban proletariat in Madrid, Barcelona, Valencia and Seville, and from the mining areas of Asturias and Vizcaya, rarely entered a church, and were unaware of Catholic doctrines and ritual. Many priests in the large estate regions of Andalusia and Extremadura would often draw attention to the growing hostility shown to them and the Church by day-labourers 'polluted' by socialist and anarchist propaganda.

As far as religious practice and the role of religion in daily life were concerned, there was a vast difference between these 'de-catholicised' areas, with no Church influence, and the rural world in the north. In Castilla la Vieja, Aragon and the Basque provinces, going to church was part of the weekly and, for many women, daily routine, a show of fidelity to religion and social conformity. The Church's influence invaded daily life and established the rules of behaviour. Nearly everyone in these regions had some member of the family in the Church, providing most of Spain's priests, monks and nuns, and it was to the well-to-do districts in these areas that nearly all resources were destined.

The gulf between these two conflicting cultural worlds, practising Catholics and hardened anticlericalists, narrowed with the proclamation of the Second Republic, and a large number of Spaniards who had hitherto displayed indifference to this struggle were caught in the middle. All the alarm bells started ringing. Lluis Carreras and Antonio Vilaplana, two priests who worked with Cardinal Vidal i Barraquer, put it plainly in the report that they sent on 1 November 1931 to the Vatican State Secretariat: under the 'apparent grandeur' of the Church during the Monarchy, 'Spain was becoming religiously impoverished', with the enlightened elite and the common people distancing themselves from religion, and the nation needing a 'restoration of Christian society'.[1]

The blame was placed on the Republic for its obsessive persecution of the Church and Catholics, while in fact the conflict was far-reaching, with its origin in previous decades. It was not that Spain was no longer Catholic, as Manuel Azaña put it so graphically in his speech in the Cortes on 13 October 1931, by which he meant that the Church no longer guided Spanish culture, having turned its back on the working classes a long time before. It was that there was one Spain that was extremely Catholic, another not so much so, and a third that was highly anti-Catholic. There was more Catholicism in the north than in the south, among landowners than among the dispossessed, among women than among men. The majority of Catholics were antisocialist and law-abiding citizens. The republican and working-class left was associated with anticlericalism. It is hardly surprising that the proclamation of the Republic meant rejoicing for some and mourning for others.

Republican legislation further reinforced the traditional correlation between order and religion, although during the early days of the Republic, before these laws appeared, a group of distinguished

---

[1] Quoted by Hilari Raguer, 'La cuestión religiosa', in Santos Juliá (ed.), 'Política en la Segunda República', *Ayer*, 20 (1995), p. 232.

Catholics, encouraged by Ángel Herrera, the editor of *El Debate*, decided to found a new association for 'the socio-political salvation of Spain'. Thus *Acción Nacional* was born, on 29 April 1931, whose aim, according to Chapter 1 of its regulations, was 'political propaganda and action under the watchwords of Religion, Family, Order, Work and Ownership'. The idea was also, as Cardinal Pedro Segura, primate of the Spanish bishops, wrote in a 'confidential and highly classified' letter to Cardinal Vidal i Barraquer on 4 May, 'the serious and effective union of all Catholics' for the General Election, with the aim of ensuring 'the election of candidates who are guaranteed to defend the rights of the Church and social order'.[2]

From the outset it had the blessing of the Vatican, the Nuncio, Tedeschini and most of the bishops, and it soon prevailed over the republican Catholicism of Niceto Alcalá Zamora and Miguel Maura; it also marginalised the Carlist cause, which at the time did not enjoy the official patronage of the Catholic Church. Even so, notable well-to-do fundamentalists donated funds to the movement, such as the Count of Rodezno in Navarre, the rich wine-producers Domecq and Palomino in Jerez, and José María Lamamié de Clairac in Salamanca, a prosperous, powerful landowner and a descendant of French legitimists. In fact, for the vast majority of Catholics, *Acción Nacional*, which had to change its name to *Acción Popular* in April 1932, following a government order restricting the use of the word *nacional*, was, to paraphrase the words of Martin Blinkhorn, a convenient façade behind which was hidden a number of private interests and a common hostility towards the Republic and all it stood for.[3]

Acción Nacional did badly in the General Election in June 1931; the Catholic right was in the throes of being organised and was lacking direction. In this organisation there were (at least at first; later they were to split) some who opted for the legal way, for the 'accidentalism' of forms of government, who quickly understood that it was not a question of Monarchy or Republic, but 'the defence of religion and social order', alongside others who preferred, and began to put into practice, the path of violence to overthrow the Republic.

[2] *Arxiu Vidal i Barraquer. Església i Estat durant la Segona República Espanyola 1931–1936*, Publications de l'Abadia de Montserrat, Barcelona, 1971, pp. 41–2.
[3] Martin Blinkhorn, *Carlism and Crisis in Spain 1931–1939*, Cambridge University Press, 1975.

Some historians have called these two options the 'accidentalist' and 'catastrophist' right. The former designation was favoured by Ángel Herrero and José María Gil Robles; the latter by Antonio Goicochea, an ex-minister from the time of the Monarchy. Gil Robles later wrote that it was he who, at a meeting in Ávila on 9 April 1931, a few days before the city council elections that saw the end of the Monarchy, proclaimed for the first time 'the accidental nature of the forms of government'.[4]

Thus, what mattered, more than the form of government, was the defence of the 'fundamental, basic principles of any society' and religion was one of these. Few of the movement's candidates were elected, but those who were made their presence felt in the opening session of the Cortes by speaking out against the 'explosive radicalism' of the government's legislation proposals, particularly with reference to the religious issue, which, after the passing of Article 26 on 13 October 1931, became, in Gil Robles' words, the 'seed of discord'.[5]

In this battle there were fundamental issues affecting the Church, such as the non-confessional nature of the State, the ending of State financing of the clergy and the ban on teaching activities for those in holy orders, although we should not forget other issues that fuelled the day-to-day conflict between the pro- and anticlericals, such as the divorce and civil marriage laws passed in March and June 1932. Many priests and Catholics also came into conflict with the local authorities elected in April 1931, over religious rites and symbols of marked significance for the Catholic faith, including bell-ringing, processions, baptisms, weddings and funerals. The abolition of processions caused a great many conflicts in many towns, as is borne out by the large number of telegrams sent by mayors and civil governors to the Interior Minister. Some wanted to abolish them, or replace them with 'purely civic processions', while others were eager to organise 'tumultuous' parades of the local church's images of the saints. The same sources suggest that it was very common for Catholic women to be involved in this type of protest.

With so many wrongs to redress, political Catholicism burst onto the republican scene with a vengeance. As Santos Juliá has pointed out, the founders of the Republic, with Manuel Azaña at the head, never

---

[4] José María Gil Robles, *No fue posible la paz*, Ariel, Barcelona, 1968, p. 31.
[5] Ibid., p. 54.

took it seriously enough, rejecting it as a reaction from a Church which it saw as being decayed, with the air of a dethroned monarchy, a marginal force that was no match for a regime supported by its people.[6] The reality, however, was different: in two years, Catholicism took root as a mass political movement that was to influence the future of the Republic, firstly through free elections, and subsequently with the force of arms.

Some of the merit for turning Catholicism into a mass political movement must go to José María Gil Robles, a young and hitherto little-known lawyer in Salamanca, from a Carlist family and protégé of Ángel Herrera, who very soon made a name for himself as a parliamentarian for his questions to the government over religious matters. He was 34 years old. His strategy consisted of hoisting the 'banner to unite Catholics and attract a large mass of the detached', mobilising them and uniting them politically. This meant involving the Church hierarchy to organise all Catholics into one party, electing members to Parliament, and demanding a review of any articles in the Constitution that were prejudicial to the interests of the Church. Also clear in Gil Robles' mind was how to organise this mass Catholic response: protests against sectarian politics; providing to the right, 'through mass public demonstrations, the awareness that it had previously lost of its own strength'; 'getting it into the habit of standing up to leftist violence and fighting, whenever necessary, for public pressure'; and 'spreading an ideology and proselytising, through the explanation of its doctrine'.[7]

Naturally, not all the merit belongs to Gil Robles. The close link between religion and land-ownership in Castilla, the mobilisation of hundreds of thousands of Catholic farm-workers, poor and 'extremely poor' landowners, and the almost total control wielded by landowners over organisations that were supposedly set up to improve the lot of these farm-workers, also played their part. And money and the pulpit worked wonders: the former served to finance, among other things, an influential local and provincial press network; from the latter, the clergy took it upon itself to unite, more than ever, the defence of religion with that of order and decency. And this met with the support of

---

[6] The attitude of the Catholics towards Manuel Azaña and the scant attention paid by Azaña to this emerging Catholic movement is analysed extensively in Santos Juliá, *Manuel Azaña, una biografía política. Del Ateneo al Palacio Nacional*, Alianza Editorial, Madrid, 1990, pp. 243–56.

[7] Gil Robles, *No fue posible la paz*, p. 64.

bishops, lawyers and professional sectors of Catholicism in the cities; fundamentalists and powerful landowners such as Lamamié and Francisco Estévanez, who so zealously defended the Castilla cereal producers' interests in the Cortes; and the hundreds of thousands of Catholics with little property but with a great love for order and religion.

This campaign of mobilisation and organisation outside the Cortes, the denouncing of the Constitution and the government's socialising politics, took its decisive step with the founding of the *Confederación Española de Derechas Autónomas* (CEDA; Spanish Confederation of the Autonomous Right). This took place in Madrid, in a Congress that opened on 28 February 1933, attended by 400 delegates who claimed to represent 735,058 members. It was a great political umbrella covering different regional and sectorial organisations, including *Acción Popular*, the *Juventudes de Acción Popular* (the Youth Wing of *Acción Popular*), the *Asociación Femenina* and the *Derecha Regional Valenciana* (the Valencian branch of *Acción Popular*), whose leading figure, Luís Lucia, was largely responsible for this idea of grouping together all the Catholic organisations into a large confederation. It did not include the most radical anti-republican sector, which had split from *Acción Popular* in January 1933, with Antonio Goicochea, José María Pemán and Pedro Saínz Rodríguez at the head, to set up *Renovación Española* (RE), a small group in favour of the restoration of Alfonso XIII, which found solid support among the aristocracy and the old rural *caciquismo*, and which tried to reach out to the Carlists.

The CEDA channelled widely diverse interests, from the small landowners to those in a sector of the agrarian and financial oligarchy, which is why its propaganda was often able to say that it was not a class-based organisation. It is true that its social composition was very broad, with many women in the main cities, but its identity and intentions seemed to be reasonably clear from the outset. Dominated and led by large landowners, urban professionals and many ex-Carlists who had evolved towards 'accidentalism', including Luís Lucia, this first mass party in the history of the Spanish right set itself up to defend 'Christian civilisation', combat the 'sectarian' legislation of the Republic and 'revise' the Constitution.[8]

---

[8] The coming onto the scene and consolidation of this popular Catholic movement is described in José R. Montero, *La C.E.D.A. El catolicismo social y político en la II República*, Ediciones de la Revista de Trabajo, Madrid, 1972.

Its initial expansion coincided with the outcry over the discussion and passing in the Cortes of the *Ley de Confesiones y Congregaciones Religiosas* (Religious Confessions and Congregations Act). The CEDA handled itself well in the midst of this clamour, with the bishops and the Vatican reacting to 'the harsh attack against the divine rights of the Church'. The calls grew for disobedience and defiance. Bishop Manuel Irurita had written in the Lérida Diocesan Journal on 20 February 1933, before the Bill had passed into law, that civil power could not interfere in matters that belonged to ecclesiastical authority, that in matters of religion 'we recognise just one legitimate power, the power of the Church', and that 'we are not willing to comply with any laws or regulations that come out against the rights of God and His Church'. In both the Alfonsine and Carlist camps, the clamour against the Republic was now unanimous. According to Manuel Fal Conde, the leader of the *Comunión Tradicionalista*, Catholics had a duty to defend themselves from all these attacks, 'even with their blood'.[9]

The confrontation between the Church and the Republic, between clericalism and anticlericalism, divided Spanish society in the 1930s as much as agricultural reform or the major social conflicts had done. Officially established as the State religion, the Catholic Church had, during the Restoration and Primo de Rivera's dictatorship, made full use of its monopoly in education, its control on people's lives, to whom it preached doctrines that were historically connected with the most conservative of values: obedience to authority, redemption through suffering and confidence in gaining reward in heaven.

With the proclamation of the Republic, the Church lost, or felt that it had lost, a large part of its traditional influence. Privilege gave way to what the ecclesiastical hierarchy, and many Catholics, considered to be open persecution. The Spanish Church found it harder to take root among the urban workers and rural proletariat. There was ever clearer evidence of the 'failure' of the Church and its 'ministers' to understand social problems, exclusively concerned as it was with the 'kingdom of the sacred' and the defence of the faith. This is what a reformist, liberty-driven regime such as the Republic revealed, as well as legislative persecution, popular anticlericalism and sporadic violence. The Church fought hard against losing all this influence, and prepared itself to combat this throng of Spaniards that it considered to be its enemy, a feeling that was reciprocated by the Spaniards. And

---

[9] Quoted in Blinkhorn, *Carlism and Crisis in Spain.*

Catholicism, used to being the religion of the status quo, moved onto the attack and became, in the words of Bruce Lincoln, 'a religion of counter-revolution'.[10]

The mobilisation of Catholics against the articles of the Constitution that were detrimental to the Church's interests was embodied in an open attack against Manuel Azaña and his republican–socialist coalition government. Azaña was adamant that the Religious Confessions and Congregations Act would be complied with 'from beginning to end, with complete adherence, with total stringency', because, as he stated on various occasions, this Act was the expression of Article 26 and 'the Constitutional mandate' had to be complied with 'in all its requirements'. The Catholics classed it as a despotic and authoritarian Act that ignored the essentiality and traditions of the Spanish nation. They set into motion all the many mechanisms at their disposal to defeat it. Azaña and the republican government rejected the power of the Church and the Catholics, yet two years after the proclamation of the Republic, there they were, mobilising in the streets, in the media and in the pulpit. The opponent was indeed powerful, a genuine national bureaucracy, with some 115,000 clergy distributed throughout all the villages, towns and cities, exercising an ideological control that was without comparison in western societies. It was also a Church that had no respect for secular authority, unless this authority submitted to its commandments.

The Catholics were not alone, either, because from spring 1933 onwards, their offensive coincided with that of employers' organisations, the *Partido Radical*, the emerging extreme right, and disturbances and strikes called by the anarchists following the ugly events in Casas Viejas. Prior to this massacre and CEDA opposition, some members of the military and landowners had already attempted to overthrow the Republic by force of arms.

The anti-republican offensive

There had already been some sabre-rattling in the summer of 1931, when the first measures of Manuel Azaña's military reform became known. In June of that year, two monarchist generals, Emilio Barrera and Luis Orgaz, were arrested due to rumours of a conspiracy against

---

[10] Bruce Lincoln, 'Revolutionary exhumations in Spain, July 1936', *Comparative Studies in Society and History*, 27, 2 (1985), pp. 241–60.

the republican regime, and a few days later, a group of generals who had been appointed by Primo de Rivera, including José Cavalcanti, Miguel Ponte and Barrera, initiated a more organised conspiracy with funding from certain exiled aristocrats, such as the Duke of Alba, and support from former collaborators of the dictatorship, such as the Marquis of Quintanar, the Count of Vallellano and the journalist Juan Pujol, editor of the Madrid daily, *Informaciones*, and representative of the millionaire Juan March. The monarchists, as Julio Gil Pecharromán, an acknowledged expert on the authoritarian right, has pointed out, 'were fully aware of the possibilities that military discontent opened up to them'.[11]

The first conspiracy attempt was quickly neutralised by the government, who in September banished General Orgaz to the Canary Islands, but the plot was taken up again by General Ponte working from France, with other generals, such as Barrera, Rafael Villegas and Manuel González Carrasco, and an important group of Alfonsine civilians, ex-ministers of the Monarchy and dictatorship, who were living in peaceful exile in Biarritz: Juan de la Cierva, José Calvo Sotelo and Eduardo Aunós. It was also the first time they sought external support, specifically in Italy, which was to become a common factor in military and civil conspiracies during the Republic. In April 1932, General Ponte and the aviator Juan Antonio Ansaldo, as the latter subsequently related, went to Rome to meet Italo Balbo, the Air Minister in Mussolini's Fascist government, and apparently they were promised machine guns and ammunition, material backing which, however, they never received.[12]

While this conspiracy of generals and notable monarchists was running its course, former constitutionalists, such as Manuel Burgos y Mazo and Melquíades Álvarez, were nurturing another conspiracy to change the course of a Republic which, according to Burgos y Mazo, was beginning to resemble 'a soviet and, unavoidably, anarchy'. The aim of this plot was to attract General José Sanjurjo, the hero of the Morocco campaign in the 1920s, for which he was known as 'the

---

[11] Julio Gil Pecharromán, *Conservadores subversivos. La derecha autoritaria alfonsina (1931–1936)*, Eudema, Madrid, 1994, p. 108, provides a good summary of the plot that culminated in the uprising led by General Sanjurjo (pp. 108–13).

[12] Juan Antonio Ansaldo, *¿Para qué ...? (De Alfonso XIII a Juan III)*, Editorial Vasca Ekin, Buenos Aires, 1951, pp. 31–6.

Lion of the Riff', and who, as Director-General of the Civil Guard, had managed to keep it 'neutral' in the transition from Monarchy to Republic. Burgos y Mazo had already contacted Sanjurjo in November 1931, and Melquíades Álvarez tried again nine months later. The apparent aim of the military intervention was to replace Azaña's government with one made up of republican moderates, as a sort of 'rectification' of the Republic; a restoration of the Monarchy was out of the question, due to its unpopularity in that period.

At first, Sanjurjo did not show much interest, but his dismissal as Director-General of the Civil Guard following the deplorable events in Arnedo and his transfer to the command of the Carabineros, a lower-category post, made him change his mind. He considered it a punishment and began to think that there were grounds for replacing this Republic with a military dictatorship: disorder, the military reforms and the debates taking place at that time over the Agrarian Reform Act and the Statute of Catalonia. At the beginning of the summer of 1932, Sanjurjo joined the rebel military junta, which for some months had been led by General Barrera.

Sanjurjo's commitment encouraged and united the various conspirators, although the organisation was fairly flawed and the lack of discretion enabled the State security forces to monitor it. In addition, the preparations experienced various contretemps which undermined the future coup. In May, José María Albiñana, leader of one of the first Alfonsine radical right groups, the *Partido Nacionalista Español* (PNE), was banished to a village in Las Hurdes, accused of spreading monarchist propaganda, although actually the Interior Minister knew that his party was one of the firmest political backers of the military conspirators. In fact, on 5 August, a few days before the uprising, the police in Madrid arrested several PNE leaders and closed their premises in Madrid, Bilbao, Burgos and Vigo.

More serious setbacks for the plotters' plans were the arrest on 15 June of General Luis Orgaz, one of the principal organisers, and the refusal of the *Comunión Tradicionalista* to subscribe to the uprising and provide the services of the *Requeté*, an armed militia that received military training and instruction. But the rebellion was definitely on now, and before the government could fully break up the plot, the conspirators set the date for 10 August.

In the early hours of that day, a group of armed military and civilians, under the command of Generals Barrera and Cavalcanti, tried to take the War Ministry and the nearby Palace of Communications. Various units of the Civil and Assault Guard put down the rebellion, in which nine rebels died and several others were injured. General Barrera flew to Pamplona in Ansaldo's plane to try to convince the Carlists to join in. He failed, and fled to France. In other provinces in the south, the insurrection failed too, and General González Carrasco, in charge of the coup in Granada, also fled to France, together with the Marquis of Las Marismas del Guadalquivir.

In Seville, however, General Sanjurjo managed to draw in the military garrison and units of the Civil Guard. He declared a state of emergency and, in the classic tradition of the military *pronunciamiento*, published a manifesto written by the journalist, Juan Pujol, announcing a dictatorship, but not the restoration of the Alfonsine Monarchy. The government and the Cortes had brought Spain, it said, to the brink of 'ruin, iniquity and dismemberment'. Outside Seville, however, nobody joined the coup and General Sanjurjo, on learning that he was alone and that his subordinates refused to fight troops coming from Madrid, left the city. He was arrested in Huelva, a day later, when he was trying to make for the Portuguese border. Thus ended what came to be known as the *Sanjurjada*, the first military uprising against the Republic, just over a year after its proclamation.

The Interior Minister received telegrams from many cities and towns requesting an 'exemplary punishment' for Sanjurjo, including 'the ultimate penalty'. Nevertheless, Manuel Azaña realised from the outset that he should not be made a martyr, as the Monarchy had done with Galán and García Hernández after the failure of the Jaca uprising, as he noted in his diary on 25 August 1932: 'let us try not to make the same mistake. We must put an end to a long tradition of uprisings and firing squads, to show that these actions result in no glory at all. A more exemplary lesson is a Sanjurjo who has failed, alive and serving a prison sentence, than a Sanjurjo who is glorified in death'.[13]

And so it was. Condemned to death by a court martial, his sentence was commuted to life imprisonment, in spite of the objections of Casares Quiroga, the Interior Minister, who thought that the reprieve 'weakens the resolve of the government, encourages conspirators,

[13] Manuel Azaña, *Diarios 1932–1933 (los 'Cuadernos robados')*, Crítica, Barcelona, 1997, p. 45.

and prevents us from being stringent with extremists'. The reprieve caused disturbances in several cities, 'sparks of popular fury against Sanjurjo', as Azaña wrote.[14] Sanjurjo was held in El Dueso prison, in the province of Santander, until his pardon by Lerroux's government in April 1934, when he established his residence in Portugal. From there, he was at the forefront of another coup against the Republic, this time with fatal consequences, in July 1936.

The punishment for the military, aristocracy and extreme right sectors that had taken part in the uprising was severe. Several hundred members of the army were dismissed for their intervention or complicity, and 145 officers were deported to the Saharan base of Villa Cisneros, under the terms of the Defence of the Republic Act, the same fate that had befallen the anarchists several months previously. The coup also galvanised a radicalisation of the agrarian reform, although the initial proposal to confiscate land from the nobility, for the financial backing that some aristocrats gave to the conspirators, was reduced to affect just the Grandees of Spain, a total of 262 individuals. Many conservative newspapers were temporarily shut down, the activities of Albiñana's PNE were banned and prominent monarchists, including some who had not taken part in the coup, were arrested or had to flee the country.

Azaña's government reinforced its authority and made major changes in the security forces. Cabanellas, who had had some contact with Burgos and Mazo during the early days of the conspiracy, resigned as Director of the Civil Guard and Azaña abolished this post, 'an independent stronghold that no one has hitherto dared to attack', and also the post of Director of the Carabineros, which had been occupied by Sanjurjo since February. The Agrarian Reform Act and the Statute of Autonomy of Catalonia, which had caused interminable discussions and provoked obstacles of all kinds, were finally passed. Azaña was elated, at the high point of his term of office. What the Republic had managed to achieve under his mandate in less than a year was hard to surpass. And up to then, the enemies were, with the odd exception, predictable.

There was doubt as to whether Alejandro Lerroux had been involved in the *pronunciamiento* or not. Azaña knew that Lerroux and Sanjurjo had met and talked, Alcalá Zamora also believed that the head of the *Partido Radical* was at least aware of it, and recent

[14] Ibid., p. 22.

research by Nigel Townson provides many details of the old politician's relationship with some of the plotters. Lerroux met Sanjurjo several times before the Republic and at least twice in the months leading up to the coup in August 1932; he was aware of all the plotters' plans and of the proposals that some of them made to him that he should head the government that resulted from the uprising.[15]

Juan March, the magnate whose bid for the tobacco concession in Ceuta and Melilla had been turned down by the government, financed this coup and subsequent monarchist conspiracies. When Lerroux became Prime Minister after the election in November 1933, he organised an amnesty for those involved in the coup, despite opposition from the President of the Republic, Alcalá Zamora, and leading members of his party. As the judge in the Sanjurjo trial observed, the deal between Sanjurjo and Lerroux was that 'if the movement triumphed, Lerroux would come to power; and if it failed, he would acquire the commitment to obtain the amnesty'.[16]

Before Lerroux got his chance to occupy this post, many things occurred that changed the course of the Republic. Despite all expectations, 1933 was a very difficult year for Azaña's government. It began with an anarchist uprising, which culminated in the Casas Viejas massacre, undermining the Republic's credibility. It was also the year that Spanish Fascism appeared on the scene, fuelled by the news from Germany of the overthrow of the Weimar Republic by Hitler and the Nazis. In the middle months of the year, bad news about the economy and unemployment coincided with the opposition shown by the employers' associations, crisis in the corporative system of the mixed committees, the bursting onto the scene of Catholicism as a mass political movement and pressure from the *Partido Radical*. By September 1933, as a result of all this, and the fact that Azaña had lost the confidence of Alcalá Zamora, the republican left and the socialists were no longer in the government.

Fascism appeared in Spain later than in other countries, particularly in comparison to Italy and Germany, and was very low-key as a political movement until spring 1936. During the early years of the

---

[15] Nigel Townson, *La República que no pudo ser. La política de centro en España (1931–1936)*, Taurus, Madrid, 2002, pp. 174–5. (Original English edition: *The Crisis of Democracy in Spain: Centrist Politics under the Second Republic (1931–1936)*, Sussex Academic Press, 2001.)

[16] Ibid., p. 131.

Republic, it was barely noticed on a stage occupied by the extreme monarchist right and the moving to the right of political Catholicism. Definitely not Fascist – despite the fact that they later sympathised with many of their ideas – were the monarchist right groups, Alfonsine and Carlist, who from the outset preached the violent overthrow of the Republic, albeit with very limited resources.

Hostility towards the Republic very soon found resonance in the *Sociedad Cultural de Acción Española*, founded in July 1931 for the dissemination of fundamentalist monarchist ideas, which in the middle of December that year launched *Acción Española*, a magazine inspired by *L'Action Française*, the mouthpiece of the authoritarian movement founded by Charles Maurras in France. Involved in this counter-revolutionary cultural society and its opinion magazine were Alfonsine aristocrats who financed it, such as the Marquis of Quintanar, monarchist intellectuals such as Eugenio Vegas Latapié and Ramiro de Maeztu, and Carlist thinkers such as Víctor Pradera. Its aim was to defend monarchist political order, with traditional roots in the Spanish nation, the basis of its new, Catholic and corporative State and, as Martin Blinkhorn has stated, to reverse the liberalisation and dechristianisation of Spanish intellectualism that they believed had occurred during the nineteenth century.[17]

These arguments were shared in essence by Carlism, the extreme right popular movement that was born a century before the Second Republic. Held back and weakened by the presence of the Alfonsine monarchy during the first third of the twentieth century, the Carlists gained great benefit from the fall of Alfonso XIII and the establishment of a republican regime in Spain. Its anti-republican ideology was accompanied in the 1930s by the active reconstruction of the *Requeté*, the military force formed by its most belligerent youth members, a modern paramilitary unit that was trained and in perfect readiness to assist in the coup d'état in July 1936.

Many of these fundamentalist monarchists, both Alfonsine and Carlist, played a leading role in the early days of *Acción Nacional*. After the elections to the Constituent Cortes, Antonio Goicochea, a former Maurist leader and minister during the Monarchy, took on

---

[17] A summary of its principal opinions can be found in 'Right-wing utopianism and harsh reality: Carlism, the Republic and the "crusade"', in Martin Blinkhorn (ed.), *Spain in Conflict 1931–1939. Democracy and Its Enemies*, Sage Publications, London, 1986, pp. 183–205.

the leadership of the party, and his executive committee was joined by two further Alfonsines, the Count of Vallellano and Cirilo Tornos, as well as the Carlist Count of Rodezno. However, their influence within the party began to diminish with the advance and consolidation of the possibilist leanings of Ángel Herrera and Gil Robles. The failure of the *Sanjurjada* also meant the temporary failure of insurrectional action against the Republic and they were forced to leave a party that had decided to function solely through legal channels. Goicochea resigned from all his duties in *Acción Popular*, and at the end of January 1933 he founded *Renovación Española*, whose birth, according to Gil Pecharromán, was 'almost clandestine, more in keeping with a nucleus of conspirators or an old *caciquil* organisation than with a modern party aspiring to mass appeal'.[18] From that moment on, all efforts were devoted to conspiracy, to propagating the idea of the legitimacy of a military uprising against the Republic, and to acquiring the necessary funds and support to carry it out.

None of these radical monarchist ideas had shown, up to that time, any particular interest in the Fascist ideology, whose early manifestations in Spain were pursuing different courses. They began with cultural and journalistic projects. The first initiative came from Ernesto Jiménez Caballero, with his avant-garde journal *Gaceta Literaria*, launched in 1927, although the first organised Fascist group grew up around Ramiro Ledesma Ramos, a young intellectual post office official, and his weekly journal *La Conquista del Estado*, founded in March 1931. A few months later, in October, Ledesma Ramos and Enésimo Redondo, an extreme Catholic lawyer from Valladolid, launched the *Juntas de Ofensiva Nacional Sindicalista* (JONS; Unions of the National Syndicalist Offensive). Ledesma tried to instil a revolutionary nationalism with a Fascist flavour in the JONS, using direct action, which might compete with the anarcho-syndicalists in the working classes, but he never attracted more than a few hundred sympathisers, all recruited in the heartlands of Old Castilla.

Hitler's ascendancy in Germany attracted the interest of many extreme rightists who, while still knowing little about Fascism, saw in the Nazis a good example to follow in their attempts to overthrow the Republic. In Spain, however, any Fascist project that wanted to flourish had to count on the monarchists to obtain funds, and this

---

[18] Gil Pecharromán, *Conservadores subversivos*, p. 125.

was the road that led to the founding of the *Falange Española* (FE) that year. José Antonio Primo de Rivera, the son of the late dictator, was the link between monarchist authoritarianism and the Italian-flavoured Fascist ideas. Together with Rafael Sánchez Mazas and Julio Ruiz de Alda, he founded a splinter group, the *Movimiento Español Sindicalista*, which managed to obtain an undertaking from the Alfonsines of *Renovación Española* to finance the new party, in exchange for a brief mention in their political programme of the authoritarian concept of order advocated by traditional Catholicism.

This gave José Antonio Primo de Rivera better financial backing than the JONS had, and even enabled him to be elected to the Cortes as the rightist candidate for Cádiz. In that electoral campaign, Primo de Rivera and Ruiz de Alda held an 'act of rightist affirmation' in the Comedy Theatre in Madrid on 29 October 1933, which was considered to be the origin and founding of *Falange Española*. Also present was Alfonso García Valdecasas, an intellectual and pupil of Ortega y Gasset and former member of the *Agrupación al Servicio de la República* (Group in the Service of the Republic), who, a few months previously, during a period in which there was a mushrooming of pro-Fascist splinter groups, had founded the *Frente Español*.

At the beginning of 1934, the Falangists merged with the JONS to form the *Falange Española de las JONS* (FE JONS), remaining until the spring of 1936 a minuscule organisation with just a few thousand affiliates, which tried to obtain funding from monarchists and from Italy with limited success. It also failed to gain a footing among the working classes, although its leaders attempted to do so with the setting up of a nationalist and anti-Marxist syndicalist movement, the *Confederación Obrera Nacional-Sindicalista* (CONS). All attempts to copy the Fascist and Nazi models, by planting roots in Spanish society, failed until its big chance came with the violent civil war. Meanwhile, its militants agitated in the streets, came into conflict with leftist supporters and created the disorder required to make people think that things were going from bad to worse.

The limited appeal of a mass Fascist movement in Spain before the civil war, fourteen years after Mussolini's march on Rome, has given rise to explanations to suit all tastes. Spain did not take part in the First World War, and therefore, unlike other countries, particularly those on the losing side or those for whom victory brought hardship, such as Italy, did not have thousands of demobbed servicemen who joined the ranks of paramilitary organisations, an essential breeding ground for Fascism as a political and social movement. Neither did Spain suffer the consequences of the 1929 economic crisis as brutally as other countries did. At the same time, however, the weakness of Spanish nationalism and the weight of traditional, reactionary bureaucracies, such as the army and the Catholic Church, hindered the advance of a movement whose principles were identified with a modern, radical nationalism to mobilise the middle classes against the revolution, but also against the political practices of the established ruling classes.

Yet barely three years after their appearance, these Fascist splinter groups, together with *Renovación Española*, Carlism and political Catholicism, were at the forefront in the tormenting and overthrow of the Republic. They did their best, using all the social and economic means at their disposal, to sabotage the republican reformist project, the consolidation of workers' rights and the representative power obtained by left-wing organisations. As such, although a 'genuine' mass Fascist party had not taken root in Spanish society, what had germinated and gathered strength was a counter-revolutionary politico-cultural tradition, which, like 'pre-Fascism' in Italy and *völkisch* nationalism in Germany, was able to be mobilised to play a similar role.

Also absent from Spanish society in those years was Communism, the other major ideology and political movement to arise from the First World War. The Partido Comunista de España (PCE; Communist Party of Spain), founded at the beginning of the 1920s in line with the essential principles of the Communist International, came to the Republic while still in its infancy, compared to socialism and anarchism, and was an organisation that brought together several hundred militants. The party was isolated and immersed in a marked anti-socialism. It saw the Republic as a 'bourgeois-landowners' dictatorship', and until the summer of 1934 the party line followed the tactic of the 'single front', the theory of 'social fascism' and the 'class war policy'. Not one of its candidates was elected to the Constituent Cortes in June 1931, and it received barely 40,000 votes in the whole of Spain. It was essentially a city-based party, with limited presence in peasant struggles, and its young militants came mainly from small workshops and the services sector.

Despite a radical change of leadership, in which José Bullejos was expelled from the party at the end of 1932 and replaced by José Díaz,

Jesús Hernández, Vicente Uribe and Dolores Ibárruri, *La Pasionaria* –
the leading lights of Spanish Communism until the end of the civil
war – during the early years of the Republic the PCE remained true to
the Stalinist slogans of the man who was in charge of the situation, the
Argentine Vittorio Codovilla, the delegate of the Third International
in Spain. However, the organisation attracted new members in 1933,
with the fall of Azaña's government and the radicalisation of certain
socialist sectors, and began to acquire influence in Spanish society
for the first time in 1934, when the Comintern changed its 'class war'
policy and criticism of bourgeois democracies for the setting up of
anti-Fascist fronts. In the elections of February 1936, the PCE won
seventeen seats. It was not yet a major party, but it had come out
of isolation. Although late, and thanks to a war, Communism, like
Fascism, ended up by exerting a marked influence on politics and
Spanish society in the 1930s.

In 1933, neither the Falangists nor the Communists were strong
enough to hinder the reformist projects of Manuel Azaña's government or to destabilise the Republic. The pressure came from other
fronts: from the *Partido Radical*, from the employers' associations,
from a new confederation of the right formed by the Catholics, and
from anarchism. At the beginning of the year, after the ugly events in
Casas Viejas and during the fall-out from the *Sanjurjada*, Azaña noted
in his diary: 'Today the Republic is caught between two pincers: the
monarchists and the anarchists'. And to deal with these pincers he tried
to bring to an end the legislative work of the Constituent Cortes and
have this function carried out by normal legislative process as soon as
possible. That same day, 15 January 1933, he wrote: 'Lerroux's predominance in the government of the Republic would be immoral and
vacuous'.[19] Eight months later, Lerroux was Prime Minister.

'The Republic between two pincers'

Lerroux and the radicals had left the government in December 1931,
after the passing of the Constitution, when they had asked Azaña
to form a government without the socialists. As Azaña ignored their
request and kept the socialists, the radicals withdrew and broke the
coalition that had governed the Republic since 14 April. Lerroux was

[19] Azaña, *Diarios*, p. 138.

to wait for the moment to present himself as an alternative to the government made up of leftist republicans and socialists. As Azaña noted in his diary on 14 December 1931, after a meeting with Lerroux at his home: 'The radicals, in competition with the socialists, want to be in the opposition, in order to be the *reserve* and dissolve the Cortes. They want the rest of us to *wear ourselves out* and one day come to power as a guarantee of order, et cetera, et cetera'.[20]

Azaña was right. The *Partido Radical*, the oldest and biggest of the republican parties, had its main base, as Nigel Townson's study has shown, in the urban and rural middle classes, among traders, shopkeepers and small businesses. Until the coming onto the scene of Catholicism as a political movement, the radicals became the surest guarantee of order against Azaña and the socialists, and in many places the party became a haven for caciques and hardened monarchists. With this mixture of classes, the party's propaganda was directed 'towards all Spaniards', and aimed to exploit, using any means, any sign of unrest against all socialists.

Lerroux's attacks on the socialists were directed above all towards the employers, in rallies, meetings with businessmen and electioneering on stages that he dominated, outside parliament, where his interventions were very infrequent. He was particularly harsh in Zaragoza on 10 July 1932, when he accused the socialists of exercising 'a type of dictatorship', and asked Alcalá Zamora to withdraw his support from the government, hinting that if the leftist republicans and socialists continued in power, the military might rise up, which is exactly what happened a month later; this gave rise, as we have seen, to all types of doubts and speculations over his participation in that first serious conspiracy against the government of the Republic.

The proclamation of the Republic had not sat well with the business world, which saw the socialists' participation in government, particularly with Largo Caballero in the Ministry of Labour, as a threat to its interests and to the nation's wealth. Criticism against Largo Caballero, who remained in the Ministry from April 1931 to September 1933 – a considerable time in which to implement his wide range of legislation – centred on his plans for worker intervention in industry, which the employers' organisations managed to block, and

[20] Manuel Azaña, *Memorias políticas y de guerra*, 4 vols., Crítica, Barcelona, 1981, vol. I, p. 341.

in the implementation of the system of mixed arbitration committees, which they considered to be unacceptable meddling in private company management. 'Socialists out' became the unanimous war cry of businessmen and employers in the spring and summer of 1933, when economic crisis and unemployment were at their height, and the CNT was concentrating its strikes and mobilisations against the mixed arbitration committees.

In an assembly of agrarian organisations held in Madrid in March, the landowners requested that the Agrarian Reform Act be revised, as it was 'anti-juridical and anti-economic'. Shortly afterwards, the recently founded *Confederación Española Patronal Agrícola* (Spanish Confederation of Agricultural Employers) accused the socialists and their policy in the Ministry of Labour of transferring 'the loathsome class struggle' from the city to the country. The continuous complaints and hounding of the socialists came to a head in the *Magna Asamblea Nacional*, held in Madrid in July 1933, under the auspices of the three main business and employers' organisations: the *Confederación Gremial*, the *Confederación Patronal* and the *Unión Económica*. There, a fresh demand was made for the modification of the structure of the mixed arbitration committees, one of the employers' bêtes noires when dealing with the socialists.

The other was agrarian reform and all that that meant for them: the threat to ownership and the break-up of class harmony in the country. Order and religion were invoked as the essence of the rural world. The CEDA and the employers' organisations, dominated by the interests of the agricultural oligarchies, attracted the massive support of hundreds of thousands of small and midsize landowners in Castilla, Levante and Aragon, using all the resources of the system of local domination, but also sheltering it under the ideological umbrella of Catholicism. Thus emerged a marked agrarianism, the apology of the true roots of the rural medium and the rejection of cities and modernisation as hubs of revolutionary agitation. Against this, the left, from republicans to anarchists, as well as the powerful FNTT, which changed its name to the *Federación Española de Trabajadores de la Tierra* (FETT), as a consequence of the ban on using the word 'national', ignored the interests of these small and midsize landowners, who finally embraced the cause of reaction against the Republic and socialisation.

The opposition of radicals, employers and landowners, and the arrival of the CEDA as a mass political movement, generated a great deal of tension between a Parliament dominated by left-wing republicans and socialists, and broad sectors of society, including the CNT unions who were attacking its legislation. Furthermore, during 1933, there were clear signs that the governing coalition was losing support from the electorate. This tension was also perceived by Alcalá Zamora, the President of the Republic, who ended up playing a major role in solving the political crisis.

April saw local elections in the town halls designated in April 1931 by Article 29 of the former Electoral Act, which had since then been governed by administrative commissions. At stake were some 19,000 councillors' seats in almost 2,500 councils, although only 2 per cent of electors in the whole of Spain were involved, and most of these small towns were in traditionally conservative zones in the north of Spain. The results gave a substantial boost to the Catholic right and were very good for the *Partido Radical* at the expense of the socialists. Azaña thought, and so he noted in his diary on 30 April, that these results could not be termed 'decisive', and that a 'minor election' should not suggest 'a general change in politics', although he warned that in future elections to the Cortes, the right would reach 'its highest point, as a consequence of the women's vote and the wear and tear that always occurred with governing parties'.[21]

Furthermore, the Religious Confessions and Congregations bill was being discussed at that time, which had brought about forceful Catholic mobilisation, and which served to present the recently founded CEDA to society. The Act was passed in the Cortes on 17 May, but the Catholic Alcalá Zamora did not sign it until 2 June, and did not hide his annoyance with the government. Azaña wanted to know whether he enjoyed the confidence of the President of the Republic and proposed a government reshuffle, taking advantage of the fact that he was forced to replace the Finance Minister, Jaume Carner, who had terminal cancer. Alcalá Zamora tried to exploit what was merely a change of ministers to suggest a government crisis and dismiss Azaña. He began consultations with a long list of politicians at the Presidential Palace, with himself taking centre stage, as in the old days of the Monarchy, although only Indalecio Prieto, of the PSOE, and Marcelino Domingo, of the *Partido Radical Socialista*, had any possibility of forming a government. As neither of the two accepted,

---

[21] Ibid., pp. 612–13.

Alcalá Zamora had to go back to Azaña. He formed a government on 13 June, incorporating into the coalition *Esquerra Republicana*, with Lluís Companys as the Navy Minister, and the *Partido Republicano Federal*, a small party whose leader, José Franchy Roca, became the new Minister of Trade and Industry. Carner was replaced in the Finance Ministry by the economist Agustín Visuales, a party colleague of Azaña's.

The composition of the new government seemed to have left things as they were before the crisis, but there was no respite. Opposition from the Catholics and radicals mushroomed, as did unemployment and labour conflicts. Three Madrid newspapers, *El Sol*, *Luz* and *La Voz*, changed hands and the plaudits for Azaña were transformed into criticism, hounding and calls for his defeat. The *Partido Radical Socialista* entered a stage of deep division, until, at the end of the summer, it split into two sectors: one led by Félix Gordón Ordás, head of an alliance of workers, and small and midsize landowners, highly critical of Azaña and opposed to the socialists remaining in the government; and the other, the centre-left, led by Marcelino Domingo and Álvaro Albornoz. This split aggravated even more the difficult internal relations between the various partners in the governing coalition, and this state of affairs was to be found reported in Manuel Azaña's diary. He was regularly asked at this time to appoint Gordón Ordás to a ministry, 'to shut him up and keep him happy'. But the Prime Minister was adamant: 'I am not going to reward Gordón's attitude within his party against me by giving him a ministry right now, nor will I have someone who is vehemently opposed to socialist participation in the government'.[22]

This was because Azaña still had the conviction, originating from his first constitutional government in December 1931, when Lerroux's radicals withdrew, that in order to build a democratic parliamentary system, what was needed was the collaboration of the socialists and control of their trade union force. And the socialists also made it quite clear on various occasions that their commitment to participation in the government depended on Azaña continuing as Prime Minister. Such was their position until Alcalá Zamora took action to change the situation.

---

[22] Azaña, *Diarios*, pp. 359–60.

An opportunity to break this alliance was presented to Alcalá Zamora at the beginning of September, following the elections to the Constitutional Safeguards Tribunal, an institution whose remit included hearing appeals against laws for their non-constitutionality or conflicts over powers to act between the State and the Autonomous Communities. According to the law that regulated it, twenty of its thirty-five members had to be elected by the Cortes and designated by various institutions, but the election of the other fifteen was by city councils from all over Spain on a regional basis.

The opposition turned this election into a plebiscite on Azaña's government. The vote took place on 3 September. The government parties received most votes, but the distribution of the seats favoured the parties of the right, who won six seats, while the radicals obtained four and the republican–socialist coalition six. The radicals exploited these results alongside their well-known argument, which Lerroux had not stopped spreading since their withdrawal from the government in December 1931, that society was divorced from the Cortes. The *Partido Radical* obtained more votes than any other republican party, including the PSOE, and its press took great pains to state that, but for them, the Constitutional Safeguards Tribunal would have turned into 'a rightist redoubt against the Constitution and the Republic'. What Lerroux wanted was a change of government, consisting of republicans only, and presided over by him.

Azaña asked for a vote of confidence in the Cortes. He won, but on the next day, 7 September, Alcalá Zamora withdrew his confidence for the second and final time, this being tantamount to dismissal. Azaña was defeated not by the Cortes but by a decision of the President of the Republic, who asked Alejandro Lerroux to form a government that would re-establish 'brotherly understanding between all republican factions'.

There would be no socialists in this government, something that all the parties of the right and almost all the republicans had been wanting for a long time. Nor did the socialists want to form part of it under these conditions, with a government headed by Lerroux; in the executive committee on 11 September, its members unanimously passed a motion proposed by Largo Caballero that declared 'broken all the commitments agreed upon between the republicans and socialists in the gestation of the revolutionary movement, and that, therefore, each political group and each party fully regained their independence to follow the path that they deemed pertinent to the defence of their interests'. The 1930 commitment, the one that had helped to give birth to the new regime, was breaking up, and this rupture was to have major repercussions for the socialists and the Republic.[23]

A day later, Lerroux formed a government with seven radicals, five leftist republicans (including a post for Claudio Sánchez Albornoz, of *Acción Republicana*, Azaña's party, who became Minister of State) and one independent. After almost half a century of toiling away in politics, always for the republican cause, Lerroux was now Prime Minister of the Republic. He had been born in La Rambla, in the province of Córdoba, on 4 March 1864. By the time he had achieved his life's wish, he was 69 years old.

On 2 October, Lerroux presented his government to the Cortes, an institution that, with its current composition, he did not respect and that he wanted to dissolve. The republicans of the left and the socialists did not back the government. Furthermore, a few days previously, in an extraordinary Congress, the radical socialists had ratified their definitive split. Gordón Ordás was quite happy to collaborate with Lerroux and the radicals, but the sector led by Marcelino Domingo, made up of the *Partido Radical Socialista Independiente*, walked out with almost half the deputies, who did not want to make a pact with Lerroux. Lerroux had survived less than three weeks as Prime Minister, although other opportunities were to come his way, and his government did not even receive the confidence of the Parliament.

That was also the last session of the Constituent Cortes. This was because Alcalá Zamora, after a frustrated attempt to create a government of luminaries, gave the task to Diego Martínez Barrio, vice-president of the *Partido Radical*, who tried to return to the broad coalition of republicans and socialists. The latter were no longer interested, and on the day after the composition of Martínez Barrio's new government was known, 9 October, the decree for the dissolution of the Cortes was published. Although Lerroux was not given the job of organising the elections, a government led by the radicals was, and the first round of polling was to take place on 19 November, with the second round on 3 December.

[23] Quoted in Santos Juliá, *Los socialistas en la política española, 1879–1982*, Taurus, Madrid, 1996, p. 196.

In July 1933, the Cortes had passed a modification of the electoral system which fostered the formation of broad electoral alliances and raised the quantity of votes required for a list of candidates to win in the first round to 40 per cent. In the second round, which would be held in the event of no candidate attaining this 40 per cent, only those who had obtained more than 8 per cent in the first round could be elected. Polling was to be by constituencies, with cities with over 150,000 inhabitants having their own constituencies, a condition that was only met then by Madrid, Barcelona, Seville, Valencia, Málaga, Zaragoza, Bilbao and Murcia. The big novelty, however, was the women's vote in a general election for the first time in Spain's history, which was to incorporate over 6,800,000 new electors – more than half the census.

Now that the government coalition between socialists and republicans was broken, the leftist parties stood separately, and the republicans were now divided at the polls. The non-republican right, however, formed the *Unión de Derechas y Agrarios* on 12 October, an electoral coalition which brought together CEDA sympathisers, farmers, traditionalists and Alfonsines. The Union set forward a slimmed-down three-point programme, which was really the embodiment of the hard line they had taken in the two previous years against the leftist government: a revision of the Constitution and reformist legislation, particularly in religious and social matters; the suppression of agrarian reform; and amnesty for political crimes, a measure that would basically benefit all those condemned for the unsuccessful military coup of August 1932, or those accused of spreading monarchist propaganda and conspiracy against the Republic.

The radicals came to the polls in an optimistic mood, because, as Nigel Townson said, they were expecting to obtain the reward for their opposition campaign during the two years of the Azaña government, which, as the election successes of 1933 had shown, had been very well received by public opinion. They presented themselves as an option of the centre, in an attempt to appeal to left and right with their proposal of 'Republic, order, freedom, social justice, amnesty', an option reaching out to all classes in which the basic enemy was the Socialist Party, with a more benevolent attitude towards the non-republican right, aware as they were that they needed their support to govern in the Cortes.[24]

[24] Townson, *La República que no pudo ser*, pp. 222–3.

Never before had there been an election campaign with so much propaganda deployed and so much money spent. The amount of funding obtained by the rightist coalition easily exceeded that of the radicals and the leftist parties. The CEDA printed 10 million leaflets and 200,000 colour posters, and used the radio and cinema, together with aerial propaganda drops. It was also a passionate campaign, with the mobilisation of Catholic voters in defence of order and religion, and a socialist left that was beginning to show that it had lost touch with the bourgeois Republic. One point of concern was how the women, commonly identified with Catholicism and the Monarchy, would vote. The fear of the Church's influence in the women's vote and, through them, that of their husbands, was a favourite topic among sectors of the anticlerical left, and stimulated pithy comments, both sexist and hardly democratic, in *La Tierra*, an extremist and provocative Madrid newspaper.

The anarchists of the CNT and the FAI were not so concerned about this matter because, from the moment the elections were called, they started stirring unrest in favour of abstention. Never had so much been written on the subject in so little time. Insults against the 'voter animal': 'In the whole of the animal kingdom, there is no creature more unhappy and odious than voter-man'. Invective against the left and the right: 'Vultures, red and yellow, and tricolour vultures. All vultures. All birds of prey. All of them, filthy swine that the working man will sweep away with the broom of revolution'. A return to old arguments, but with new targets. The workers, 'fed up with being cannon fodder, factory fodder, prison fodder, Mauser fodder', would not turn up to the polls: 'Nobody should vote, because politics means immorality, shameful business practices, growing fat, excessive ambition, uncontrolled hunger to become rich, to dominate, to impose oneself, to possess the privileges of the State, both in the name of democracy and in the name of God, the Fatherland and the King'.[25]

And the CNT, in the run-up to the elections, ratified its commitment with a new uprising. At a plenary meeting in Madrid on 30 October 1933, the regional delegates voted for a kind of revolutionary 'recipe', an initiative from Aragon, which made an uprising unavoidable.

---

[25] The quotes are taken from the two main anarchist newspapers, *Solidaridad Obrera*, in Barcelona, 21 October 1933, and *CNT*, in Madrid, 28 October 1933.

They would step up the anti-election campaign, aware that they were thus incurring 'an immediate responsibility with the Spanish proletariat'. If the 'Fascist tendencies' won the elections, then the CNT would make their 'libertarian Communist aim' a reality. Promising revolution if the right won was a threat that the CNT, obviously, had never previously had the opportunity to carry out. The right did win and they were forced to keep their promise, because if they did not, as they declared months later, 'it would have meant destroying our moral principles, and as our moral principles are paramount for us, we entered the struggle'.[26]

Even those who did not enter the struggle helped, with their abstentionist stances, to accelerate its arrival. Benito Pabón, who in February 1936 was to be elected for Zaragoza for the Popular Front, toured Spain recommending 'absolute abstention'. Miguel Abós, a leading light in Aragon who was constantly under the scrutiny of the anarchists in this region for his moderation, and who admitted having voted in the municipal elections of 1931, sang the same tune: 'a rightist victory would be the call for the implantation of libertarian Communism in Spain'. On 19 November, the day appointed for the 'voter animal' to operate as such, the Barcelona CNT newspaper, *Solidaridad Obrera*, added its voice: 'Do not be taken in, do not vote for the leftist parties, because their victory would mean keeping back your emancipation; take no notice of anyone who tells you that if you do not vote, the right will win. It is preferable that they do win, because their victory will favour our plans'. The following day, with things having gone as forecast, there was no possible turning back. 'People: join the social Revolution!' Revolution was imminent: 'The victory of the right has opened the doors to Fascism. The proletariat will use revolution to prevent their coming to power'.

The result of the two rounds – caused by insufficient percentages in sixteen constituencies – represented a resounding victory for the *Partido Radical* and the CEDA. There are various reasons to explain this victory and the defeat of the left. The 1933 Electoral Act favoured broad coalitions, and the socialists and leftist republicans, despite

[26] *Report of the National Revolutionary Committee to the General Meeting of the Regional Committees of CNT*, held in Madrid on 23 June 1934 and days following. The other quotations are taken from the *Actas* [Proceedings] *del Pleno de Regionales de la Confederación Nacional del Trabajo*, held in Madrid on 30 October 1933 and days following.

having voted for it in the Cortes, stood alone (the former) and dis-
united (the latter). The more conservative forces, directionless and
disorganised in 1931, had reorganised and united around the defence
of order and religion. And the radicals had also shifted to the right.
There is no doubt that there were many Catholic women in Spain who
had voted for the CEDA in 1933. But to say that women were responsible for the victory of the right, including under this label the CEDA
and the *Partido Radical*, as particularly the republicans and some
socialists who had spoken against women's suffrage in the debates of
1931 had done, seems to be unfounded. The electorate's shift to the
right in 1933 was a general phenomenon, not just the result of the
female vote. Women also voted in 1936, many of them for the CEDA
and the rightist parties, and yet it was the leftist parties, who had
grouped themselves into the Popular Front coalition, that won those
elections.

It might also be argued that the electoral defeat of the left was influenced by the anarchist propaganda in favour of abstention and the
aggressive stance they had taken against the governing republicans
and socialists up to that moment. Abstention in 1933 was higher than
in 1931 and 1936, and was particularly noticeable in cities such as
Seville, Barcelona, Cádiz and Zaragoza, where the anarchists wielded
more influence. But evidence from Catalonia, the region where revolutionary syndicalism was most deeply rooted, has shown that electoral
abstention for ideological reasons – in this case, anarchist propaganda – would have been limited to minority sectors of the working
class. The majority of workers adopted a 'sporadic attitude', more
abstentionist in 1933 and less so in 1936, which basically depended
on socio-economic factors and the degree of expectation regarding
change of working conditions. In 1933, the dashing of expectations,
the energetic abstentionist campaign of all the CNT leaders, and
the confrontation between the two workers' syndicalist groups, the
CNT and the UGT, took votes away from the republican and socialist
candidates.

At any event, the composition of the Cortes that resulted from these
elections bore little similarity to the Constituent Cortes of June 1931.
Alcalá Zamora's decision to withdraw his confidence from a government with a parliamentary majority, and to declare the job of the
Constituent Cortes concluded, opened a period of political instability
that had not hitherto been seen. It is often said that the governments

of the Republic were weak ones and that, according to the tally and argument established years ago by Juan Linz, there was a change of government every 101 days. But this assessment does not hold true for the situation in the first two years. Azaña formed his first constitutional government on 15 December 1931, which lasted, crisis-free, until 8 June 1933, and following his return four days later, he remained in office until 8 September that same year. The governments under the *Partido Radical* after the 1933 elections never lasted more than an average of three months, and between September 1933 and December 1935 there were twelve governments, with five different prime ministers and fifty-eight different ministers. Azaña was, in the opinion of Santos Juliá, one of his most illustrious biographers, 'the only politician of the Republic capable of running, with reasonable stability, a coalition government made up of parties that were distinct and even at loggerheads with each other'.[27]

The reformist projects of the republican–socialist coalition and the legislation undertaken by the Constituent Cortes had led to the appearance of vehement reaction and tension within Spanish society. Alcalá Zamora believed, as did others at the time, that the opinions of the man in the street did not match those that prevailed in the Cortes. This is why he sought, as he explained in the preamble of the dissolution decree, 'decisive orientation and harmony, through direct consultation of the general wish'. Harmony was one thing he did not get, and his decision to withdraw his confidence from Azaña and his government did not benefit the Republic. But the elections that followed were fair, as befitted a parliamentary democratic system, and the Cortes that was thereby elected did represent the general wish, including, for the first time, that of women. A new alternative was dawning for the Republic, without the socialists and leftist republicans. The time had come for the *Partido Radical* and the Catholic right.

---

[27] Santos Juliá, 'Introducción', in Azaña, *Diarios*, pp. xxv–xxvi.

4 | Reshaping the Republic

The CEDA received the most votes in the 1933 elections, winning 115 seats in the new Cortes. The radicals won 104 seats, but after two years in opposition, the party had won only ten seats more than in the elections for the Constituent Cortes. *Acción Republicana*, Manuel Azaña's party, lost 23 of the 28 seats it had obtained in 1931, and the socialists went down from 115 to 58 seats. In all, the non-republican right went from 40 seats in 1931 to 200 in 1933, and the left from 250 to around a hundred. It was a highly fragmented parliament, with twenty-one groups represented and a good many new deputies: over 60 per cent of the radicals were in this category and only ten CEDA deputies had had previous parliamentary experience. With these results, it was going to be hard to establish a stable coalition.

Alcalá Zamora asked Lerroux to form a 'purely republican' government of the centre, which would not include leftist republicans, with whom Lerroux had broken back in December 1931, or the CEDA, which had failed to declare publicly its adherence to the Republic. The veteran leader of the *Partido Radical* thought that a parliamentary alliance with the CEDA would ensure a majority, and therefore governability, and would enable this 'accidentalist' right to be incorporated into the Republic, isolating the monarchist extreme right. The CEDA strategy, as Gil Robles explained on various occasions, consisted of first collaborating with the radicals in parliament, then entering the government, and finally heading it. They would then revise the Constitution and if that tactic failed, according to Gil Robles in an interview in *Renovación*, the mouthpiece of the radicals, 'we shall have to look for other solutions', outside the democratic context.[1]

---

[1] *Renovación*, 2 January 1934, quoted in Nigel Townson, *La República que no pudo ser. La política de centro en España (1931–1936)*, Taurus, Madrid, 2002, p. 240. (Original English edition: *The Crisis of Democracy in Spain: Centrist Politics under the Second Republic (1931–1936)*, Sussex Academic Press, 2001.)

The CEDA threatened violence unless they were allowed to govern, and the socialists proclaimed their intention of unleashing a revolution if the CEDA entered the government. As far as the leftist republicans were concerned, this government of radicals backed by the Catholic right was a betrayal of the Republic, and if Martínez Barrio, who was acting Prime Minister at the time of the elections, is to be believed, Azaña, Casares Quiroga and Marcelino Domingo put pressure on him to call new elections before the recently elected Cortes was convened. However, the Cortes held its opening session on 8 December, and on 19 December, Lerroux presented his government, made up of seven radicals, two independent republicans, one liberal democrat and the landowner and monarchist, José María Cid. Thus began what Lerroux called 'a Republic for all Spaniards'.

A government of the centre

Lerroux formed his government when the dead from the third and last of the anarchist insurrections, the one with the most planning and most fatalities, were still being buried. On 26 November 1933, a CNT National Assembly, held in Zaragoza, the new headquarters of its National Committee, entrusted the job of organising this insurrection to a revolutionary committee that included Buenaventura Durruti, Cipriano Mera, Isaac Puente and several leading syndicalists in Zaragoza, including Antonio Ejarque and Joaquín Ascaso. They chose to ignore various messengers sent to Zaragoza telling them to put the operation on 'hold' because other regions 'were not ready'. The die had been cast. The anarchists of Aragon, who had for a long time been telling all and sundry that their region was home to a strain of inborn rebellion, took the crucial step.

On 8 December, the day of the opening session of the Cortes, amidst rumours of preparations for a revolution, the Civil Governor of Zaragoza, Elviro Ordiales, who had 'noted the presence of outsiders among the extremists of Zaragoza', ordered the closure of all CNT premises. The forces of order patrolled the streets and, according to government sources, were set upon first. The following day, Saturday, the clashes and shooting spread through all the central districts of the city. All shops, taxis, trams and buses were on strike, and there were attempts to burn some convents. Having declared a state of alarm, the Governor issued a decree banning the printing of leaflets, meetings and strikes. The revolutionary committee responded with a manifesto: 'The time for revolution has come. We shall implement libertarian Communism'. The shooting could be heard all over the city. By nightfall, there had been twelve deaths and a large number of wounded.

The incidents continued until 14 December. The army intervened and the strike meant that public transport was driven by the Assault Guards, escorted by soldiers. The police looked for the most active militants in flats and public premises; they found some women 'who were dispensing munitions to the extremists' and on 16 December, the revolutionary committee, minus Durruti, who was found later in Barcelona, was arrested. The day before, the National Committee of the CNT had given the order to return to work, and the Chamber of Commerce recommended 'prudence' to its members, who had begun firing and sanctioning workers. Law-abiding citizens clamoured for tributes to be paid to the Governor, and the authorities, with the chairman of the Employers' Federation at their head, visited him to thank him for his good work, while a group of distinguished ladies presented his wife with an image of the Virgin of the Column.

The battle between the authorities and the insurgents was also unleashed in a large number of towns and villages in the region. Leaving aside the places where there were only minor disturbances or just sympathisers of the revolutionary movement, events were at their most serious wherever there was an attempt to proclaim libertarian Communism, where a common sequence would ensue: groups led by anarchists would go to the Civil Guard barracks, which they would take over or not, depending on the strength of the two sides; they would take over the town and arrest the authorities, other law-abiding citizens and the wealthy, usually without any violent reprisals; they would explain their social project to the population, burn land registry deeds and official documents, and even start supplying produce 'following the rules of libertarian Communism'; they would not spread the rebellion to other places and, in fact, would wait passively for the arrival of government forces, which had been mustered to put down the uprisings; they would then flee and, in any event, suffer a swift defeat, accompanied by harsh repression.

This is how it happened in various places in Huesca, Teruel and La Rioja. Outside the epicentre, tremors from the uprising reached isolated spots in Extremadura, Andalusia, Catalonia and the coalfields of León. By 15 December, it was all over. The uprising that concluded the libertarian Communist trial run had lasted just five days. Of the three, it was the one that left the deepest mark: 75 dead and 101 wounded among the insurgents; 11 civil guards killed and 45 wounded; 3 assault guards killed and 18 wounded. Prisons were filled and there were denouncements of torture. Emergency tribunals came into play, as envisaged by the Public Order Act passed in July of that year, and they heard a large number of cases in the Provincial Courts of Aragon and La Rioja from the day after the uprising. The CNT was broken, in disarray, with no mouthpiece. In short, just a remnant of what, two years earlier, promised to be a devastating force.

As had already happened on the two previous occasions, the more moderate syndicalist leaders, who had been expelled from the CNT, reacted harshly. 'Between the FAI and the rank and file of the CNT', wrote Joan Peiró a few days after the uprising, 'prevails the bitterest of divorces'. He accused the former of using 'substantial sums of money in an anti-election campaign that only served to stimulate reaction'. Revolutions, he concluded 'come about by joining forces, not dividing them' and this was 'the harsh lesson' that 'the FAI herd' needed to learn. Peiró was merely echoing the official assessment made by the *Federación Sindicalista Libertaria*, the organisation that grouped together the unions that had split from the CNT: it had been 'a movement of small groups, of guerillas'; nothing like a mass movement.[2]

Just when the anarchists were exhausting their insurrectional options, and criticisms were being voiced from within the movement of the futility of these actions by 'rash minorities', the socialists were announcing revolution. After their exit from government in September 1933 – 'expulsion', some of their representatives would say – there was no point in the legal struggle and reformism; a parliamentary Republic was no longer any use, and social revolution became the only perspective possible. In fact, they were beginning along paths that had previously been trodden by the anarchists: denouncements of persecution and repression, general strikes and frustrated uprisings that were independent of daily working-class struggles. Paradoxically, October 1934 found a good many anarcho-syndicalists jaded by

---

[2] There is an account of this insurrection and the reactions of the moderate syndicalists in Julián Casanova, *Anarchism, the Republic and Civil War in Spain: 1931–1939*, Routledge, London, 2004, pp. 74–8.

strikes, uprisings and protests, and instead musing over the futility of sporadic actions that did not enjoy wide social backing.

The socialists' change of direction had already begun in the spring and summer of 1933 as a reaction to the sluggishness in the application of the Agrarian Reform Act, and its moderate, far from socialist essence. During the first two years of the Republic, the UGT, in particular its land labourers' section, fuelled by its high expectations for change and the official protection of the Ministry of Labour, became a mass syndicate of unskilled workers and peasants; they began to reject the policy of negotiation and *jurados mixtos* when the economic crisis, rising unemployment and employers' pressure hampered the corporatist structure that formed the basis of Largo Caballero's policy as a minister.

As proposed from the outset, the socialist notice of revolution that followed their exit from the government and their break with the republicans was a defensive strategy to stop the CEDA, the non-republican right, from coming to power in a Republic that they, as its founders along with the republican left, considered to be theirs. The revolutionary uprising depended on a third-party decision – that Alcalá Zamora, the President of the Republic, would agree to admit the CEDA into the government; but the socialists spent several months preparing the way, in case that occurred. In late January 1934, Julián Besteiro and other leaders who were against the revolution resigned from the executive committee of the UGT. A few days later, supporters of Largo Caballero also took over control of the FETT. Ricardo Zabalza replaced Lucio Martínez Gil, a Besteiro supporter. The struggle for control of Spanish socialism clearly went Largo Caballero's way; by that time he had accumulated the posts of Chairman of the PSOE, Secretary-General of the UGT and undisputed leader of the *Juventudes Socialistas*.

And so began the government of a centrist republican coalition under Lerroux: with one recent anarchist uprising steeped in blood and the announcement of another socialist uprising to come. Lerroux wanted to revise the policies of the first two years without the need to repeal some of its reforms. As some *Partido Radical* leaders said, he wanted to shift the Republic to the centre. But from the outset the non-republican right, whom he depended on to be able to govern, put pressure on him for a thorough revision that would act on the essential points of the reforms implemented by the republican/socialist coalition in the two previous years. Gil Robles warned him time and again in his speeches: either the government implemented a 'complete rectification' or the CEDA would be forced to bid for power.[3]

One of the non-republican right's first objectives was to prevent the implementation of the Religious Confessions and Congregations Act, which had been passed in June 1933. And they got their way. Catholic schools continued operating normally, the government initiated talks with the Vatican to sign a new Concordat, and priests' wages were partially reinstated: under a law passed on 4 April 1934, the State would pay two-thirds of the salary applicable in 1931 to priests over 40 years of age operating in small villages. The effects of this highly anticlerical law had been frozen, and religious displays, particularly rosaries and processions, were once again to be seen in many locations in Spain.

The radicals had never liked the socialist-type labour legislation, and the main employers' associations, happy with the centre-right election victory, called for 'proper rectifications'. Although they did not disappear, the *jurados mixtos* changed the procedure for electing their presidents; they were now to be elected from among professionals, not appointed by the Ministry, and the power of these arbitration committees was transferred from the unions to the employers. The Municipal Districts Act was modified and, in practical terms, repealed. The landowners discriminated against the most contentious of the socialist militants and anarchists, lowered wages and recovered a large part of the power they had lost in the early days of the Republic. The socialists denounced the situation in their media, and in the Cortes the more moderate radicals acknowledged that *caciquismo* had come back to many villages. The *Partido Radical*, which many people had long considered to be the epitome of nepotism and influence-peddling, now attracted caciques and monarchists, and its leaders received hundreds of letters seeking favours. 'They all want jobs, they all ask for posts', wrote the Galician deputy, Gerardo Abad Conde, in a letter to Lerroux.[4]

Repeal of the socialist and republican left reforms was regarded by the *Partido Radical* as 'not only consistent with its centrist appeal', but

---

[3] José María Gil Robles, *No fue posible la paz*, Ariel, Barcelona, 1968, pp. 105–6, 108–9.
[4] Quoted in Townson, *La República que no pudo ser*, p. 247.

also, in the opinion of Nigel Townson, 'a necessary price to pay for the support of the non-republican right'.[5] However, this pact with the CEDA was soon to cause major tension within the party, which eventually led to a split between them. Diego Martínez Barrio, the party's vice-president, complained about this shift to the right on several occasions. In an interview published in February 1934 in *Blanco y Negro*, the Sunday supplement of *ABC*, he declared himself to be 'a left-winger' and said that he would go on criticising collaboration with the CEDA for as long as that party refused to declare itself republican publicly.

Gil Robles again threatened to 'withdraw support from the government'. Some conservative *Partido Radical* deputies began to support CEDA pleas for the revision of the Constitution. Martínez Barrio felt isolated, and in late February he resigned from his post as Minister of War, as did another radical minister, Antonio Lara, from the Finance Ministry. Just two and a half months after coming to power, Lerroux was forced to reorganise the government. Furthermore, Alcalá Zamora asked for another radical to be replaced, José Pareja Yébenes, the Minister of Education. Thus, three new ministers were brought in: the academic and diplomat, Salvador Madariaga, the Aragonese businessman, Manuel Marraco and a Madrid lawyer, Rafael Salazar Alonso, a young political hardliner of 38 years of age, who took over the Cabinet Ministry. This was the first of the various crises that the CEDA would provoke in the radical governments.

The crisis that was to come shortly afterwards had worse consequences for the *Partido Radical*. The government brought before the Cortes a proposal for amnesty for those involved in the military uprising of August 1932, particularly for General Sanjurjo: an amnesty that was part of both the CEDA and the *Partido Radical* election programme, and which revealed the possible debt that Lerroux owed to the insurgents. Following intense parliamentary confrontations between the Minister of Justice, the liberal democrat Ramón Álvarez Valdés, and the socialist Indalecio Prieto, which cost Álvarez Valdés his post, the law was passed on 20 April, and in the end it included all those involved in the *Sanjurjada* and those who were in prison for the anarchist uprising of December 1933. The headquarters of *Acción Española* would be able to reopen and José Calvo Sotelo was allowed to return to Spain.

[5] Ibid., pp. 238–9.

Alcalá Zamora refused to sign it, as he had warned he would, because in his opinion, this law weakened the Republic by releasing its enemies. He wanted to send it back to the Cortes for its reconsideration, but not one government minister backed him, a prerequisite for these cases under Article 84 of the Constitution. So Alcalá Zamora signed the new law, but attached a thirty-four-page memorandum listing all his personal objections. Gil Robles tried to take advantage of the situation to force the President's resignation, but Lerroux refused to cooperate and was forced to present his resignation as a matter of protocol. This happened on 25 April, and the following day, Alcalá Zamora invited the Minister of Labour, Ricardo Samper, a jurist and veteran republican from Valencia, to form a government. Lerroux, in order not to exacerbate the crisis, offered no objection, in spite of the pressure he received from his allies, his only condition being that Salazar Alonso would continue as a minister. It was the third radical government in four months and the crisis also showed that by his excessive meddling, Alcalá Zamora would not let the parliamentary system operate normally. Stanley Payne believes that Alcalá Zamora was trying to replace Lerroux – whom he saw then as a personal rival – as leader of the republican centre. At any event, Samper was not the leader of the radicals, and soon after taking office, the party split, leaving his position even weaker.

The split came from the left wing of the *Partido Radical* and was led by Martínez Barrio just over two months after he had left the government. The dissidents, as they explained in a manifesto published on 19 May, were leaving the party because it had moved away from the 'old radical ideology'. A few days later, Martínez Barrio declared that Lerroux had changed the centrist policy of the radicals for one of 'sectarian' right that rejected the 'liberal, democratic theories' of the Republic. Nineteen deputies abandoned the *Partido Radical*, almost one-fifth of its parliamentary group; it was now down to 85 members, below the 94 it had in the Constituent Cortes. The split also affected a large number of radical officials in the provinces. Nigel Townson wrote that the schism not only shifted the party *to* the right, but also made it more dependent *on* the right.[6]

This profound crisis of Lerroux radicalism coincided with a long, slow recovery of the leftist republicans. In April 1934, *Acción*

---

[6] Ibid., p. 277.

Republicana, Casares Quiroga's *Partido Republicano Gallego* and Marcelino Domingo's independent socialist radicals joined forces in a new party called *Izquierda Republicana* (IR), with Manuel Azaña as the leader. The radical dissidents, meanwhile, formed the *Partido Radical Democrático*, which in September of that year merged with Gordón Ordás' socialist radicals to form *Unión Republicana* (UR). The founding of IR and UR had no effect on the composition of the Cortes, where the alliance between radicals and the CEDA provided the centre-right with a comfortable majority to govern, but this policy of leftist republican groupings put a brake on the marked tendency for disintegration, which had started in 1933 and whose effects were so harmful in the elections.

Ricardo Samper governed from 28 April 1934 to the beginning of October that same year. During that time, he had to deal with a growing trade union mobilisation, major social conflicts in Madrid, Barcelona and Zaragoza, a general land-workers' strike, a conflict over powers with the *Generalitat* of Catalonia and a protest by Basque town and city councils, which included nationalists, leftist republicans and socialists, in defence of the *Concierto Económico* (Economic Pact), a historic right that was being called into question by tax measures proposed by the Minister of Finance, Manuel Marraco. Beleaguered by these conflicts, and harshly criticised by the employers, who accused it of weakness and of failing to support their interests against the unions, Samper's government was at the mercy of the CEDA and the strategy of Gil Robles, who was now thinking of the second phase of his plan: entering government.

The land-workers' strike was already in motion when Samper replaced Lerroux as Prime Minister. In late February 1934, the FETT National Committee had warned that the labour and social legislation passed by the provisional government of the Republic and by the Constituent Cortes was not being complied with, and was being systematically breached by the employers following the right's victory in the elections. It announced that a general strike for the beginning of June would take place if the government ignored its claims. These included demands regarding compliance with working conditions, the regulations referring to employment of outsiders, at a time when the repeal of the Municipal Districts Act was being debated, and the restriction on the use of agricultural machinery. Furthermore, unemployment was on the increase. In March of that year, the number of unemployed in the agrarian sector was 415,000, 63 per cent of the total unemployed. Official figures placed the figure at 700,000 unemployed, 18 per cent of the active population, but socialist calculations claimed that the true unemployment rate was double that figure.

On 14 May, various FETT leaders, with Ricardo Zabalza, the secretary-general, at their head, visited the Minister of Labour, the radical José Estadella, to inform him of 'the serious consequences that would follow from the calling of a general strike throughout Spain', specifying that it was a 'land-worker and union' conflict, not a revolution. The Prime Minister, Estadella and the Minister of Agriculture, the radical Cirilo del Río, tried negotiating to prevent the strike, but they came up against the hardline attitude of the Cabinet Minister, Salazar Alonso, who defended the stance of the agrarian employers. Convinced that the strike was just the beginning of a revolutionary movement, as he stated in an interview in *Blanco y Negro*, he ordered the civil governors to 'suspend and ban all types of assembly' and impose press censorship on anything that referred to the land-workers' protest.[7]

The negotiations fell through, and on 5 June the strike began, with marked repercussions in the provinces of Andalusia, Extremadura and Castilla-La Mancha. According to research by Manuel Tuñón de Lara, the strike affected over 700 municipalities in 38 provinces, and lasted between five and fifteen days, depending on the socialist presence. Confrontations between strikers and blacklegs or strikers and the forces of order were frequent, and on 20 June, when it was all over, official figures showed a balance of thirteen dead and several dozen wounded. Several thousands of workers were imprisoned, although they were soon released, and the Cabinet Minister, Salazar Alonso, took advantage of the situation to dismantle the organisational structure of the FETT in the south, and replace a large number of socialist mayors with management boards presided over by members of the *Partido Radical*.

Largo Caballero and several leaders of the PSOE and UGT executive committees were worried that this strike would interfere with the preparations for the revolutionary uprising that had been announced

---

[7] The land-workers' general strike is addressed extensively in Manuel Tuñón de Lara, *Tres claves de la Segunda República. La cuestión agraria, los aparatos del Estado, Frente Popular*, Alianza Editorial, Madrid, 1985, pp. 130–53, from which the information used in this chapter is taken.

in the event of the CEDA entering the government. They decided that the urban trade unions would not join the conflict. As the CNT, weak as it was and unconcerned with the specific demands of the FETT, did not join either, the protest only led to the repression and undermining of the socialists' biggest syndicate. The right came out of it strengthened, and the landowners rid themselves of union and insurgent pressure for a time.

However, the summer of 1934 was not such a quiet one for Ricardo Samper's government. At the end of March, the Catalan Parliament had passed the *Ley de Contratos de Cultivos* (Crop Contracts Act), proclaimed by Lluís Companys on 14 April, in a bid to help the *rabassaires*, rentiers and sharecroppers in the wine-growing sector with close links to the *Esquerra*, enabling them to buy any land that they had worked for fifteen years. The *Instituto de San Isidro*, the organisation of landowners in Catalonia, supported by the *Lliga*, the employers' organisations and the CEDA, attacked the law, and several rightist deputies moved in the Cortes for the government to lodge an appeal before the Constitutional Safeguards Tribunal, claiming that the Catalan Parliament and the *Generalitat* had no powers to act in this matter. On 8 June, the Tribunal handed down a decision in favour of the government and the landowners. Four days later, the Catalan Parliament ratified the Act that had been declared unconstitutional.

The deputies of the *Esquerra* and, in solidarity with them, those of the *Partido Nacionalista Vasco* (PNV), walked out of the Cortes. Samper, and some of his ministers, including Rafael Guerra del Río and Filiberto Villalobos, tried to broker an agreement between the two sides in order to avoid conflict with Catalonia, but Salazar Alonso and the CEDA placed obstacles in the way. On 30 June, Gil Robles wrote to Samper, asking him to 'impose respect for the law and protect the prestige of public authority'. Azaña defended the *Generalitat* as being 'the only republican authority left in Spain', and the socialists, angry at the repression of the land-workers' unions, saw in this dispute complete submission by the government to the radical right. Although Samper and Companys, with the help of Alcalá Zamora, looked for a legal formula to solve the conflict of prerogatives, Gil Robles decided to draw in the reins. After the parliamentary summer recess, but before the first session of the Cortes on 1 October, he officially withdrew CEDA support from Samper's government, asked for a reshuffle and announced that the CEDA should enter the new government.[8]

The radicals, with Lerroux at their head, knew that they could not continue in government without the CEDA. Samper tried to defend his record in the opening session of the Cortes, but Gil Robles publicly repeated his proposal: a government that reflected the parliamentary majority. Samper resigned. Alcalá Zamora did not want to dissolve the Cortes, because the Constitution only allowed him to do so twice, so he gave in to the non-republican right's proposal and asked Lerroux to form a new government; it was announced on 4 October and included three CEDA ministers: Manuel Giménez Fernández in Agriculture, Rafael Aizpún in Justice and José Oriol Anguera de Sojo in Labour. Samper's centrist policies, which involved a moderate revision of the legislation from the 1931–33 period, but not its repeal, was unworkable. The non-republican right began to govern the Republic with the most traditional republican parties. The republican left warned of the 'betrayal' involved in 'the monstrous act of handing over the government of the Republic to its enemies'. Martínez del Barrio, Lerroux's former lieutenant who was no longer in the party, asked Alcalá Zamora to give power to the left to save the Republic. The socialists declared their revolution. Nothing would be the same after October 1934.

Insurrection

The revolution, according to the socialist revolutionary committee, should have started with a general strike in the main cities and industrial centres, followed by sympathetic sectors of the armed forces. There were major strikes in Madrid, Seville, Córdoba, Valencia, Barcelona and Zaragoza, with brief outbreaks of armed uprising in certain locations in the latter province. In the mining area to the west of Bilbao, the army and the Civil Guard fought the insurgents for a few hours, and in Eibar and Mondragón, the violent actions of the revolutionaries touched well-known rightists, such as the Carlist deputy, Marcelino Oreja. Nowhere, however, did the soldiers leave their

[8] The obstacles placed by the CEDA against Samper's government are summarised in Townson, *La República que no pudo ser*, pp. 303–10.

barracks to support the revolution, and armed rebellion was limited to Asturias, although the *Generalitat* government's rebellion against central power also had a strong political impact.

The general strike started in Catalonia on 5 October without the official backing of the CNT, despite the fact that some scattered anarchist groups wanted to implant libertarian Communism, albeit with little chance of success. At 8 pm the following day, President Lluís Companys announced that the government of the *Generalitat* was breaking all links with 'spurious institutions', as all the republican left parties had already done when the CEDA entered the government. He proclaimed 'the Catalan State within the Spanish Federal Republic' as a measure against the 'monarchist and Fascist forces ... who had seized power'; he also invited the 'provisional government of the Republic' – in other words, the republican and socialist forces who had formed it in April 1931 – to install itself in Catalonia. It was, according to Enric Ucelay da Cal, an attempt to repeat the revolutionary gesture of 1931, to put an end to the problem between the Catalan government and the centre-right government in Madrid that was a result of the tension that had built up over the matter of the *Ley de Contratos de Cultivos*, and to keep Catalan nationalism on track. 'They can no longer say that I am not a Catalan nationalist', Companys is said to have murmured after proclaiming the 'Catalan State' from the balcony of the *Generalitat*.[9]

Despite the preparations for rebellion carried out by Josep Dencás, the *conseller de Governació*, General Domingo Batet, the head of the military garrison in Barcelona, ignored the orders given by Companys as the highest authority in Catalonia, and took over the city. In the early hours of the following day, he placed his troops outside the *Generalitat* building, and after limited resistance and artillery fire, the Catalan government surrendered. Miguel Badia, the head of the services of public order and a colleague of Dencás in the most radical sector of Catalan nationalism, tried to organise some sniper fire from roof terraces. When they saw that all was lost, Badia, Dencás and their military advisers escaped via a secret passage in the Cabinet Office, or via the sewers according to other sources, and fled to France. The

[9] Enric Ucelay da Cal, *La catalunya populista. Imatge, cultura i política en l'etapa republicana (1931–1939)*, Ediciones de La Magrana, Barcelona, 1982, pp. 216–17.

fatal balance of the failed uprising was forty-six deaths, eight soldiers and thirty-eight civilians.

This failure occurred at the same time as the failure of most of the strikes and attempted uprisings that had observed the order of the revolutionary committee. The aim was to stop the CEDA entering the government, but it was unsuccessful. Quite a different story was what happened in Asturias, with revolutionary violence and subsequent brutal repression hitherto unseen in Spain. It was a genuine attempt at social revolution: October 1934, 'red' October.

In Asturias, the *Alianza Obrera*, the only alliance that had managed to group together the forces of the UGT, the CNT and the Communists, had organised or backed major mobilisations in the previous months, with various general strikes between February and October in the mining areas. Furthermore, the movement had armed itself with stolen weapons, rifles, machine guns and sticks of dynamite. These arms were not enough to defeat the security forces and the army, but they were enough to launch thousands of militants in a struggle against the Civil Guard in their barracks, from where they were to obtain more arms. The arming of the uprising, in which the mobilisations of syndicalists and miners were not involved, was carried out by the *Juventudes Socialistas* and anarchist groups who set up paramilitary combat squadrons. This preparation, which was not enough to ensure victory, but which was more intensive than in other areas of Spain, where preparation was virtually non-existent, explains, as Paco Ignacio Taibo wrote years ago, 'the Asturian difference', because, in short, there was a movement there that managed to take control of various towns and villages over several days.[10]

The uprising began on the night of 5 to 6 October, when several thousand trade union militants seized the Civil Guard posts in the mining areas, took control of Avilés and Gijón, took over the ordnance works in Trubia and occupied the centre of Oviedo. Fierce fighting ensued there between the forces of order and the revolutionaries in the area of the civil government building, the State telephone company building and the cathedral. The regional committee of the *Alianza Obrera*, led by the socialist Ramón González Peña, coordinated the

[10] Paco Ignacio Taibo, 'La diferencia asturiana', in Gabriel Jackson *et al.*, *Octubre 1934. Cincuenta años para la reflexión*, Siglo XXI Editores, Madrid, 1985, pp. 231–41.

large number of local committees that sprang up in the various towns and tried to guide the 'revolutionary order'. Swift control was established over public services, transport and supplies for besieged locations; in some places, the official coinage was suppressed and the first examples of violence against employers, the upper classes and the clergy appeared.

Thirty-four priests, seminarists and brothers from the Escuelas Cristianas in Turón were killed, with the legislative persecution of the first biennium giving way to the physical destruction of members of the Church, something that had not occurred in the history of Spain since the massacres of 1834–35 in Madrid and Barcelona. Furthermore, the purifying fire appeared once more in Asturias: fifty-eight churches, the bishop's palace, the seminary, with its magnificent library, and the *Cámara Santa* in the cathedral were burnt or blown up.

The subsequent repression carried out by the army and the Civil Guard was, as we shall see, extremely harsh, an exemplary lesson, and thousands of socialists and anarcho-syndicalists filled gaols all over Spain. But the Church and the Catholic press devoted themselves to remembering the atrocities suffered by their martyrs, by calling for punishment and repression as the only remedy against the revolution. The Church's blinkered attitude with regard to social matters was what Canon Maximiliano Arboleya, familiar with the working-class environment in Asturias, deplored in a letter to his friend in Zaragoza, Severino Aznar, following the storm of 'hatred and dynamite': 'Nobody, but nobody, has stopped to wonder whether this atrocious criminal revolutionary movement of 50,000 men has any explanation other than the usual perverted socialist propaganda; nobody ever thinks that we too may be largely responsible'.[11]

Apart from the rural areas of the north of Spain, this social Catholicism, which was led by people such as Maximiliano Arboleya or Severino Aznar, had not gained much ground. As far as the miners and inhabitants of the industrial suburbs of the major cities were concerned, the Catholic Church sided with 'oppressive' capitalism, and the only aim of the Catholic syndicates was to defend the Church and

[11] Quoted in Domingo Benavides, 'Maximiliano Arboleya y su interpretación de la revolución de octubre', in Gabriel Jackson *et al.*, *Octubre 1934. Cincuenta años para la reflexión*, Siglo XXI Editores, Madrid, 1985, p. 262.

capitalism. 'Whether we like it or not', reflected Arboleya, this was the view taken by 'nearly all our workers'.

To put down the rebellion, the government was forced to use the Spanish Legion and the *Regulares* from Morocco. The Minister of War, the radical Diego Hidalgo, decided to pass over the Chief of General Staff, General Carlos Masquelet, and instead chose General Franco, whom he had met recently during army manoeuvres in León, to coordinate the military operations and the repression, and this made Franco, for at least a few days, the true Minister of War. General Eduardo López Ochoa, in command of the main relief column, moved in from Galicia with a contingent of nearly 400 troops. On 10 October, two companies of the Legion and two *tabores* (battalions) of *Regulares* disembarked in Gijón and began to advance towards Oviedo. In response to the advance of these troops, many of the militia began to withdraw. González de la Peña ordered a withdrawal to the mountains, although there were groups of armed miners who refused to obey and continued fighting in the streets between 14 and 17 October. López Ochoa now had over 15,000 soldiers and 3,000 civil guards available, who, together with Colonel Yagüe's colonial troops, began to clean up the area. On 18 October, Belarmino Tomás, the chairman of the revolutionary committee that had stayed behind with the last of the resistance groups, discussed surrender terms with López Ochoa.

As well as the revolutionary violence, there were also summary executions under martial law. The most accurate estimate of victims suggests 1,100 deaths among those who supported the rebellion, some 2,000 wounded, and some 300 deaths among the security forces and the army. In the first phase of repression, hundreds of prisoners were beaten and tortured, a measure in which the Civil Guard Major Lisardo Doval played a leading role by imposing genuine police brutality, until he was dismissed in December. Luis de Sirval, a journalist who had investigated and denounced the excesses of Yagüe's mercenaries, was murdered by a foreign officer in the Civil Guard, Lieutenant Dimitri I. Ivanov. A large number of leading republican and socialist politicians, including Largo Caballero and Azaña, were arrested. The gaols filled up with prisoners, revolutionaries and leftist militants, and the repression was turned into a recurrent theme in political debate over the following months.

Although this uprising was better organised and had more backing and weaponry than the anarchists had had in 1932 and 1933, its failure is easily explained. It was sparked by the CEDA's entry into the government and not by a wide-ranging State or social crisis. Outside Asturias, it was only small and highly localised groups, unlike the protest actions and strikes conducted by the CNT and UGT during the republican years, that stepped forward when the time for the revolution to start arrived. The peasant syndicates of the FETT did not take part, following the repression of the June 1934 strike, and nor did the CNT (except in Asturias), deeply divided and weary of useless rebellions, because, as its media hastened to declare, 'the dilemma is not between a government of the right or government of the left, but between a bourgeois Republic or Libertarian Communism'. The socialists were treading what was, for them, a new path after their time in government, one that even the most radical anarchists were suggesting was leading them nowhere: 'We can no longer move forward, as we have been doing up to now, using trial and error. All trials have their limit, and for the FAI this limit was reached on 8 December 1933', declared *Tierra y Libertad* on 11 October, when only Asturias remained as the focal point of the rebellion.

But even allowing for the poor preparation and the lack of peasant and anarchist backing, the failure of the revolution was not surprising. Against a State that keeps its armed forces intact and united, a revolutionary strategy based on scattered support can never spark widespread disruption and ends up being easily repressed. All the police and Civil Guard, as well as the army forces, were loyal to the government, and there was no chance of them joining the revolutionaries or refusing to repress them. The military preparation for the uprising was left in the hands of groups of young people who were able to erect barricades in certain *barrios* in the cities, or to fight with more arms in the mining areas, but not to oppose a united army. Following the Russian precedent in 1917, where the army was demoralised after heavy defeats and hundred of thousands of casualties in the First World War, no worker or peasant uprising succeeded in Europe, with the exception of Béla Kun's regime for a few months in Hungary in 1919.

The strategy based on the hope that the army and forces of order would take part in the rebellion failed, in the first place, in Madrid, and without Madrid and without the seizing of even the public buildings, the revolution had no chance of succeeding. And this was in spite of the fact that, as Sandra Souto made clear, the capital saw massive worker mobilisation and the most far-reaching and longest-lasting general strike during the whole of the time of the Republic.[12] For armed revolutions to succeed, they need to have some of the army on their side. And, as the military coup in July 1936 proved, the revolutionary process requires the collapse and division of the mechanisms of strength and defence of the State. None of this happened in October 1934.

With this rebellion, the socialists showed the same condemnation of the representation system as the anarchists had done in previous years. The very announcement of the revolution, determined by the CEDA's entry into the government, was a means of coercion against the established legitimate political authority. Leaving aside the alleged circumstances of their radicalisation, the socialists broke with the democratic process and the parliamentary system as a means to press for a reorientation of politics. The movement's leaders, at the instigation of the younger members, who formed militias and developed a taste for a military framework, tried to copy the Bolshevik model in Spain.

The militants in the *Juventudes Socialistas* were the first to applaud the socialists' exit from the government in 1933 and the tearing up of all their agreements with the republicans; it was this that closed the 'bourgeois democracy' phase and saw the start of their headlong rush to social revolution. The increase in calls for violent action matched the loss of confidence in the legality of the republic. The appearance of the *Falange Española*, Hitler's rise to power, the crushing of the Austrian socialist movement by Chancellor Dollfuss in February 1934, the verbal aggression of Gil Robles, with his constant rants against democracy in favour of the 'totalitarian concept of the State', and the obvious Fascist leanings of the youth wing of *Acción Popular* (JAP), mobilised young people, both students and workers; in the first few months of 1934, they launched violent political confrontations such as had not been seen in the early years of the Republic. In January, as a consequence of a general strike of students called by the socialist and Communist-led *Federación Universitaria Escolar* (FUE), a group from the Falangist militia, *Primera Línea*, led by Agustín Aznar and Matías Montero, stormed the FUE premises and some students were

---

[12] Sandra Souto Kustrín, 'Y *¿Madrid? ¿Qué hace Madrid?' Movimiento revolucionario y acción colectiva (1933–1936)*, Siglo XXI Editores, Madrid, 2004.

set upon. On 9 February, Matías Montero was murdered while selling Falangist newspapers, and he became a martyr for this minority Fascist organisation. The socialists had their martyrs too, such as Juanita Rico, a young woman of 20, who was murdered by Falangists in July. Their funerals gave a chance for uniforms to be shown off, as well as their symbols, hymns, and blue, black or red shirts.

Yet to suggest that the October uprising marked the end of any possibility of constitutional coexistence in Spain, the 'prelude' or 'opening battle' of the civil war, is to place a workers' uprising, defeated and repressed by republican order, on the same plane as a military rebellion carried out by the armed forces of the State. The Republic always repressed uprisings and imposed order. After October 1934, socialists and anarchists alike abandoned rebellion as a stratagem and the possibilities of trying it again in 1936 were practically nil, now that their ranks were split and considerably weakened. For the non-republican right, however, October 1934 marked the way. They always had the army, the 'backbone of the Fatherland', as José Calvo Sotelo would often refer to it then.

After October 1934, the left tried to re-establish its democratic political activity, win at the polls and surmount its insurrectional failures. The CEDA grew, defended repression to the hilt, and shed any possibility of stabilising the Republic with its coalition partner, the *Partido Radical*. Any potential centrist solutions proposed by Lerroux and his team ended up swamped by the CEDA's conquest of power strategy, and by the scandals that, barely a year after that October, engulfed them until they were eliminated from the political scene.

The road to authoritarianism

The brunt of the blame for the rebellion was placed, at the instigation of the CEDA and one sector of the *Partido Radical*, on Manuel Azaña, the socialists and the Statute of Catalonia as a symbol of the 'disunion of the Fatherland'. Azaña had gone to Barcelona on 28 September to attend the funeral of Jaume Carner, his ex-Finance Minister. There he met Indalecio Prieto, and he tried to 'caution him against' the proposed revolution, as he 'considered that it lacked any chance of success'. In his conversations with Prieto and another former socialist minister, Fernando de los Ríos, who had also attended the funeral, he once again showed that relations with the socialists had been broken off and that *Izquierda Republicana* was not involved in the socialist plans for an uprising. After the funeral, Azaña remained in Barcelona, 'following the advice of a number of friends in Madrid to stay away from the capital for a short period during which political upheaval was promised'. He noticed that in Catalonia, too, there was an atmosphere of unrest over the possible entry of the CEDA into the government, and he advised the Catalan politicians against embarking on 'a situation of violence against the State, because, as well as having little or no chance of success, it would provoke a reaction throughout Spain that would only serve to strengthen the position of the right'.

Azaña took no part in what was known as the rebellion of the Catalans that began in the afternoon of 6 October; and three days later, on Tuesday 9 October, he was arrested in the home of Doctor Carlos Gubert. Lerroux, who had sent a telegram to the authorities in Barcelona, saying that the former Prime Minister was involved in the uprising, told the press that he had been found in possession of 'extensive documentation of great interest' that proved that he had gone to Barcelona on some 'important undertaking'. The monarchist newspaper, *ABC*, charged him with going on radio to 'call on the Catalans to prepare for war against the invading army that Lerroux's factious government might send'. *El Debate*, the mouthpiece of the CEDA, referred to him as a mason to explain his complicity with Companys and separatism. And the leader of the *Partido Radical*, Joaquín Pérez Madrigal, after seeing the events in Asturias, declared that 'my first conclusion is that Azaña is largely responsible for what has happened'.[13]

While awaiting trial, Azaña was held in a prison ship anchored in the port of Barcelona, later to be moved to two further floating gaols, accused by the Chief Prosecutor of the Republic of the crime of rebellion, until he was released following a Supreme Court decision on 28 December 1934. But this did not satisfy his political enemies, now in government, and they brought before the Cortes various motions for impeachment against him for gunrunning. Bringing Azaña to Parliament, where he was in his element, was a blunder on the part of his adversaries. He was cheered by the crowds when he left the Cortes after the debate on 21 March 1935, and although his accusers set up

---

[13] Information on the repression in Asturias is in Townson, *La República que no pudo ser*, pp. 315–24.

a parliamentary commission to prove his guilt, the strategy did not prosper. As the Count of Rodezno said before this debate: 'they are insisting on putting Mr Azaña on a pedestal, and they are going to succeed'.[14]

The next step in the search for scapegoats was to try to discredit the Statute of Catalonia and have it abolished. Following a debate between the government coalition partners, in which some wanted it modified and others abolished, a law was passed on 14 December suspending Catalonia's autonomy indefinitely, until the government and the Cortes saw fit to reinstate it. The *Ley de Contratos de Cultivos* was repealed, and the central administration reclaimed the powers to act that had been transferred to the *Generalitat* during the two previous years. The whole of Catalonia was being punished for the rebellion by certain members of its governing party. A few days later, Lerroux's government appointed a veteran politician of the monarchist *Partido Liberal*, Manuel Portela Valladares, Governor-General, and he handed the Barcelona city council over to the radicals.

More than 3,000 people were arrested in Catalonia, and the first death sentences were handed down by the military courts for the October rebellion onto Major Enrique Pérez Farrás and Captains Escofet and Ricart, who had been involved in the uprising as heads of the autonomous police force, the *mossos d'esquadra*, and the *somatén*. On 17 October, the government voted for the executions, although the President of the Republic, Alcalá Zamora, reminded them that they had pardoned those responsible for the military uprising of 10 August 1932, and, despite the vehement opposition of the CEDA and others such as Melquíades Álvarez, who advocated a firm hand, he managed to persuade Lerroux to commute the death sentences on 31 October. However, the trials continued, and this time it was Companys and his *consellers* (government team) who, on 6 June 1935, were sentenced to thirty years' imprisonment for 'military rebellion'.

Meanwhile, in Asturias, the beatings in the gaols went on, and the repression aggravated the division in the governing coalition. The prisoners signed letters denouncing the use of torture, and British and

---

[14] Quoted in Santos Juliá, *Manuel Azaña, una biografía política. Del Ateneo al Palacio Nacional*, Alianza Editorial, Madrid, 1990, p. 385, from which the information on the persecution of Azaña after the insurrection of October 1934 is taken.

French socialist politicians visited the region and pleaded amnesty for those on trial. Only two death sentences were carried out in February 1935: a sergeant who had deserted the army to fight on the side of the revolutionaries, and a worker accused of several murders. The rest of the death sentences were commuted, although when the Cabinet met on 29 March to discuss the cases of Ramón González Peña, the most prominent leader of the insurrection, and Teodomiro Menéndez, the government was split, with Lerroux and six other radicals voting in favour of a reprieve, and the three CEDA ministers, the Agrarian and the Liberal Democrat against.

Protests about the arbitrary and, as time went on, unnecessary repression left the radical ministers 'consumed within', as César Jalón, the radical Minister of Communications in the government that Lerroux formed on 4 October 1934, later wrote: 'Asturias, it's always Asturias ... The nightmare of revolution and the nightmare of Spain would always be the spectre that followed us until it overthrew us'.[15]

Indeed, the CEDA and the non-republican right wanted to take revenge to its ultimate consequences, and they provoked the government crises that were needed to achieve their aim of seeing Gil Robles as Prime Minister, the final phase of their strategy. Taking the reprieve of Pérez Farrás as his excuse, Gil Robles sounded out the possibility of the army imposing a 'solution of force' to restore the 'legitimacy violated by the President'. The anti-Azaña generals, Joaquín Fanjul and Manuel Goded, leading figures in all the conspiracies against the Republic from 1932 until it was overthrown in 1936, advised the CEDA leader to maintain their collaboration in government, as the army could not yet guarantee a united position of strength to squash the left.[16]

A few days later, in the light of accusations made by José Calvo Sotelo in the Cortes against Ricardo Samper, the former Prime Minister, and Diego Hidalgo, the Minister of War, for not having put down the revolution earlier, Gil Robles asked Lerroux to dismiss them. The following day, 16 November, Lerroux realised one of his dearest ambitions: holding the post of Prime Minister as well as Minister of War, albeit at the cost of getting rid of Diego Hidalgo, 'my very good friend'. Juan José Rocha, who was dubbed *Miss Ministro*, because he

---

[15] Quoted in Townson, *La República que no pudo ser*, p. 323.
[16] Gil Robles, *No fue posible la paz*, pp. 145–8.

was in all the radical governments, dancing from one post to another, was appointed Foreign Minister, replacing Samper. One month after the October uprising and the formation of Lerroux's third government, the right had its first trophy. That was just the start, because before the end of the year, on 29 December, the CEDA also engineered the departure of another Liberal Democrat, Filiberto Villalobos, the Minister of Education, who had been trying since April 1934 to prevent cuts in education costs and simultaneously maintain some of the educational reforms of the first biennium. The argument for getting rid of Villalobos was that he defended secular tendencies and that his Ministry was still dominated by a 'Marxist revolutionary policy', but he himself was convinced that the CEDA's real aim was to 'boycott those ministers who loyally defend the Republic'.[17]

Three ministers in three months. Nigel Townson maintains that the CEDA was constantly eroding the foundations of the radical government to clear the way for its own rise to power. The next opportunity for eroding the radicals and coming closer to power came with the debate on the scope of the repression in Asturias. On 3 April, the three CEDA ministers resigned over the reprieve of twenty prisoners condemned to death by the military courts, including the socialists Rafael González Peña and Teodomiro Menéndez. In new consultations set up by Alcalá Zamora as a result of the crisis, the CEDA and José Martínez de Velasco's Agrarians requested more posts in the government. The President of the Republic, who was reluctant to give the CEDA more power, invoked Article 81 of the Constitution, which enabled him to suspend the Cortes for thirty days, and he appointed a government presided over by Lerroux, with a radical majority that excluded the CEDA, and with General Masquelete, the Chief of General Staff, under Azaña, as Minister of War.

It did not work. The CEDA threatened to dissolve the Cortes; the JAP demanded 'all the power for the *jefe*' in a rally with all the Fascist paraphernalia held in Madrid on 23 April; and Lerroux agreed to form a new government with the CEDA. But this time it was with a non-republican right majority, the first time this had occurred during the Republic. There were only three radical ministers, with the ever-present Juan José Rocha in the Foreign Ministry, two Agrarians and five CEDA ministers. The remaining three posts were occupied by

---

[17] Townson, *La República que no pudo ser*, pp. 319–20.

two independents, Manuel Portela Valladares in the Cabinet Ministry, Joaquín Chapaprieta in Finance, and a liberal democrat, Joaquín Dualde, in Education. José María Gil Robles entered the government as Minister of War. It was 6 May 1935. Since Azaña's departure in September 1933, the radicals had formed seven governments in barely twenty months.

This was when the real 'rectification' of the Republic began, with the radicals, who had broken any possible links with the leftist republicans and socialists, subject to the will of the CEDA and the demands for revenge from employers and landowners. Hundreds of mixed arbitration committees were disabled or suppressed, with an express amendment of the labour reforms passed in the first two years by Francisco Largo Caballero. A decree issued on 1 December 1934 by the CEDA minister José Oriol Anguera de Sojo outlawed 'unreasonable strikes' – in other words, those that were not authorised by the government, although his bill to repeal the *Ley de Asociaciones Profesionales*, which would have made political parties and trade unions illegal, did not prosper. However, workers lost their rights, and thousands of them were dismissed for belonging to unions or on the pretext of having taken part in the October uprising and strikes. The employers, who at the beginning were confident that the radicals would look after their interests and summarily dispense with the socialist reforms, went into action and recovered the status they had lost with the coming of the Republic.

This offensive was most noticeable in the rural environment and in the conditions of the land-workers, a collective that had already more than paid the price for their insubordination with their strike in 1934. In October 1934, the Agriculture portfolio was in the hands of Manuel Giménez Fernández, a law lecturer from Seville who defended social Catholicism in a CEDA dominated by reactionary and authoritarian postures. His first measure, the *Ley de Yunteros*, dated 21 December, extended the occupation of lands by the peasants of Extremadura, who had benefited from the *Intensificación de Cultivos* decree of October 1932 and were now about to be evicted through pressure from the owners. However, when he tried to benefit rural tenants, whom he saw as a counterweight to the big landowners, he was met with opposition from Gil Robles and his party. His bill, which materialised as the *Ley de Arrendamientos Rústicos* (Law of Rural Lettings), passed on 15 March, proposed that tenants could

take possession of any land that they had worked for at least twelve
years. The extreme right labelled this 'Marxism in disguise', his colleagues in his own party called him a 'white Bolshevik', and when
the CEDA returned to the government on 6 May 1935, following its
one-month absence, Giménez Fernández was no longer Minister of
Agriculture.

Giménez Fernández's defeat, as Edward Malefakis points out,
meant that any hope of serious social reform vanished. Following
the new conditions established after October 1934, a coalition of
extreme right and CEDA deputies finally saw their ambition to overthrow the September 1932 *Ley de Reforma Agraria* accomplished.
This included figures such as José Antonio Lamamié de Clairac, the
traditionalist who had so strongly opposed the Act in the Constituent
Cortes, and representatives of the landowners in the reactionary wing
of the CEDA, such as Cándido Casanueva and Mateo Azpeitia.[18]

Giménez Fernández was replaced by Nicasio Velayos y Velayos, a
rich, ultra-conservative Valladolid landowner, of the *Partido Agrario*.
The *Ley de Yunteros* was disregarded, and thousands of families
were evicted from the lands they were occupying. On 3 July, Nicasio
Velayos presented his *Reforma de la Reforma Agraria* bill. It needed
just five days of debate in the Cortes to be passed, while discussions
over the 1932 *Ley de Reforma Agraria* had taken five months. This
counter-reform Act annulled the inventory of seizable property and
rejected the principle of confiscation, meaning that the Institute of
Agrarian Reform (IRA) was forced to compensate the Grandees of
Spain who had had their lands expropriated since 1932, and the IRA's
budget was drastically reduced.

In practice, this Act marked the end of agrarian reform. The rightist majority in the Cortes wanted no land reform at all, either radical
or conservative. It was the culmination of the new domination of the
rural oligarchy following the land-workers' strike in June 1934 and
the uprising in October that same year. The FETT was disorganised,
the *jurados mixtos* did not work and wages were lower for those who
did find work, because unemployment in the rural environment was
continually on the increase. Furthermore, this was all made possible
because the government decided that over 2,000 socialist and leftist

---

[18] Edward Malefakis, *Reforma agraria y revolución campesina en la España
del siglo XX*, Ariel, Barcelona, 1976, p. 409.

republican town councils, 20 per cent of Spain's total, were to be replaced by management committees of the *Partido Radical* and the CEDA from October 1934.

Nobody believed any more in the *Partido Radical*'s promise of a 'Republic for all Spaniards', at a time when the government, controlled by the most reactionary sector of the CEDA, only looked after the interests of the big landowners and the employers. Some radicals protested, although Lerroux had decided that in order to hold on to his position as Prime Minister, he needed to avoid public confrontation with the CEDA. Clara Campoamor, the only female *Partido Radical* deputy, who had fought so hard for women's suffrage, left the party, and was also unable to do anything as Director-General of *Beneficiencia* (Charity), a post attached to the Ministry of Labour, in the hands of the CEDA since October 1934.

Gil Robles, Minister of War from May to December 1935, did not have time to undo all the reforms of earlier years in military matters, but with his appointments policy he did reinforce the power of the anti-Azaña officers and introduced a rightist element into the army. He appointed General Joaquín Fanjul, a former extreme right Agrarian deputy, Under-Secretary in the Ministry. General Emilio Mola became head of the army in Morocco, and Manuel Goded Director-General of Aviation, appointing Colonel Monasterio his aide-de-camp. When he moved in Cabinet for the appointment of General Franco as Chief of General Staff, a motion that was carried on 17 May 1935, Lerroux voted in favour and Alcalá Zamora against, with the latter, according to Gil Robles, repeating several times in the meeting: 'Young generals tend to be would-be coup warlords'.[19]

The President of the Republic was right. Without exception, all these officers played leading roles in the uprising against the Republic in July 1936. On the other hand, many officers with a republican background were dismissed from their posts and suffered professional reprisals. And it is highly likely that some officers appointed by Gil Robles, such as General Fanjul, encouraged and protected the *Unión Militar Española* (UME), the semi-clandestine association organised and led since the end of 1933 by Captain Bartolomé Barba Hernández and Lieutenant Colonel Valentín Galarza, both of the General Staff.

---

[19] Gil Robles, *No fue posible la paz*, p. 235.

The final project was the reform of the Constitution, one of the pet objectives of Gil Robles and the CEDA. Stanley G. Payne says that the tactic was basically to counteract anti-Catholic legislation, introduce aspects of the CEDA social programme, strengthen conservative institutions (such as the armed forces) and prepare a fundamental constitutional reform – a reform so fundamental that it was to destroy the 1931 Constitution. But the CEDA was in no hurry, because under the terms of Article 125b of the Constitution, any reform adopted before 9 December 1935 – in other words, 'during the first four years of the life of the Constitution' – needed the agreement of two-thirds of the Cortes, but after that date an absolute majority was enough. Furthermore, if the reform was passed, the law stipulated the dissolution of the Cortes and fresh elections, and what Gil Robles wanted was to be Prime Minister before undertaking this constitutional reform. On 1 September, at a JAP rally in Santiago de Compostela, with clearly Fascist trappings, Gil Robles announced that he sought the 'complete revision' of the Constitution. And if the Cortes failed to pass this revision, he added, 'the Cortes are dead and must disappear'.[20]

As the *Partido Radical* also sought a reform of the Constitution, albeit less far-reaching, Lerroux's government presented a bill before the Cortes on 5 July, to reform forty-one articles dealing with religion, the family, property and regional autonomy. A parliamentary commission was set up, chaired by Ricardo Samper, but because of the divergence between the *Partido Radical* and the CEDA over the scope of the revision, it did not start to function until October. By then, however, Lerroux was no longer Prime Minister. Yet another crisis was to remove him from this post, a post that he would never hold again.

The crisis began unexpectedly with the resignation on 19 September of the Minister for the Navy, Antonio Royo Villanova, a fierce opponent of Catalan nationalism from Zaragoza and a member of the *Partido Agrario*, in protest over the delegation of powers regarding certain State highways to the restored *Generalitat* of Catalonia. He was backed by another *Partido Agrario* member in the government, the Minister of Agriculture, Nicasio Velayos. Lerroux resigned to reorganise the coalition, this time without Agrarian support, but

[20] Stanley G. Payne, *Spain's First Democracy: The Second Republic, 1931–1936*, University of Wisconsin Press, 1993.

Alcalá Zamora asked the Speaker of the Cortes, Santiago Alba, a former monarchist now in the *Partido Radical*, to form a government. In view of the problems he perceived, Alba gave up, and on 25 September the task was finally handed over to Joaquín Chapaprieta, a liberal financier, friend of Alcalá Zamora, who had been Finance Minister in the outgoing government.

Chapaprieta, who in the previous months had introduced an austere public spending plan, reduced the Cabinet from thirteen ministers to nine: three for the *Partido Radical*, three for the CEDA, one for the Agrarians, and he incorporated one member of the *Lliga Catalana*, Pere Rahola, as Minister for the Navy. Chapaprieta himself took the Finance portfolio. Lerroux was Foreign Minister and Gil Robles continued as Minister of War.

However, this government was extremely short-lived. Even as it was formed, Alcalá Zamora already knew that 'relatives and friends' of Lerroux's were involved in a corruption scandal with bribes included. Daniel Strauss, a shady businessman who passed himself off as Dutch, but who in fact was of German origin and had Mexican nationality, tried to introduce into Spain a roulette-type game, and to obtain a permit he gave various sums of money and gold watches to certain members of the *Partido Radical*, including Joan Pich i Pon, since April 1935 the President of the restored *Generalitat*, and Aurelio Lerroux, the adopted son of the radical leader. In spite of the sums of money paid out, the permit was not forthcoming, and the inventors and promoters of the game, Strauss and Perle, sought compensation and publicised the scandal.

At the beginning of September 1935, Strauss sent Alcalá Zamora a comprehensive dossier detailing all the interviews, promises and pay-offs, with the names of all those involved. The President of the Republic presented it to Lerroux just before the September crisis, but the old radical leader was unconcerned and replied that it would be very hard to prove his contacts with Strauss. At the beginning of October, Alcalá Zamora revealed the details to Chapaprieta, the matter was raised in the Cortes and a judicial inquiry was opened. The radical ministers were forced to resign on 29 October. Chapaprieta formed a government without the radicals. This marked the breaking of the *straperlo* scandal, a neologism that combined the surnames of the game's two promoters, and which became, particularly after the civil war, the most common term to denote the black market.

Everyone, left and right, including Alcalá Zamora, who was keen to occupy Lerroux's centre, exploited the scandal. It had immediate and devastating consequences for many of the leading figures in the party. Soon afterwards, moreover, when Lerroux was announcing a reform, 'a new era of bountiful life' for the organisation, another scandal involving the radicals came to light over irregularities in the illegal payment of public funds to the owner of a company which, years earlier, had won a public contract to run a ferry service between the colonies of Equatorial Guinea and Fernando Poo, a contract that had been cancelled in 1929. Antonio Nombela, the Inspector General of the Colonies, refused to compensate Antonio Tayá, the owner of this company, who had contacts with Lerroux, and he was dismissed in July 1935. Nombela was upset over this decision, and after an unsuccessful bid for redress, he complained to Chapaprieta and the Speaker of the Cortes. Chapaprieta, isolated, without a party, and with his economic reforms blocked by the CEDA, tendered his resignation on 9 December. This was Gil Robles' opportunity to govern and undertake the revision of the Constitution.[21]

But Alcalá Zamora blocked Gil Robles' appointment as Prime Minister because, as he wrote later in his memoirs, he had never made an 'explicit declaration of his total adherence to the regime'.[22] Gil Robles, on the other hand, thought that this refusal to hand over power to him was what led many 'conservatives' to see violence as the only solution. There were rumours of a coup d'état. General Fanjul, Under-Secretary in the Ministry of War, told Gil Robles that if he were so ordered, he would mobilise the troops, and according to Gil Robles himself, who years later sought to make it quite clear that he did not back this measure, it was Francisco Franco, the Chief of General Staff, who convinced Generals Fanjul, Varela and Goded 'that at this time, the army cannot and should not be counted on to stage a coup d'état'.[23]

On 14 December, with the *Partido Radical* discredited by the scandals, and the CEDA vetoed by the President of the Republic, Manuel Portela Valladares formed a government with independents and

---

[21] The best information on these scandals is in Nigel Townson, *La República que no pudo ser,* pp. 368–80.
[22] Niceto Alcalá Zamora, *Memorias*, Planeta, Barcelona, 1977, pp. 341–4.
[23] Gil Robles, *No fue posible la paz*, pp. 365–6.

liberal democrats. Three weeks later, on 7 January 1936, faced with the impossibility of governing without the support of either of the two major parties, Alcalá Zamora signed the decree to dissolve the Cortes and gave Portela the job of organising new elections. Short-lived governments were now to become a thing of the past. Fresh elections would decide the course of the Republic.

In the months leading up to this, Manuel Azaña and Indalecio Prieto had corresponded about the need to build a coalition similar to the one that had governed in the first two years of the Republic. Largo Caballero, the leader of the UGT, opposed this agreement, although with the calling of elections he agreed to join in on condition that after the elections, if the coalition won, only republicans would govern, and that the PCE would be part of this electoral coalition. The Communists called this coalition the *Frente Popular*, a name that was never accepted by Manuel Azaña, and the pact was officially announced on 15 January, signed by the leaders of the leftist republican parties, Azaña of *Izquierda Republicana* and Martínez Barrio of *Unión Republicana*, the socialist movement, including the PSOE, the UGT and the *Juventudes Socialistas*, the PCE, the *Partido Obrero de Unificación Marxista* (POUM), a new organisation set up in September 1935 resulting from a merger of Joaquín Maurín's *Bloc Obrero y Camperol* and Andreu Nin's *Izquierda Comunista*, and, finally, the *Partido Sindicalista*, founded by Ángel Pestaña after his expulsion from the CNT.

This time the right was not so united, and the CEDA, which was stronger in the provinces, set up electoral pacts with conservative republicans, radicals or monarchist and Fascist movements. In Catalonia, the CEDA, the *Lliga*, radicals and traditionalists formed a comprehensive *Front Català de l'Ordre*. The radicals, discredited and in array, were forced to field their candidates separately from the two main alliances.

The left published a manifesto calling for 'comprehensive amnesty' and reinstatement of the dismissed as common themes. The nucleus of the CEDA's campaign, 'Against the revolution and its collaborators!', presented a catastrophist view of what the Republic had represented up to then. For the left, two years of destruction of republican reforms, the 'black biennium', were over. The CEDA, which had been unable to fulfil its aim of totally reversing the course of reform, promised a complete revision of the Constitution. The extreme right, under Calvo Sotelo, considered the Republic was now finished, and promised an unequivocal authoritarian and corporatist State. The date for the elections to decide all this, resulting in either a new course for the Republic or its conclusive end, was set for Sunday 16 February 1936.

5 | *The seeds of confrontation*

The *Frente Popular* coalition won the polls and for many people this represented the second act of a play that had begun in April 1931, only to be interrupted in the summer of 1933. It was indeed a second opportunity for Manuel Azaña, once more in power and with rejoicing in the streets; for the socialists, who once again had a strong influence on local powers; and for the anarcho-syndicalists, who were able to recover their capacity for unrest, and some of the social benefits they had lost.

The leading players may have returned, but the atmosphere after the left's victory bore little relation to the one that reigned in the spring of 1931 that saw the birth of the Republic. The *Partido Radical*, the oldest of the republican parties, the founder of the Republic and the governing party between September 1933 and December 1935, sank without trace in the elections. The upper classes felt threatened by the new thrust from the trade union organisations and social conflicts. The defeated non-republican right now thought only of force as a resource against the government and the Republic. A significant sector of the army plotted against them and did not stop until they were defeated. February 1936 saw free democratic elections; July 1936, a coup d'état. History accelerated over those five months.

The *Frente Popular* and the return of Azaña

In February 1936, 72 per cent of the Spanish population, men and women, voted – the highest turnout of the three general elections held during the Second Republic. As Javier Tusell showed years ago, it was also a clean election, in a country with democratic institutions and with many sectors of the population believing that this election was decisive for the country's future.[1] This is why the election campaign

---

[1] Javier Tusell, *Las elecciones del Frente Popular en España*, Edicusa, Madrid, 1971.

125

was so intense, so feverish. The *Frente Popular* presented a moderate programme that attracted many former *Partido Radical* voters, with amnesty and a return to the reforms and political solutions as its basic points. The non-republican right used vast sums of money on printed material to remind people of the horrors of the revolution in Asturias, and never tired of saying that it was a battle 'for God and for Spain', between 'Catholic Spain ... and appalling, barbaric, horrendous revolution'. The extreme right, monarchists and Fascists, were already advocating armed struggle, with dictatorship as the solution.

Apart from this verbal aggression, there were very few incidents during the election campaign. The winner, by very few votes, was the *Frente Popular*, although the majority system established by the electoral regulations gave it a comfortable majority in the Cortes. The parties that received the most votes were the CEDA and the PSOE, followed closely by *Izquierda Republicana*, while the *Partido Radical*, which fielded almost all its candidates separately from the main coalitions, was, after the revision of the scrutiny, reduced to four seats, ninety-nine fewer than in 1933. Alejandro Lerroux, standing for the *Front Català d'Ordre*, failed to win a seat.

The *Frente Popular* won 263 seats, the right 156 and the various parties of the centre 54. The electorate voted mainly for the socialists, republican left and Catholics. In the *Frente Popular*, the leading positions on the lists were almost always taken by the republicans of Azaña's party, and on the right, by the CEDA, which does not, contrary to what others have said at times, confirm a victory for the extremists. The Communist candidates were always the last to figure on the *Frente Popular* lists, and the sixteen seats they obtained, having received only one in 1933, were the result of having managed to join this coalition, not a reflection of their real strength. The *Falange* managed just 46,466 votes, 0.5 per cent of the all votes cast. Thirty-three parties were represented in the Cortes, of which only eleven won more than ten seats. It was a highly fragmented, rather than polarised, parliament, in which the party that had run the government in the two previous years became a mere spectator.

The *Frente Popular*'s victory was wildly celebrated in many cities. In some gaols, the prisoners rioted and demanded their freedom. Amnesty and the reinstatement of all dismissed workers were the demands that were most prevalent among the demonstrators who roamed the streets in various provincial capitals as soon as this victory was announced. This was the case, for example, in Zaragoza, where the CNT and UGT called a general strike and announced a demonstration to demand freedom for the 'political and social' prisoners. General Miguel Cabanellas, a month into his command of the 5th Division, sent military units to occupy the official buildings and the main streets. The following day, after a state of emergency had been declared, the city woke up paralysed. The demonstration, led by the newly elected deputies, Benito Pabón and Eduardo Castillo, and made up of several thousand people, was dispersed by the Assault Guard. There were scuffles and shots, with one fatality and several demonstrators wounded.

Gil Robles tried to persuade Portela Valladares, the Prime Minister, not to resign and to declare a state of emergency. General Franco, the Chief of General Staff, telephoned General Sebastián Pozas, Director-General of the Civil Guard, to join in a military action to occupy the streets to prevent unrest and revolution. Pozas, an old *africanista* loyal to the Republic, refused, and Franco then put pressure on General Nicolás Molero, the Minister of War. General Goded wanted to mobilise the Montaña barracks in Madrid, and two other generals who had taken part in all the plots against the Republic, Joaquín Fanjul and Ángel Rodríguez del Barrio, sounded out other garrisons in the capital. Franco felt that the time was not ripe, and he backed off, although between 17 and 19 February he was, says Paul Preston, 'closer than ever to mounting a military coup'. This was avoided by the firm attitude of Pozas and General Miguel Núñez de Prado, the police chief.[2]

Pressured on all sides to declare a state of emergency and annul the election results, and scared by rumours of a military coup and by the agitating in various cities to release political prisoners, Portela resigned on 19 February. Niceto Alcalá Zamora, the President of the Republic, called on Manuel Azaña to form a government. The republican leader and one-time Prime Minister was not happy with this way of receiving power, before the constitution of the new Cortes, and without even knowing the official result of the elections: 'I have always been afraid that we would come back to govern in adverse conditions', he wrote in his diary on 19 February. 'They could not be worse. Once more, the corn must be harvested before it is ripe'.[3]

[2] Paul Preston, *Franco: A Biography*, HarperCollins, London, 1993, p. 119.
[3] Manuel Azaña, *Memorias políticas y de guerra*, 4 vols., Crítica, Barcelona, 1981, vol. II, p. 11.

The government consisted of republicans only, as Azaña had agreed with the socialists before the elections, particularly because the socialists rejected the possibility of again forming a coalition government with the republicans. Nine ministers were from *Izquierda Republicana*, three from *Unión Republicana*, and there was also one independent, General Carlos Masquelet, a former adviser to Azaña in the early years of the Republic, who was now made Minister of War. It was a moderate government (to call it a *Frente Popular* government would be a misnomer), mostly made up of university professors and lawyers, some of whom, including José Giral, Santiago Casares and Marcelino Domingo, had been close allies of Azaña between 1931 and 1933. But the two parties represented in this government occupied less than a quarter of the seats in the Cortes, and this potentially threatened its stability. Azaña asked for union under the same banner that included 'republicans and non-republicans, and all those who love the Fatherland, discipline and respect for established authority'.[4]

There were urgent jobs to do and promises to be met. On 21 February, the Permanent Deputation of the Cortes, summoned by Azaña, passed the granting of a general amnesty for all those in prison for 'political and social crimes', a measure that affected, it was said at the time, nearly 30,000 people. Among them was Lluís Companys and his councillors from the *Generalitat*, who were serving thirty-year terms in the gaol at El Puerto de Santa María. A government order authorised the Catalonia autonomous parliament to resume its duties and Companys was received by an enthusiastic crowd in Barcelona. From then on he adopted a conciliatory attitude towards the government in Madrid: 'Our souls are imbued with feeling. No vengeance at all, instead a new spirit of justice and redress', he said from the balcony of the *Generalitat* building.

The granting of amnesty, the reinstatement of councillors and mayors elected in April 1931 and suspended since December 1933, and the rehiring of dismissed workers were all weighty matters that the government was under pressure from the people to resolve. Demonstrations and mobilisations over these and other matters were to raise the temperature of the disagreeable, wet atmosphere of the dying days of that winter. Much was expected of the government, and once it had dealt with those matters, the demonstrations ceased.

---

[4] Ibid., pp. 19–20.

Since the day after the elections, the press and the new government had been constantly repeating the need to keep the law, re-establish calm and guarantee order. 'The neutrality of the streets must be re-established at all costs', said *El Sol* on 4 March 1936, three days after the mass demonstration through the streets of Madrid to celebrate the election victory and support the new government. Streets that were free 'for traffic, the symbol of activity and work, the material expression of circulating wealth ... to enable people to pursue their goals, their obligations, to earn their daily bread'. Because the streets were 'nobody's and everybody's. Just like the Fatherland'.

'The street is still nobody's. It remains to be seen who conquers it', Ramón J. Sender had written in *Siete domingos rojos* some years earlier.[5] It was all about the street. Occupying or clearing it. For many people, filling the streets was a symbol of power. Empty, or serving as 'a place of law-abiding relaxation for the crowded cities', they were, for others, a sign that order was working. Opposing viewpoints that served to identify and classify. This was why there was so much interest in returning to this setting again and again. It was also why the state of emergency lasted so long during those months. In short, it was why one sector of the army plotted a real occupation of the streets. To save a Fatherland that would end up as belonging to them and a few others, but not to everyone.

The trade union organisations, each acting independently, began to mobilise with claims that would attract the most members: wage rises, shorter working hours, control of hiring and firing. A union's success in securing employment for its members depended partly on its strength, the pressure it could exert on the building-site foreman, or on the small workshop or factory owner. This issue once again drove a wedge between the two organisations and led to strikes and confrontations, such as those in Málaga, particularly when a large section of the UGT emulated the procedure that had been so successful for the CNT in the building sector: turning up at the site and making an outright demand that any person hired had to come from the union.

Social conflicts were more intensive during the early months of 1936 in the countryside. Although there was not much new in the *Frente*

---

[5] Ramón J. Sender, *Siete domingos rojos*, Colección Balagué, Barcelona, 1932. (A recent edition was published by the Instituto de Estudios Altoaragoneses, Huesca, 2004.)

Popular programme compared to the first biennium as regards agrarian reform, the election victory and the forming of a new republican left government brought the land struggle to the fore once more. The 1932 Act did not go far enough, but even so, during the CEDA radical biennium, attempts had been made to reverse its most threatening social effects. Making up for lost time and speeding up the application of these reforms were undoubtedly two issues that appeared at the top of the government's agenda. Among the potential beneficiaries there were no longer expectations, but burning desire that all the promises would be kept.

The government naturally wanted to control the change that was coming. The rural unions, representing farm-hands, day-labourers, small sharecroppers and land-workers in general, saw it as a question of justice, restitution of their full rights to lands that they were farming, and in some cases, as happened with the *yunteros* in Extremadura in 1935, from which they had been evicted. Now, with the decisive backing of many of the reinstated local authorities, they began an offensive that, from March 1936 onwards, became open conflict. That month, the 1932 *Intensificación de Cultivos* Decree was re-established, and the Ministry of Agriculture, under Mariano Ruiz-Funes, of *Izquierda Republicana*, authorised the Institute of Agrarian Reform, once more chaired by Adolfo Vázquez Humasqué, to occupy as a 'social utility' all estates 'that can solve the agrarian problem in any municipal region, thereby avoiding heavy concentration of ownership, an excess of peasants and predominance of extensive crops'.[6]

But just in case this did not work out, starting on 25 March, the *Federación Española de Trabajadores de la Tierra* organised a mass occupation and ploughing up of estates in the province of Badajoz, involving some 60,000 labourers who invaded over 2,000 estates. Similar occupations, albeit on a lesser scale and more controlled by the IRA, occurred in Cáceres, Jaén, Córdoba, Seville and Toledo, the area where socialist trade unionism was at its strongest. Between March and the military uprising in July, much more land – seven times more, according to Malefakis – was distributed than in the five previous years of the Republic. Some 550,000 hectares are thought to have been occupied by some 110,000 peasants, although these figures are

---

[6] Edward Malefakis, *Reforma agraria y revolución campesina en la España del siglo XX*, Ariel, Barcelona, 1976, p. 430.

disputed by some.[7] This was not many, bearing in mind that the commission set up to apply the 1932 Act had planned to distribute land to 150,000 peasants in the first two years. But it did serve to alarm the employers, the upper classes and all those who were beginning to think that the government was not in control of the situation, because it took no action, and that these invasions were an outright challenge to existing class structures.

With the figures at our disposal, it is somewhat speculative to agree with the cut-and-dried claim that in the spring of 1936 Spain began to experience an unprecedented wave of strikes, particularly where the CNT held sway, or that these months represented, as Stanley G. Payne suggests, the most notable period of civil disorder in Spain's history.[8] If, as Payne admits, the available statistics are flawed, the most that one can conclude is that there were as many strikes in those five months as in the whole of 1933, assuming that the Ministry of Labour Gazette's method of gathering statistics was equally as flawed for those two years. But in order to characterise this wave, other sources need to be considered, and another type of ingredient introduced into the analysis.

Firstly, the CNT did not play a very big role in this round of strikes. It might have done so in Madrid, Málaga and other less important cities, but not in Barcelona, Seville or Zaragoza, the cities where the union had its strongest presence in the first three years of the Republic. In Seville and Barcelona, the anarcho-syndicalists were weak, and their support was the lowest it had ever been during the time of the Republic. With insurrection no longer an option for them, they also had to cut the ideological ties that had distanced them from the republican regime. And by cutting them, they were back to where they had been in the spring of 1931.

The indications, at least for Barcelona and Zaragoza, were very clear: to cooperate with the republican authorities, instead of constantly mobilising their affiliates against them; and to display a willingness to negotiate agreements to fight unemployment rather than employing direct action. Nobody suggested renouncing their ideas.

---

[7] Malefakis, *Reforma agraria y revolución campesina en la España del siglo XX*, pp. 432–3.

[8] Stanley G. Payne, 'Political violence during the Spanish Second Republic', *Journal of Contemporary History*, 25, 2–3 (1990), p. 279.

But now that their prisoners had been released, and with no martyrs to venerate, the principal concerns in the first few months of 1936 were unemployment, working conditions and, particularly, union reorganisation. The victimist tone of their declarations and their aggressive language against republicans and socialists were things of the past. The pervading atmosphere among the CNT unions was very different to that of 1932 and 1933. Workers' meeting places were reopening. The wounds opened by the schism were healing with the return of all the leaders and unions, except for the group led by Ángel Pestaña, who had won a seat in the February 1936 elections. Their media outlets, censored, but with no suspensions, were recovering.

The beginning of May saw a meeting in Zaragoza of 649 CNT delegates, representing 988 unions and 559,294 affiliates. The most notable outcome of this extraordinary Congress has always been considered to be its famous pronouncement on libertarian Communism, a resounding victory for the reactionary communal ideas vehemently defended by Isaac Puente and Federico Urales, the father of Federica Montseny, during the republican years. And, bearing in mind what seemed to be on the horizon, it was indeed astonishing to see a group of anarchists, including Federica Montseny, Juan García Oliver and Joaquín Ascaso, discussing subjects as bizarre as the family and sexual relationships in the free communes of the future.

However, it should be remembered that this was the first time that the CNT had publicly admitted the errors of pursuing insurrection as a tactic, and it set aside any speculations over agrarian reform to follow a new tack, specific claims regarding wages, working conditions and the return of communal assets. 'The constructive preparation of the peasants, in accordance with our principles, is the anarcho-syndicalist movement's most important and most difficult mission in the countryside', reads the pronouncement on the 'agrarian problem'. The aim was 'from now on to steer away from occasional actions that regions initiate of their own accord, without the slightest control, under circumstances that show that the time is not right for revolution, and without the preparation required to overcome the capitalist system from the outset'.[9] Organisation, preparation and canvassing social support among the peasants – it is hard to imagine how far this

---

[9] 'Dictamen sobre el problema agrario', in *El Congreso Confederal de Zaragoza, mayo de 1936*, CNT, 1955.

approach would have gone, because two months later the military uprising forced them to change tack once more.

Furthermore, the idea that this was not a decisive period of social conflict in the rural environment is something that recent monographs have affirmed. The quantity, nature and intensity of the conflicts were no higher than they had been between 1931 and 1934. Compliance with social legislation, working conditions and the introduction of compulsory contributions to offset the unemployment problem were among the most common demands during those months. Acts of violent repression against rural workers' demonstrations were rare, if compared to their frequency during the first biennium, and the massacre at Yeste (Albacete) on 29 May, where seventeen peasants were riddled with Civil Guard bullets, failed to produce any social mobilisation, any outcry against the Civil Guard, and did not even revitalise the cult of martyrdom that was so common on previous occasions.

History should not be assessed, however, merely by the deaths it causes. The threat to social order and the subverting of class relations were perceived with greater intensity in 1936 than in the first few years of the Republic. The political stability of the regime was also under greater threat. Class distinction, with its talk about social divisions and its incitements to malign the adversary, had gradually permeated the atmosphere in Spain since the reformist plans of the early republican governments began to meet insurmountable obstacles. Violence, too, was present, with assassination attempts against prominent people; and the armed clashes between left and right political groups, occasionally with bloodshed, served to give practical expression to the verbal excesses and aggression of certain leaders. And as if that were not enough, neither of the two leading parties in the Cortes, the PSOE and the CEDA, contributed during those months to the political stability of the democracy and the Republic. Spanish politics and society displayed unequivocal signs of crisis, although this did not necessarily mean that the only solution was a civil war.

Crisis

On 12 March, in Madrid, several Falangist gunmen fired on Luis Jiménez de Asúa, a prominent socialist leader and a professor of law, one of the main drafters of the 1931 republican Constitution. He was unharmed, but his police escort, Jesús Gisbert, was killed. The

funeral of the police officer gave rise to displays of condemnation and
serious incidents, including the burning of churches and the premises of the right-wing newspaper *La Nación*. The police arrested various Falangists, although the perpetrators of the shooting managed to
escape to France in a light aircraft piloted by the military aviator Juan
Antonio Ansaldo. The Directorate-General of Security, on government instructions, ordered the arrest of the *Falange*'s political board
and national leadership. On 14 March, José Antonio Primo de Rivera
was arrested in his home, as were other leaders, such as Julio Ruiz
de Alda, Raimundo Fernández Cuesta, Rafael Sánchez Mazas and
David Jato. The instructing judge said that the *Falange* programme
that they defended was unconstitutional, and ordered that they be
held on remand before trial for unlawful assembly. They were sent to
the political prisoners' wing in the Modelo gaol.

A month later, on 13 April, Manuel Pedregal, the magistrate who
had just sentenced some of those involved in the assassination attempt
against Jiménez de Asúa, was also murdered. During the military parade the following day, the fifth anniversary of the proclamation of the
Republic, presided over by Niceto Alcalá Zamora and Manuel Azaña,
there were fresh incidents. As the Civil Guard units marched past, one
sector of the crowd booed them and various shots were heard, resulting in the death of Anastasio de los Reyes, a Civil Guard lieutenant
who was there in plain clothes, and several spectators injured.

Right and left accused each other of the incident. At the funeral of
the lieutenant, attended by the deputies Gil Robles and Calvo Sotelo,
together with several armed Falangists, there was a confrontation with
leftist groups. The result was six dead and thirty-six wounded. One of
those killed was a student, Andrés Sáenz de Heredia, a Falangist and
first cousin of José Antonio Primo de Rivera.

The clandestine *Falange* continued with what they called 'Front
Line' violent actions. Many of the affiliates were armed and practised
at shooting ranges. Between April and July 1936, according to Julio
Gil Pecharromán, the *Falange* 'was involved in a fierce struggle against
leftist workers' organisations which cost it some forty dead and over
a hundred injured, but caused more casualties among the ranks of its
adversaries'.[10] Most of these incidents, in which right and left groups

---

[10] Julio Gil Pecharromán, *José Antonio Primo de Rivera. Retrato de un
visionario*, Temas de Hoy, Madrid, 2003, pp. 425–9.

showed very little concern for human life, occurred in Madrid, while for Barcelona, which had between 1931 and 1934 experienced a large number of violent conflicts and uprisings, it was a quiet spring, with considerably fewer strikes and less political violence than in the Republic's capital. The one exception to this rule was the assassination, on 28 April, of the Badia brothers, members of a group known as *Estat Català*, possibly at the hands of FAI gunmen, although several Falangists were arrested. Miquel Badia was the head of the *mossos d'esquadra* at the time of the insurrection of 6 October 1934.

Meanwhile, the Cortes, which had been inaugurated on 15 March, with Diego Martínez Barrio as Speaker, were somewhat paralysed by debate over the official election results and, above all, by the process of replacing the President of the Republic. This was a crisis, all experts agree, that weakened the leftist republican government and smoothed the way for a military plot.

Nobody wanted Alcalá Zamora to stay on as President of the Republic. The CEDA, under Gil Robles, believed he had robbed them of the chance to hold total power in December 1935. The left, and Azaña in particular, never forgave him for having withdrawn his confidence in September 1933, leading to the fall of Azaña's government and the breaking up of the coalition between socialists and republicans that had governed in the two previous years. Furthermore, Alcalá Zamora had tried to assemble a centrist party for the February 1936 elections, using the mechanisms of presidential power, and the ballot boxes were testimony of his failure. He was not the President that the republican left wanted on its return to power, and the right was not going to lift a finger to impede his removal either.

Article 81 of the Constitution allowed for the removal of the President of the Republic in the event of his dissolving the Cortes twice, and the new Parliament considered that the latest dissolution, on 7 January 1936, was inadmissible. The debate was held on 7 April; 238 deputies voted in favour of his dismissal and only 5 of Portela's deputies voted against. The right, which had supported the measure, abstained. Alcalá Zamora was thus dismissed by the Cortes. A new President of the Republic was to be elected.

The Speaker, Diego Martínez Barrio, took over as interim Head of State, and his party, *Unión Republicana*, put forward as its candidate Manuel Azaña, who had widespread support, although Largo Caballero and the socialist left preferred Álvaro de Albornoz. If we accept the view of Santos Juliá, one of his foremost biographers, Azaña too wanted this post, because his idea was to form once more a republican and socialist coalition government, under Indalecio Prieto. The two offices, those of President of the Republic and Prime Minister, would thus be held by two people with authority and the backing of the main parties that had won the February elections.[11]

The President of the Republic, according to the Constitution, was to be elected by indirect suffrage. In the voting for representatives for the electoral college, held on 26 April, most of the right abstained. The *Frente Popular* obtained 358 representatives, and the opposition 63. Two weeks later, on 10 May, in the *Palacio de Cristal* in the Retiro, Manuel Azaña was elected President of the Republic by an overwhelming majority and the blank votes of the CEDA.

However, things did not turn out as Azaña had planned. Azaña's invitation to Prieto to form a government was opposed by the UGT and the socialist left, who threatened to break the pact with the *Frente Popular* if Prieto became Prime Minister. The socialist parliamentary group, under Largo Caballero, discussed this matter, and the motion that the socialists should form part of the government again was defeated by a comfortable majority of forty-nine votes against and nineteen in favour. Now that a coalition government led by the socialists was not an option, Azaña turned to one of his most loyal collaborators, Santiago Casares Quiroga, who became Prime Minister of the new government and also took on the War portfolio. Made up of leftist republicans only, including the Catalan *Esquerra*, it has passed into history as the weak government that permitted conflicts and political violence, instead of repressing them, and that was unable to stop the military coup, the blame for which has tended to be placed on Casares Quiroga's shoulders. Yet, in this case, history is somewhat more complex.

The schism that had existed in socialism since December 1935, with two independent leaders in confrontation with each other – the PSOE in the hands of Indalecio Prieto's 'centrist' faction and the UGT in the power of Francisco Largo Caballero's 'leftist' wing – impeded any opportunity of reinforcing the republican government. Indalecio Prieto, who had already committed the grave error of condoning and

---

[11] Santos Juliá, *Manuel Azaña, una biografía política. Del Ateneo al Palacio Nacional*, Alianza Editorial, Madrid, 1990, pp. 483–7.

collaborating in the preparation of the October 1934 revolutionary movement, embarked on the process of replacing Alcalá Zamora without having assured his alternative policy of leading the government and, with Azaña, strengthening the republican State.

Meanwhile, Largo Caballero was unable to offer any solution other than waiting for the revolution, which would come as a response to any coup by the right or the military, and radicalising his ideas. He was supported in this endeavour by the *Juventudes Socialistas*, ever more intent on creating militias, a paramilitary framework and armed confrontations with groups of young Fascists. In June, under the leadership of Santiago Carrillo, they merged with the young Communists, thereby creating the *Juventudes Socialistas Unificadas*, a prelude to the Communist dream of uniting the two Marxist workers' parties. During those months, the PCE set out its moderate policy of fighting Fascism, putting a brake on strikes and focussing its political struggle in parliament, but at the same time it benefited from the split in socialism, the bolshevisation of its youth, to grow and make inroads into the UGT unions.

At the opposite extreme of parliamentary politics, the CEDA began a decisive shift to authoritarian ideas, something that had been extremely evident for months in its youth movement, with their language and Fascist salutes and the uniforms they wore. The February 1936 elections marked the end of 'accidentalism' in the Catholic movement. When it became obvious that the corporatist-based 'revision' of the Republic could not be achieved via the acquisition of power in parliament, an objective that was shared by Gil Robles and the Church hierarchy, they began to think of more effective methods. Following the electoral defeat of February 1936, everyone got the message: they needed to abandon the ballot box and take up arms. The fundamentalist idea of the 'right to rebelliousness' advocated in a book published in 1934 by Aniceto de Castro Albarrán, the canon preacher of Salamanca, of a rebellion in the shape of a patriotic and religious crusade against the atheistic Republic, started gathering followers.[12] The *Juventudes de Acción Popular* were swelling the ranks of the *Falange*, with over 15,000 affiliates transferring from one organisation to the other; and in the Cortes, Gil Robles endorsed the anti-system rants of José Calvo Sotelo.

---

[12] Aniceto de Castro Albarrán, *El derecho a la rebeldía*, Gráfica Universal, Madrid, 1934.

These catastrophist stances engulfed what little was left of social Catholicism: people such as Maximiliano Arboleya, who had drawn attention to the mutual hatred between the Church and the working class; moderate Catholics such as the Basque politicians Manuel Irujo and José Antonio Aguirre; and radical sectors of Catalan Catholicism, with Cardinal Vidal i Barraquer at their head. Not even Francesc Cambó's *Lliga Catalana* was exempt from this ultra-Catholic image, labelled by many, according to Borja de Riquer, as '*el partit dels rics i dels capellans*' (the party of the wealthy and the clergy).[13] With peaceful 're-Catholicisation' through the trade unions and the Church's social action no longer an option, it took just a few months to shift to violent 're-Catholicisation' via a holy and patriotic war.

And this was the direction taken from the day after the *Frente Popular* coalition election victory. As early as 20 February, the Carlist-leaning daily *El Pensamiento Alavés* was saying that 'it will not be in Parliament that the final battle is fought, but on the terrain of armed struggle'. It was to be a struggle that would originate in an 'essentially counter-revolutionary region', made up of Castilla, León, Álava and Navarre, which would act 'if necessary as a new Covadonga which would serve as a place of refuge for those who fled from the revolution and undertook the Reconquest of Spain'.

It was no coincidence that it was Navarre and Álava that would see during those months the consolidation of the *Requeté*, the 'red berets', a 'military organisation, well disciplined, with a firm structure and a strong threat to the republican regime', which, as both Martin Blinkhorn and Javier Ugarte have shown in detail, had numerous locations for manoeuvres and military training that were attended by priests and the upper classes of the region.[14] In fact, military training and instruction had, for some time, carried more weight in Carlist circles than traditionalist political theory. Jaime del Burgo, who as a student had begun to carry a weapon since the proclamation of the Republic, classified the headquarters in Pamplona as 'a barracks' where, as in most of the Carlist premises, the *requetés* would occupy

[13] Borja de Riquer, *El último Cambó 1936–1947. La tentación autoritaria*, Grijalbo, Barcelona, 1997, p. 31.
[14] Martin Blinkhorn, *Carlismo y contrarrevolución en España*, Crítica, Barcelona, 1979; Javier Ugarte, *La nueva Covadonga insurgente. Orígenes sociales y culturales de la sublevación de 1936 en Navarra y el País Vasco*, Biblioteca Nueva, Madrid, 1998.

the ground floor, equipped and on permanent watch. When the time came, the *Requeté*, with its strict hierarchy and intensive training, was the civil militia that the military rebels would most rely on.

The Catholic and extreme right-wing press incited their readers to rebellion against the disorder that they attributed to the 'tyrannical *Frente Popular* government', 'the enemy of God and the Church'. And the confrontation between the Church and the Republic, between clericalism and anticlericalism, once more dominated current affairs after the February 1936 elections. Once more, there were disputes over symbolic matters, with local authorities banning processions, bell-ringing and open-air religious activities. Back came the proposal to replace confessional education, as envisaged in the 1933 Religious Confessions and Congregations Bill, paralysed by the victory of the radicals and the CEDA in that year's elections. First Azaña's, and then Casares Quiroga's government reopened some of the issues that had already divided Catholics and republicans during the early years: the closing of Church schools, co-education and the consolidation of public education at the expense of religious tuition. But of the more than 250 deaths that are said to have occurred between February and July as a result of 'political violence', not one cleric was killed, which contradicts the memory that is often still conveyed about that spring of 1936, echoing all that was written then to sanction the Church's support of the military coup: that the 'extermination of the Catholic clergy' had begun before July 1936.

In fact, when Tomás Domínguez Arévalo, the Count of Rodezno, wrote in autumn 1936, once the war had started, about the 'anarchic and despotic social situation' that Spain had been in during the months prior to the military uprising, he mentioned not only the 'more than two hundred churches burnt down', but also the 'constant strikes, employers and landowners murdered, estates arbitrarily invaded'. Rodezno was a Catholic traditionalist deputy, as well as the owner of various estates in Navarre, Logroño and Cáceres, with influential contacts in Madrid, and a solid background in politics and finance in Navarre. Further down the social scale, religion was used not only to keep landowners and poor labourers united against the Republic, but also to ensure that these less favoured sectors would accept the dominance and supremacy of the ruling classes as something 'natural'.[15]

---

[15] Blinkhorn, *Carlismo y contrarrevolución en España*, pp. 319–47.

But none of this offensive launched by the monarchist oligarchies and the Catholic masses of the CEDA would have achieved the desired result – overthrowing the Republic and eradicating the threat of socialism and libertarianism – had they not been able to rely on the weaponry of a large sector of the army. In the first few weeks after the February elections until the middle of March, Azaña's recently elected government acted on a proposal by General Carlos Masquelet, the Minister of War, and ordered major changes and transfers affecting high-ranking officers who were suspected of taking part in plots or had stated the need for military intervention. Franco was replaced as Chief of General Staff and was sent out to the Canary Islands. Fanjul, the Under-Secretary at the Ministry of War who had been appointed by Gil Robles, was left without a posting, as were other significant *antiazañista* and anti-republican officers, such as Orgaz, Villegas and Saliquet. General Goded, the Director-General of Aviation, was posted to the Balearic Islands and Mola was transferred to the 12th Brigade stationed in Pamplona. They were replaced by officers who were republicans or supposedly loyal to the established rule, although events were soon to prove that this transfer policy failed to put a brake on the plotting and the coup. In addition, some of the transferred officers felt insulted. Franco, for example, says Paul Preston, 'perceived it as a demotion and another slight at the hands of Azaña', and 'banishment'.[16]

In charge of the organisation of the plot were various right-wing officers, including some from the *Unión Militar Española* (UME), a semi-clandestine anti-leftist organisation consisting of several hundred officers. On 8 March, Francisco Franco, who was due to leave for the Canary Islands the next day, Generals Mola, Orgaz, Villegas, Fanjul, Rodríguez del Barrio, García de la Herrán, Varela, González Carrasco, Ponte, Saliquet and Lieutenant Colonel Valentín Galarza met in Madrid, at the home of José Delgado, a stockbroker and friend of Gil Robles, 'to agree on a rising to re-establish internal order and the international prestige of Spain', according to surviving documents on 'the preparation and development of the National Rising'. They also agreed that General Sanjurjo, who was then living in Portugal, would head the uprising.[17]

[16] Preston, *Franco*, p. 120.
[17] Copy of the documents provided by Lieutenant Colonel Emiliano Fernández Cordón, regarding the preparation and running of the National Rising (75 pp.), housed in the Servicio Histórico Militar, Madrid. The quotes that follow by General Mola also come from this document.

In the end, however, the main player in the plot was General Mola, who talked to the leaders of the rebellion and issued, under the pseudonym of 'El Director', various reports, instructions and enclosures for the leaders' eyes only. He signed the first of the 'five confidential instructions' on 25 May, somewhat later than the date proposed for the coup at the meeting on 8 March, in which he explained the conditions required 'for the rebellion to be an outright success'. It was also in this first 'confidential instruction' that Mola proclaimed the need for violent repression: 'Bear in mind that the action will need to be uncommonly violent in order to bring down the enemy, who is strong and well organised, as soon as possible. Naturally, all leaders of political parties, companies or unions that are not sympathetic to the *Movimiento* will be imprisoned, and they will be dealt exemplary punishments to stifle any rebellious or strike movements'.

The officers were slow to respond to the call to participate in the coup, but when Mola drafted this first 'confidential instruction', he already knew that the garrisons in Morocco were prepared to revolt. Also important were Mola's contacts with Gonzalo Queipo de Llano, the head of the Carabineros, and the discussions he had on 7 June with General Miguel Cabanellas, commander of the 5th Division, confirming Cabanellas' participation in the coup, and establishing the resources he would need to confront the opposition that in Zaragoza 'will almost certainly come from the union masses', as well as the organisation of the 'columns that will be needed to prevent the Catalans from invading Aragonese territory'. By the end of June, everything was ready in the 5th Division for the rebellion, with Colonel Monasterio, who had been Gil Robles' military adviser and confidant in the Ministry of War, at the centre of the plot. Also by this time the military conspirators had assigned tasks to the various regions. On 4 July, the wealthy businessman, Juan March, agreed to provide the money for a plane to fly Franco from the Canary Islands to Morocco. The aircraft, a De Havilland Dragon Rapide, was chartered two days later in England by Luís Bolín, *ABC*'s London correspondent, for £2,000.

The assassination of José Calvo Sotelo convinced the plotters of the urgent need to intervene and brought into the fold many of the undecided, who were waiting for things to become clearer before agreeing to participate in the coup and risk their salaries and their lives. On the afternoon of Sunday 12 July, in a street in central Madrid, several right-wing gunmen – traditionalists, according to Ian Gibson's research – killed José del Castillo, a lieutenant of the Assault Guard, whose socialist sympathies were widely known.[18] In the early hours of the following day, some of his colleagues, led by a Civil Guard captain, Fernando Condés (who, like Castillo, had previously served as an army officer in Morocco), went to the home of Calvo Sotelo, in the Calle Velásquez, and, while they were supposedly taking him to the central barracks of Pontejos, murdered him and left his body in the morgue at the Almudena cemetery.

Calvo Sotelo, the leader of the *Bloque Nacional*, had in previous months been involved in harsh confrontations with the left in the Cortes, and his murder by members of the Republic's police naturally caused indignation among his followers and politicians of the right. The monarchist leader Antonio Goicochea, speaking at his funeral, uttered these words that were subsequently repeated many times: 'We swear a solemn oath to dedicate our lives to this threefold task: to imitate your example, avenge your death and save Spain'. During a session of the Permanent Delegation of the Cortes, held on 15 July, Gil Robles said to the leftist deputies that 'the blood of Señor Calvo Sotelo is on your hands'. The government was not involved in the murder, said the CEDA leader, but it was 'morally responsible' because it 'sponsors violence'.[19]

When General Franco received the news on the morning of 13 July, he said to the messenger, Colonel Teódulo González Peral, in words that were later constantly quoted by apologists for the coup, to show the connection between this murder and Franco's ultimate decision to intervene: 'The fatherland now has another martyr. We cannot wait any longer. This is the signal!'[20] The next day, the Dragon Rapide arrived in the Canary Islands. On the evening of 17 July, the garrisons of Melilla, Tetuán and Ceuta rose in Morocco. In the early hours of 18 July, Franco signed a declaration of martial law and pronounced himself in opposition to the government of the Republic. On 19 July, he arrived at Tetuán. Meanwhile, many other military garrisons in the peninsula joined the coup. Peace was over in the Republic.

[18] Ian Gibson, *La noche en que mataron a Calvo Sotelo*, Argos Vergara, Barcelona, 1982.
[19] Gil Robles, *No fue posible la paz*, Ariel, Barcelona, 1968, pp. 749–65.
[20] Quoted in Preston, *Franco*, p. 137.

Why did the Republic not survive?

Up to the beginning of the Second Republic, Spanish society seemed to have managed to avoid the problems and troubles that had beset most European countries since 1914. Spain had not taken part in the First World War, and therefore had not undergone the upheaval that this war had caused, with the fall of empires and their subjects, the demobbing of millions of ex-combatants and massive debt caused by the vast spending on the war effort. But it did share the division and tension that accompanied the process of modernisation between those who feared Bolshevism and the various manifestations of socialism, lovers of order and authority, and those who dreamed of this new, egalitarian world that would arise from the class struggle.

The programme of political and social reforms that followed the proclamation of the Republic highlighted some of the tensions that had been germinating during the previous decades, with industrialisation, urban growth and class conflicts. This opened up a breach between various clashing cultural worlds, between practising Catholics and hardline anticlericalists, bosses and workers, Church and State, order and revolution.

The problems Spain faced in consolidating democracy and the Republic originated from various fronts. Firstly, it was extremely difficult to consolidate a stable coalition between republicans and socialists, between the representatives of a broad sector of the middle classes and those of an equally broad sector of the urban working classes. This common project, whose origin lay in the summer 1930 San Sebastián Pact and which directed the orientation of the early months of the Republic, lasted barely two years. In October 1931, Alcalá Zamora and Miguel Maura, the Prime Minister and the Interior Minister, both monarchists who had embraced the Republic, left the government over the debate on the religious question. They did not have much force or support – barely 30 deputies of the 470 that made up the Constituent Cortes – but the most conservative republicans and Catholics distanced themselves from the scheme. And it was not only over the disputed Article 26 of the Constitution, the one that was considered the most anticlerical; their decision was also influenced by their disagreement over the scope of other reformist projects, mainly agrarian reform and the labour legislation that had already been set in train by the socialists.

Indeed, its hostility towards the socialists was the reason why the *Partido Radical*, the hub of the republican alliance, left the government and passed over to the opposition in parliament in December 1931. Azaña, the Prime Minister after the Constitution was passed, preferred to dispense with Lerroux and his demands that the socialists leave the government, and continue with the representatives of a major sector of the working classes in the executive, in the belief that this was the best way of stabilising the Republic. The government and its reformist programme was backed only by leftist republicans and socialists, although its parliamentary support was considerably reduced because the radicals had won ninety-four seats in that year's elections and the middle classes were even more divided. Behind the *Partido Radical* were a good many civil servants, teachers, skilled workers and members of the liberal professions, as was the case with the leftist republicans, but there were also businessmen and employers who were not sympathetic to the ideas and projects of the republican left. Furthermore, in many areas, the *Partido Radical* became the refuge of caciques and confirmed monarchists, an excellent platform from which, during the two years they were in power, to hound the republicans, socialists and their ambitious programme of reforms.

At the other extreme, what was intended to be the incorporation of the working class into the government and administration of the State was hampered from the outset, because there was a powerful anarcho-syndicalist movement in Spanish society, represented by broad sectors of agricultural day-labourers and the urban working classes, in major cities such as Zaragoza, Seville, Valencia and, especially, Barcelona and its industrial belt, who preferred revolution as an alternative to parliamentary government. Some of the hardline leaders of this movement, typified by the FAI and the group led by Buenaventura Durruti, Juan García Oliver and Francisco Ascaso, embraced insurrection as a method of coercion against the established authority. Behind this series of insurrection attempts, in January 1932 and January and December 1933, was essentially a rejection of the system of representation and the belief that force was the only way to abolish class privilege and what they considered to be its accompanying abuse of power.

Mobilisations by the CNT, strikes rather than insurrection, soon made it clear that the forces of order, the Civil Guard, and also the recently created Assault Guard, acted with the same brutality as they had done under the Monarchy. It was clear that those responsible for this repression were not from the UGT. Yet this seemed to make no difference to the libertarian propaganda: they were governing in coalition with the republicans, they enjoyed official privilege – *socialenchufistas* they called them – and therefore they were jointly responsible for the serious errors committed by the authorities. The traditional enemies of the working class, capitalism and the State were now joined by the 'socialist hordes'. From autumn 1931 onwards, this posture spread with tiresome insistence, although it was after January 1932, following the massacre at Arnedo, the insurrection in Fígols and the subsequent deportation of CNT leaders, that it became firmly rooted in the anarchist media. After the events at Casas Viejas, the rupture between the two syndicalist groups was irreparable.

The struggle for control of the distribution of labour and the socialists' use of the State as a tool to reinforce the UGT and to resolve conflicts were elements that were behind many of the confrontations between the two union organisations in the early years of the Republic. The economic crisis, public spending restrictions and the lack of money to tackle major reforms almost certainly hindered the consolidation of republican democracy. Two and a half years after the proclamation of the Republic, following numerous conflicts and with several uprisings behind it, the CNT was severely weakened and, with the odd exception such as Madrid, had seen a sharp fall in its membership. Things were not much better for the UGT: the socialists were no longer in government – something that the employers and *Partido Radical* republicans had been demanding all through 1933 – and the inability of the party and the UGT to channel the workers' interests led to a fragmentation of the socialist movement, giving rise to considerable political weakness in the second biennium of the Republic.

With the break-up in 1933 of the coalition between republicans and socialists, the aim of which was to incorporate major sectors of the middle classes and urban workers into its projects, the PSOE distanced itself from its position of gradual and peaceful progress towards socialism and hoisted the banner of revolution. The socialists started to advocate force as a resource to be used against the parliamentary regime, with their first insurrection in October 1934, the very time that even the most radical anarchists had exhausted its potential.

Against the republican reforms and revolutionary deeds and words, anti-republicanism, anti-democratic postures and counter-revolution were advancing rapidly, and not only among the most influential sectors of society, such as businessmen, industrialists, landowners, the Church and the army. After the fall of the Monarchy and the first few months of disorganisation among the right, political Catholicism burst onto the republican scene like a whirlwind. The close link between religion and land-ownership could be seen in the mobilisation of hundreds of thousands of Catholic farm-workers, poor and 'extremely poor' landowners, and the almost total control wielded by landowners over organisations that were supposedly set up to improve the lot of these farm-workers.

Dominated by large landowners, urban professionals and many ex-Carlists who had evolved towards 'accidentalism', the CEDA, the first mass party in the history of the Spanish right, set itself up to defend 'Christian civilisation', combat the 'sectarian' legislation of the Republic and 'revise' the Constitution. When it became obvious that the corporatist-based 'revision' of the Republic could not be achieved via the acquisition of power in parliament, its leaders, affiliates and voters began to think that violence might be more effective. Its youth movements and the monarchist parties had already started out on the road to *fascistisation* some time before. After their electoral defeat in February 1936, everyone had got the message, and they joined forces to bring about the destabilisation of the Republic and rushed to support the military coup.

The downfall of the *Partido Radical* left the Republic without a political centre. There was no liberal right, and the Catholics were not going to support reforms, however moderate they were. Giménez Fernández tried it with his agrarian policy and he lasted only six months in the Ministry of Agriculture, having been dubbed a 'white Bolshevik' by his party colleagues. The year that the CEDA was in government, in coalition with centrist republicans and the non-republican right – in other words, the middle classes, the land-owning bourgeoisie and peasant farmers – was the most unstable year of the Republic. And that despite the fact that the workers' syndicates had been closed down and a large proportion of the socialist and republican left opposition was in gaol. Thus the Republic could not be consolidated from above either, basically because these groups did not believe in it, and the government coalition of the second biennium broke up. In the early months of 1936, CEDA's political territory was beginning to be occupied by the extraparliamentary and anti-system forces of the extreme right.

Reform and social conflicts, confrontation between the Church and the republican State, caused a deep divide in Spanish society in the 1930s. In view of the fact that, as leading studies of economic history have shown, economic factors did not play a decisive role in the final outcome of the republican regime, in comparison, for example, with the final crisis of the Weimar Republic, some authors have ascribed the 'failure' of the Republic – the term that tends to be used – to politics, specifically political 'polarisation' and violence.

The Second Republic was, according to Stanley G. Payne, the author who best summarises this theory, 'the most polarised of all the modern European democratic systems'. During the first three years, there was less violence and in no way did it threaten the stability of the system. The real violence, however, began in 1934, 'after political polarisation became extreme' and those responsible for the 'polarisation' and the violence were the socialists. Between 1931 and 1935, governments adopted a heavy hand against violence, whatever its source. Yet in 1936, the Azaña–Casares Quiroga government was reluctant to adopt really harsh measures because its policy depended on an alliance with the revolutionaries, and its only repressive measures were ineffectively directed against Falangist activists and military plotters. All this – in other words, 'society's leaning towards violence' and the republican left governments' weakness and incompetence in 1936 – created a higher degree of 'polarisation' and violence in Spain than existed in Italy, Germany and Austria before the collapse of their democracies. And if that happened in those three countries, it was bound to occur in Spain, where the whole situation was much worse.[21]

This may also be interpreted another way. After the Russian revolution, any attempt at revolt or revolution by the left was defeated, in country after country, be it Germany, Hungary or Italy, and no liberal democracy (the dominant system in western Europe until Hitler's rise to power) was defeated by the use of arms by the left. Wherever

---

[21] Payne, 'Political violence during the Spanish Second Republic', pp. 285–6.

they tried it, the mechanisms of repression used by the State, united in order to safeguard social order, either prevented it or left the way clear, with their consent and backing, to the setting up of Fascist or counter-revolutionary dictatorships.

In Spain, the anarchist uprisings of 1932 and 1933, and particularly the insurrectional movement in October 1934 in Asturias, Catalonia and other scattered locations, were serious disturbances that were cruelly put down by the armed forces of the republican State. Of the nearly 1,400 killed in the Asturias uprising, over 1,100 were revolutionaries, or those considered as such by the security forces, and the same proportion applied, albeit with fewer deaths, in the three anarchist uprisings.

As with General Sanjurjo's rebellion in August 1932, these violent disturbances hindered the survival of the Republic and the parliamentary system; they showed that violence was a resource commonly employed by certain sectors of the left, by the army and by the guardians of traditional order, but they did not cause the end of the Republic, let alone the beginning of the civil war. And this was because when the army and the security forces were united and loyal to the regime, insurrectional movements were easily put down, albeit at the cost of heavy bloodshed. In the early months of 1936, leftist as well as anarchist insurrection had ceased to be viable, as was the case in other countries, and the syndicalist organisations were much further from promoting a revolution than they had been in 1934. There had been free elections in February, without any government rigging, in which the CEDA, like the other parties, had invested considerable resources in its bid for victory, and there was a government which had once more set out on the road to reform, but this time with a society that was more fragmented and a harmony that was more undermined. The political system was shaky and, as occurred in all the countries of Europe, with the possible exception of the United Kingdom, the rejection of liberal democracy in favour of authoritarianism was rife.

Yet none of this need have led to a civil war. The war began because a military uprising weakened and undermined the ability of the State and the republican government to maintain order. The death blow to the Republic was dealt from within, from the very heart of its defence mechanisms, the military factions that broke their oath of loyalty to this regime in July 1936. The division of the army and security forces thwarted the victory of the military rebellion, as well as the achievement of their main objective: the rapid seizure of power. But by undermining the government's power to keep order, this coup d'état was transformed into the unprecedented open violence employed by the groups that supported and those that opposed it. It was only then, not October 1934 or the spring of 1936, that the civil war began.

PART II

Civil war

6 | *From coup d'état to civil war*

The generals who were due to command the rebel forces knew that a large proportion of officers supported the rebellion. They thought that only a few would oppose it. And any resistance from the unionised workers, which they forecast would be strong in Madrid, Zaragoza, Seville and Barcelona, could be overthrown 'immediately'. That was the plan: an uprising, with all the violence necessary, and a quick victory. Things did not turn out that way, and the result of this uprising was a long civil war, lasting nearly three years.

Rebellion

Confidence in the swift success of the uprising was quickly dispelled when the rebels were defeated in most of the big cities. The combined resistance of the security forces loyal to the Republic and militants of political and syndicalist organisations was crucial in crushing the revolt in Barcelona, Madrid, Málaga, Valencia, Gijón and San Sebastián. However, wherever this combination was absent (such as Seville and Córdoba) or the Civil Guard and Assault Guard backed the actions of the rebels (Zaragoza and Valladolid, for example), the struggle was so one-sided that it did not take long for the rebels to gain their objective.

Seville fell very quickly into the hands of General Gonzalo Queipo de Llano, the Inspector General of the Carabineros, who arrived there on 17 July to head the coup, although the planning had been done by José Cuesta Monereo, a major in the High Command stationed in the city. Queipo de Llano, who immediately began to use Radio Seville to broadcast his macabre sense of humour and threaten the 'reds', claimed that he had taken the city with two or three dozen men, although in fact he had needed almost 4,000. He used artillery to shell the city hall and the civil government building, and from the outset he employed indiscriminate violence. According to Antonio

Bahamonde, Queipo's propaganda agent and a Catholic editor who escaped after this inferno and left a detailed account of the repression, the soldiers, with the help of Carlists and Falangists, left so many bodies lying on the ground that 'they had to stack them up against the walls of the houses to leave room for cars, equipped with machine guns, to patrol the city'.[1]

Equally costly, in terms of lives, was the quelling of the uprisings in Madrid and Barcelona, the two biggest cities in Spain, very soon to become symbols of popular resistance – 'the people in arms', as the anarchists were popularly known. Barcelona had a well-equipped garrison, divided between troops loyal to the Republic, such as Captain Federico Escofet, linked to left-wing Catalan nationalism, and others, such as General Álvaro Fernández Burriel, who were involved in the plotting. The uprising began on 19 July, led by Fernández Burriel, while waiting for Manuel Poded, the general commander of the Balearic Islands who had at the last minute been given the responsibility for leading the rebellion in Barcelona, to take command of operations. It was all in vain, because the Civil Guard, the *Generalitat* security forces and anarchist groups already had the situation under control. By the time the last rebel troops in Barcelona, holed up in the Carmelite convent, had surrendered on 20 July, and General Manuel Goded had announced their defeat and surrender on the radio, the fighting in the Catalan capital had left a balance of 450 deaths. And the war and the revolution had not even started yet.

That same day, groups of armed workers and troops loyal to the republican government stormed the La Montaña barracks in Madrid, defended by some 2,000 rebels under the command of General Joaquín Fanjul, supported by 500 Falangists. The outcome was tragic: the enraged attackers, who had seen many of their comrades fall in this action, killed over a hundred soldiers and Falangists right there, after they had surrendered. Fanjul survived a few days before he was tried and shot. This first massacre caused despair among some of those who defended the legitimacy of the republic. As the socialist Julián Zugazagoitia wrote, 'the officers were executed by the most violent element of the militia who felt that now was not the time for

---

[1] Antonio Bahamonde and Sánchez de Castro, *Un año con Queipo. Memorias de un nacionalista*, Ediciones Españolas, Barcelona, 1938, p. 27.

mercy'.[2] Indeed, mercy was not a quality to be found in abundance during those warm July days, and even less so in the years and decades that were to follow. It was denied to Zugazagoitia in 1940, for example, when, after being handed over to the Francoist authorities by the Vichy regime, he was shot in the selfsame Madrid in which he had so vehemently expressed his horror at the lack of concern for human life imposed by the war.

It was very important that the rebellion should succeed in Zaragoza in order to control the large area of the Ebro corridor, march on Madrid and halt the Catalans, decided Generals Mola and Cabanellas in their first meeting, on 7 June 1936 at Las Bardenas, a military base halfway between Pamplona and Zaragoza. Miguel Cabanellas, who had played a highly ambiguous role as director of the Civil Guard in the *Sanjurjada* in August 1932, managed to fool the republican authorities and a fair number of CNT and UGT members, because of his membership of the masons and his early statements declaring his 'democratic tradition' and his 'love for Spain and the Republic'. As he said in a communiqué broadcast on the radio on 20 July 'to the Zaragoza proletariat': 'Have no suspicion, have no fear, I have promised in the past, and still do on my honour that [the military] is bound to the Fatherland and the Republic, and that all the legitimate rights you have won will be maintained and even improved'.[3]

When Cabanellas learnt of the beginning of the rebellion in Morocco on the evening of 17 July, he received a telegram from the Minister of War ordering the arrest of Colonel Monasterio and Lieutenant Colonel Urrutia, the leading figures in the plot in Zaragoza, who had already agreed with Mola to take part in the coup. The next day, the Prime Minister, Casares Quiroga, telephoned Cabanellas, asking him to go to Madrid to report on the situation in the 5th Division. Cabanellas refused, and General Núñez del Prado, Director-General of Aviation, travelled to Zaragoza to speak to Cabanellas, or, according to other sources, to take over the command of the 5th Division. As soon as he landed, however, he was arrested by General Álvarez Arenas, another of the rebels, transferred to Pamplona and shot.

---

[2] Julián Zugazagoitia, *Guerra y vicisitudes de los españoles*, Tusquets, Barcelona, 2001, p. 86.

[3] Reproduced in Emilio Colás Laguía and Antonio Pérez Ramírez, *La gesta heroica de España. El movimiento patriótico en Aragón*, Editorial Heraldo de Aragón, Zaragoza, 1936, p. 19.

A tightly knit garrison, and the incorporation of the Civil and Assault Guard forces into the rebel army ensured that Zaragoza very quickly fell to the rebels, in spite of the fact that the syndicalist organisations went on strike and put up some armed resistance for a few days.

By the end of July, the military coup's destiny was decided. It had met with success in almost the whole of northern and north-west Spain (Galicia, León, Old Castilla, Oviedo, Álava, Navarre and the three capitals of Aragon); the Canary and Balearic Isles, except for Menorca; and large areas of Extremadura and Andalusia, including the cities of Cáceres, Cádiz, Seville, Córdoba, Granada and, after 29 July, Huelva. Any chance of victory would mean having to bathe the streets and districts of most of these provincial capitals in blood. To eradicate any resistance, the rebels had to work hard, firstly, against their own military colleagues loyal to the Republic or those who were doubtful about the uprising. This patriotic movement could not afford any opposition. Any attempt at opposition cost the perpetrators dearly, beginning with several field and general officers who faced summary firing squads in Tetuán and Melilla. This is what happened in Tetuán to General Manuel Romerales, arrested at gunpoint in his office by some of his subordinates. Among those court-martialled and executed in Galicia were Rear Admiral Antonio Azarola in El Ferrol on 4 August 1936, and Generals Enrique Salcedo, head of the 7th Division, and Rogelio Caridad in La Coruña on 9 November.

Not even pleas for clemency could prevent the shooting of Generals Miguel Campíns and Domingo Batet. The former, the military governor of Granada, opposed the uprising and was arrested at gunpoint by several officers, who forced him to sign the declaration of martial law. He was taken to Seville and sentenced to death for 'rebellion' on 14 August. He was shot two days later. Franco, a friend of Campíns, interceded on his behalf before Queipo, but without success. Batet, who had been head of the 4th Catalonia Division in October 1934, restoring central government authority over the *Generalitat*, was in July 1936 head of the 6th Division based in Burgos. He had only been there a few days, having been sent by Casares Quiroga's government to replace General Pedro de la Cerda, to halt the plot. This he could not do and he refused to join the rebels, for which he was sentenced to death and shot on 12 February 1937. Franco ignored a plea for clemency from Queipo, and even took part in the trial against Batet. It was his revenge against Queipo for Campíns' execution.

Thus it was not the army en masse that rose up against the Republic; neither could it be called 'the rebellion of the generals', although this term is still being used. Of the eighteen division generals, including those in the Civil Guard and the Carabineros – in other words, those who commanded the most important units of intervention – just four took part in the uprising: Cabanellas, Queipo, Goded and Franco, and only one of them, Cabanellas, commanded troops in the peninsula. There were two further division generals, at that time without a posting, who took part in the uprising, Fanjul and Saliquet, while Generals Riquelme and Masquelet, who were in special postings, remained loyal to the republican government. Nor were the brigade generals unanimous in their support for the uprising: fourteen of the fifty-six that were serving on 18 July rebelled against the government.

The most active role in the uprising was played by the corps of field officers, whose action drew in several senior officers who were not involved at the beginning, and who were not averse to using violence against the undecided or those who opposed their plans. Of the 15,301 officers in all branches, corps and services serving in July 1936, just over half clearly supported the rebellion. The rebels initially had some 120,000 armed men, of the 254,000 in the peninsula, the islands and Africa at that time, including the forces of public order. However, various factors came together to give superiority to the rebels and lessen the effectiveness of those who remained loyal to the republic. Firstly, the order from the republican government to demobilise the troops, with the idea of undermining the military rebels, achieved the opposite result, because many of these soldiers, in areas where the uprising failed, subsequently refused to go back to their units and, in response to the popular and revolutionary call, joined the militias. Secondly, the anarchists and socialists, the first to organise militias, were traditionally anti-militarist, which led them to distrust many of these officers, even though they had not risen up against the Republic. A substantial part of what could have been the republican army was fragmented from the beginning, in scattered units and with no possibility of imposing its discipline on the militias, 'the people in arms', that were emerging everywhere.

Among the rebels, however, things were very different, because, despite the fact that the peninsular army was also underprepared for war, they did have disciplined and organised troops, and above all they had the Africa army from the outset, with almost all its 1,600 officers and 40,000 men under their command. Its best-known and best-trained troops were the *Tercio de Extranjeros* and the Legion, founded by Millán Astray and Franco in 1920, and made up of deserters, criminals, outcasts and fugitives, who were trained to venerate virility and violence. At the time it had two regiments, one in Melilla and the other in Ceuta, the latter under the command of Lieutenant Colonel Yagüe, Franco's right-hand man in the repression in Asturias in October 1934 and Mola's representative for the plot in Morocco. Alongside the Legion were the *Fuerzas Regulares Indígenas*, made up of Moroccan mercenaries and some Spaniards.

By 19 July, Franco was in Tetuán, in command of this powerful Morocco garrison, and it was this post that gave rise to what Paul Preston calls 'the making of a Generalísimo'.[4] The problem now was to transport these troops to the mainland, as the Strait of Gibraltar was under the control of the crew of the republican fleet that had mutinied against their rebel officers, and only a small contingent of African troops had managed to reach Andalusia in the early hours of the rising.

So Franco turned to Hitler and Mussolini for help. He used two German businessmen resident in Spanish Morocco, and local representatives of the Nazi Ausland (Foreign) Organisation, Adolf Langenheim and Johannes Bernhardt, to meet Hitler, via a series of elaborate contacts. On 23 July, Bernhardt, who in fact had offered his services to Franco, flew to Berlin with a message from Franco to the Führer, asking for fighter and transport aircraft. He first met Rudolf Hess, Hitler's right-hand man, and two days later, the Führer himself. Hitler was hesitant at first, but after being convinced by Bernhardt that what Franco wanted was to save Spain from an imminent Bolshevik revolution, he decided to send this aid. On 29 July, some twenty Junkers 52 transport aircraft and six Heinkel fighters set out for Tetuán.

According to Enrique Moradiellos, Hitler initially decided to support the military rebels and later intervene in the war 'for political and strategic reasons': if the military coup in Spain were successful, it would deprive France of a certain ally on its south flank, while a

---

[4] Paul Preston, *Franco: A Biography*, HarperCollins, London, 1993, pp. 144–70.

government victory would 'reinforce Spain's link to France and the USSR, the two powers that surrounded Germany from the east and west, and which opposed the Nazis' expansionist plans'.[5]

Mussolini, who received repeated calls for help from Franco through the Italian consul in Tangier and his military attaché, also decided to help the rebels for geostrategic reasons: he would gain an ally in the western Mediterranean and thereby weaken France's military position. On 28 July, he sent a squadron of twelve Savoia-Marchetti S.81 bombers and two merchant ships with Fiat CR.32 fighters. By so doing, Hitler and Mussolini, says Preston, 'helped turn a *coup d'état* going wrong into a bloody and prolonged civil war'.[6] All these aircraft, with their crews and technicians, enabled Franco to evade the republican navy blockade, transport his troops to Andalusia and thus begin his advance on Madrid. On 7 August, one day after a convoy of African troops had crossed the Strait, Franco installed himself in Seville.

Franco had at his disposal the military forces of the Moroccan protectorate, and in Navarre, General Emilio Mola had the unanimous support of the *Requeté*, the 'red berets', a disciplined military organisation that had instructed and prepared hundreds of local militants, young people, students, priests and law-abiding citizens for rebellion against the Republic. The network set up by the plotters in Navarre was the most valuable structure in the mainland. General Mola, five years older than Franco, had spent a large part of his career in the army of Morocco. He was tried by the Republic for his performance as Director-General of Security under Berenguer throughout 1930 until April 1931, pardoned in 1934, and rehabilitated when Gil Robles was Minister of War and Franco Chief of General Staff. After the *Frente Popular*'s election victory in February 1936, he was transferred from the command of the military forces in Morocco, an appointment made by Gil Robles in 1935, to the 12th Infantry Brigade, a post which included the Military Command in Pamplona. It was there, from 14 March 1936 onwards, that he issued the various 'confidential instructions' as 'Director' of the conspiracy and organised the deployment of the various generals and officers who were to command the rebel forces.

[5] Enrique Moradiellos, *El reñidero de Europa. Las dimensiones internacionales de la guerra civil española*, Península, Barcelona, pp. 88–9.

[6] Paul Preston, *La guerra civil española*, Debate, Barcelona, 2006, p. 130.

On Sunday 19 July, the rumour went round the towns and villages of Navarre that the army had risen in Pamplona. When the rumour was confirmed, the Carlists noisily took to the streets, hoisted the monarchist and Carlist flags on the *Círculos* (community centres) and, to the cry of 'Every man to war!', set out for Pamplona. In Artajona, they brought out the *Requeté* banner, embroidered with the image of the Virgin of Jerusalem, which they believed would surely protect them in this war they were about to wage against the unbelievers. The young men, with the priests at their side, made their confession and took communion before saying goodbye to their families, as if they were going to the Crusades. All this had, as Javier Ugarte rightly put it, an air of 'mystic-warlike rapture'. Community ties, coming from the same village and family networks were what enabled 'this immense ability to mobilise large sectors of the population', a genuine 'mass mobilisation', which accompanied the uprising from the start – a magnificent example that the army and the clergy cited whenever they came across lack of enthusiasm or faintheartedness in other regions.[7] In just those last few days in July, over 10,000 volunteers arrived in Pamplona and more than 1,000 in Vitoria.

Mola had so many men in Pamplona that he was able to deploy 2,000 *requetés* to crush the resistance along the Ebro and help to consolidate the rebellion in Zaragoza. On 20 July, Mola travelled to Burgos, the headquarters of the 6th Division responsible for the military command in Pamplona; here too, the city had been steeped in patriotic and religious fervour since Sunday 18 July, with solemn masses and monarchist flags. The same day, General Sanjurjo was killed trying to take off in the light aircraft that was supposed to be taking him to Spain, from his exile in Portugal, to head the rebellion. The day before, the Falangist pilot, Juan Antonio Ansaldo, had arrived at Sanjurjo's summer residence in Estoril, having been sent by Mola to collect the head of the insurrectionists. The aircraft, a flimsy two-seater Puss Moth, which was also carrying an enormous suitcase belonging to Sanjurjo, crashed immediately after take-off and burst into flames near the aerodrome at Cascais. Ansaldo escaped unhurt from the accident.

---

[7] Javier Ugarte, *La nueva Covadonga insurgente. Orígenes sociales y culturales de la sublevación de 1936 en Navarra y el País Vasco*, Biblioteca Nueva, Madrid, 1998, pp. 87–9.

With Sanjurjo dead, and Fanjul and Goded under arrest after their risings failed in Madrid and Barcelona, the military rebels were forced to change their plans. On 21 July, Mola flew to Zaragoza to talk to Cabanellas and invite him to preside over the *Junta de Defensa Nacional*, the senior board for military coordination in the rebel zone, which was set up in Burgos three days later. As well as Cabanellas, it was made up of Generals Saliquet, Mola, Dávila and Ponte, and Colonels Montaner and Moreno. On 30 July, General Gil Yuste, who had been head of the civil government in Vitoria since 18 July, took command of the 5th Division based in Zaragoza, although a few days later he joined the *Junta de Defensa* and General Ponte was transferred to the 5th Division.

A large proportion of the rebel senior officers had been affected by the major corporate controversy over the review of the promotions conceded illegally by Primo de Rivera's dictatorship, and subsequently revoked by the Republic in a decree issued in January 1933. Such was the case with Generals Orgaz, Aranda and Varela, and Colonel Monasterio, although other officers, such as Asensio Torrado, Romerales and Hidalgo de Cisneros, while in the same situation, were loyal to the republican government. Some of them had also taken part in plots against the republican regime. This was the case with Colonels Serrador and Martín Alonso and General Ponte, an aristocratic monarchist who had applied to join the reserves under the terms of Azaña's law and was discharged for his role in Sanjurjo's uprising.

The accountability for actions during the dictatorship trials, the review of promotions and Azaña's Military Reform Act fed the hostility of many officers against the Republic. 'Order and unity in the Fatherland', the 'total absence of public power', were phrases that appeared in all the insurrectionist communiqués proclaiming martial law, but one of their main themes was the heaping of insults on politicians whom they rejected and despised as leftist and Bolshevik lackeys.

Of course, this was not the first time that the army had tried to save the Fatherland. But the rising initiated in Melilla on 17 July by forces of the *Tercio* and *Regulares* was not just any rebellion, a mere *pronunciamiento* as had occurred so often in Spain's recent history. After five years of a Republic, of opportunities to remedy unresolved problems, of times of instability and political and social mobilisation, a new, violent and decisive solution was required, such as was already a feature of Fascist regimes elsewhere in Europe, to end the crisis and repair, once and for all, the fissures opened up – or widened – by the republican regime.

And if saviours were needed, they had one in General Francisco Franco, who believed that this was his mission – to save a Fatherland in which there was no room for liberals, republicans, militant workers' organisations or *Frente Popular* voters. They were all leftists, reds, despicable enemies, no better than the tribes he had so often fought against in Africa: 'Spreading terror ... by eliminating, without any scruples or hesitation, anyone who does not think the same as us', declared General Mola, another saviour, on 19 July. And therein lay one of the clues as to what was about to occur: the elimination of anyone who did not think the same, 'throwing out all this rubbish about the rights of man, humanitarianism and philanthropy', as one of his subordinates, Colonel Marcelino Gavilán, declared the same day, after taking the civil government building in Burgos by force – in short, removing the words 'mercy' and 'amnesty' from the dictionary, in the words of General Gonzalo Queipo de Llano, number three in the ranking of saviours following the death of Sanjurjo. Historic utterances, incitements to violence, which Franco repeated in an interview on 28 July 1936, with the North American journalist, Jay Allen, who, surprised at the general's height, 'remarkably small', declared: 'Another little guy who wants to be a dictator'.[8]

The language of arms

Right from the start of the military coup, and quite some time before it evolved into open war and generated the beginning of a revolutionary process wherever it had failed, the rebels put into action a terror mechanism that destroyed the resistance capabilities of the workers' and republican organisations, intimidated their less active adversaries, and physically wiped out their political and ideological enemies.

[8] Mola's and Marcelino Gavilán's utterances are taken from José María Iribarren, *Con el general Mola. Escenas y aspectos inéditos de la guerra*, Editorial Heraldo de Aragón, Zaragoza, 1937, p. 211; Franco's belief in his mission is from Preston, *Franco*, pp. 145–6; Allen's sentence is quoted in Ian Gibson, *Queipo de Llano. Sevilla, verano de 1936*, Grijalbo, Barcelona, 1986, pp. 81–2.

The course of events was very similar in all the cities where the rising was successful. The army left their barracks, swarmed into the streets and proclaimed martial law, thus banning meetings, strikes and the possession of arms. Military squads with their machine guns installed outside the main public buildings showed that this was serious. Civil governors were replaced by officers. From their new post, they dismissed the political authorities, beginning with the mayors and regional council leaders, and ordered the Civil Guard in the various towns and villages to join the uprising.

Thus began mass gaolings, selective repression to eliminate resistance, systematic torture and 'hot-blooded' terror, the type of terror that abandoned people wherever they had been shot, in roadside ditches, against cemetery walls, in rivers or in disused wells and mines. Mayors, civil governors, local councillors, trade union and *Frente Popular* leaders were the first to suffer the terror of the *paseos*. One could come across a corpse anywhere, still warm or in an advanced state of decomposition, due to the high temperatures of that summer of 1936. For example, a milkman came across the republican mayor of Salamanca, the Professor of Medicine, Casto Prieto Carrasco, in a ditch beside the road to Valladolid. Another doctor, Manuel Pérez Lizano, president of the Zaragoza Provincial Council, was discovered by members of the Red Cross, an institution over which he also presided, on the banks of the Aragon Imperial Canal.[9]

Compliance with the law was replaced by the language and dialectic of arms, by the rejection of human rights and the veneration of violence. Now that this new scenario of total war was under way, in which politics came to be assessed exclusively in military terms and one was either a friend or an enemy, the legitimation of the use of physical violence met no serious obstacles. It was enough to say that the enemy was not a human being to kill him without remorse. They were rats, 'red scum', 'rotten limbs' that needed to be amputated 'to save the nation, the Fatherland'. Political and ideological adversaries, or simply adversaries, no longer had the right to be considered fellow countrymen.

Under these circumstances, with no law to be obeyed, and with no fear of punishment, gangs of killers appeared everywhere, protected

[9] Unless indicated otherwise, the analysis of the political violence in both camps comes from Julián Casanova, 'Rebelión y revolución', in Santos Juliá (ed.), *Víctimas de la guerra civil*, Temas de Hoy, Madrid, 1999, pp. 57–185.

by the army, by landowners and the middle class fearful of revolution; they organised shooting parties to settle old scores, dominated by young Falangists, students and respectable citizens, but also by predatory and spiteful people who, unfettered by the inhibitions that had previously restrained their violent instincts, now gave free rein to their aggression and cruelty. Thus it is hardly surprising that the greatest bloodshed took place in the two months that followed the rising, before this violence was legalised.

Indeed, the final days of July and the months of August and September 1936 saw the highest number of killings in almost every region that had been under the control of the rebels from the start: between 50 and 70 per cent of the total number of victims of this repression during the civil war and afterwards were concentrated in this short period. If we extend this period to the end of 1936, the percentages border on the upper limit, which shows that this was not just a wartime repression, a war that still had two years to run, but also an emergency 'surgical' extermination. Over 90 per cent of the close to 3,000 killings in Navarre, and 80 per cent of the 7,000 in Zaragoza occurred in 1936. But the percentages were very similar in Córdoba, Granada, Seville, Badajoz and Huelva, the provinces in which, together with Navarre and Zaragoza, the stench of death was at its strongest in that wave of summer terror. In none of these provinces was the death toll below 2,000 victims, in barely seventy days.

The killings were rife wherever there was the most resistance, wherever old conflicts and influential leftist organisations triggered the settling of scores. Rational behaviour took a back seat amidst so much torture and death. Apparently peaceful citizens killed with impunity when they were given a uniform or acted collectively. An apparently trivial event, a commemoration, was all it took for the death toll to soar. The night of 10 to 11 August 1936 in Seville was such a case: to celebrate Sanjurjo's anti-republican coup in 1932, various left-wing figures were murdered, including the city's first republican mayor and Cortes deputy in 1933 and 1936, José González Fernández de Labandera; the socialist deputy Manuel Barrios; the secretary of the Andalusian masons, Fermín de Zayas; and the Andalusian nationalist notary, Blas Infante. August, the festive month par excellence in Spain, was, in 1936, the month of death.

And death came in the form of *paseos* on the blood-stained stage of that summer. The victims would be arrested in the streets or in their homes for being 'well-known leftists', for opposing the 'glorious National Movement', sought because they appeared in the documents seized on the premises of political and trade union organisations, denounced by their neighbours or singled out for their irreligious behaviour. They would be held for a few days in the many buildings that had been equipped as gaols, where they would stay until the *saca* (cull) – another word that gained a place of honour in the vocabulary of repression on both sides during 1936. Those chosen for the *sacas* would be 'taken for a walk' at night, just before dawn. Sometimes the coroner would be in attendance to authorise the removal of the bodies, but usually, in those early days, they would be left abandoned, after a priest had tried to give spiritual comfort to the prisoners.

The avalanche of killings in this major 'cleansing' operation gave rise to all types of anomaly. Thousands of deaths were never registered, while many others appeared as 'an unidentified man or woman'. For example, 581 men and 26 women appear as such in the city of Zaragoza. In Huelva, 827 were inscribed with no date of death. This was the time of mass killings in the area covered by Queipo de Llano's 2nd Division, in Galicia, in Extremadura, in Aragon, executions carried out by civil guards, by armed police in plain clothes, by 'paramilitary' patrols that killed for pleasure. There was no longer any room for the dead in the cemeteries, so large mass graves were dug, as in the case of Lardero, a small village near Logroño where close to 400 people were shot and buried; or, in the case of Víznar, a few kilometres from Granada, where García Lorca met his death. Common graves were rapidly dug by the victims themselves or on the orders of the competent authority, as was the case with the Zaragoza City Councillor, García Belenguer, who on 5 August 1936 requested that compressors be taken to the cemetery to 'check the earth-moving works with greater speed'.[10]

This 'hot-blooded' terror needed no procedures or safeguards. Three-quarters of the 1,830 killed in Cáceres were 'taken for a walk', almost all of them in the first few months, while only 32 of the 2,578 victims of repression in the city of Zaragoza during 1936 faced a court martial, eight of whom were members of the army, shot in their barracks. In fact, being a member of the army was practically the only circumstance that enabled one to avoid the *paseo* in the rebel zone,

---

[10] Minutes of the Zaragoza City Council session, 5 August 1936.

although, as we have seen, this did not mean that officers loyal to the Republic or who were hesitant about joining the uprising escaped the cruel persecution of their rebel colleagues.

The breakdown of order

The coup did not overthrow the Republic, but by opening a wide breach in the army and the security forces, it did destroy its cohesion and caused unrest. The Prime Minister, the republican Santiago Casares Quiroga, fearful of revolution and the popular unrest that might break out, ordered the civil governors not to distribute arms to the workers' organisations. There was little else he could do, because events very soon overtook him. He resigned on the night of 18 July. The person who might have succeeded him, the experienced Diego Martínez Barrio, spent the whole night trying to reach an impossible compromise with Mola, by offering him, if various sources are to be believed, a post in government. The task was finally accepted on the morning of 19 July by José Giral, a friend and confidant of Manuel Azaña. This government consisted of leftist republicans only, practically the same faces as had previously served under Casares Quiroga, with the addition of two army officers: General Pozas as Interior Minister and General Castelló in the War Ministry. It was Giral who decided to arm the most politically committed militant workers and republicans, and they took to the streets to fight the rebels wherever the loyalty of certain military commanders, or the indecision of others, permitted. Madrid and Barcelona were good examples of this, as were Valencia, Jaén and San Sebastián.

Thus there is no need to continue feeding the myth. It was not the people, 'the people in arms', who, alone, defeated the rebels in the streets of the major cities of Spain. The republican State, however, by surrendering its monopoly on arms, was not capable of preventing the beginning of a sudden and violent revolutionary activity, aimed at destroying the positions of the privileged classes, wherever the insurgents were defeated. The streets were taken over by new players, armed men and women, many of whom had become known for their vehement opposition to the existence of this selfsame State. They were there, not exactly to defend the Republic, which had had its chance, but to take part in a revolution. Wherever the Republic had not gone far enough with its reforms, they would with their revolution. Political measures gave way to armed action.

A counter-revolutionary coup d'état, whose intention was to halt a revolution, ended up by unleashing one. The was not the first time, nor would it be the last, that this had happened in history. It is very likely that, but for the coup, and the collapse of the State's coercion mechanisms, this revolutionary process would never have got off the ground. Naturally, if support for the rising among the armed forces had been unanimous, any resistance would have easily been put down. The trade union militias, even with arms, would not have been able to do anything against a united army. The revolutionary organisation had the ability to undermine and destabilise the Republic, but not to overthrow and replace it. In the Spanish army in July 1936, there was hardly any sympathy for revolutionary ideas, while a large number of officers were clearly in favour of the authoritarian and counter-revolutionary cause.

And once the wheels of this military uprising and revolutionary response had started turning, it was only arms that had the right to speak. The response given to the rebels who failed in their attempt, and who were considered responsible for the violence and bloodshed that was spreading all over Spain, was brutal. Most of the rebels arrested in Barcelona were transferred to the SS *Uruguay*, moored in the harbour. Obviously, the leaders of the revolt headed the list of executions. After a trial on the vessel on 11 August, General Manuel Goded and Alvaro Fernández Burriel faced a firing squad the following day in the castle of Montjuïc, where Francisco Ferrer y Guardia had been shot in 1909, and hundreds of anarchists had been imprisoned and tortured since the end of the nineteenth century. The officers who acted as judge and prosecutor in this court martial, Colonel Carlos Caballero and Lieutenant Pedro Rodríguez, would later be shot in Barcelona in 1939, after the city had been taken by Franco's troops.

Almost a hundred officers who joined the revolt in the Barcelona garrison were executed between September 1936 and February 1937, after being condemned by the *Jurado Popular Especial*, later called the *Tribunal Popular Especial*, set up on 2 September for the 'repression of Fascism', one of whose members was the notorious publicist, lawyer and regular contributor to the libertarian press, Ángel Samblancat. On 8 November, all the prisoners were moved from the

Uruguay to the military prisons in the castle of Montjuïc, and from then on all trials were held in the Catalonia Appeals Courtroom.

A few days after Goded, it was General Joaquín Fanjul's turn to face the firing squad, a scene that was repeated in Menorca, Almería, Málaga, Albacete, Guadalajara and other cities in which the uprising failed. It should be made clear, however, that most of the defeated officers were not given the chance to face a court martial, unlike in Barcelona, although even there, in the final days of August and 1 September 1936, a group of militiamen removed ten officers (closely linked to Goded in the rising) from the *Uruguay* and shot them.

'Impatient' militiamen, who wanted the officers well and truly dead before they could be tried, were rife in the summer of 1936. On 25 July, in Lérida, a city in which the 'popular' terror wrought havoc in the early days, militiamen who were on their way to the Aragon front removed from the gaol twenty-six army and Civil Guard officers, who had been held there since 20 July, and summarily shot them. In San Sebastián, Colonel León Carrasco Amilibia, who had led the rising there, was taken from the regional council building, where he had been detained for a few hours, and was murdered alongside the railway track. One day later, at dawn, a group of militiamen went to the provincial gaol, where they killed fifty-three people, forty-one of whom were army officers. Examples of unpunished actions against officers in prison following their defeat reached levels of exceptional cruelty in Madrid, where in all the *sacas*, particularly the mass *sacas* of autumn 1936, members of the army were picked out for execution. This initial atmosphere of impunity was ideal for settling old scores. Such was the case with General Eduardo López Ochoa, who had commanded the troops in the putting down of the revolt in Asturias in October 1934. The July 1936 coup found him as a patient in the military hospital in Carabanchel. According to the data in the *Causa General* (a special court set up after the civil war to judge those accused of crimes against the Nationalists), he was taken from there by the militias and, 'urged on by the mobs, they paraded the general's head through the central streets of Madrid'.

All these officers were assumed to be 'proven' Fascists, and 'proven' Fascists, as the Barcelona CNT newspaper, *Solidaridad Obrera*, declared on 1 August 1936, had to be killed. The military, and particularly the clergy, were the prime targets of the violent purges that predominated in the summer of 1936, wherever the defeat of the rising opened the gates to revolution. In addition, this purifying flame also engulfed, during these first few weeks, conservative politicians, landowners, smallholders, farmers, the middle classes, shopkeepers, workers who were known in the factories for their moderate ideas, engineers and personnel managers in the various industries, and Catholics – above all, Catholics. And the source of this river of blood was the multitude of works, *barrio* and village committees set up and fuelled by the revolution; militias, 'investigation and vigilance groups' charged with ridding the scene of 'unhealthy' people. And all 'for the good of public health'. It is telling that this obsession for 'cleanliness', 'hygiene' or 'public health' was shared in that summer of 1936 by those on both sides of the line dividing the success or failure of the military rising.

The press and propaganda of the various political and trade union organisations took it upon themselves to remind people of the need for bloodshed to fight the 'Fascists' and consolidate the revolution. Thus, in the early weeks of the war, 'hunting for Fascists', the defence of the revolution and the persecution of its opponents were elements that were closely linked, and in practice it was hard to find the dividing line. The unrestrained terror began with the elimination of those who had taken part in the rising against the Republic, continued as an urgent task to suppress 'reaction', and ended up contaminating the very foundations of republican law and order. At last, the time had come for the people to cast off their shackles, and many enthusiastically subscribed to this extremist rhetoric. The anti-Fascist committee in the town of Ascó, in the province of Tarragona, which, like other revolutionary and militia committees had taken on judicial duties, respected those individuals who belonged to collectives and 'worked keenly for them', but meted out to others, 'the justice that they deserved', under the ambiguous accusation of 'being well-known elements'.[11] Examples such as this were to be found all over republican – or revolutionary, as others put it – Spain until autumn 1936. From that moment, reprisals and 'acts of individual terrorism', as they were called by the CNT leader, Joan Peiró, declined, until they had almost completely disappeared by the first three months of 1937.[12]

---

[11] Document signed by the Committee on 27 September 1936, housed in the Civil War Archive, Salamanca, file 839 for Barcelona.
[12] Article by Joan Peiró in *Solidaridad Obrera*, 7 September 1936.

Until this cooling down arrived, the radical elimination of all these
representatives of power was achieved by the *paseo*, the method used
in the 'practice of summary justice' to settle scores, feed class hatred
or exact revenge. The description of this method left to us by the
anarchist Juan García Oliver, Minister of Justice between November
1936 and May 1937, makes the matter quite clear: 'Since the military rising meant the breaking of all social constraints, because it
was carried out by the classes that traditionally maintained social
order, the attempts to re-establish legal equilibrium saw the spirit of
justice reverting to its oldest and purest origin: *el pueblo: vox populi,
suprema lex*. And while this abnormality lasted, the people created
and applied its own law and procedure, the *paseo*'.[13]

'Murder on wheels' is what Agustín de Foxá called it in *Madrid de
corte a checa*. Patrols would requisition property, palaces, mansions
and cars, particularly large cars, in which they would take their victims 'for a spin'. Some of the members of these patrols were common
criminals, who had been let out of gaol by the militias after the defeat
of the rebels, and they were now settling old scores or venting their
accumulated resentment. 'Out of control', they were dubbed, although
this term should not be used lightly. Many people, who had nothing
to do with common criminals, were convinced that the revolution
consisted, firstly, of cleaning the atmosphere, taking the scalpel to the
rotten organs of society – in other words, the middle class, the military, priests and landowners, 'parasites' all of them. And there were
also many, represented then by intellectuals such as Rafael Alberti,
who believed in 'necessary killing', in the class war that would overthrow an outdated, bourgeois world, to allow the world of the proletariat family to rise from its ashes. This same radicalism with regard
to the middle classes had already been proclaimed by the leading
character in *Siete domingos rojos* by Ramón J. Sender: 'I go outside.
A bourgeois is not a person. Not even an animal. He is the lowest of
the low. He is nothing. How am I going to feel sorry about the death
of a bourgeois – me, who goes out to kill them?'[14]

[13] Juan García Oliver, *El eco de los pasos*, Ruedo Ibérico, Madrid, 1978, p. 347.
[14] There is an edition of Agustín de Foxá's novel, *Madrid de corte a checa*,
published by Planeta, Barcelona, 1993 (original edition was published by La
Ciudadela, Madrid, 1938); Ramón J. Sender, *Siete domingos rojos*, Colección
Balagué, Barcelona, 1932 (a recent edition was published by the Instituto de
Estudios Altoaragoneses, Huesca, 2004); Rafael Alberti's comment comes

Nobody in those early weeks of committee and militia power was able to provide a satisfactory response to these excesses. The most talked about event of that month occurred in Madrid, which, as we shall see, would experience many more such events in the months that followed. On the night of 22 to 23 August, a group of militiamen selected several out of the almost 2,000 inmates who were crowded into the Modelo prison at the time. Right there, they killed several officers, right-wingers and politicians, just because of who they were: people like the Falangists Fernando Primo de Rivera and Julio Ruiz de Alda; the founder of the *Partido Nacionalista*, Jose María Albiñana; the ministers in Lerroux's December 1933 government, Ramón Alvarez Valdés and Manuel Rico Avello; the agrarian José Martínez de Velasco, who had also been a minister in the two Chapaprieta governments towards the end of 1935; and the old and experienced politician, Melquíades Álvarez, aged 72, the champion of reform in Spain during the first third of the twentieth century. It is of little interest to this story that the origin or excuse for these thirty-odd killings was a fire that had been started by common prisoners or Falangists in an escape bid. The cleansing and the blood, which besmirched what it was supposed to clean even more, only added discredit to the cause of the legality of the Republic. Manuel Azaña, who was still President of this Republic, recalled a year later, in his *Cuaderno de la pobleta*, his consternation, sadness and desolation at the murder of these well-known people: 'Whether they were well-known or not, it would still have been an atrocity, but their fame made the case worse from a political point of view'.[15]

Attacks on prisons, *paseos* and *sacas* were, therefore, how the terror unleashed by the revolutionary storm in the name of the sovereign people manifested itself in the summer of 1936. All through that summer, as with the other 'hot-blooded' terror initiated and served up by the military, bully boys and landowners, judicial procedures

from Derek Gagen, '¿El "asesinato necesario"? Violencia inevitable en *De un momento a otro* de Rafael Alberti', in Derek Gagen and David George (eds.), *La guerra civil española. Arte y violencia*, University of Murcia, Murcia, 1990, pp. 29–51.

[15] *El cuaderno de la pobleta*, published in 1937, may be found in Manuel Azaña, *Memorias políticas y de guerra*, 4 vols., Crítica, Barcelona, 1981, vol. II, pp. 22–383.

were considered superfluous. The *paseo* was much quicker. And like that meted out by the other side, the terror wrought in the republican zone by the militias, 'revolutionary justice', the 'investigation groups' or any killer with an arm and vengeance in his heart, was at its height in the months of August and September, with the major exception of Madrid, where several thousand people met their death as a result of the *sacas* in November 1936.

Over 50 per cent of the 8,352 killings in Catalonia during the war had occurred by 30 September 1936, rising to 80 per cent by the end of the year. Similar percentages were to be found, albeit with considerably fewer victims, in the eastern regions of Aragon, Córdoba, Jaén, Málaga and Almería. In Gijón, the 430 killings that occurred during the year that the city remained under the power of the various committees had taken place by October 1936.

This violence against people of order and the clergy did immense harm to the republican cause abroad. Images of burning convents and the annihilation of the clergy were made available all round the world, while the large-scale massacres perpetrated by the military rebels in the summer of 1936 warranted no negative reaction in the political, diplomatic and financial circles of London or Paris. Furthermore, the 'red terror' damaged the efforts of the Republic to obtain international support, although it was naturally not the principal reason why the democratic powers decided to leave the Republic abandoned and almost on its own against the Nazi and Fascist threat.

José Giral and his government soon became aware of the problems the Republic was going to face to obtain international aid. On 19 July, according to the socialist Léon Blum, the Prime Minister of France, the recently appointed Spanish Prime Minister, José Giral, sent him a telegram: 'We have been caught unawares by a dangerous military coup. Please contact us immediately to supply us with arms and aircraft'.

The initial reaction of the French Popular Front government, made up of socialists and radicals, was to 'implement an aid plan ... to provide materiel to the Spanish Republic'. This seems to have been motivated by political and military reasons: both countries were democratic republics, and it was in France's interest to have a friendly regime on the Pyrenean border, which, in the case of a European war, would guarantee safe passage between France's African colonies, where a third of its army currently was, and France itself.[16]

However, this aid plan was never put into practice because the military attaché in the Spanish embassy in Paris, an agent of the rebels, leaked the information about Giral's request and Blum's response to the right-wing daily *Echo de Paris*, and the paper began 'a vigorous campaign exposing in all their detail the resolutions taken, thereby stirring up considerable unrest'. Public opinion was divided. While the left in general expressed its sympathy for the republican cause, the political right, Catholics and broad sectors of the administration and the army, rejected 'the aid plan'. By the end of July, the right-wing press had already made it quite clear that an intervention in Spain would mean 'the beginning of the conflagration in Europe that Moscow so ardently hopes for'. The leaders of the *Partido Radical* had also advised their colleague, Yvon Delbos, the Minister of Foreign Affairs, of their 'apprehension over the initiative'. Delbos and Édouard Daladier, the radical Minister of National Defence, paid heed to this pressure and began to express their opposition.

As if this internal opposition were not enough, the attitude of the British government, France's main ally in Europe, ended up by tipping the scale against the initial decision to send aid. The British Conservatives, in power since 1931, were afraid that any intervention in the Spanish conflict would hamper their policy of appeasement with Germany. Meanwhile, British commercial groups, with substantial interests in Spain at the time, reacted adversely to the revolution unleashed in the major Spanish cities as a consequence of the coup. 'I urge you to be cautious', said Anthony Eden, the British Foreign Minister, to Blum on 24 July. Albert Lebrun, the President of the French Republic, also warned Blum that 'handing over arms to Spain might mean war in Europe or revolution in France'. On 25 July 1936, after the first of three French government cabinet meetings held to discuss the events in Spain, the decision was announced 'not to intervene in any way in Spain's domestic conflict'.

This saw the start of the non-intervention policy that would be implemented from the summer of 1936. The French Popular Front authorities, with Blum at the head, believed that this was the best way

---

[16] The request to Blum, and what follows regarding the positions of France and Britain, comes from Moradiellos, *El reñidero de Europa*, pp. 77–88.

of bringing calm to the internal situation, maintaining the vital alliance with the United Kingdom, and avoiding the internationalisation of the Spanish Civil War. Things did not turn out that way, because Franco's requests for aid from Hitler and Mussolini had more success, and, furthermore, Nazi Germany and Fascist Italy never respected this non-intervention policy. Consequently, the Republic, a legitimate regime, was left initially without aid, and the military rebels, lacking all legitimacy, received, almost from the opening shot, the aid that was vital to wage a war that they themselves had started. The rebels were already starting with a clear advantage. The coup d'état, which had not achieved its principal aim, the seizure of power, evolved into a civil war because Italo-German aid enabled the rebels to transfer the army from Africa to the mainland. The transfer of over 10,000 troops during the summer was essential for the domination of Andalusia and the advance through Extremadura towards Madrid.

Spain split in two

The coup d'état and the subsequent civil war had disastrous effects for the Republic. Its administration went to pieces, as did its army and police forces. José Giral's government, which lasted barely a month and a half, took some very important decisions, in spite of appearing to be a makeshift government with no support: it authorised the civil governors to distribute arms to the political and trade union organisations, asked for aid from abroad (aware that this was the only way of defeating the rebels) and, through its Finance Minister, the leftist republican Enrique Ramos, began to use the Bank of Spain's gold reserves to finance the war against the rebels. All this was acknowledged months later by Manuel Azaña to José Giral: 'One has to admire the quiet courage with which you accepted the post, when nobody was willing to obey and when one and all were oiling the wheels for their escape'.[17]

But this 'quiet courage' was bearing little fruit in the part of Spain not occupied by the rebel forces. The existing order collapsed, the owners of many farms and factories fled or were killed, and the trade unions were organising their occupation and collectivisation. Losses in the harvests were immense and the economy was paralysed. Even

---

[17] Quoted in Pablo Martín Aceña, *El oro de Moscú y el oro de Berlín*, Taurus, Madrid, 2001, p. 37.

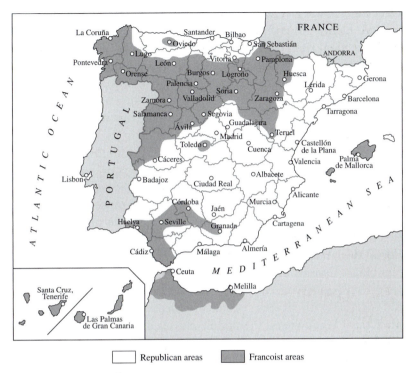

Map 1 Spain, 31 July 1936

so, the republican zone still had the main cities, the main industrial and mining centres, Catalonia, the Basque Country and Asturias, and the headquarters of the principal companies and banks. Most of all, the Republic had the Bank of Spain and its large gold reserves, some 700 tons, with a value of around 2,500 million pesetas.

The republican zone's financial advantage was very clear at the beginning. According to Pablo Martín Aceña, 'when the conflict began, 30 per cent of agricultural produce was to be found in the republican zone, and 70 per cent in the National zone. Conversely, around 80 per cent gross value of industrial production was to be found in the republican zone and 20 per cent in the National zone. Republican territory accounted for 70 per cent of the State budget'.[18]

[18] Pablo Martín Aceña, 'La economía española de los años treinta', in Santos Juliá (ed.), *Historia de España de Menéndez Pidal. República y guerra civil*, 42 vols., Espasa Calpe, Madrid, 2004, vol. XL, p. 400.

Over time, as the war progressed, the shortage of staple products was to have highly adverse consequences for the Republic, particularly when the main cities began filling up with refugees, while the military rebels were able to make up for their lack of an industrial base with aid received from Germany and Italy. But that was how things were in the summer of 1936, when Spain lay bleeding and the Republic was forced to face a civil war, a violent struggle that involved both the military and the civilian population.

The war forced many people to take part unwillingly, to take sides despite their beliefs, or to defend themselves in the hope of better times to come. But this was not a good time for the weak-willed. The rebels, in the areas where they held sway, and those who defeated them in others, knew from the outset whom to train their bullets on. It is hardly surprising that the rebels were supported by most of the clergy, the landowners and industrialists most under threat from the republican reforms and claims of the workers; after all, in previous years they had rehearsed various ways of destabilising the Republic. But together with all these people of order were poor and extremely poor rural landowners, the middle classes and urban workers who did not seem to be on the right side of the social barrier. 'Essentially, it was a class war', as George Orwell noted with his customary lucidity.[19] And he was mostly right, although it would be truer to say that the classes, their struggles and their interests were in fact major players in this war, but not the only ones. There were really several wars within the one we know as the civil war. This is why its analysis has always been so complex, yet at the same time so fascinating. And it is also why the purifying flames that engulfed even the most insignificant opponent spread so quickly and destructively over the whole of Spain.

The weeks that followed the military rising saw a large number of people changing sides, in what many people summarise with the comment 'first some came over, and then the others', meaning that both sides were guilty of killing. The advance from the south of troops from Africa gave the rebels control of Extremadura and large areas of Castilla-La Mancha. In the first fortnight of August, *Regulares* and the Legion left their footprints in Almendralejo, Mérida, Zafra

---

[19] George Orwell, *Homenaje a Cataluña*, Ariel, Barcelona, 1983, pp. 2–4. (First published in English in 1938.)

and other locations, providing the peasants with their 'agrarian reform', the small plot of land in which they would rest for ever after being murdered: land 'rent-free and in perpetuity', as Zugazagoitia wrote.[20] On 14 August, General Juan Yagüe's troops took Badajoz, showing, for all the world to see, that success on the war front was only achieved by leaving no possible enemies in the rear. Hundreds of prisoners were taken to the bullring, where, again in the words of Zugazagoitia, 'leashed like hunting dogs, they were pushed into the arena as a target for the machine guns which, well positioned, remorselessly mowed them down'. Such a massacre, naturally, merited the defiant reply given by General Yagüe to the *New York Herald* journalist, John T. Whitaker: 'Of course we shot them. What do you expect? Was I supposed to take four thousand reds with me as my column advanced racing against time? Was I expected to turn them loose in my rear and let them make Badajoz red again?'[21]

Yagüe was right. The province of Badajoz never fell into the hands of the reds again, although to achieve this it was necessary to eliminate several thousand people – 6,610 according to figures from 85 locations provided by Francisco Espinosa.[22] Salazar's dictatorship in Portugal also lent Yagüe a hand. As had happened previously in other towns in Extremadura, quite a few people fled to Portugal after the fall of the city. Salazar's police refused them entry or else handed them over to the rebels. A fair number of them were executed on 20 August, one week after the slaughter in the bullring. Those who met their death included the mayor, Sinforiano Madroñero, and Nicolás de Pablo, who had been elected to the Cortes for the PSOE in the February 1936 elections.

After the fall of Badajoz, Yagüe's columns continued their rapid advance on Madrid. On 3 September, they reached Talavera, where a sector of the population also received their fair share of violence. That same day, in the north, where General Mola had launched an attack on Guipúzcoa, Irún fell. On 12 September, it was San Sebastián's turn. The conquest of Guipúzcoa was an important victory for the rebel army's plans; it had now joined one part of Spain from the north, via

---

[20] Zugazagoitia, *Guerra y vicisitudes de los españoles*, p. 134.
[21] John Whitaker, 'Prelude to world war: A witness from Spain', *Foreign Affairs*, 21, 1 (October 1942), pp. 104–6.
[22] Francisco Espinosa, *La columna de la muerte. El avance del ejército franquista de Sevilla a Badajoz*, Crítica, Barcelona, 2003.

Castilla and the west, to the south, while leaving Vizcaya, Cantabria
and Asturias cut off, unable to communicate with the rest of the republican zone except by air and sea. Before the loss of Guipúzcoa, retreating militia groups had time to tinge the dying days of the summer with
more blood. As almost always, there was no lack of memorable figures
among the dead, including the traditionalist Víctor Pradera and the
Renovación Española leader, Jorge Satrústegui.

The summer was over. The bloodshed begun by the military rebels
from the first day met its response among those for whom the coup
d'état was the signal to eradicate the symbols of this clerical, bourgeois
and reactionary society. In barely two months, the lust for revolutionary and counter-revolutionary cleansing had sent tens of thousands
of citizens to their graves. In military terms, the revolutionary zeal
of the trade union organisations reaped very few benefits and a great
many setbacks for the republican cause, with losses from Huelva to
Guipúzcoa, via Badajoz and Toledo. These military victories were
boosted on the rebel side with the concentration of political and military power in the person of General Franco, a factor that could not be
replicated in republican Spain; this was despite the fact that, since the
beginning of September, her government had been led by Francisco
Largo Caballero, a trade union leader who was much more in tune
than Giral with the scenario that had resulted from the defeat of the
rebels in the major cities.

These military victories and the concentration of political and military power among the rebels, as opposed to the fragility and disorder
to be found in the republican zone, should not, however, blind us to
the real foundation on which all this was based: the call to violence
and the extermination of the adversary, enduring values in the regime
that emerged from this war, a regime that was to last for almost four
decades.

7 | *Order, revolution and political violence*

The military rebels gave a taste of their sword to tens of thousands of citizens. Nobody knew better than they did how useful terror could be to paralyse any potential resistance and eliminate their opponents. Many of them had cut their teeth in the colonial wars, ideal settings for learning to reject human values and civic virtues, to become educated in the veneration of violence. The premeditated violence before the coup, during the plotting stage, was nothing compared to what was to begin in July 1936. They started by spreading terror from the very first day, intimidating, killing, crushing any resistance. With the declaration of martial law, anyone defending the Republic was deemed a 'rebel'.

When the military coup evolved into a war, the destruction of the enemy became the absolute priority. And in this transition from politics to war, the opponents, either political or ideological, lost their status as compatriots, 'Spaniards', and became an enemy against whom the use of violence was totally legitimate. 'If I see my father in the enemy ranks, I shoot him', said General Mola.[1] War was no longer the continuation of politics by other means, as Karl von Clausewitz, the leading military theorist of the nineteenth century, had written. A century later, it was a case of using it to resolve social conflicts, something which matched perfectly the pattern of that turbulent epoch of wars, revolutions, Fascism and democracies in crisis. In Europe, in the period between the two world wars, political styles, according to Richard Vinen, 'became aggressively masculine', and the words 'struggle', 'battle' and 'the enemy' dominated political speeches.[2]

---

[1] José María Iribarren, *Con el general Mola. Escenas y aspectos inéditos de la guerra*, Ed. Heraldo de Aragón, Zaragoza, 1937, p. 211.
[2] Richard Vinen, *A History in Fragments: Europe in the Twentieth Century*, Abacus, London, 2002, p. 154.

In Spain, it was not just the military rebels who considered the Republic to be illegitimate or believed that the true social values, the values of order, were in danger. The policy of extermination initiated by the military rebels was fervently subscribed to by conservative sectors, landowners, the bourgeois, property owners and 'respectable people', who rejected once and for all the defence of their order via the law because, 'once the social peace had been broken', this was now impossible, as they never tired of saying in the spring of 1936. 'The urgent re-establishment of the principle of authority' is what the representatives of the Chambers of Commerce asked for in their convention held in Madrid at the end of June that year.[3]

This 'principle of authority' began to be re-established with the declaration of martial law, a procedure that enabled the military rebels to implement a series of exceptional regulations in order to exercise their power without restrictions. In areas where the military coup was unsuccessful, the State ceased to exist outside Madrid – if indeed it existed even there – and groups of varying postures and beliefs took to the public stage with arms. The moment had come for the power of committees, 'vigilante' patrols, 'investigation' groups, for the setting up of local and regional powers isolated from José Giral's republican government in Madrid, which, harking back to the past, was still referred to as the 'central' government.

From the collapse of the State, the disintegration of the administration and the distribution of arms among those who were willing to take them, emerged a wave of militant egalitarianism, millenniumism, a 'spontaneous revolution', which, in the view of many witnesses, would collectivise factories and land, with wages suppressed and with the establishment of the earthly paradise that the people had been dreaming of for so long. This was the happy image of revolution that was handed down, for example, by George Orwell in his *Homage to Catalonia*, published in 1938.

But before any building, the 'social ill' and its main causes had to be weeded out. This was what revolution meant for many anarchosyndicalist leaders and militants, but also for many other socialists and UGT members: the radical elimination of the symbols of power; the overthrow of the existing order; propagating an aggressive

---

[3] *Memoria de la Cámara Oficial de Comercio e Industria de Zaragoza, 1936*, pp. 21–5.

rhetoric that spoke of a society with no classes, no parties, no State. Revolution meant cleaning the atmosphere, applying the scalpel to diseased organs. And all this was a throwback to the Jacobins, the revolutionaries of the nineteenth century or those of the Russian revolution, reflected in the 'Public Health Committees', which, as in Lérida or Málaga, for example, devoted themselves to the cleansing of 'the unhealthy' in the summer of 1936.

Cleansing was a recurrent theme in the two zones created as a result of the uprising. The Spanish Civil War has gone down in history, and in memory, for the way it dehumanised its adversaries and for the horrific violence that it generated. If we go by the meticulous research carried out in the last few years, there were at least 150,000 lives lost to this violence during the war: close to 100,000 in the zone controlled by the military rebels and somewhat fewer than 60,000 in the republican zone. Figures aside, we are fully aware of the principal manifestations of this terror in the 'two cities', one 'celestial', the other 'earthly', recalled by the bishop of Salamanca, Enrique Pla y Deniel, quoting Saint Augustine.[4] The entrance of the Church onto the stage, far from reducing the violence, increased it, blessing it on the one hand and kindling even more the popular feeling against the clergy that had broken out at the same time as the defeat of the military uprising. It is now time to give an account of this immeasurable violence.

In the service of Spain and Christian civilisation

The repression dealt out by the military rebels was of a selective nature from the outset. The first to fall were the political authorities, distinguished republicans and political and trade union leaders. They were public figures, who appeared in the papers, with known addresses, and who, in most cases (particularly civil governors and mayors), had attended the same events, meetings and even parties as some of the military personnel who ordered their liquidation. They were intellectuals, professionals, small businessmen, members of the middle class who had attained political, cultural and social standing

---

[4] Enrique Pla y Deniel, 'Las dos ciudades', 30 September 1936, reproduced in Antonio Montero Moreno, *Historia de la persecución religiosa en España, 1936–1939*, BAC, Madrid, 1961, pp. 608–708.

largely through the Republic. They were killed not to serve as a lesson to their followers, as is sometimes said, but to overthrow the model of society and system of freedoms that they defended. There were political, but also social values involved, although both victims and executioners came from the same social background. We might call it political repression. Queipo de Llano had already said as much in November 1936, when the cleansing was well under way: 'Spain cannot be reconstructed until the entire political rabble is swept away'.[5]

There are many different examples, and it is worthwhile looking at just a few of them. The civil governors of the four Galician provinces were killed. The civil governor of La Coruña, Francisco Pérez Carballo, aged 25, had worked as an assistant lecturer in Roman law at the University of Madrid, and gained a position as a legal adviser in the Cortes by competitive examination. On 20 July, when a sector of the army declared martial law in this city, he tried to put up resistance in the civil government building, with several members of the military loyal to the Republic. As was the case in so many places, the huge disproportion in the number of forces neutralised the resistance. On 24 July, he was shot, together with Major Quesada and Captain Tejero, who had accompanied him in the defence of the civil government building.

That was not the end of it. Pérez Carballo was married to Juana Capdevielle, an arts graduate and archivist at the University of Madrid. In July 1936, she was heavily pregnant. After the declaration of martial law, she took refuge in the house of López Abente, a pharmacist. She was arrested, and while in gaol she learnt of the death of her husband, which provoked a nervous attack and apparently caused a miscarriage; she was attended to by the doctor and *Esquerda Republicana* deputy, García Ramos, who was also being held there. She was released, but in the middle of August she was arrested again by Falangist paramilitary groups. They raped and murdered her, leaving her body in a spot near Rábade.

Whenever they could not find the governor, they would pick on his family, which at the same time served to intimidate the fugitive

---

[5] The declaration of the state of war in Seville, with the persecution of trade unions and political organisations, as well as Queipo de Llano's declarations, may be found in Ian Gibson, *Queipo de Llano. Sevilla, verano de 1936*, Grijalbo, Barcelona, 1986, pp. 72–80.

and force him to turn himself in. For example, they failed to capture Ignacio Mateos Guija, the recently appointed Civil Governor of Cáceres. But his family, living in Navalmoral de la Mata, which was taken by the rebels on 21 July, was taken for more than its fair share of *paseos*, and was left in pieces. They began with his father, José Mateos, a republican shopkeeper, who had been a member of the town council, and one of his brothers, Antonio Mateos Guija, aged 19; they were executed on the bridge spanning the Tagus at Almaraz, and were then thrown into the water. They continued with two other brothers and an uncle, the brother of his father. They sent the rest of the family to prison. They looted his father's shop and the Falangists shared out the spoils.

The *sacas* and *paseos* accounted for the lives of most of the political authorities and party leaders of the *Frente Popular* coalition. Mayors, provincial government presidents, city council representatives and hundreds of holders of political posts were killed in this way, dumped in meadows, outside towns or against cemetery walls. The shootings were carried out here and there, usually as dawn was breaking, with the killers themselves as the only witnesses. Only exceptionally were they tried together, as occurred in León on 4 November 1936, in a trial that was held in the regional government chamber, an event that aroused a great deal of interest, 'with a queue forming in *Botines* [the regional government building] to hear the sentence'. Among the accused were Emilio Francés, the Civil Governor; Miguel Castaño, the mayor; Ramón Armesto, President of the Provincial Government; and Félix Sampedro, President of the *Frente Popular*. They faced the firing squad two weeks later, in spite of the intervention of the bishop of León, Álvarez Miranda, a gesture that was unusual for such times. According to the register, however, the cause of death in all cases was 'cardiac arrest'.[6]

The fury of the army and Falangists was aimed particularly at the *Frente Popular* coalition deputies elected in February 1936. A report drawn up by the secretariat of the *Congreso de los Diputados*, published on 22 August 1938, stated that forty had been murdered and twelve were either prisoners or 'missing' in 'rebel territory'. This was not a bad haul, considering that most of the 263 deputies in this coalition

---

[6] Secundino Serrano, *La guerrilla antifranquista en León (1936–1951)*, Siglo XXI Editores, Madrid, 1988, pp. 101–3.

were elected in provinces and cities in which the rebellion had been put down. Of those killed, twenty-one were socialists, two Communists and the rest republicans. Eighteen belonged to Andalusian provinces and five to Galicia, a region in which leftist and nationalist politicians were wiped from the map. One of them was Ángel Casal, an editor in the *Partido Galleguista*, Mayor of Santiago de Compostela and Vice-President of the La Coruña Provincial Government in 1936. He had been a member of the commission that presented the Galician Statute of Autonomy in the *Congreso de los Diputados*. His body was found in a ditch on 19 August that year.

Some of these politicians, intellectuals and professionals were also masons, and many others were falsely accused of being members of free-masonry. In fact, as José Antonio Ferrer Benimelli has shown, the fervent zeal of the Fascists in the summer of 1936 decreed that being a mason was considered to be a 'crime against the Fatherland'. And a genuine process of extermination was what the military rebels and the Falangists set in motion against freemasonry, with lodges demolished and all their members murdered, as was the case in several cities in Galicia, and in Zamora, Cádiz, Granada, Huelva, Las Palmas and Zaragoza.[7]

What happened in Huesca warrants particular attention. Close to a hundred people were accused of masonry and then shot in the first few days, although there were barely a dozen masons in this city, all members of the *Triángulo Joaquín Costa*. Such was the fate of the republican mayor, Mariano Carderera, and the ex-mayor, Manuel Sender, the brother of the writer Ramón J. Sender, who were named in proceedings that were opened a long time after their deaths, almost as if by doing so they could be executed all over again. Also falsely accused of being a mason was the anarchist Ramón Acín, a painter and sculptor, the art lecturer at the Huesca Teacher Training College, who had organised CNT syndicates in Upper Aragon, plotted against the Primo de Rivera dictatorship, struck up a friendship with Fermín Galán, the 'martyr' of the Jaca rising, and become one of the founding fathers of revolutionary trade unionism in Aragon. He was killed on 6 August, a few days before his wife, Concha Monrás Casas: they left two daughters, Katia and Sol, aged 13 and 11. The register lists Acín as having died 'in a brawl'.

[7] José Antonio Ferrer Benimelli, *La masonería española*, Itsmo, Madrid, 1995, pp. 144–5.

'The law was enforced' was what the police reports tended to say. Schoolteachers were one such group who for a long time experienced the law being enforced. The hatred felt by conservatives, Catholics and Falangists for the members of this group who had most closely identified with liberal, republican or socialist ideas, or for their battle against religious education, knew no bounds. The Falangist newspaper published in Zaragoza, *Amanecer*, expressed it thus: 'for fertile poets, puffed-up philosophers and young schoolteachers and their ilk, we can only suggest what the classical romance expressed: a monk to hear their confession and a harquebus to kill them'.[8]

The bureaucratic web that was set up to 'purge' them was highly intricate. An order issued on 19 August 1936 by the *Junta de Defensa* required local mayors to inform the university rectors, before 30 September, of the 'politico-social conduct and moral education' of the teachers in their locality. Several hundred schoolteachers were summarily killed in those early weeks: in Burgos, a fairly conservative province, twenty-one met their death; a few more, thirty-three, in the province of Zaragoza; and nearly fifty in León.

The military and Falangist terror destroyed the political victories and dreams of these intellectual, professional and administrative sectors who had developed a common political culture, marked by its anticlericalism, republicanism, democratic radicalism and, in some cases, Messianism for the working classes. This destruction, which spread like a relentless tide through the towns and cities in the rebel zone, caused others, who at the beginning supported the 'glorious movement to save Spain', to think it might not have been so glorious or saviour-like. These people, like the republicans who had been murdered, were intellectuals, professionals or civil servants. Some had been republicans since the declaration of the Republic on 14 April 1931, and they were proud of it. The intense social mobilisation and political radicalisation of subsequent years, culminating in the spring of 1936, had caused them to call for what they considered to be a necessary rectification of the Republic. And maybe this was what the military uprising would achieve. Clean up what was necessary and put the Republic back on the road it had first followed in 1931.

Such a person was Don Miguel de Unamuno. The rector of the University of Salamanca thought and said on those decisive days in

---

[8] *Amanecer*, Zaragoza, 13 March 1937.

July that everything was under control, that it was a mere 'cleaning operation'. This was why, when the first city council after the military rising was assembled on 25 July, with Major del Valle as mayor, and whose members included representatives of Salamanca's business and banking sectors, Unamuno agreed to serve on the council once more, having previously been elected on 12 April 1931.

'I am at your disposal', he said to the councillors on the day the city council was set up. 'Western civilisation, Christian civilisation, is under great threat and must be saved', at a time when 'towns and villages are being run by the lowest of the low, almost as if they had sought discharged convicts to run things'.[9]

The theme of 'saving western civilisation' was to be heard repeatedly during this time. There were some who did not stop repeating it for years, in spite of the fact that they were drenching the countryside in blood and cramming the prisons. Many were the bodies that Unamuno saw passing by, bodies that were unavoidable, and even necessary, in this 'flare-up of passions'. But that was just the start. The bodies were no longer those of anonymous people, people who were running the towns and villages incompetently, 'discharged criminals'. They were the bodies of friends, university lecturers, schoolteachers, doctors and civil servants. And his correspondence, as Luciano González Egido tells us, 'was full of letters from women pleading for mercy, justice and hope for their imprisoned husbands'.

One of these women was the widow of Prieto Carrasco, the mayor and Professor of the Faculty of Medicine, who had been killed in those first few turbulent days by Falangists from Valladolid. News also came from Granada of the killing of Salvador Vila Hernández, the rector of Granada University, an ex-student of Unamuno's whom he had seen in Salamanca in July, before he was arrested and taken back to Granada. He was not the only rector to be executed by the saviours of 'Christian civilisation'. The same fate befell Leopoldo Alas, the son of the writer 'Clarín' and the rector of the University of Oviedo.

While he was suffering these bitter blows, other things were happening in Salamanca. As from 1 October, Franco was 'Head of Government of the Spanish State', and a few days later he moved into

---

[9] Quoted in Luciano González Egido, *Agonizar en Salamanca. Unamuno (julio–diciembre 1936)*, Alianza Editorial, Madrid, 1986, pp. 40–50, 104–13.

the bishop's palace in Salamanca. On 12 October, the university was set to host an event to commemorate the Discovery of America – the 'Festival of the Race', as it was called in those days of patriotic fervour. Unamuno, as rector, and representing General Franco, chaired the event in the main hall of the university, accompanied by Carmen Polo, Franco's wife, and by military and ecclesiastical authorities. Speeches were heard from these military and ecclesiastical authorities, as well as from the intellectuals who supported them, in which they attacked the evils of Russia, anarchy, and the iniquitous Catalans and Basques.

Unamuno was the last to speak. And he unleashed his tongue. He said that he, too, had believed in the idea of an 'international war to defend Christian civilisation'. But not this war; this was an 'uncivil war'. 'Winning is not convincing ... and you cannot convince with hatred that leaves no room for compassion, the hatred for intelligence'.

General José Millán Astray, the founder of the Foreign Legion, interrupted him: 'Death to the intellectuals!' and 'Long live death!', his favourite slogan. Legionnaires approached the platform. They threatened and insulted the old professor. Carmen Polo, escorted by her personal guard, took him out by the arm. But Unamuno still had time to finish: 'You lack reason and right in the struggle. It is useless to ask you to think of Spain'. That was his last public appearance. He died on 31 December 1936. A few days earlier, a firing squad had executed his friend, Atilano Coco, who had spent the previous months in prison, without knowing 'whether I am here on the order of some judge or the military commander'. Atilano Coco was a protestant minister. And a mason. What chance did he have of survival in a Spain so fervently Catholic?[10]

As well as civil governors, *Frente Popular* deputies, political, intellectual and professional elites, this selective repression also included a considerable number of workers' organisations' leaders and militants: some, also well known, went to the same informal gatherings and meetings as these republicans, and some were even related to them; others, the majority, were separate from these elites because of their revolutionary passion, their radical workers' views and their hatred of the class system. Isaac Puente, a doctor who preached libertarian Communism, met his death in Vitoria on 1 September 1936.

[10] Ibid., pp. 129–42.

José Villaverde, a syndicalist in the mould of Joan Peiró or Ángel Pestaña, was 'taken for a walk' in La Coruña the same month, after rejecting the regional Falangist head's offer to spare his life in return for organising the Fascist syndicates.

Socialists and anarchists, Communists, UGT and CNT union members fell like flies. Officers, Falangists, bosses, owners and people of order settled old scores with them, fed up as they were with workers' disputes, revolutionary threats, their social aspirations and their agrarian reform. In general terms, the repression was a great deal more systematic and there was more of it in places where social conflicts had been most intensive – areas where socialist trade unionism or anarcho-syndicalism had been consolidated, and those places where the *Frente Popular* had been successful in the February 1936 elections.

This wave of extermination also caught up thousands of people who had never been conspicuous for their public actions, or so they thought. Because under this new lawless order, someone only had to state that such-and-such a person never attended mass, used to frequent the local party headquarters or the *ateneo libertario*, had celebrated republican election victories or was simply 'known to be against the *Movimiento Nacional*'. Thus men and women were ruthlessly chopped down, never knowing why, men and women who had the misfortune to run foul of Falangist university students, or do-gooder landowners who refused the dispossessed even the right to breathe.

It was a reflection of opposition and confrontation between two worlds, of the socio-economic and cultural imbalance between the haves and the have-nots, between those who had had the chance to acquire culture and the illiterate. In short, it was a reflection of class repression, from the top down, accompanied and reinforced by the political persecution examined earlier, although personal and family quarrels, or religious, nationalist and linguistic divisions, mean that the more conventional images regarding class conflict propagated by militant literature should be rejected.

The purge was massive and dramatic in the rural environment, where close personal relationships favoured the flourishing of old disputes and passionate family quarrels, mixed with political and class hatred, and the thirst for vengeance by landowners cowed by popular threats. For long years afterwards, many of them were yet to discover where their dead were, scattered as they were in the most unlikely places, until they found them in registry office and cemetery lists published in various studies. Others have been less lucky, and have been deprived of this sentimental and symbolic satisfaction, because their dead were never registered.

They were also dark days for many women, countless numbers of whom were killed, although in no province did the number of executions reach 10 per cent; but, above all, they suffered humiliations ranging from having their hair shorn to sexual harassment, as well as being given castor oil laxatives or being forbidden to show their grief through mourning. There were women who had to open their doors to Falangists at night and tell the murderers where they would find their absent husbands and sons. Thousands of widows and orphans, who had lost their parents and husbands in the prime of life – most of the murdered were between 19 and 40 years old, according to the most comprehensive studies – with their own lives shattered and in ruins, and with the stigma of being related to dead reds.

There were women who died for having overreached what people of order considered to be their station in life, or for being the partner of a well-known red. Such was the case of María Domínguez, one of the first women to breach the barriers to political office, something which, particularly in the rural environment, radically divided the male and female genders; and Amparo Barayón, the wife of the writer Ramón J. Sender, a pathetic example of the torment endured by many women who were subject to the stifling atmosphere to be found in many towns and provincial capitals.

María Domínguez was the first woman to obtain the office of mayor in a Spanish town. She was born in 1882 in the village of Pozuelo de Aragón, in the province of Zaragoza, to a poor, illiterate family. Her marriage of convenience, arranged by her parents at the end of her adolescence, lasted less than eight years. In 1907, tired of being badly treated, she left her home and village and went to Barcelona to look for a new life. She had been a keen reader and writer ever since she was a girl, and she began to carve a niche for herself as a contributor to the republican weekly, *El Ideal de Aragón*, published between 1914 and 1920. At the age of 36, she accepted the offer of a post as schoolteacher in a small hamlet in the Baztán valley in Navarre, and she arrived there, laden with a collection of books by authors such as Victor Hugo, Zola, Blasco Ibáñez and Kropotkin, but 'without knowing the rule of three'. From there, she went to Zaragoza, where she met Arturo Romanos, a socialist who lived in Gallur, whom she married and with whom she shared a life of intense militancy that led her to organise sections of the UGT and contribute articles for the socialist weekly, *Vida Nueva*. In October 1932, the Civil Governor of Zaragoza appointed her President of the Gallur Management Committee, a post she held for only a few months, as she was hampered by the opposition of the most conservative sectors of the Committee and the incomprehension of some of her socialist colleagues.

Republican, socialist, feminist and, what is more, with experience of political office – no wonder she was accused by the good burghers of the town, arrested and 'taken for a walk'. They took her to another town, Fuendejalón, where her entry in the register on 7 November 1936 reads 'bullet wounds'. She was aged 55 and was 'a housewife', the entry went on. A few days earlier, in Tabuenca, also nearby, her husband met a similar fate, in 'an act of violence', according to the duty registrar.[11]

Amparo Barayón first met Ramón J. Sender in a literary salon in Madrid at the beginning of the Second Republic. They had a son, Ramón, in 1934, and they were married in a civil ceremony at El Escorial at the end of 1935, shortly before the birth of their daughter, Andrea, in February 1936. Amparo learnt of the military rising in San Rafael, a favourite summer resort of the Madrid bourgeois, where her husband, who had been awarded the National Literature Prize that year for his novel *Mister Witt en el Cantón*, had rented a house.

Sender managed to escape from San Rafael before the arrival of the rebel troops, and Amparo decided to go to Zamora, her city of birth, thinking that she and her children would be safer with her family. It was not to be. She was arrested at the end of August, while protesting about the murder of her brother Antonio. On 10 October, the secretary of the prison governor snatched her baby daughter from her arms, saying that 'reds do not have the right to bring up children'. As had been the case with other women who had had their children taken away from them, this was a sign that her hours were numbered. That night, the Falangists took her to the cemetery in a truck. She

---

[11] Julita Cifuentes and María Pilar Maluenda, 'María Domínguez: la primera alcaldesa de España', *Trébede* magazine, 50 (2001), Zaragoza, pp. 19–24.

wanted to make her confession, but a priest refused to grant her absolution as she had not married in church and was living in sin. She had been denounced by her brother-in-law, Miguel Sevilla, 'the assassins' friend', and she was shot by Segundo Viloria, who had unsuccessfully courted her years earlier. Before she died, she wrote a note to her 'darling' Ramón: 'Never forgive my killers who have robbed me of Andreína, nor Miguel Sevilla, who is guilty of having denounced me. I feel no sorrow, because I am dying for you. But what will happen to the children? They are yours now. I shall love you always'.[12]

The mention of Viloria raises the subject of the executioners, among whom we find hot-headed killers, such as Viloria himself, Falangist or Carlist fanatics, and also people of order, the cream of society. For example, it was an ex-CEDA deputy, Ramón Ruiz Alonso, a well-known figure in Granada, who arrived at the home of the Rosales family to take away Federico García Lorca, who was in hiding there. It was in the afternoon of Sunday 16 August 1936, and that same morning, his brother-in-law, Manuel Fernández-Montesinos, the ex-mayor of Granada, who was married to Concha García Lorca, had been shot.

According to Ian Gibson, when Ruiz Alonso knocked at the door of the Rosales home in the Calle Angulo, he was accompanied by two CEDA colleagues: 'Juan Luis Trescastro – a well-known landowner and typical loudmouth to be found among the young Andalusian upper classes – and Luis García Alix, the party secretary in Granada'. He was taken to the civil government, then under Major José Valdés Guzmán, who had been purging Granada of 'reds' since the military rising. Because of García Lorca's reputation, Valdés discussed what to do with the poet with General Queipo de Llano, who apparently answered him with the famous phrase, 'give him coffee, plenty of coffee'.[13]

The most reliable indications suggest that he would have been given his coffee at dawn on 18 August in Víznar, where the Falangists had ordered the opening of common graves dug by Granada masons and 'reds' before they were murdered by volunteers of the 'Black Squad'.

[12] Ramón Sender Barayón, *Muerte en Zamora*, Plaza & Janés, Barcelona, 1990, p. 173.
[13] Quoted in Gibson, *Queipo de Llano*, p. 106. The information on the murder of García Lorca may be found in Ian Gibson, *Federico García Lorca: A Life*, Faber and Faber, London, 1989.

He met his death alongside a schoolteacher and two anarchist *banderilleros*, and among his killers was José Luis Trescastro. His death certificate used another euphemism of the many that we have already seen here: 'from wounds produced by acts of war'.

Falangists, *requetés*, citizen militias and volunteers were the most visible manifestation of this rightist mobilisation, unprecedented in the history of Spain, which had been facilitated by the military uprising. All these reactionary sectors accompanied the army in carrying out the terror; and while it often left the cleansing work to these paramilitary groups, it was the army that was in charge of the violence by declaring martial law, taking on all powers related to public order, and submitting ordinary justice to the military. During these early months, its commanders and officers never put a brake on a repression that they controlled at all times, in spite of the appearance of 'unrestraint' that encompassed many *sacas* and *paseos*.

'Popular justice' and organised terror

There was much talk of 'unrestraint' and 'disorderly mobs' on the opposing side, in the zone where the uprising was defeated. And despite the growth in the number of armed groups in those first few weeks, the absence of government, vox populi, *suprema lex*, as the anarchist García Oliver put it, and the fact that anyone could carry a pistol or a rifle to exact revenge or kill at will, we should not attach too much blame to the 'disorderly mobs', those who seemed to act on their own initiative, those who have so often been mentioned in order to explain the extreme violence in the republican zone.

Of course, there was no lack of 'disorderly mobs'. They were to be found in Barcelona, a major sea port, with a large immigrant population, centres of low life and prison fodder. They were to be found in the earliest days in the militias that were formed to overthrow the rebels in the large cities, in the 'vigilante patrols', in armed groups of various types, peopled by murderers seeking revenge and thieves for whom the unlocking of the prison gates presented an opportunity to rob at will. But the instigators and perpetrators of many of these killings belonged to the political organisations of the *Frente Popular*; they were Communists, republicans, socialists and anarcho-syndicalists, who responded to the military coup with arms, killing their political and class enemies in the belief that behind their elimination lay redemption, and that the time for 'popular', 'revolutionary' justice had arrived.

Not everyone wanted bloodshed, and from the outset there were plenty of voices raised against the massacre, something conspicuously absent among the crusaders on the other side. However, the defeat of the uprising released shackles, bringing about complete liberation from the yokes of the past, and saw the arrival of the long-awaited revolution and final judgement for the rich, exploitative bosses, a favourite theme in the most radical propaganda and rhetoric. With no rules or government, with no mechanisms for forcing people to comply with laws, the 'thirst for justice', revenge and class hatred spread with devastating force to wipe out the old order.

Those considered to be oppressors were liquidated in their hundreds and thousands during the early weeks, the end of July and the rest of the summer of 1936. And almost certainly there was an angry, immediate reaction against the military rebels, who were seen as being directly responsible for what was happening. What was certainly angry, immediate and extremely swift was the reaction against the clergy, who, as the most easily attainable target at the beginning of the breakdown of social order, went through a living hell.

There are data that clearly confirm this argument. With the exception of Madrid, where the wave of repression peaked in the autumn, most executions of military personnel took place in the summer of 1936. The rage against the clergy occurred during the same months, in Madrid as well, and by the end of September 1936, the number of ecclesiastical personnel murdered was almost 90 per cent of the total for the entire civil war. August was the bloodiest month in many areas of Catalonia and Aragon, Murcia, Toledo, Badajoz and Castellón.

But the number of killings was still very high in October in Catalonia, and particularly in the Community of Valencia, with percentages slightly lower than those of September, the month with most deaths in the provinces of Alicante and Valencia. There were numerous stormings of prisons in September and October, with dozens of fatalities, and these were repeated in December in Guadalajara and Santander, and in January 1937 in Vizcaya. Some of these stormings took place several days after 4 September 1936, the date that Francisco Largo Caballero took over as Prime Minister. And, most significantly, despite the fact that the end of August saw the first decrees setting up special courts to deal with the crimes of 'rebellion' and 'sedition', was that thousands and thousands of citizens were 'taken for a walk' with no legal safeguards. The protection that this legislation was supposed to give was of little use to them.

This 'ardent' terror became diluted from late November 1936 onwards, and until the first quarter of 1939, with the new outbreak of violence by retreating troops in Catalonia and Levante, cooled down to such an extent that there were many places where there were no more killings. And not because there was no one to kill, as some have suggested: the same 'crimes', the same 'reasons' that in July and August 1936 served to send many to their graves were given a different treatment by the Popular Tribunals in 1937 and 1938. The lives of thousands of prisoners were saved by the order and discipline imposed in the background by political organisations represented in the governments of Francisco Largo Caballero and Juan Negrín, from the UGT to the CNT, as well as Communists, republicans and Basque and Catalan nationalists.

There are some remarkable aspects surrounding the violence unleashed in the republican zone, which, in view of the fragmentation of powers and the variety of situations that came out of the defeat of the rebels, can only be investigated by a thorough examination of the various zones in which the most significant cases were concentrated.

In Barcelona, the wave of repression was clearly class-based; it spread through the factories and the suburbs and settled old scores with the owners and employers, as well as *somatenistas* and the gunmen of the free syndicates. Despite what has often been assumed and what had been written in the anarchists' writings about a future society, in the early months of the persecution of their adversaries, the CNT committees were more concerned with combating the 'counter-revolution' than with collectivising production resources. However, this was not an unusual situation or unlike anything that had happened in other revolutions. Hence the first thing that the Central Committee of Anti-Fascist Militias (which had been operating since 20 July as a revolutionary government) did was to decree the setting up of special 'teams' to maintain 'revolutionary order'. 'Investigation Groups' and 'control patrols' they were called, and they were made up of several hundred armed men, led by FAI members such as Aurelio Fernández, or anarchists well known for their radical views, such as Dionisio Eroles, who had spent half his life in prison. Both were later to hold important posts directing the police and public order in the government of the *Generalitat*, which the CNT joined on 26 September 1936.

Until the disappearance of these control patrols, following the events of May 1937, the 'patrolmen' devoted themselves to 'social hygiene'; they set up their own prisons, took the rich, the clergy and right-wingers 'for a walk', and vied with the republicans and Communists for the 'control' of order away from the front. Given the fragmentation of powers that prevailed in the city that summer, it cannot have been very hard for these armed groups to spread panic among the well-to-do.[14]

Armed control of the revolution spread to other cities and towns in Catalonia, with committees and militias eliminating the bourgeois, holders of political and administrative posts, *requetés* and traditionalists who, as well as having been involved in the rising, had been members of the *somatén* and free syndicates. A great many factory and workshop managers were killed, but not many eminent *Lliga* members or major industrialists, as they managed to flee before they were hunted down. There were plenty of enemies to hunt down in the rural environment, in the interior districts that had always seen constant confrontations over tenancies, with owners and farm labourers being killed in their hundreds. And although a third of the 8,532 victims of this terror in Catalonia met their death in Barcelona, the persecution, as a ratio of the number of deaths over the number of inhabitants, was harsher and more intense in the agricultural districts of the interior than in the more industrialised areas along the coast.

The purifying fire hit the clergy with particular brutality. Stories of the public burning of religious images and artefacts, the use of churches for stabling and storage, the melting down of church bells for ammunition, the suppression of religious acts, the exhumation of monks and nuns, and the killing of regular and lay clergy were recounted and spread in all their grisly detail throughout Spain and beyond the Pyrenees, as the symbol of terror par excellence of anarchist control. It was hardly surprising: 1189 priests, 794 monks and 50 nuns were killed, and the overall figure rises to 2,437 if we count the towns of Aragon and the Community of Valencia that belonged to dioceses based in Catalonia. Over a third of all the clergy shot in republican Spain perished there.

[14] Julián Casanova, *Anarchism, the Republic and Civil War in Spain: 1931–1939*, Routledge, London, 2004, pp. 101–15.

It is hardly necessary to mention that the clergy were killed without trial. If there was a terror that was 'hot-blooded', it was the terror that was visited on the clergy, who were rarely sent to prison. Only 240 clergy were sent to the Modelo prison in Barcelona during the whole war, 1.8 per cent of the total number of inmates, and up to the end of 1936 only forty-six were sent there.

There was hot-blooded terror aplenty against the clergy, military personnel and right-wingers in Lérida, a city in which the militias also left their mark. A Committee of Public Health was operating there and, from 18 August, a Popular Justice Tribunal, the first to appear in republican territory, and together they constituted a unique revolutionary model, with the presence of the POUM, a blend of Jacobin and Bolshevik influences, which did not go down well with certain anarchists who defended the 'spontaneous' justice of the people.

In short, Catalonia witnessed the various paths trodden by revolutionary violence during the second half of 1936: unrestrained *paseos*; mass killings directed by committees and control patrols, who had their own gaols, the *checas*, with the Sant Elías *checa* in Barcelona being one of the most notorious; militiamen who looked after 'public safety'; and popular tribunals, with their self-conferred licence to carry on killing. The result was that 6,400 people were killed in five months, 80 per cent of the 8,352 killed in the entire war. This was revolutionary retribution of the highest order, the brutality of which would have been just as harsh had the number of victims been several hundred higher or lower.

But there is persuasive evidence that there was a large number of people, including the CNT leader Joan Peiró, senior politicians in the *Generalitat* and ordinary militants, as well as Pere Bosch-Gimpera, the rector of the university, who tried to prevent the bloodshed, something that can hardly be said for the rebel officers and authorities on the other side. They also saved a good many lives, the best-known example being that of Cardinal Vidal i Barraquer; and they helped several thousand citizens, particularly civil servants, army personnel, politicians and clergy, to leave the country during this period of 'hot-blooded' terror.

Although these efforts to put a brake on this uncontrolled killing were repeated in Madrid – where, at the beginning of 1937, there were nearly 8,500 people who had taken refuge in various embassies – the results were patently dwarfed by the magnitude of the slaughter that occurred there. The image of Madrid that was forever engraved on the collective memory of the republicans and the International Brigade volunteers was its heroic resistance displayed in November 1936. The image for the winners of the war was that of the *sacas* and killings that occurred during this same period.

Paseos, *sacas* and *checas*: these were the three elements that were linked to the wave of terror that engulfed Madrid in the summer and autumn of 1936. *Checa* was the name given to the gaols, both improvised and organised, in requisitioned buildings where 'committees of investigation' met, set up by left-wing political parties and syndicalists, with carte blanche to make arrests, requisition or kill. *Checa* was the Russian acronym for the 'Pan-Russian Extraordinary Commission for the Suppression of Counter-Revolution and Sabotage'.

If we are to give credence to Agustín de Foxá's opinion, later recycled by Francoist writings, this was 'organised crime': 'for the first time in history, the entire bureaucratic mechanism of a State was an accomplice to murder'.[15] The *Causa General* was later to be even more apocalyptic about the legend of the *checas*, when it presented a detailed list of over 200 of them, with a large number of accusations of torture and killings.

In fact, in the summer and autumn of 1936, the whole of Madrid, which had previously been the seat of the royal court, was to become one big *checa*, although the figures – not the legend – say that most of the *sacas* were from the prisons, particularly the Modelo, which witnessed some unforgettably horrific events. Unforgettable were the names of some of the politicians killed in the *saca* of 22 August, and over half those shot in Paracuellos on 7 and 8 November came from this prison. One week before this massacre, thirty-one men faced a firing squad in Aravaca, following a *saca* from the Las Ventas prison. Two of them, Ramiro de Maeztu and Ramiro Ledesma Ramos, were later to figure particularly prominently in the memory of the winners of the civil war. Maeztu, the founder and editor of the magazine *Acción Española* in 1930 and author of the famous *Defensa de la hispanidad*, was remembered because he was the most distinguished intellectual the Francoists could display as a martyr, although his popularity was later superseded by that of Pedro Muñoz Seca, the

---

[15] Agustín de Foxá, *Madrid de corte a checa*, Planeta, Barcelona, 1993, p. 272. (Original edition published by La Ciudadela, Madrid, 1938.)

author of *La venganza de don Mendo*, who was killed in Paracuellos at the end of November. As far as Ledesma Ramos, the author of *La Conquista del Estado* and founder of the JONS, was concerned, it was because impoverished Spanish Fascist thought needed its myths, fearless souls who had died for the Fatherland in the flower of youth.

All the stormings, or *sacas*, were dwarfed by the one in Paracuellos del Jarama, an event that was never repeated in the civil war, because the situation that provoked it was also unrepeatable. On 6 November 1936, Franco's troops arrived at the gates of Madrid. The Council of Ministers, including the four CNT leaders who were new arrivals in the government, unanimously decided to transfer the government from Madrid to Valencia. Just before the transfer, Largo Caballero ordered the setting up of a *Junta de Defensa* under General Miaja, which was to exert authority in a Madrid that was under siege from that day until 22 April 1937. Santiago Carrillo was appointed Councillor in Charge of Public Order.

At that time, there were over 5,000 people being held in the prisons and *checas* of Madrid. Around 2,000 were removed on 7 and 8 November and taken in buses operated by the Madrid tram company to Paracuellos del Jarama and Torrejón de Ardoz. The *sacas* and killings went on for several days and escalated towards the end of the month. On 4 December, the new Inspector General of Prisons, the anarchist Melchor Rodríguez, halted the *sacas*. In one month, this process had accounted for some 2,700 prisoners, who were positively identified after the war, although in the veneration of the martyrs promoted by the eventual victors, this number was inflated to eight or nine thousand. Some 1,300 people had faced the firing squad in the first of these *sacas*.[16]

It was a bad time for the republican cause, with Madrid, with no government, under siege, during which armed groups systematically murdered prisoners. Not surprisingly, the affair gave rise to a string of justifications, accusations and controversial statements, which are to be found in writings even now. Socialists and anarchists, according to the proceedings of the CNT National Committee of 8 November,

---

[16] An analysis of the repression in the republican zone, which the Nationalists called 'red terror', may be found in Julián Casanova, 'Rebelión y revolución', in Santos Juliá (ed.), *Víctimas de la guerra civil*, Temas de Hoy, Madrid, 1999, pp. 117–77.

reproduced by Jorge M. Reverte, had agreed to classify the prisoners into groups and to the 'immediate execution, dealing with the responsibility', of the first of these groups, made up of 'Fascists and dangerous elements'.[17]

A major role in this decision would also have been played by militant Communists of the Juventudes Socialistas Unificadas, the high command of the police system: Manuel Muñoz, the Director-General of Security; Santiago Carrillo, the Councillor in Charge of Public Order; and Segundo Serrano Poncela, the delegate for the Directorate-General of Security. And although it is highly likely that the typical 'disorderly mobs' – those who were always at home in chaotic situations – were acting of their own accord, the November *sacas* in Madrid suggested a full-scale cleansing dictated by the war, but one that was also coveted, a unique chance to eliminate the political, ideological and class enemy.

Madrid symbolised the *checas*, mass *sacas* and 'organised terror' in the same way that Barcelona, during the summer, symbolised the *paseo*, the 'control patrols' and the 'popular' and 'spontaneous' justice of the anarchists. It is fair to say that in Madrid, the fury was directed primarily against military personnel and leading politicians, while in Barcelona it was the clergy and business owners who bore the brunt. It is clearly significant that it was the socialists and Communists who took the leading role in this mass lynching of the enemy in Madrid, and that it was the anarchists who were behind the chaos that was responsible for the thousands of killings in Catalonia by so many different factions.

Clergy, right-wingers, the military, professionals and tradespeople, textile and footwear businessmen, Catholic workers and many farm owners, 'individualists' who opposed collectivisation made up the sectors that were most affected by the radical elimination of the adversary that sent 5,000 people to their graves in the Community of Valencia. Most of the almost 4,000 who were murdered in the areas of Aragon where the militias had settled were rich labourers, owners of small and medium-sized businesses, tradespeople, craftsmen and day-labourers, with a high percentage of clergy in the diocese of Barbastro. In Badajoz, Córdoba, Jaén and La Mancha, the

[17] Jorge M. Reverte, *La batalla de Madrid*, Crítica, Barcelona, 2004, pp. 577–81.

victims were mainly landowners, agricultural land and industry owners' families, members of the aristocracy, and conservative and right-wing politicians.

A special place with regard to these 5,000 dead is held by José Antonio Primo de Rivera, the martyr of the crusade, the *ausente*, to whom buildings were dedicated, as were hundreds of streets, squares and schools; and many churches bore the inscription 'José Antonio Primo de Rivera, *Presente!*'

He was born in April 1903 into a well-to-do Andalusian military family, with close links to the land-owning oligarchy, and he was educated as a monarchist aristocrat, at all times loyal to the memory of his father, the dictator Miguel Primo de Rivera. At the time of the military rising, he was in prison in Alicante, where he had been taken on 5 June from Madrid. He had been arrested, along with other FE JONS leaders, on 14 March, two days after three Falangists tried to assassinate Luís Jiménez de Asúa, a professor of law and a PSOE deputy.

So the rising found him in prison, but confident, having supported it unreservedly in a manifesto drawn up on 17 July, that it would succeed and thus bring about his release. But it did not turn out that way in Alicante, and several months went by in which, while his allies were planning his escape or an exchange of prisoners – something that other leading right-wingers such as Ramón Serrano Suñer or Raimundo Fernández Cuesta managed to secure – the Committee of Public Order in Alicante was thinking of 'taking him for a walk' on the pretext of a transfer to the gaol in Cartagena.

On 16 November, along with his brother Miguel, he faced a Popular Tribunal, made up of three magistrates and a fourteen-man jury, and answered questions about his connections with the conspirators and the preparation of the military uprising. José Antonio denied both his participation in the plot and the *Falange*'s responsibility for acts of violence. On 18 July, the magistrates accepted the prosecutor's request for the death penalty, while the sentence for his brother Miguel was life imprisonment. Miguel's wife, Margarita Larios, *Margot*, who had gone to Alicante a few days before the rising, was sentenced to six years and one day. José Antonio was shot at dawn on 20 November 1936. He was 33, and he has always been said to have died bravely and honourably.

This marked the beginning of the legend of the *ausente*, cleverly cultivated by Franco. And there were plenty of *ausentes*. The other two members of the triumvirate that were behind the FE JONS, Ruiz de Alda and Ledesma Ramos, had been assassinated in Madrid. Onésimo Redondo, the founder of the JONS in October 1931 (together with Ledesma Ramos), was killed on the Sierra de Guadarrama front at the beginning of the war, although there were plenty who believed that he had been killed by Falangists from a rival group.

Among the victims of violence on the republican side, there were very few women. Except for Madrid, where several hundred disappeared in the *sacas*, the number of victims was very low in most of the provinces, ranging from five in Murcia to sixteen in Alicante and seventeen in Ciudad Real. It hardly needs saying that the wives of many of the victims of revolutionary and leftist violence were also threatened, and in some cases ill-treated; but it was nothing like the ruthless treatment meted out by the military, Falangists and Catholics to the sisters, daughters, wives and mothers of the 'reds'. Despite the widespread conventional image of anarchist militiamen raping and killing women, only seventeen were killed in the eastern areas of the province of Zaragoza, while in the rest of the province, nearly 300 faced rebel firing squads.

The conclusion seems clear: the violence was inextricably linked to the coup d'état and the progress of the civil war. Symbolised by the *sacas*, *paseos* and mass killings, it served the two sides in their struggle to eliminate their respective enemies, whether natural or unforeseen. It was an essential part of the 'glorious National Movement', its onslaught against the Republic and the gradual conquest of power, skirmish by skirmish, massacre by massacre, battle by battle. It also became a basic ingredient of the diversified chaotic response provided by left-wing political and trade union organisations to the military coup. Contrary to appearances, this violence was not so much a consequence of the war as the direct result of a military uprising, which, from the outset, went hand in hand with unpunished murder and the coup de grâce. It was a strategically designed plan, which, in the places where it failed, was met by a sudden armed response against the main players in the uprising and those considered to be their material and spiritual brothers-in-arms.

While carrying out this extermination, the rebels were also given the inestimable blessing of the Catholic Church from the very beginning. The clergy and sacred objects, however, were the prime target of popular rage by those who took part in the defeat of the military rebels and who led the 'cleansing' undertaken in the summer of 1936.

'Religious zeal', 'satanic rage'

On 20 July 1936, General Emilio Mola arrived in Burgos, a city that since Sunday 18 July had been experiencing a wave of patriotic and religious fervour, with solemn masses and the pre-Republic red and gold flag on every mast. The cathedral bells announced the general's arrival to the population. 'Traditionalist and Fascist squads' escorted the procession to the Palace of the 6th Division, in the Plaza Alonso Martínez. This was followed almost instantly by the arrival of the archbishop of the diocese, Manuel de Castro, to 'pay his respects' to the general, accompanied by his private secretary, Canon Alonso Hernández. When the public realised the prelate was there, 'they applauded him enthusiastically'.[18]

Some days later, on 16 August, it was General Francisco Franco who visited Burgos, then the capital of the rebel military command, the *Junta de Defensa Nacional*, presided over by General Miguel Cabanellas. After greeting the 'brave race of the North of Spain' that was cheering him, Franco went to the cathedral to hear mass. With him went Generals Mola, Cavalcanti and García Alvarez. Waiting for them on the steps that were 'packed with people' was the arch-priest Pedro Mendiguren. The archbishop took his seat near the great altar. The generals heard Mass 'with unction'.

It had been exactly a month since Spain became engulfed in a civil war caused by a failed military rebellion. The Catholic Church was quite clear about its position. Its mission was to oppose anarchy, socialism and the lay Republic. And all its representatives, except for the very few who did not share this warlike zeal, offered their help and blessing to the rebels. The Fatherland, order and religion, three things that were basically the same, had to be saved. And they lent their full weight to this cause from the pulpit, with sermons, exhortations and episcopal declarations. Nor was there any lack of priests or other religious personnel to sport the red beret and a pistol, masquerading as soldiers, Falangists or *requetés*.

The uprising was 'providential', wrote Cardinal Isidro Gomá in his 'Report of the military-civilian rising', which he sent to the Secretary

---

[18] Information is taken from the newspaper, the *Diario de Burgos*, 21 July 1936. The arguments in this section come from Julián Casanova, *La Iglesia de Franco*, Crítica, Barcelona, 2005.

of State of the Vatican, Cardinal Eugenio Pacelli, on 13 August 1936; 'providential' because 'it has been proved, from documents now in the hands of the insurgents, that the Communist revolution was due to break out on 20 July'.

The 'military-civilian' rising found Isidro Gomá in Tarazona, in the province of Zaragoza. He had gone there from Toledo on 12 July to spend a few days in the city that had been his first see in 1927, and he was due to stay there until 25 July, to attend the consecration of his suffragan Gregorio Modrego. But, 'caught unawares' by the military coup, he went to the spa resort of Belascoain, in Navarre, 16 kilometres from Pamplona. He established himself in Pamplona, and from there exerted his authority as primate of the Spanish bishops during the civil war.[19]

Another Catalan bishop, Enrique Pla y Deniel, was, like Gomá, a conspicuous ideologist for the crusade and an apologist for a 'necessary war'. On 30 September 1936, when General Franco was about to be invested, thanks to this 'necessary' war, with the highest powers a leader could aspire to on this earth, Pla y Deniel published his famous pastoral letter, 'Las dos ciudades', in Salamanca. In this letter, he defined the Spanish war as a struggle between 'two concepts of life, two sentiments, two forces that are preparing for a universal struggle among all the peoples of the world': on one side, the earthly city of the 'godless'; on the other, 'the heavenly city of the children of God'. It was not, therefore, a civil war, but a 'crusade for religion, the Fatherland and civilisation'.[20]

What Pla y Deniel wrote in 'Las dos ciudades' implanted in the minds of Spanish Catholics two ideas that the course of the war, Franco's victory and time converted into myths, the cornerstones of the explanation given by the Catholic Church to justify its involvement. The first was that the Church hierarchy, in keeping with its 'absolute lack of any party political leanings', acted with 'cautious reserve' from the beginning, following the line that 'the Church does not interfere with what God has left to be disputed by man'. And while they were aware

---

[19] 'Informe acerca del levantamiento cívico-militar de España en julio de 1936', signed in the spa resort of Belascoain (Navarre), 13 August 1936, reproduced in *Archivo Gomá. Documentos de la Guerra Civil. Julio–diciembre de 1936* (ed. José Andrés Gallego and Antón M. Pazos), 12 vols., CSIC, Madrid, 2001, vol. II, pp. 80–9.

[20] Pla y Deniel, 'Las dos ciudades'.

of 'the true nature of the movement and the integrity of its promoters' intentions and moral stance', they were waiting while 'the two camps emerged and the difference between them was made clear'.

Once this occurred, when the sacrilegious actions, the burning of religious buildings and the killing of clergy spread without control, and the republican government was unable to 'put a brake on these excesses', overwhelmed by 'anarchy-supporting mobs', then, and only then, did the Church take sides, openly and officially declaring itself 'in favour of order against anarchy, the implantation of a hierarchical government against the disintegrating properties of Communism, the defence of Christian civilisation and its bases, religion, the father-land and the family, against the godless, the heathen, those without a Fatherland and the down-and-outs of the world'.[21] In short, it was violent anticlericalism and disorder that brought about the Church's intervention in favour of the camp that respected religion and in which order prevailed.

This Manichean version of the civil war, which for the Church was not a civil war but a crusade, seems to be at odds with data supplied by recent research: from the very first rebel shot, the Church stated its position and acted accordingly. It only kept quiet to cover up the systematic elimination of the adversary that the army, landowners and the bourgeois, alarmed by the revolution, put into practice close to home, with hundreds of clergy as witnesses to the terror.

The first bishops to speak out were those who felt safer alongside the military rebels, basically because the coup had been a resounding success in the zone that contained their dioceses. These were the dioceses of almost the whole of northern Spain, from Pamplona and Zaragoza to Galicia, with Burgos, Valladolid, Salamanca and Zamora in between; thirty-two sees of the sixty-one dioceses that existed then in Spain were to be found in the rebel zone in the second half of August. According to data furnished by Alfonso Álvarez Bolado from ecclesiastical gazettes, 'in no fewer than 11 dioceses ... through 18 interventions, the bishops had made their position absolutely clear' before the first official declaration by Pope Pius XI on 14 September 1936. Furthermore, three of them, the bishop of Pamplona and the archbishops of Zaragoza and Santiago de Compostela, had labelled the civil war as a 'religious crusade' before the end of August.

[21] Ibid.

All these declarations followed a substantially identical line: they unblushingly sided with the military coup, which they celebrated, with the Catholic masses, as a liberation; they urged people to join in the struggle against the 'lay-Jewish-Masonic-Soviet elements', an expression used by the bishop of León, José Alvarez Miranda; and they saw no outcome to the conflict other than the resounding victory of 'our glorious army' over 'the enemies of God and Spain'.[22]

The Church has always tried to justify its postures and attitudes by citing the vicious anticlericalism that was unleashed in areas where the rising was defeated – a message with a clear impact – although the enthusiastic support for the coup by many ecclesiastical personnel came before, and in many cases ran parallel with, the clergy killings. It was not the 'satanic hatred' of the 'Communist hordes' that caused the Church and Catholics to take sides with the military rebels. It is true that it did reinforce their posture. But it was not the cause.

Furthermore, the clergy's complicity with the terror unleashed by the army was absolute and did not need anticlericalism to manifest itself. From Gomá to the humble priest who lived in Zaragoza, Salamanca or Granada, all were aware of the killings, heard the shots, saw how the people were taken off, how relatives of the prisoners or the missing would come to them and desperately beg for help and mercy. And except for rare occasions, the most they did was attend to the spiritual needs of the condemned. The most common attitude was silence, either voluntary or imposed by their superiors, or else accusation and denunciation. The violence of the military insurgents was legitimate because it was used 'not to promote anarchy, but legally, to the benefit of order, the Fatherland and religion', declared the archbishop of Zaragoza, Rigoberto Doménech, on 11 August.[23]

Even before the Spanish Church hierarchy had officially termed the war a crusade, a trend that started in the second half of August, large numbers of Catholics, less Catholic conservatives and non-Catholic Fascists had classified the assault on power as a *bellum sacrum et justum*, a 'necessary' war against the enemies of Spain, in favour of centralism and authoritarianism, and the preservation of the socio-economic

---

[22] Alfonso Álvarez Bolado, *Para ganar la guerra, para ganar la paz. Iglesia y guerra civil: 1936–1939*, Universidad Pontificia de Comillas, Madrid, 1995, pp. 50–3.

[23] *Heraldo de Aragón*, Zaragoza, 11 August 1936.

order. As Gomá said to Pacelli, this was 'the true, traditional Spanish people': some were motivated by 'the religious ideal, their Catholic conscience having been deeply wounded by the sectarian and anti-religious laws, and by uncontrolled persecution'; others, because 'their material interests were under threat'; many were motivated by the desire 'to re-establish the material order that had been profoundly disrupted'; and there were plenty, added Gomá, who were motivated 'by the feeling of national unity, under threat from separatist tendencies in certain regions'.[24]

There was nobody better than the Church and the Catholic movement it supported, with its own tradition, press and 'national structure', to provide social backing for the cause of war, to 'unify', in the words of Fernando García de Cortázar, 'the variety of possible rationales for the war into a single exclusive, integrated principle'. Catholicism was, in the words of Frances Lannon , the 'short cut', 'the ideal focus', both respected and positive, for all those who were truly seeking to protect their sectorial interests and their social position.[25]

The appearance on the scene of the sacred and religion also set in motion a persuasive, Baroque-style liturgical ritual of religious sentiment and patriotism, which became an integral part of the war's progress in Catholic Spain. The success of this religious mobilisation, this liturgy that attracted the masses in the dioceses of 'liberated' Spain, encouraged the army to adorn its speeches with references to God and religion, hitherto absent from the proclamations of the military coup and declarations during the subsequent days. It convinced them of the importance of this emotional link, as well as of destroying the enemy. The symbiosis between 'religion and patriotism', the 'virtues of *la Raza*', reinforced national unity and legitimised the violence that they had meted out in the summer of 1936.

The restoration of traditional customs, with crucifixes, Sacred Hearts, images of the Virgin of the Column and the red and gold flag, attracted an enthusiastic response. Old religious customs were

---

[24] *Archivo Gomá*, pp. 80–9.

[25] Fernando García de Cortázar's analysis is in 'La Iglesia y la guerra', in Edward Malefakis (ed.), *La guerra de España (1936–1939)*, Taurus, Madrid, 1996, pp. 511–40; Frances Lannon's pioneering interpretation of the Catholic Church in the contemporary history of Spain is in *Privilege, Persecution and Prophecy: The Catholic Church in Spain 1875–1975*, Clarendon Press, Oxford, 1987.

brought back, religious feast days were restored to the official calendar, and others of a 'national' character began to be celebrated, which were maintained throughout Franco's dictatorship until his death.

While this was going on, the other half of the Church, in the areas where the rebellion had failed, was undergoing what Gomá called 'satanic rage', a devastating retribution of vast dimensions. Over 6,800 churchmen, both lay and regular clergy, were killed; a large number of churches, hermitages and sanctuaries were burnt or suffered looting and desecration, with their works of art and items of worship totally or partially destroyed. Nor did cemeteries or graveyards fare any better, with a great number of priests' graves desecrated and the remains of monks and nuns exhumed.

Burning a church or killing a priest was the first thing that was done in many villages and towns where the military uprising was unsuccessful. 'Direct action', nothing less: that was what the clergy deserved. Andreu Nin, one of the big names in the POUM, publicly stated as much at the beginning of August 1936. Nin, who, a few months later, was to be kidnapped and murdered by the Communist secret services, thought and said the same as many other revolutionaries, leftist republicans and union leaders: the 'bourgeois' Republic's anticlerical legislation had done nothing to solve the 'problem' of the Church. It had had to be solved by the working class in the revolutionary flare-up initiated by the military coup. And it had been solved by the workers and revolutionaries in the way that they knew how, by 'attacking the roots', leaving no church standing, suppressing 'the priests, churches and worship'.[26]

'They asked for it' was a phrase found repeatedly in the libertarian and socialist press. And they asked for it because 'the powers of the clergy constantly stood alongside the powers of the sabre'. No one should be surprised, they added, that churches, 'Fascist redoubts par excellence, have been reduced to ashes'. There could be no pacts with the clergy. *Solidaridad Obrera* might have been trying to reassure the middle classes over possible revolutionary excesses in mid-August 1936, but in the matter of the clergy it was not yielding any ground: 'Religious orders must be dissolved. The bishops and cardinals must be shot. And Church property must be confiscated'.[27]

[26] *La Vanguardia*, Barcelona, 2 August 1936.
[27] *Solidaridad Obrera*, Barcelona, 15 August 1936.

Without a doubt, the treatment meted out to the clergy by the 'hordes' and their leaders in the summer of 1936 was merely the ful-filment of what many had been saying would happen since the begin-ning of the century, when leftist intellectuals, radical politicians such as Alejandro Lerroux and militant workers saw the Church and its representatives as the ultimate enemies of freedom, the people and progress, a designation that had hitherto been reserved for capitalism and the State. They all promised that one of the many contributions of the revolution would be 'the purifying firebrand' for church build-ings and the cassock-wearing 'parasites'. And when the time came, they put it into practice.

The Church was persecuted for many reasons, and here one should remember the opinion of its detractors and persecutors, even though what they expressly stated did not always match their innermost motivations. José Álvarez Junco argues that this long-winded, repeti-tive criticism of the Church, full of nuances, 'responded to fundamen-tally ethical recriminations, rather than to an analysis of the social power of the Church and its consequences'. Naturally, there was a harsh battle between the Church and anticlericalism over basic themes related to the organisation of society and the State. But the issues that gave rise to demonstrations and counter-demonstrations, the burning of convents and violence against the clergy were 'more symbolic and cultural', with strong popular support.[28]

The Catholic clergy was accused of 'betraying the Gospel', 'pharisa-ism', abandoning the original virtues of brotherhood and poverty – a recurring feature in the anarchist press which Gerald Brenan seized on as an explanation. In Brenan's view, anticlerical violence was the expression of a 'deep religious feeling' in an 'intensely religious people who feel they have been deserted and deceived'. This view was shared by some Catholics, who felt that anticlericalism was not only an expression of 'popular rage' manipulated by demagogues and revolutionaries. 'I always maintained that deep down, the burning of churches was an act of faith', Ronald Fraser was told by one of these Catholics, Maurici Serrahima, a lawyer and leading member of *Unió Democràtica*, who gave shelter to eleven Capuchin friars from the

---

[28] José Álvarez Junco, *El emperador del Paralelo. Lerroux y la demagogia populista*, Alianza Editorial, Madrid, 1990, pp. 397–418.

convent at Sarriá, and helped Cardinal Francesc Vidal i Barraquer of Tarragona to flee the country.

In other words, it was an act of protest because, in the eyes of the people, the Church was no longer what it should have been. It was the disenchantment of someone who believed, loved and was betrayed. It came from the idea that the Church should have been on the side of the poor, but it wasn't, and in fact it had not been for many years, except for some of its members. It was a protest against the Church's submission to the well-to-do.[29]

Spain in 1936 had some 110,000 clergy, out of a population of 24 million. Of these, nearly 60,000 were nuns, 35,000 priests and 15,000 monks. According to the study published by Antonio Montero Moreno in 1961, 4,184 diocesan priests, 2,365 monks and 283 nuns were murdered. Twelve bishops and the apostolic administrator of Orihuela met the same fate. Of the 6,832 victims of the anticlerical violence, 839 were killed in July following the coup and 2,055 in August. In other words, 42.35 per cent of the total number of victims met their death in the first forty-four days, and ten of the thirteen bishops were killed before 31 August – irrefutable proof of the swiftness and immediacy of the torment experienced by the clergy.

It was hard to believe that such atrocities could be committed by locals, people whom everyone knew as members of the community. Time and again, descriptions of violence against Church property and persecution of the clergy referred to 'outsiders', 'strangers', 'militiamen' or, in the cities and bigger towns, the 'mob', the 'rabble' or 'the masses'. It was a case of blaming the 'disorderly mobs' who forced the locals to violate rules that would never have been broken but for these 'intruders'. These expressions were also used in the *Causa General* conducted by the Supreme Court prosecutor after the civil war, to gather evidence of 'criminal acts' committed during the 'red domination'.

But there is also evidence to the contrary, suggesting that all these acts had been committed by locals; that, at least, is what was reported by various priests who assessed the damage left behind by the anticlerical

---

[29] Gerald Brenan, *The Spanish Labyrinth*, Cambridge University Press, 1990, p. 245 (originally published 1943); Ronald Fraser, *Recuérdalo tú y recuérdalo a otros. Historia oral de la guerra civil española*, 2 vols., Crítica, Barcelona, 1979, vol. I, p. 207.

turmoil in Aragon and Catalonia, where the militias had passed through. For example, in Aspa in Lérida, 'all Church property was looted and they burnt the churches and altars; also looted were the hermitage of San Sebastián and the palace chapel in this parish, and it was all the work of the local parishioners, with no outsiders involved'.[30]

The fires were witnessed, amid tumult or expressions of horror, by children, women and many others who showed no reaction at all. The 'impassiveness' of most of the inhabitants of these towns and villages was particularly noted in the reports drawn up after the civil war by various bishops. It was the men who burnt the churches, and rarely were the women involved; they would watch the conflagrations from the doorways of their houses. According to many accounts, the locals were 'mesmerised' by the magic of the flames, and rarely confronted the arsonists, as seems to have been the case in the burning down of the Capuchin convent in Igualada.[31]

There were those who were to be seduced by the well-worn argument that the anarchists were responsible, although this anticlerical violence was often taken to excess in many areas dominated by socialists, Communists and republicans. In fact, with the exception of the Basque Country, where only forty-five clergy were murdered, wearing a cassock became a symbol of relentless persecution in the whole of the republican zone, albeit to a lesser degree in Murcia, Albacete, Badajoz and Santander.

The persecution of the clergy transformed the Church into a victim, infecting it with disdain for human rights and the veneration of violence unleashed by the coup d'état, and ruined any faint hopes there might have been for an understanding between the more moderate Catholics and the Republic. From then on, relentless intransigence was the order of the day. And although the anticlerical violence ended a long time before the violence backed by the clergy did, the Church, from Cardinal Isidro Gomá downwards, rejected any mediation or conclusion to the war other than the unconditional surrender of the 'reds' – in other words, the same demand as that made by all the rebel generals with Franco at their head.

---

[30] Manuel Viola, *El martirio de una Iglesia. Lérida, 1939–1936*, Lérida, 1981, p. 198.
[31] Miguel Termens i Graells, *Revolució i guerra civil a Igualada (1936–1939)*, Publicacions de l'Abadia de Montserrat, Barcelona, 1991, p. 54.

Catholicism and anticlericalism were passionately involved in the battle over basic themes related to the organisation of society and the State that was being unleashed in Spanish territory. Religion was extremely useful from the outset, because, as Bruce Lincoln maintains, it proved to be the only element that systematically generated a current of international sympathy for General Franco's Nationalist cause.[32] On the other hand, the violent anticlericalism that broke out with the military rising brought no benefit at all to the republican cause. The fact that the violence of the military rebels was meted out in the name of values as elevated as the Fatherland and religion made things much easier, in comparison with the other side's violence 'in the service of anarchy'. This was how it was perceived in Spain and beyond its frontiers. It was yet another battle that the Republic lost in the eyes of the rest of the world.

[32] Bruce Lincoln, 'Revolutionary exhumations in Spain, July 1936', *Comparative Studies in Society and History*, 27, 2 (1985), pp. 241–60.

8 | *An international war*

Although the Spanish Civil War was clearly internal in its origin, the international situation played a decisive role in the duration, progress and final result of the conflict. The rearmament policies followed by the principal countries of Europe since the beginning of that decade created a climate of uncertainty and crisis that undermined international security. The Soviet Union began a large-scale programme of military and industrial modernisation that was to position it as the leading military power over the next few decades. At the same time, the Nazis, under Hitler, committed themselves to overturning the Versailles agreements and restoring Germany's dominance. Mussolini's Italy followed the same path, and its economy was increasingly devoted to preparing for war. France and the United Kingdom began rearming in 1934, and this process escalated after 1936. The world arms trade doubled between 1932 and 1937. According to Richard Overy, 'the popular antiwar sentiment of the 1920s gradually gave way to the reluctant recognition that major war was once again a serious possibility'.[1]

Under these circumstances, none of these countries showed any interest in stopping the Spanish Civil War. International support for both sides was vital for fighting and continuing the war during the early months. Italian and German aid enabled the military rebels to move the Africa army to the peninsula at the end of July 1936, and Soviet aid made a decisive contribution to the republican defence of Madrid in November 1936. The USSR's military support for the Republic served as a pretext for the Axis powers to increase their military and financial support to Franco's side. These manifestations of support were maintained almost unchanged until the end of the

[1] Richard Overy, 'Warfare in Europe since 1918', in T. C. W. Blanning (ed.), *The Oxford History of Modern Europe*, Oxford University Press, 2000, p. 220.

war, while the rest of Europe, with the United Kingdom at the head, appeared to observe the Non-Intervention Agreement.

The basic ingredients of this international dimension are well known, from the pioneering works of Ángel Viñas in the 1970s, to the most recent studies by Enrique Moradiellos. Ever since Hitler's rise to power at the beginning of 1933, the British and French governments had embarked on an 'appeasement policy', which consisted of avoiding a new war in exchange for accepting the revisionist demands of the Fascist dictatorships, as long as they posed no risk for French or British interests. According to Moradiellos, the response of these two countries 'to the outbreak of the Spanish Civil War and its international implications was at all times subject to the basic objectives of this general appeasement policy'. On the other hand, said Viñas, 'the Third Reich's support was a key element in transforming the 1936 military coup into a civil war, and its development as such'.[2]

The Spanish conflict became one more link in a chain of crises, spreading from Manchuria to Abyssinia via Czechoslovakia, which led to the outbreak of the Second World War. The Spanish Civil War was, in origin, a domestic conflict between Spaniards, but in its progress it evolved into an episode of a European civil war that ended in 1945. In such a heated atmosphere, the civil war could never be a struggle between Spaniards or between revolution and counter-revolution. For many Europeans and North Americans, Spain became the battlefield of an inevitable conflict in which at least three contenders were involved: Fascism, Communism – or revolution – and democracy.

Non-intervention

Barely two weeks after the military rising, the governments of the principal European powers had already shaped their policies with regard to this fledgling conflict in Spain. The British Foreign Office declared 'strict neutrality' and asked the French to do the same. In Paris, Léon Blum went back on his original decision to help the government of the Republic and opted for non-intervention. Germany and Italy were

---

[2] Enrique Moradiellos, *El reñidero de Europa. Las dimensiones internacionales de la guerra civil española*, Península, Barcelona, p. 56; Ángel Viñas, *Franco, Hitler y el estallido de la guerra civil*, Alianza Editorial, Madrid, 2001, p. 518.

willing to help the military rebels. And although Russia would very soon change its posture, it initially kept a guarded distance. Outside Europe, the United States followed the United Kingdom's neutral line. Many other small countries in Europe and South America showed no outward signs of concern, although there was unspoken support for the military rebels. The only country to express clear support for the Republic was Mexico.

The non-intervention policy was an initiative of the French Popular Front government. After discovering on 30 July that the Nazis and Italian Fascists had started to help the military rebels, because two planes sent by Mussolini landed in Algeria by mistake, the French proposed that the principal countries of Europe sign a Non-Intervention in Spain Agreement. In the words of Léon Blum's secretary, it was 'in order to stop others doing what we were unable to do'.[3] Since it could not help the Republic, because that would have created an internal conflict with unforeseen consequences in French society, it would at least force Germany and Italy to call off their support for the rebel side. The posture of non-intervention of the Minister of Foreign Affairs, the radical Ivon Delbos, was strictly enforced from the first week of August. The French High Command also wanted to avoid an intervention that would turn Italy against France and endanger peace in the Mediterranean. France's proposal also included a ban on the export and sale of arms to the republicans and rebels. On 13 August, the government closed the Pyrenees border.

The United Kingdom, through its ambassador in Paris, Sir George Clerk, immediately informed Delbos of the need to speed up the putting into practice of the non-intervention agreement, and in the meantime, above all, not to supply any arms that would jeopardise everything. Clerk made no secret of his sympathies for the military rebels, whom he considered to be the only ones capable of defeating 'anarchy and the soviet influence'; nor did Anthony Eden, the British Foreign Secretary, or the Ambassador in Spain, Sir Henry Chilton, who, instead of returning to Madrid, remained in Hendaye, expecting a swift rebel victory. According to Antony Beevor, 'the naval base of Gibraltar had been flooded with pro-nationalist refugees', and Luís Bolín, Franco's new press officer, and the Duke of Alba, who was also

---

[3] Moradiellos, *El reñidero de Europa*, p. 95.

the Duke of Berwick, influenced the upper echelons of British politics with their declarations on the 'atrocities of the reds'.[4]

Some of these British authorities very soon began to term the members of the republican government in Madrid 'reds'. On 29 July, the British consul in Barcelona, Norman King, who believed that the Spanish were 'a blood-thirsty race', informed the Foreign Office that 'if the government wins and puts down the military rebellion, Spain will rush headlong into the chaos of some form of Bolshevism'.[5] The aristocratic diplomatic circles, the middle class and the Anglican Church authorities, with the exception of the bishop of Cork, supported the military rebels, while the Labour Party, the trade unions and many intellectuals were behind the republican cause. As K. W. Watkins' study showed some time ago, British society suffered a deep schism. And Paul Preston stressed the idea of a 'divided' United Kingdom: while public opinion was 'overwhelmingly' behind the Republic, the inner circle that took the really 'crucial decisions' declared themselves to be in favour of the military rebels. For these conservatives, the Spanish Civil War was also a class conflict, and they knew perfectly well whose side they were on.[6]

London and Washington, who had never shown any sympathy for the Republic during its five years of peace, very soon took a position of what Douglas Little called 'malevolent neutrality'.[7] The non-intervention policy would serve, following the diplomatic objectives set by the Foreign Office, to confine the struggle within the Spanish borders and avoid confrontation with Italy and Germany. This policy put a legal government and a group of military rebels on the same footing.

At the end of August 1936, the twenty-seven European states (all except Switzerland, whose constitution decreed its neutrality) had officially subscribed to the Non-Intervention in Spain Agreement,

---

[4] Antony Beevor, *The Battle for Spain: The Spanish Civil War 1936–1939*, Weidenfeld & Nicolson, 2006, pp. 202–3.

[5] Cited in Enrique Moradiellos, *La pérfida Albión. El gobierno británico y la guerra civil española*, Siglo XXI Editores, Madrid, 1996, p. 61.

[6] Kenneth William Watkins, *Britain Divided: The Effects of the Spanish Civil War on British Political Opinion*, Thomas Nelson & Sons, London, 1963; Paul Preston, *La guerra civil española*, Debate, Barcelona, 2006, pp. 149–50.

[7] Douglas Little, *Malevolent Neutrality: The United States, Great Britain, and the Origins of the Spanish Civil War*, Cornell University Press, Ithaca, NY, 1985.

whereby they deplored 'the tragic events being enacted in Spain', decided 'to strictly abstain from all interference, either direct or indirect, in the internal affairs of this country', and banned 'the exporting ... re-exporting and delivery to Spain, Spanish possessions or the Spanish zone in Morocco, of all types of arms, munitions and war materiel'.[8] The monitoring of this agreement was conducted by a Non-Intervention Committee, set up in London on 9 September under the chairmanship of the Conservative Lord Plymouth, the parliamentary under-secretary to the Foreign Office, and a Non-Intervention Subcommittee, made up of representatives from the states bordering Spain and the major arms producers, including Germany, France, the United Kingdom and the Soviet Union.

In practice, non-intervention was a complete 'farce', as it was termed by people at the time who saw that it put the Republic at a disadvantage with the military rebels. The Soviet Union, which had little faith in the agreement, decided in principle to observe it in order to keep on good terms with France and the United Kingdom. But Germany, Italy and Portugal systematically flouted the commitment and continued sending arms and munitions. For Germany and Italy, intervention in the civil war marked the consolidation of a new diplomatic alliance, which, via the official setting up of the 'Rome–Berlin Axis' in October 1936, was to have major repercussions on international politics in the future. It was made clear that Germany and Italy were not going to respect the agreement they had signed when, on 28 August 1936, Admiral Wilhelm Canaris and General Mario Roatta, the heads of their respective countries' military intelligence, met in Rome and decided to 'continue (in spite of the arms embargo) supplying war materiel and munitions deliveries, in response to the requests of General Franco'.[9]

The reasons for the Nazis' decisive intervention in the Spanish Civil War had much to do with military strategy, as well as certain economic considerations and their alliance policies. As Walther L. Bernecker observed, from the very start, the Nazis and their propaganda machine, controlled by Paul Joseph Goebbels, spread the idea that the war in Spain was a confrontation between 'Fascists' and 'Marxists', although in internal reports and discussions, this anti-

[8] The document is reproduced in Moradiellos, *El reñidero de Europa*, p. 99.
[9] Ibid., p. 101.

Communist ideological view carried less weight. Blaming the Soviet Union and international Communism for causing the Spanish Civil War, an argument which both Hitler and Franco clung to, bore rich fruit for the Nazis, as was perceived by the French ambassador in Berlin, André-François Poncet, in a report sent to Delbos on 22 July: it urged 'peace-loving countries' not to fall out with Germany, thereby making it the principal guarantee against the Bolshevik peril.[10]

After the Second World War, Hermann Goering, the Third Reich's Minister of Aviation, declared before the International Tribunal at Nuremburg that he had urged Hitler to intervene in favour of Franco, 'firstly to counteract there the spread of Communism, and secondly, to try out my young air force ... fighters, bombers and anti-aircraft guns, thus enabling me to see whether the materiel was fit for purpose'.[11] The Nazis used Spanish soil as a testing ground, and the volunteers of the Condor Legion, both officers and men, were paid, in Preston's words, executive salaries to fight in Spain.[12]

Hitler considered, as Ángel Viñas' research showed, that aiding Franco favoured the interests of Germany's foreign policy. It meant overthrowing the *Frente Popular* forces in Spain, thereby avoiding the creation of a leftist block in Europe led by France. For Hitler, the defeat of France, his prime objective for realising his expansionist ambitions in central and eastern Europe, would be much easier with a Spain under the control of anti-Communist generals. A victory for the Republic, on the other hand, would reinforce Spain's links with France and the Soviet Union, the two powers, one in the east and the other in the west, that opposed the Third Reich's imperialist aspirations. Hitler said as much to Wilhelm von Faupel, a retired general and the Reich's first chargé d'affaires to Franco, in November 1936: 'Your mission consists solely and exclusively in ensuring that, once the war is over (with Franco victorious), Spain's foreign policy is not influenced by Paris, London or Moscow'.[13]

---

[10] Walther L. Bernecker, *Guerra en España, 1936–1939*, Síntesis, Madrid, 1996, pp. 47–8.
[11] Ibid., pp. 49–50.
[12] Preston, *La guerra civil española*, p. 165.
[13] Quoted in Ángel Viñas, *La Alemania nazi y el 18 de julio. Antecedentes de la intervención alemana en la guerra civil*, Alianza Editorial, Madrid, 1977, p. 363.

Although the Italian Fascists had had much more contact with Spanish monarchist and far-right groups during the Second Republic than the Nazis, Fascist Italy, as a political regime, like Nazi Germany, took no part in the preparations for the coup that unleashed the civil war. However, a few days after the military rising, Mussolini acceded to Franco's request for aid and took this decision when he learnt that Hitler was going to support Franco once it was clear that France and the United Kingdom were not going to intervene. Mussolini's propaganda also exploited the ideological aspect of his intervention, anti-Communism, but his reasons for supporting the military rebels, like Hitler's, had much more to do with the benefits that he reckoned this intervention would bring to his foreign policy: it would weaken France's and the United Kingdom's military position and provide an ally in the western Mediterranean.

Nazi and Fascist military aid was considerable and decisive for Franco's victory. Between the end of July and the middle of October 1936, twenty German Junkers 52 and six Heinkel 51 fighters transported over 13,000 men of the Africa army and 270 tonnes of materiel. Later, with the Condor Legion, which from November 1936 took part in all the major battles of the war, Nazi Germany sent 600 further aircraft that dropped a total of approximately 21 million tonnes of bombs. For their part, the Italians began by sending twelve Savoia 81 bombers to transport the Moroccan troops to the mainland, and, during the course of the war, according to John F. Coverdale, their military aid consisted of materiel worth over 6 billion lira (64 million pounds sterling at 1939 exchange rates), including nearly 1,000 aircraft, 200 field guns, 1,000 armoured vehicles and several thousand machine guns and automatic weapons.[14]

With not so much publicity, but still significant, was the aid provided by the dictatorship of Antonio de Oliveira Salazar. Portugal offered the rebels a logistics base for their arms purchases, and in the early days of the conflict, as well as handing over to rebel Spain all the republicans who had fled from the repression in Andalusia and Extremadura, the Portuguese government gave them the use of the country's roads, ports and railways to connect the north-western

---

[14] John F. Coverdale, *La intervención fascista en la guerra civil española*, Alianza Editorial, Madrid, 1979, pp. 152–71, 372–3. (Original English edition published by Princeton University Press, 1975.)

zone with Andalusia. Salazar's aid was also very useful in the defence of the rebel cause in the Non-Intervention Committee, the League of Nations and other international fora. The danger was posed by the 'reds', not Italy or Germany, and this was how Armando Monteiro, the Portuguese Foreign Minister, expressed it to Anthony Eden on a visit to London on 30 July 1936: 'a victory for the army would not necessarily mean an Italian- or German-type political victory, while a victory for the reds would be a disaster – a victory for anarchy, with serious consequences for France, and therefore for Europe, where the force of Communism is now overwhelming'.[15]

International diplomacy was making its move just when the Second Republic's diplomatic corps had been left divided and fragmented as a consequence of the coup d'état. Most of the embassy and consular staff in the main countries of Europe abandoned the Republic, and those who had not done so were actually serving the military rebels' cause. The ambassadors in Rome, Berlin, Paris and Washington resigned in the first few weeks, after doing all they could to hamper republican attempts to redefine its foreign policy. The socialist Julio Álvarez del Vayo, the new Foreign Minister in Largo Caballero's first government, formed on 4 September 1936, calculated that 90 per cent of the diplomatic and consular corps had deserted. According to a study by Marina Casanova, 'only sixty-two diplomats remained loyal to the Republic throughout the war'.[16]

In order to obtain foreign support, both the government of the Republic in Madrid and the *Junta de Defensa Nacional* in Burgos had to reconstruct and create their respective diplomatic corps. The Republic did so with prominent intellectuals and university professors, almost all of them with a socialist background: Fernando de los Ríos was the ambassador to Washington; Luís Jiménez de Asúa in Prague; Marcelino Pascua in Moscow; Luís Araquistain in Paris and Pablo de Azcárate, the only one who had actually had any experience of foreign service, in London. The military rebels, on the other hand, boasted distinguished members of the aristocracy and diplomatic and financial circles, with good connections with the elite

---

[15] Quoted in Moradiellos, *El reñidero de Europa*, p. 100.
[16] Marina Casanova Gómez, 'Depuración de funcionarios diplomáticos durante la guerra civil', *Espacio, tiempo y forma*, Series V, *Historia Contemporánea*, 1 (1988), p. 372.

groups of international diplomacy, such as the Duke of Alba and Juan de la Cierva in London; José María Quiñones de León in Paris; and the Marquis of Portago and the Baron of Las Torres in Berlin. On 4 August 1936, José Yanguas Messía, who had been Foreign Minister in Primo de Rivera's dictatorship, and recently appointed head of the Diplomatic Office of the *Junta de Defensa Nacional* in Burgos, reported that 'the general tone of the diplomatic situation is favourable to our movement ... because all over the world the overwhelming influence of the totalitarian States is being felt', and he forecast that 'the capture of Madrid' would 'be the determining factor for the official recognition of the absolute legitimacy of our movement'.[17]

The 'capture of Madrid' was not possible because, among other reasons, when what seemed to be the final battle began, in autumn 1936, the first shipments of Soviet military aid to the Republic broke the pattern of continuous rebel victories and republican defeats that had been the norm during the summer. The first Soviet shipments of heavy weaponry arrived at the port of Cartagena on 4 and 15 October. The troops led by Franco, now head of the rebels, were advancing unfalteringly on Madrid. The Italians and Germans had managed to strengthen the system of military aid to the rebels, while the United Kingdom and France were strictly observing the Non-Intervention Agreement. In an international context, all this seemed to favour the military rebels. Things changed when Stalin decided to intervene. Two months had gone by since the conflict had broken out.

Moscow did not even have an ambassador in Spain in July 1936, because the Republic, despite having established diplomatic relations with the Soviet Union in July 1933, had never put this agreement into practice. On 25 July, José Giral, the new Prime Minister after the coup d'état, asked the USSR, through the Soviet ambassador in Paris, for arms and munitions 'of all types and in large quantities', to defeat the military rebellion. But Stalin, worried about the German threat after Hitler's rise to power, and aware of the need to gain the cooperation of France and the United Kingdom to counter this threat, did not respond to this request. For Stalin and Soviet foreign policy,

[17] Quoted by Enrique Moradiellos in 'El mundo ante el avispero español: intervención y no intervención extranjera en la guerra civil', in Santos Juliá (ed.), *Historia de España de Menéndez Pidal. República y guerra civil*, 42 vols., Espasa Calpe, Madrid, 2004, vol. XL, p. 253.

the outbreak of an armed conflict in Spain created a serious dilemma. It was not in his interest to leave the Republic abandoned, something that would strengthen Hitler's position, but neither did he want to harm his relations with the democratic powers. If he supported the Republic, it would fuel the theory that behind any aid he might give lay 'international Communism'.

At first, the Spanish Civil War provided no advantage to the interests of the Soviet Union, and on 22 August, Maxim Litvinov, the Foreign Affairs Commissar, signed the Non-Intervention Agreement. A few days later, he officially stated that he would not be supporting the Spanish Republic with arms, and he appointed an ambassador for Madrid, the diplomat Marcel Rosenberg. The instructions given to him were very clear: 'Our support would give Germany and Italy the excuse to organise an open invasion and aid of such volume that we would be unable to equal it'. However, the instructions went on, 'if there is evidence that in spite of the non-intervention declaration aid is still being given to the rebels, then we might change our decision'.[18]

The evidence that Hitler and Mussolini were aiding the rebels, in spite of the Non-Intervention Agreement, alarmed Stalin. If the Republic were defeated quickly, France's strategic position with regard to Germany would be radically weakened, and the increase of Nazi and Fascist power would also have negative repercussions for the Soviet Union. Stalin prepared the way. He notified the Non-Intervention Committee that he would be forced to breach the agreement if Germany and Italy continued doing so, and he calculated the potential costs of the aid so that the British government did not see it as support for a revolution that was spreading throughout the republican zone, and the Nazis did not take it as open intervention. Preston maintains that Stalin helped the Spanish Republic not to hasten its victory, but rather to keep it in existence long enough to keep Hitler occupied in a costly venture.[19]

In October, the first shipments of arms arrived in Spain. The Soviet Union began to do what Italy, Germany and Portugal were already doing: breaching the non-intervention accords without officially

---

[18] Quoted in Antonio Elorza and Marta Bizcarrondo, *Queridos camaradas. La Internacional Comunista y España, 1919–1939*, Planeta, Barcelona, 1999, p. 460.

[19] Preston, *La guerra civil española*, p. 162.

abandoning this policy. From that moment on, Soviet military aid to the Republic – paid for, as we shall see, with the Bank of Spain's gold reserves – was continuous until the end of the war and was vital for sustaining the Republic's cause against Franco's army and the support of Hitler and Mussolini. As well as war materiel, a substantial quantity of aircraft and armoured vehicles, numbering some 700 and 400 units respectively, the USSR also sent food, fuel, clothes and a considerable number (around 2,000 in total) of pilots, engineers, advisers and members of the secret police, the NKVD, under the command of Alexander Orlov. The Russian people contributed millions of roubles for the purchase of clothes and food, generating, according to Daniel Kowalsky, the biggest mobilisation of foreign humanitarian aid in history, destined for the Iberian peninsula.[20]

At the same time as the first arms shipments, the first foreign volunteers for the International Brigades began to arrive, recruited and organised by the Communist International, which was well aware of the impact of the Spanish Civil War on the world, and of the desire of many anti-Fascists to take part in this struggle. With the Soviet intervention and the International Brigades, the Nazis and Fascists increased their material aid to Franco's army and also sent thousands of professional servicemen and volunteer fighters. The war was not a Spanish domestic matter. It became internationalised, thereby increasing its brutality and destruction. Spanish territory became a testing ground for new weaponry that was being developed during those rearmament years, prior to a great war that was on the horizon.

Foreigners

The decision to send volunteers to fight in the Spanish Civil War was adopted on 18 September 1936 by the Comintern Secretariat. The recruitment centre was Paris, and the organisational aspects were put into the hands of French Communist Party leaders, with André Marty at the head, and other leading agents of the International, such as Luigi Longo ('Gallo') and Josep Broz ('Tito'). According to Antonio Elorza and Marta Bizcarrondo, this decision 'is well documented

---

[20] Daniel Kowalsky, *La Unión Soviética y la guerra civil española*, Crítica, Barcelona, 2003. (English edition: *Stalin and the Spanish Civil War*, Columbia University Press, New York, 2004.)

and belies the typical interpretations that have hitherto been circulating' since the beginning of the Communist International, that the International Brigades were spontaneously made up of 'freedom volunteers', and other interpretations that present them as 'the army of the Comintern', 'an instrument of Stalin's Machiavellian policy with regard to Spain'. There were a good many in the Brigades who were Stalinists, especially at the organisational level, but there were thousands who were not.[21]

They started arriving in Spain in October, from Poland, Italy, Germany and other countries under the control of dictatorships and Fascism, although it was France that provided the largest number. Those from North America arrived later, at the end of the year, and the Lincoln Battalion, the subject of some of the legends most widely spread by writers and intellectuals, did not enter into action until the Battle of the Jarama, in February 1937. Before them, several hundred left-wing sympathisers, who at the time of the coup happened to be in Barcelona, attending the Popular (also known as Anti-Fascist) Olympics, organised as an alternative event to the Olympic Games being held in Berlin, had already joined the anarchist and socialist militias.

The number of brigadists varies according to sources, from the 100,000 quoted by the Nationalists, to exaggerate their influence and the significance of international Communism, to the 40,000 referred to by Hugh Thomas in his classic study on the civil war. One of the latest and most exhaustive studies on the International Brigades, by Michel Lefebvre and Rémi Skoutelsky, provides a figure of nearly 35,000, accepted today by quite a few historians, although there were never more than 20,000 combatants at a time, and in 1938 the number had reduced considerably.[22] Some 10,000 volunteers died in combat; they came from over fifty countries, with France providing almost 9,000, while barely 150 came from Portugal. The military reports logging their presence in the training base in Albacete tell us that the two greatest concentrations of volunteers there coincided with the first few months of their intervention, from October 1936 to March 1937, and with the battles of Teruel and Aragón, from December 1937 to April 1938.

[21] Elorza and Bizcarrondo, *Queridos camaradas*, pp. 459–63.
[22] Michel Lefebvre and Rémi Skoutelsky, *Brigadas Internacionales. Imágenes recuperadas*, Lunwerg Editores, Barcelona, 2003.

Many of the volunteers arriving in Spain were unemployed, but many others left behind their jobs. There were also adventurers, looking for excitement, intellectuals and middle-class professionals, who were the ones who later wrote about their experiences. Most of them, however, were convinced that Fascism was an international threat and that Spain was the right venue to combat it. So wrote an English worker, neither a poet nor an intellectual, in a letter to his daughter, reproduced by Watkins in his study on the division caused by the Spanish Civil War within British society: 'Now I want to explain to you why I left England. You will have heard about the War going on here. From every country in the world working people like myself have come to Spain to stop Fascism here. So although I am miles away from you, I am fighting to protect you and all children in England as well as people all over the world'.[23]

These manual labourers, making up 80 per cent of the volunteers from the United Kingdom, had felt drawn by the Communist Party, which provided them with protection and a solid doctrine to adhere to. This was also the time that vast numbers of exiles from eastern and central Europe and the Balkan States converged on Paris, fleeing from Fascist and military repression. From there, they went through Barcelona and Valencia, to end up in Albacete, where they were galvanised into action by André Marty, the head of the International Brigades, about whom much has been written, including the story that he had 500 brigadists shot, although no one has presented any proof as to when and how 'the butcher of Albacete' did this.

During the first few months of recruitment, five International Brigades were organised, numbered from XI to XV. The XI, under the command of the Soviet General Emilio Cléber, and the XII, under the Hungarian writer Maté Zalka 'Luckács', played a decisive role in the republican defence of Madrid in November 1936, although some authors, including Beevor, consider that their exploits were exaggerated by the Francoists and conservative and anti-Communist Britons, such as the ambassador Henry Chilton, who thought that Madrid was being defended by foreigners only. The Thälmann battalion, made up of German and some British Communists, had its first taste of action in the battle for Madrid. One of them, the Briton

[23] Watkins, *Britain Divided*, p. 170.

Esmond Romilly, later recalled many of the dead in that battle: 'I remember hearing them speak of their lives as exiles ... persecuted by the immigration laws and relentlessly persecuted – even in England – by the Nazi secret police'.[24]

There were also many foreigners fighting with Franco's troops. They, like the International Brigades, came from a wide range of countries. Not many of them were volunteers, because the majority of those who fought, particularly Germans and Italians, were regular soldiers, well prepared, who were paid in their countries of origin. Chief among the genuine volunteers, between 1,000 and 1,500, were Irish Catholics, under the command of General Eoin O'Duffy, who subscribed to the idea of a crusade as held by the Spanish Catholic Church and Pope Pius XI in the Vatican. They bore various religious emblems, rosaries, images of the *agnus dei* and the Sacred Heart, as did the Carlists, and they left Ireland, according to O'Duffy himself, to fight Christianity's battle against Communism. They only fought in the Battle of the Jarama, in February 1937, where, in view of their lack of military experience, they failed to acquit themselves well, and a few months later they returned home.

As well as these Irish 'blueshirts', among Franco's troops were White Russians who had honed their skills in the struggle against the Bolsheviks, a mixed group of Fascists and anti-Semites from eastern Europe, and some 300 Frenchmen from the ultra-right *Croix de Feu* making up the Jeanne d'Arc battalion. The almost 10,000 *Viriatos* (Portuguese volunteers) who had enlisted and were paid in Portugal were not volunteers, however. Although Franco's camp always presented them as such, with all these new forces and the intensive recruitment of Rif tribesmen for the Africa army, Franco's troops numbered some 200,000 men by the end of 1936.

In answer to the International Brigades, Germany and Italy sent tens of thousands of soldiers to fight alongside the military rebels. So that there would be no doubt as to the purpose of this intervention, on 18 November 1936, the month of the major Francoist offensive on Madrid, the governments of the two Axis powers officially recognised Franco and his *Junta Técnica del Estado*, set up on 2 October to replace the *Junta de Defensa Nacional*, and soon afterwards the first

---

[24] Quoted in Preston, *La guerra civil española*, p. 181.

two ambassadors arrived in Burgos: General Wilhelm von Faupel and the Fascist journalist, Roberto Cantalupo.

At around this time, Hitler decided to send an airborne unit that would fight as an independent corps, with its own officers, in the Francoist ranks. Called the Condor Legion, it arrived in Spain by sea in the middle of November under the command of General Hugo von Sperle, and later of Colonel Baron Wolfram von Richthofen, both Luftwaffe officers. It consisted of some 140 aircraft, divided into four fighter squadrons with Heinkel 51 biplanes, plus another four squadrons of Junkers 52s, backed up by one battalion of forty-eight tanks and another of sixty anti-aircraft guns. Thus the Spanish Civil War became the Luftwaffe's testing ground, a rehearsal for the fighters and bombers that would shortly afterwards be used in the Second World War.

Research by Raymond L. Proctor reveals that the total number of Condor Legion combatants during the course of the war amounted to 19,000 men, including pilots, tank crews and artillerymen, although there were never more than 5,500 at a time, as they were frequently relieved so that as many soldiers as possible could gain experience. The Condor Legion took part in nearly all the military operations conducted during the civil war, and 371 of its members lost their lives in action.[25]

A much larger contribution was made by the Italians, who began to arrive in Spain in December 1936 and January 1937, after the secret pact of friendship signed by Franco and Mussolini on 28 November. Up to that time, the Italians piloting the Savoia 81s and Fiat fighters had been fighting in the Foreign Legion. After the signing of this pact, Mussolini organised the *Corpo di Truppe Volontarie* (CTV), commanded by General Mario Roatta until the disaster at Guadalajara in March 1937, and then by Generals Ettore Bastico, Mario Berti and Gastone Gambara. The CTV had a permanent force of 40,000 soldiers, and its total number, according to figures published by John Coverdale, rose to 72,775 men: 43,129 from the army and 29,646 from the Fascist militia. They were joined by 5,699 men from the *Aviazione Legionaria*, thus bringing the total number of Italian combatants to 78,474, much higher than the German or International Brigades figures.[26]

[25] Raymond L. Proctor, *Hitler's Luftwaffe in the Spanish Civil War*, Greenwood Press, Westport, CT, 1983.
[26] Coverdale, *La intervención fascista en la guerra civil española*, pp. 152–71, 372–3.

Thus tens of thousands of foreigners fought in the Spanish Civil War. It was, in fact, a European civil war, with the tacit sanction of the British and French governments. A little over 100,000 fought on Franco's side: 78,000 Italians, 19,000 Germans, 10,000 Portuguese, plus more than 1,000 volunteers from other countries, not counting the 70,000 Moroccans who made up the native *Regulares*. On the Republican side, the figures given by Rémi Skoutelsky show nearly 35,000 volunteers in the International Brigades and 2,000 Soviets, of whom 600 were non-combatant advisers. Contrary to the myth of the Communist and revolutionary threat, what in fact hit Spain through an open military intervention was Fascism.

Furthermore, the Fascists went home later, with the end of the war and Franco's victory, while the members of the International Brigades had laid down their arms beforehand. On 21 September 1938, Juan Negrín, the Prime Minister of the Republic, announced in Geneva, before the League of Nations General Assembly, the immediate, unconditional withdrawal of all non-Spanish combatants in the republican army, in the hope that Franco's camp would do the same. At the time, about one-third of all those who had come to fight against Fascism were still in Spain, and on 28 October, one month after their withdrawal from the front, the International Brigades paraded in Barcelona in front of over 250,000 people. Presiding over the farewell ceremony were Manuel Azaña, Juan Negrín, Lluís Companys and Generals Rojo and Riquelme. 'You can leave with pride. You have made history ... you are a heroic example of the solidarity and ubiquity of democracy', they were told by Dolores Ibárruri, *La Pasionaria*. 'We shall never forget you, and when the leaves once more begin to bud on the olive branch of peace, together with the victory laurels of the Spanish Republic, come back!'[27]

They did not return, because the Republic was defeated a few months later, and besides, many of them, close to 10,000, had died on Spanish soil, and another 7,000 were missing. Some of those who survived later became distinguished figures, writers and politicians, in their respective countries, including Josep Broz ('Tito'), Pietro Nenni, Luigi Longo, Walter Ulbricht and André Malraux.

At the same time as the International Brigades were leaving Spain, Mussolini withdrew 10,000 combatants 'as a goodwill gesture'

---

[27] Quoted in Preston, *La guerra civil española*, p. 300.

towards the Non-Intervention Committee, just one-quarter of those who were still fighting alongside Franco's army. They were seen off in Cádiz by Generals Queipo de Llano and Millán Astray, and received in Naples by King Victor Manuel III. The last units of the Condor Legion were transported to Germany by sea after the victory parade of 19 May 1939. They were received in the port of Hamburg by Hermann Goering, Nazi Germany's Air Minister.

The Republic spent as much money losing the war as the Francoists did winning it. To pay for the war expenses, the Republic used the country's gold reserves. Franco resorted to Italian and German loans. The amount of war materiel entering republican Spain was lower than that received by Franco, and it was of poorer quality. So how did the two sides finance the war?

The gold of Moscow and the financing of the war

The Republic and its government had to defend themselves after 18 July 1936 in a war that they had not started. And they had the resources to do so. They had the gold and silver reserves of the Bank of Spain, which, as Indalecio Prieto said shortly after the start of the conflict, belonged to the legitimate Spanish government, the only entity that could touch them. This money was vital for waging a war lasting nearly three years against the military rebels and the backing of their German and Italian allies. 'Without gold', wrote Pablo Martín Aceña, 'the regime would have collapsed in a matter of weeks'. And for this reason, as well as on the battlefields and in the chancelleries, the Spanish Civil War was also fought 'in the sedate offices of Finance Ministers and governors of central banks'.[28]

The gold and silver reserves of the Bank of Spain were stored in the basement of its headquarters in the Plaza de la Cibeles. They amounted to 707 tonnes in ingots and coins, with a value at that time of 805 million dollars. It was one of the richest banks in the world, and a large proportion of these coins, particularly dollar deposits, had been there since the First World War, a time when the economic growth caused by Spain's neutrality enabled it to purchase vast amounts of gold on the international market.

[28] Pablo Martín Aceña, *El oro de Moscú y el oro de Berlín*, Taurus, Madrid, 2001, pp. 23–5.

On 21 July 1936, when the fate of the coup d'état was still being decided in certain Spanish cities, the new Finance Minister in Giral's government, the left-wing republican Enrique Ramos, ordered the Bank of Spain to organise the urgent transfer of various tonnes of gold to Paris. After negotiating various bureaucratic procedures, including a meeting of the Bank of Spain board attended by the five members who had not gone over to the rebel side, the first consignment, approximately 40 tonnes, was sent by air, for which the republican Treasury received 507 million francs, a sum that was used to purchase arms and munitions before the Non-Intervention Treaty came into effect.

Most of the gold reserves, however, remained in Madrid, and at the end of August, the Africa army troops were threatening the capital. On 4 September, José Giral, in charge of a government made up of republicans only – even though many areas of power had been controlled by workers' organisations since the military rising – handed over the reins to Francisco Largo Caballero; he formed a new government consisting mainly of socialists, but with a small number of republicans, one member of the Basque Nationalist Party, and two Communist ministers. It also saw the return of Indalecio Prieto, as Navy and Air Minister. Largo Caballero took charge of the War Ministry, and Juan Negrín, a socialist deputy since the Constituent Cortes, Finance.

On Saturday 12 September, the government, following a proposal from Negrín, decided to remove the Bank of Spain's gold reserves from Madrid. The following day, Negrín relayed this decision to Luís Nicolau d'Olwer, the Governor of the Bank of Spain, who had been Finance Minister in the provisional government of the Republic in 1931. It was a decision forced on the government by the rebel troops encircling Madrid, to prevent the gold falling into the hands of the enemies of the Republic. The destination of the gold, Negrín told him, was to be the magazines of La Algameca, in the naval base of Cartagena. The transfer was to be overseen by Francisco Méndez Aspe, whom Negrín appointed Director-General of the Treasury.

The Bank of Spain board was highly critical of this measure, and the few members who had supposedly remained loyal to the Republic deserted. The only member to stay in his post, Lorenzo Martínez Fresneda, who represented the private shareholders, 'did not waste any opportunity', says Martín Aceña, 'to leak secret deliberations' to his ex-colleagues who had gone over to the rebel side. We know this because, at the same time as the decision was taken to transfer the gold to Cartagena, a meeting of the *Consejo del Banco de España nacional* was held in Burgos, under the chairmanship of Pedro Pan, the Deputy-Governor at the time of the rising. Pedro Pan and the rest of the board that supported the military rebels thereupon decided to stop the Republic from using the gold to defend its cause.[29]

The gold bars and bags of coins were packed into wooden crates, which were taken to the Mediodía station at nearby Atocha in trucks escorted by carabineros and socialist militias. The first freight wagon to Cartagena left at dawn on 15 September and the transfer was completed on 21 September. In all, 560 tonnes of gold were transferred. It was the best security the government could have to carry on fighting. The decision to store it in Cartagena, at that time a much safer place than Madrid, was adopted by the government unanimously.

However, the gold did not stay for long in this Mediterranean port. The non-intervention policy was working with the Republic, but the western democracies were not doing anything to stop the supply of aid to the rebel army. Because of this, and in view of the Republic's desperate military situation, Arthur Stashevski, a commissar of the Soviet Union, suggested to Negrín that his government look after the gold in exchange for ensuring a permanent supply of arms. On 15 October, Largo Caballero wrote to the Soviet ambassador, Marcel Rosenberg, to tell him that he had taken the decision 'to ask you to propose to your government that it agree to a quantity of gold, some 5,000 tonnes, being deposited in the Soviet Union People's Finance Commissariat'.[30] Some days later, in a lightning operation, Spanish sailors and Russian tank crews loaded four merchant ships with 7,800 crates containing 510 tonnes of gold. The ships left Cartagena Naval Base on 25 October, bound for the port of Odessa. From there, the gold was transported by train to Moscow, where it arrived at the beginning of November.

The republican government always maintained that, with the phony policy of non-intervention imposed by the democracies, they had no alternative but to confide in the Soviet Union. More recent studies have questioned the timing and wisdom of this crucial decision.

[29] Ibid., p. 64.
[30] Ibid., p. 92.

Paul Preston agrees with Ángel Viñas when he maintains that banking circles in England and France had already shown their hostility towards the Republic by freezing Spanish assets, practically blocking any credit and systematically putting obstacles in the way of financial transactions. The Soviet Union was the only country that guaranteed the supply of arms and food in exchange for gold. On the other hand, Pablo Martín Aceña states that this decision was hastily adopted and the other alternatives, such as France or the United States, 'were not seriously examined'.[31]

What lies beyond any doubt, following the exhaustive study made by Ángel Viñas several years ago, is the fact that the money raised by the sale of the gold, some 518 million dollars, was spent in its entirety on war materiel. Almost one-third of this money stayed in the Soviet Union to pay for the supplies sent to Spain by the Foreign Trade Commissariat, and the rest was transferred to the *Banque Commerciale pour l'Europe du Nord* in Paris. Furthermore, between July 1936 and January 1937, the Bank of France acquired 174 tonnes of gold, one-quarter of the total reserves, for which the Republic's Treasury received 195 million dollars.

In conclusion, as a result of the sale of these gold reserves and other financial dealings, the republican authorities obtained 714 million dollars, and this was the financial cost of the civil war for the Republic. Three-quarters of the gold went to Moscow and one-quarter to Paris, although the Francoist authorities made no mention of this 'Paris gold'. They did, however, make sure that everyone knew about the 'Moscow gold', which they said had been stolen by the Republic and handed over to Stalin without anything in return.

The directors of the Soviet Union's Central Bank (Gosbank) made sure they charged for all their services. In Russia there was no Spanish gold left and the gold reserves had practically run out by August 1938. However, the detailed study by Gerald Howson shows that many of the rifles sold were 'old museum pieces with hardly any ammunition' and others were in a very poor state of repair. The Republic's go-betweens had to negotiate with arms dealers and acquire obsolete

---

[31] Ibid., pp. 105–9, 113–14. The ground-breaking, and what might well be considered the definitive study, judging by the figures, was Ángel Viñas, *El oro de Moscú. Alfa y omega de un mito franquista*, Grijalbo, Barcelona, 1979, later summarised in *Guerra, dinero y dictadura*, Crítica, Barcelona, 1984, pp. 168–204, from where the information here is taken.

equipment for which they had to pay much more than the true cost. Franco, on the other hand, had a constant, direct supply of high-technology arms from Germany and Italy at his disposal.[32]

The financial cost of the war on the Francoist side was very similar, between 694 and 716 million dollars, but Franco had to use credit to pay his costs, because he did not have any gold. And from what we learn from the most reliable studies on this matter, the head of the military rebels had no trouble financing his war. It was Hermann Goering, Hitler's right-hand man, who first designed the strategy for obtaining economic advantages, food, raw materials and minerals in exchange for supplying arms to the military rebels. Two companies were set up for this purpose. The *Compañía Hispano-Marroquí de Transporte* (HISMA), founded in Tetuán on 31 July 1936 by Fernando de Carranza, a naval captain and friend of Franco's, and Johannes Bernhardt, a Nazi businessman who distributed German products in Tetuán, took charge of financing the transporting of the Africa army to the mainland and the first arms purchases for the Africa army. A few months later, in October 1936, a parallel company was set up in Berlin, the *Rohstoff-und-Waren-Kompensation Handelsgesellschaft* (ROWAK), under the absolute control of Goering, which, together with HIMSA, established the trade monopoly between Germany and rebel Spain. The most valuable exports were always diverted to Germany and this enabled the two companies to control two-thirds of the bilateral Hispano-German trade.

However, the most useful aid that the Germans and Italians sent to Franco was in the form of loans: between 413 and 456 million dollars from Italy and close to 240 million dollars from Germany. The Francoist authorities became indebted to the Axis powers and they offset this by progressively increasing their exports to these two countries. Germany and Italy became Spain's largest customers, to the detriment of the United Kingdom and France. When the civil war was over, Germany was the Spanish market's largest customer and supplier.

Robert Whealey's research on how Franco financed his war has also provided conclusive data. The military rebels were not only helped by

---

[32] Gerald Howson, *Armas para España. La historia no contada de la guerra civil española*, Península, Barcelona, 2000, pp. 17–20. (Originally published in English: *Arms for Spain: The Untold Story of the Spanish Civil War*, St. Martin's Press, New York, 1999.)

the Axis powers: some of the most important capitalists and businessmen in the United Kingdom, France and the United States supported their cause from the beginning, because they saw the Spanish republicans as socialists, anarchists and Communists, even though they said that they were fighting for democracy. A good example of this, says Whealey, was the British company Rio Tinto, the biggest mining company in Spain, which cooperated with the rebel government from August until the end of the war, selling its minerals to the HISMA-ROWAK partnership. Then there were the Anglo-American oil companies, Texaco, Shell and others, who earned vast profits, some 20 million dollars, from their oil sales to Franco throughout the war. Without this oil, Franco's war machine would not have worked, since Italy and Germany, like Spain, depended on Anglo-American oil for their supplies. Franco received 3,500,000 tonnes of oil on credit, more than twice the amount of oil imported by the Republic; some of these oil magnates also hampered trade to the Republic and blocked credits in its banking system.

According to Whealey, the military rebels' juntas and governments received from the Axis, between July 1936 and March 1939, aid amounting to 637 million dollars, to which must be added 76 million dollars of exports to countries in which the dollar and sterling were the dominant currencies. These 76 million dollars, plus the moral backing of international capitalism, confirm, says Whealey, that the Non-Intervention Committee, which began to operate in September 1936 under the tutelage of the Foreign Ministers of France and the United Kingdom, was a 'farce'. The multinationals of the dollar and sterling market 'helped to crush the hopes of the Spanish republicans'.[33]

Economic aid also reached Franco from the richest capitalists in Spain, who made their fortunes available to the military rebels to annihilate the 'reds'. Juan March contributed 15 million pounds sterling, and Alfonso XIII, who in exile had supported the rebel cause from the beginning – 'your first soldier is me', he said to Generals Mola and Franco – donated 10 million dollars, part of the funds

[33] Robert Whealey, 'How Franco financed his war – reconsidered', in Martin Blinkhorn (ed.), *Spain in Conflict 1931–1939: Democracy and Its Enemies*, Sage Publications, London, 1986, pp. 244–63, developed in more detail in his *Hitler and Spain: The Nazi Role in the Spanish Civil War*, University Press of Kentucky, Lexington, 1989.

that he had managed to transfer abroad after his fall.[34] In addition, a 'national subscription' provided the rebels with jewels and gold coins; the donations were made either voluntarily or under coercion. Lists of some of the principal benefactors were published in the press, and this encouraged others to donate so that they would not be tainted as being 'disloyal'.

In the closing years of Franco's dictatorship, certain pro-Franco military historians, such as Ramón and Jesús Salas Larrazábal and Ricardo de la Cierva, attempted to show that the republicans and the military rebels had received the same amount of materiel, that foreign participation was not the factor that tipped the balance in favour of Franco, and that the claim that non-intervention had harmed the republicans was made up by the Communists and the International Left who sympathised with the Republic.

However, the foremost experts on the financing of the war and its international dimension, from Viñas to Martín Aceña, and including Howson and Moradiellos, have pointed out the imbalance in favour of the Nationalist cause not only in terms of war materiel, but also in terms of logistic, diplomatic and financial aid. The Republic had money from the sale of gold reserves at its disposal, an amount very similar to that provided to Franco in foreign aid, but the problem lay in the difficulties it had in legally purchasing arms from democratic countries. As Howson has pointed out, gold and foreign currency were not enough, because the embargo and restrictions imposed by the Non-Intervention Agreement forced successive governments under Giral, Caballero and Negrín to fall into the clutches of arms dealers, who demanded exorbitant prices and commissions and blackmailed politicians and civil servants. As a result, the Republic often had to buy overpriced and obsolete equipment, disarmed planes or bombers that had no bomb bays. Russia, Poland and other countries were continually swindling the Republic. As Martín Aceña put it, 'shoddy weaponry and bribes cost Negrín's treasury several, perhaps as much as a hundred, million dollars'.[35]

At the end of this book, once we have examined the policies of both sides and the evolution of the war, I shall suggest possible reasons

---

[34] Eduardo González-Calleja, 'El ex-rey', in Javier Moreno Luzón (ed.), *Alfonso XIII. Un político en el trono*, Marcial Pons, Madrid, 2003, p. 426.
[35] Martín Aceña, *El oro de Moscú y el oro de Berlín*, pp. 126–30.

for Franco's categorically overwhelming victory, and the Republic's crushing defeat. Nevertheless, any analysis of the varying components of the international stage that was the setting for the Spanish Civil War, the balance of support and restraint, the consequences of the non-intervention policy and the imbalance in the materiel made available to the two sides, as set out in this chapter, suggests that international intervention by Nazi Germany and Fascist Italy, and the rebuff, at best, from the western democracies, played a major, if not decisive, role in the evolution and duration of the conflict and its final result.

9 | The Republic at war

'We are waging war because it is being waged on us', said Manuel Azaña in his speech in Valencia's city hall on 21 January 1937.[1] A terrible war, which in barely half a year saw the cruel terror of the rebel army and Falangists, accompanied by a violent upheaval of the social order. And the Republic was indeed forced to fight in a war that it did not start, and the political organisations of the left had to adapt to a military activity that they knew practically nothing about. The varying ideas on how to organise the State and society held by the parties, movements and people who fought on the republican side ostensibly played a major part in frustrating a united policy against the military rebels. And there was nothing new in this situation, as it had been going on for years and had complicated the life of the Republic in peacetime as well.

Furthermore, as we have seen, the civil war was fought under the circumstances of the Non-Intervention Agreement imposed by the United Kingdom and France. For the Republic, this meant a marked international isolation, which placed it, and it alone, in a situation of material disadvantage. Non-intervention, in the words of Helen Graham, 'brought the daily erosion not only of the Republic's military capacity, but of its political legitimacy as well'. The international diplomacy that created and sustained this policy 'repeatedly blocked all the Republic's political exits, making it impossible for it to negotiate an end to the conflict in 1938'.[2] The war consumed the Republic and finished it off.

Until the end arrived, on 1 April 1939, the Republic went through three different stages, with three prime ministers. The first stage, with José Giral as premier, was marked by the resistance to the coup, the

[1] Manuel Azaña, *Los españoles en guerra*, Crítica, Barcelona, 1982, p. 19.
[2] Helen Graham, *The Spanish Republic at War 1936–1939*, Cambridge University Press, 2002, p. xi.

formation of militias, revolution and the elimination of the symbols of power and conventional citizens. Giral (1879–1962), a left-wing republican, from the same party and generation as Manuel Azaña (1880–1940), had held the chair of inorganic chemistry at the Universities of Salamanca and Madrid, was rector of Madrid University in 1931 and had taken an active part in politics during the Republic: he had been the Navy Minister in Azaña's governments between 15 October 1931 and June 1933; and after the *Frente Popular* coalition victory in February 1936, Azaña once more called on him to occupy the same post, and he stayed there in Santiago Casares Quiroga's government, until the military uprising.

As Giral did not represent this new open social and political mobilisation against the military rebellion, which was also directed against what was left of the republican State itself, nor the various revolutionary and trade union powers that were emerging – the only powers that exercised any authority in the chaos of the summer of 1936 – he had to resign and hand over to Francisco Largo Caballero. Giral continued to serve the Republic and was the Foreign Minister in Juan Negrín's first government, between 17 May 1937 and 6 April 1938, a post that was crucial for putting into practice the change in direction in Negrín's foreign policy, and was then Minister without Portfolio until the end of the war. He crossed the French border on 5 February 1939, together with Manuel Azaña (from whom he never separated during these difficult times), Azaña's wife and brother-in-law, Dolores and Cipriano de Rivas Cherif, and Diego Martínez Barrio, the Speaker of the Cortes. From France he went to Mexico, where he led the Republic's government in exile between 1945 and 1947. He died there in 1962.

The second stage began on 4 September 1936, when Francisco Largo Caballero (1869–1946) replaced Giral as Prime Minister. It was the first and only government in Spain's history that was led by a workers' leader, and the first time that there were Communist ministers in a western European government. There were not yet any anarchists, but they entered the government two months later. Between September 1936 and May 1937, Largo Caballero, with the collaboration of all the political and trade union forces fighting on the republican side, oversaw the reconstruction of the State, the militarisation of the militias, the contention of the revolution and the centralisation of power, all the while having to deal with challenges from the regions and nationalism, as Negrín would have to later. The fall of Málaga in February 1937 was the turning point in the military and political conflicts which led to the crisis in May. With his resignation, induced by the Communist Party and a sector of the PSOE executive, Largo Caballero, then 67, practically said goodbye to a long career devoted to trade union struggles, socialism and the Republic, although, by then in exile, he was yet to experience the hell of the Nazi concentration camp at Orianenburg. When it was liberated by the Russians in April 1945, he returned to France and died in Paris on 23 March 1946.

The third and last wartime premier of the Republic was Juan Negrín (1892–1956), a socialist deputy in the Republic's three Cortes, a university professor, a physiologist of international repute who had received his training in Germany, and a polyglot. His appointment was at the express decision of Manuel Azaña, with the support of the republicans, Prieto's socialists and the Communists. Demonised by his enemies and some of his alleged friends, his life and political activity has recently begun to gain a wider audience, thanks to studies by historians such as Helen Graham, Ricardo Miralles and Gabriel Jackson. Negrín hoped to win the war by combating the democratic powers' non-intervention policy, but the war was not going well, either at home or abroad. The beginning of his mandate coincided with that of Neville Chamberlain in the United Kingdom, who, by stepping up his 'appeasement' policy, gave way even more to the Fascist powers and ruled out any possibility of modifying the phony policy of non-intervention. The last year of the war was particularly difficult, with materiel and military problems, shortages of staple products, territorial losses and Francoist air-raids.

With the revolution overthrown, the Republic was unable to provide a convincing democratic solution. Resistance was not victory, although in the final months it seemed to be the only policy possible. The war lost, Negrín spent his early months of exile in France; afterwards, during nearly the whole of the Second World War, he was in England, where he led the republican government in exile, a post that was never recognised by Winston Churchill. After the defeat of the Axis powers, he returned to Paris, where he died on 12 November 1956.

Revolution

The coup d'état in July 1936 opened the floodgates to revolution. 'If the military rising has evolved into a major war, it is mainly due to our militant intervention', claimed the anarchist Diego Abad de Santillán, recalling those events, thereby fuelling the myth that everything boiled down to a confrontation between the rebel army and the worker members of the CNT: 'It was not a case of the Republic managing to defend itself against aggression; it was us who, in defence of the people, made it possible for the Republic to survive, and it was us who ran the war'.[3]

One of the most pervading images from this victory of the libertarians leading the working people was that of a CNT-FAI delegation arriving at the palace of the *Generalitat* for a meeting with the president, Lluís Companys. They went there 'armed to the teeth ... shirtless and covered in dust and smoke', according to the account written at the time by Juan García Oliver. Companys received them 'enthusiastically', to tell them that although in the past they had never been treated as they should have been, 'today you are the masters of the city and of Catalonia because you alone have defeated the Fascist forces'. 'If you have no need of me or do not want me as president of Catalonia, tell me now, and I will become just another soldier in the fight against Fascism'. And the CNT and the FAI, who had defeated Fascism, mobilised the people in the streets and had the political authorities where they wanted them, 'opted for collaboration and democracy, thereby renouncing revolutionary totalitarianism ... ... and an anarchistic confederate dictatorship'. Although they had the power to 'take it all', they rejected this ambition in an act of 'libertarian ethics'.[4]

Abad de Santillán, who was at that meeting, explained the reason for this 'exemplary' behaviour: 'we did not believe in dictatorship when it was being exercised against us, and we did not want it when we could have exercised it to harm the rest. The *Generalitat* would stay in office with President Companys at the head, and the

[3] Diego Abad de Santillán, *Por qué perdimos la guerra. Una contribución a la historia de la tragedia española*, Ediciones Imán, Buenos Aires, 1940, pp. 9–10.

[4] Juan García Oliver, *El eco de los pasos*, Ruedo Ibérico, Madrid, 1978, pp. 176–7.

people's forces would organise themselves to carry on the fight for the liberation of Spain'.[5] Thus on 21 July, the *Comité Central de Milicias Antifascistas* was set up, consisting of five anarchists, three UGT leaders, one member from the PSUC, one from the POUM, one from *Ezquerra Republicana*, one from the *Unió de Rabassaires*, one from *Acció Catalana* and several military advisers. According to the anarchist literature, it saw the birth of a model of revolutionary organisation and power, an alternative to José Giral's 'central' government in Madrid. In fact, in the two months that it existed, until its dissolution at the end of September with the entry of the anarchists into the government of the *Generalitat*, it did little or nothing to 'organise' economic and political activity in Catalonia. Instead, its decrees were aimed at creating mechanisms of control for revolutionary order, recruiting and training militias, in which García Oliver and Abad de Santillán were leading figures, and exercising the 'sole command' of war operations in the Aragon theatre.

Many anarchists felt their dreams had been fulfilled. They were living a fantasy. It was short-lived, but those summer and autumn months of 1936 were the nearest thing to what they believed revolution and the collectivised economy should be. Little did it matter that the revolution accounted for the lives of thousands of people, 'inevitable excesses', 'an explosion of concentrated rage and breaking free from the chains', in the words of Abad de Santillán.[6] The necessary destruction of this outdated order was somewhat insignificant, in any case, compared with the 'economic and social reconstruction' that was undertaken in July 1936, without precedent in world history. This was the blissful image of the earthly paradise portrayed in the anarchist literature, the declarations of Buenaventura Durruti to foreign correspondents, the press read by the workers of Barcelona and the militias on the Aragon front. 'The workers took possession of all the social wealth, the factories, the mines, land and sea transport, the large estates, the public services and major businesses'.[7]

The memory of this revolution, then, provoked conflicting reactions: for some, it represented destructive, radical upheaval; for others, it meant the creative capacity of the workers in industries and on lands

[5] Abad de Santillán, *Por qué perdimos la guerra*, p. 53.
[6] Ibid., pp. 61, 63.
[7] Ibid., p. 89.

without bosses, self-management by the workers or the imposition of the principles of a minority leadership. Furthermore, this dichotomy is to be found in all revolutions and periods of change that have historically been accompanied by wars and international pressure. For the Spanish revolution, which the anarchists claimed as theirs exclusively, the militias, the collectivisations and the committees represented its principal distinguishing features.

The militias were the most important element of what the anarchists called 'the people in arms', columns formed by workers, peasants and those of the army and security forces who had not joined the rebellion. During the early months of the war, the militias dominated large areas, created revolutionary committees to replace the old councils in any town they passed through, settled scores with the middle classes, right-wingers and the clergy, and preached a revolution of expropriation and collectivisation. All the leading lights of these anarchist columns – including Durruti and Ricardo Sanz, who succeeded him in the command of the future 26th Division after the former's death, as well as Antonio Ortiz, Cipriano Mera and Gregorio Jover, who later commanded the 28th Division (the Ascaso Column) – were 'men of action', members of the main anarchist groups of the FAI during the Second Republic.

The ardent atmosphere of the summer of 1936 also saw the birth of peasant collectivisations. Collective farming was mainly organised on lands belonging to absentee owners, or those who had either been killed or had fled, or on estates directly requisitioned by armed groups and the revolutionary committees. Obviously, the coercion was more intense in the districts chosen by the columns as centres of operations. The need to establish these militias on a broad front meant that production and consumption had to be controlled, and this asphyxiated the fragile economy of many towns and villages. Even those who professed an unshakeable faith in collectivisation as a means of doing away with social inequality had to accept this harsh reality. This was war and, as *El Frente*, the mouthpiece of the Durruti Column, said, 'it is a fact of life that armies live off the land they have conquered'.[8] A decree signed by Durruti himself in Bujaraloz, on 11 August 1936, abolished private ownership of 'large estates', declaring 'the people's ownership', under the control of the revolutionary committee, of 'all

[8] *El Frente*, 29 August 1936.

farming tools, tractors, machinery, threshing machines, etc. belonging to the Fascist owners', and he demanded from the inhabitants of Bujaraloz their 'enthusiastic and unconditional support, both material and moral', because 'the armed struggle of the anti-Fascist militias is the safeguard of the interests of the working people'.[9]

The collective farms could only be set up because of the collapse of the rule of law following the coup d'état, and were not the natural result of the thrust or intensity of the social struggles, even though, until July 1936, they had left more of a mark in the large estate areas of Castilla-La Mancha and Andalusia than in Catalonia, Valencia or Aragon. In the early days, there was only a mixture of confusion and expectation in prospect. Once the military rebels had been defeated, their weaponry and those who had helped to defeat them went over to the militias and trade unions. The presence of this armed power prevailed in all the areas in which the rising had failed, but it was particularly noticeable in the eastern half of Aragon. There, from the start, the militias hampered any balance there might have been in other parts of republican territory between trade union organisations, armed groups and civilian authorities.

These new local powers backed up by arms gave rise to the requisitions, which in turn produced the collective farms. According to IRA (Institute of Agrarian Reform) figures, based on fifteen provinces that did not include Aragon or Catalonia, 5,458,885 hectares (approximately 40 per cent of the productive surface) had been expropriated up to August 1938; and of this expropriated land, 54 per cent would have been legally collectivised. In Aragon, the region that has always been cited as the most important focus of the peasant revolution, anarchist sources claimed that 75 per cent of the land was farmed collectively, yet we have no reliable information on how much land was expropriated. If we also consider that it was in the most highly populated towns that this new ownership regime was imposed the least, then it seems reasonable not to accept this estimate.

The same problems occur when we try to determine the number of collective farms. In the majority of cases, these same sources should be treated with caution. If we accept these figures, in the Andalusian provinces there were 147 collective farms (UGT, 42; CNT, 36; UGT-CNT, 38; other organisations, 31); in Castilla-La Mancha, 452 (UGT,

[9] *Solidaridad Obrera*, 14 August 1936.

217; CNT, 186; mixed, 49); in Valencia, 353 (CNT, 264; UGT, 69; CNT-UGT, 20); in Catalonia, 95 (CNT, 43; UGT, 3; CNT-UGT, 18; other organisations, 31); in Murcia, 122 (CNT, 59; UGT, 53; mixed, 10); and in Aragon, 306 (CNT, 275; UGT, 31).

With the power vacuum created by the coup d'état, and a government whose decisions faced major obstacles to their application outside Madrid, the decision process lay in the hands of the militias and the political and trade union organisations. It was not a question of seeking alliances, but of finding an emergency solution that each organisation tried to turn into its own personal victory. And this was the reason for the chaos and improvisation that guided military actions, the trade unions' actions and the requisitions during the early months of the war.

This upsetting of the social order was also a genuine phenomenon of the revolution in industrial Catalonia. In the early days, disorganisation was rife, with owners, directors and managers either killed or fleeing their posts, panic-stricken about what lay in store for them. The time had come for the trade unions – or, to be more exact, those militants who had already made a name for themselves in the social struggles during the years of the Republic. The Regional Plenum of the Anarchist Groups of Catalonia, held on 21 August 1936, the first written record on this theme, discussed and approved 'the requisition and collectivisation of all establishments abandoned by their owners ... workers' control of banking businesses ... and particularly workers' union control of any industry that is still being run as a private company'.[10]

By the time labour activity had begun to return to 'normal' in the first half of August, the outlook for most companies was a matter for concern, and there was little hope that the crisis affecting some of the principal industrial sectors, particularly the textile industry, would now be drastically alleviated by union management. Historically, Catalonia had always experienced a shortfall in raw materials for its industry, energy sources and all types of food products. The war and the division of Spain into two zones led to a fall in demand in certain basic sectors and made it harder to import products, thereby increasing these structural problems. Industrial output fell sharply during the first two months of the conflict and wage increases were soon

[10] From the Civil War Archive, Salamanca, file 39 for Barcelona.

dwarfed by the soaring cost of living. And all this was happening in a region with a population density much higher than the rest of Spain's (91.2 inhabitants per km^2 as against 48.2) and in which the *Generalitat* estimated there were over 300,000 refugees by the end of 1936.

The *Generalitat* was slow to react. On 24 October 1936, one month after the incorporation of the CNT into its government, it issued the *Decret de Col.lectivitzacions i Control Obrer del Consell d'Economia*, the result of heated discussion among the political forces in the government, which provided a certain aura of legitimacy to the changes brought about by the revolution. It decreed the collectivisation of all businesses whose owners had been declared Fascists by a popular tribunal judgment or who had abandoned them; businesses that had more than a hundred employees before 30 June; and businesses with between fifty and a hundred employees, if this was the wish of three-quarters of the workforce. Branches of foreign businesses were given special treatment, a precaution that had previously been supported by the CNT since the early days of union control.

Many anarchists believed that with the overturning of the rule of law and this change in ownership, the revolution was now a fait accompli. The events of July 1936 had indeed caused the CNT's stock to rise dramatically. In Catalonia, the eastern half of Aragon and in certain districts of Valencia, its militants were convinced that they were absolute masters of the situation. They were no longer the 'disinherited', prison fodder, the favourite target of reactionary sentiments or those in power. Now the people – in other words, they – were armed and nothing and nobody could stop them. Everybody wanted to be a card-carrying member of the CNT. *Solidaridad Obrera*, the newspaper that was handed out free of charge in the streets of Barcelona during the first few days, soon reached its peak with so many people hungry for the latest news on the war and the revolution. Its circulation soared, from the 31,000 copies printed daily at the beginning of July, to 70,000 a few days after the rising and 150,000 by the end of August.

But for all its destruction and radicalism in the summer of 1936, the revolution had only just begun. Events immediately showed that the future was not so bright. The breach opened by the revolutionaries with their victory in Barcelona did not even reach Zaragoza. After a few weeks during which the political organisations seemed to welcome these forms of expression of popular power, the overthrow of the old order, it soon became clear that the revolutionary process – or what others termed a fight against Fascism in a civil war – was first and foremost a struggle for political and military power. It was a struggle for the control of arms and the changes wrought by them, for the reconstruction of a State weakened by the uprising, a struggle of popular impulse.

Committees sprang up everywhere. During that summer of 1936, republican Spain was a hotbed of armed and fragmented powers, difficult to keep in check. Catalonia had its Central Committee of Anti-Fascist Militias, in which the anarchists, led by Juan García Oliver, Aurelio Fernández and Diego Abad de Santillán, attempted to impose their will. Very soon afterwards, at the beginning of August, the Popular Executive Committee, with all political organisations represented, made its appearance in Valencia. In Málaga and Lérida there was a Committee of Public Health; in Santander, Gijón and Jaén, provincial committees of the *Frente Popular*; in Vizcaya, a *Junta de Defensa*; and in Madrid, as well as the National Committee of the *Frente Popular*, which organised militias and the life of the city, there was José Giral's government, which, made up as it was of left-wing republicans only, could not represent this jumble of committees, militias and control patrols, in which socialists and anarchists, UGT and CNT syndicalists were running the revolution, a revolution of destruction and murder, a revolution that was attempting to coax something new out of the ashes.

José Giral did what he could and what his duty as a loyal republican dictated. And considering that he was only a month and a half in office, what he did was fairly substantial. He asked France and the USSR for aid to defeat the military rebellion, started using the Bank of Spain's gold reserves to finance the war, dismissed any public servant suspected of siding with the rebels, and pronounced the first measures to check indiscriminate violence away from the front. This was on 23 and 25 August 1936, immediately after the killing of leading right-wingers and politicians in the Modelo prison in Madrid. Special tribunals were set up 'to try crimes of rebellion and sedition, and those committed against the security of the State'. They were made up of 'three judicial officials, who would act as *de jure* judges,

and fourteen jurypersons who would rule on the facts of the case'.[11]
This 'emergency justice' of the Republic incorporated 'summary judgment' and several other elements of military procedure, without the need to resort to 'martial law', something the republican government did not declare until 9 January 1939.

On 24 and 28 August, the *Generalitat* issued very similar decrees, setting up 'popular juries for the repression of Fascism'. And it was not just a feature of Madrid or Barcelona: popular tribunals were subsequently set up in almost all the provinces of the republican zone. It marked the change, or so it seemed, from 'abnormality', in which the 'people', as García Oliver wrote, 'created and applied its law and procedure' (in other words, the *paseo*), to 'normality', a stage in which 'suspicious elements were to be handed over to the popular tribunals and tried with impartiality, with punishment meted out for the guilty and immediate release for the innocent'.[12]

But it took time for this 'normality' to arrive, and it had to clear a way for itself among the thousands of corpses that were left behind by the *paseos*, *sacas* and attacks on prisons. The Africa army was advancing relentlessly on Madrid, after overrunning Extremadura and large areas of Castilla-La Mancha. On 3 September, Yagüe's columns arrived at Talavera. That same day, in the north, where General Mola had launched an attack on Guipúzcoa, Irún fell. 'The government of the Republic is dead. It has no authority or competence, no plan for waging all-out war and finishing it with an absolute victory for the revolution', wrote Luís Araquistain, the left-wing socialist ideologist, to Largo Caballero on 24 August.[13]

Now that the military rebels were in Talavera, Giral really believed that he had no authority or backing, and he decided to 'present to H. E. the President of the Republic all the powers received from him, as well as the resignation of all the ministers', so that he could replace them with a government that would 'represent each and every one of the

---

[11] Glicerio Sánchez Recio, *Justicia y guerra en España. Los Tribunales Populares (1936–1939)*, Instituto de Cultura 'Juan Gil-Albert', Alicante, 1991.

[12] García Oliver, *El eco de los pasos*, p. 347.

[13] Quoted in Santos Juliá, 'El Frente Popular y la política de la República en guerra', in Santos Juliá (ed.), *Historia de España de Menéndez Pidal. República y guerra civil*, 42 vols., Espasa Calpe, Madrid, 2004, vol. XL, p. 126.

political parties and trade union or workers' organisations acknowledged as having influence among the Spanish people'.[14] The hour had come for the trade unions and Largo Caballero, the undisputed leader of the UGT.

Coalition government

On 4 September 1936, Largo Caballero, who had opposed the idea of Indalecio Prieto forming a government of republicans and socialists in May 1936, and who had refused to do so after the coup d'état in July, finally agreed to lead 'a coalition government', on the advice of Luís Araquistain, in which he himself would also be the Minister for War. It was a government with a socialist majority, with Indalecio Prieto as Navy and Air Minister; Julio Álvarez del Vayo as Foreign Minister; Juan Negrín, Finance; Ángel Galarza, Interior Minister; and Anastasio de Gracia in Trade and Industry. There were also five republicans: the *Ezquerra* leader, José Tomás Piera in Employment, Health and Social Security; Julio Just in Public Works; Bernardo Giner de los Ríos in Communications and the Merchant Navy; Mariano Ruiz Funes in Justice; and José Giral as Minister without Portfolio. One of Largo Caballero's conditions was that the Communists should enter the government, and they did so with Jesús Hernández in Education and Vicente Uribe in Agriculture. Finally, he came to an agreement with José Antonio Aguirre over the participation of the Basque nationalists in return for the speedy passing of a Statute of Autonomy for Euskadi, and a few days later Manuel de Irujo joined the government as Minister without Portfolio.

That left the CNT, which was offered a ministry without portfolio, small reward for what the anarcho-syndicalist organisation considered to be its true worth. Nor was this solution to everyone's liking. Indalecio Prieto said to Mijail Koltsov, the *Pravda* correspondent, that Largo Caballero was 'a frozen bureaucrat ... capable of ruining everything', although he also admitted that he was 'the only man ... suitable for heading a new government'. Negrín agreed to take part after labelling Largo's government 'preposterous'. 'Are they

14 Ibid.

really trying to lose the war? Is this a challenge to Europe?'[15] Manuel Azaña, too, was convinced that the Spanish Lenin would be a failure. As for the idea that this government was imposed by the Kremlin, and that it would allegedly be behind all the decisions taken in republican Spain, written records belie this completely. What Moscow and the Communist International wanted at that time was for Giral to stay, with a republican majority and the participation of two socialists and two Communists. Only thus could the European democracies be spared any further apprehension.

The solution was not to the liking of certain republican heavyweights, but to others, particularly the socialist left and the UGT unions, it seemed the only one available to tackle the collapse of the republicans, win the war and, at the same time, guarantee the gains of the revolutionaries. The presence of Giral and certain republicans who had been in his government, such as Bernardo Giner de los Ríos and Julio Just, seemed to confirm that the legitimacy of the Republic was being maintained. The integration of socialists, Communists and Basque and Catalan nationalists made it a government of 'national unity' – the 'victory' government, as they were to call it.

The transfer of power from a toothless republican government to one led by the well-known, and erstwhile 'enemy', leader of its syndicalist rival put the CNT committees on alert. While the government was made up of republicans, the 'typical bourgeois', who were also despised for their inability to halt the Fascist advance, did not concern them too much. With the people armed, why create new organisms of power? What they had to do instead was to consolidate, both politically and militarily, the revolutionary changes that had spread through Catalonia, the eastern half of Aragon, Valencia and large areas of Castilla-La Mancha and Andalusia. And naturally, this was not going to be done by a phantom government that held no sway even in Madrid. However, Largo Caballero's arrival in the government, accompanied by the not markedly revolutionary socialists and Communists, changed things and also forced the rhetoric to be modified. From that moment on, the attitude of most of the CNT leaders consisted of keeping the control of the State apparatus out of the

---

[15] Ricardo Miralles, *Juan Negrín. La República en guerra*, Temas de Hoy, Madrid, 2003, pp. 79–80.

hands of all the other political organisations. It was made clear that this was a war and not a revolutionary celebration.

At the beginning they proposed a National Defence Council, made up of republicans and UGT and CNT syndicalists, to be chaired by Largo Caballero. The CNT's plan excluded the Communists, something that the UGT leader could not accept. After several weeks of negotiation, the then secretary of the CNT, Horacio Martínez Prieto, managed to persuade the other leaders that the only alternative was 'simple participation in the government'. This 'haggling' between Largo Caballero and Martínez Prieto over the exact number of ministries for the CNT occupied the closing days of October. In the end, it was four, although Largo Caballero maintained in his memoirs that they had asked for six.[16]

On 4 November 1936, the CNT brought to the Republic's wartime government four of its most noteworthy leaders. It was also clear that these four leaders represented a good balance of the two main sectors that had fought for supremacy in anarcho-syndicalism during the years of the Republic: moderate syndicalists and the FAI. Joan Peiró and Juan López, the Ministers of Industry and Trade, were seen as undisputed figures of the opposition syndicates which, after their expulsion, had returned to the fold shortly before the uprising. Juan García Oliver, the new Minister of Justice, was the symbol of the 'man of action', of the 'revolutionary gymnastics', the strategy of insurrection against the Republic in 1933, which had bubbled over since the revolutionary days of July in Barcelona. Federica Montseny, the Minister of Health, was already a familiar name because of her family: she was the daughter of Federico Urales and Soledad Gustavo, anarchists who were proud of her commitment and her pen, which she had put to good use to attack all the reformist traitors during the years of the Republic. She was also the first female minister in Spain's history.

Anarchists in the government: 'A momentous situation', said *Solidaridad Obrera* on 4 November. And they were right: 'The government … is no longer an oppressive force against the working class, just as the State is no longer the organism that divides society

---

[16] An account of the negotiation of the anarchists' entry into the government of the Republic may be found in Julián Casanova, *Anarchism, the Republic and Civil War in Spain: 1931–1939*, Routledge, London, 2004, pp. 116–21.

into classes. And what is more, neither of them will be oppressing the people, now that the CNT is in the government'. Never had the anarcho-syndicalist leaders said this about a government, or put so much trust in government action. As a result, very few noteworthy anarchists refused to support this new situation, and there was also very little resistance from the grass-roots anarchists, those who had hitherto displayed revolutionary opposition to the reformist leaders. They were to change their tune after the events of May 1937, following their expulsion from the government, and exile: for them, Largo Caballero's entry into the government had meant the absolute renunciation of every anti-political and revolutionary principle.

Yet not all reactions were as enthusiastic as those expressed by *Solidaridad Obrera*. If Largo Caballero is to be believed, the President of the Republic 'refused to sign decrees because he found the presence of four anarchists in the government repellent': he failed to realise the 'future implications of the conversion of Spanish anarchism, which had gone from terrorism and direct action to cooperation'. As Largo told him he would resign if he did not sign, Azaña 'finally signed them, albeit reluctantly'. Indeed, Manuel Azaña wrote months later that 'it was not only against my better judgement, but also despite my strongest protestations that November's ministerial changes were imposed, with the entry of the CNT'.[17]

However, their entry into the government did not come at the best of times. On the very same day, Franco's troops were at the gates of Madrid, the scene of what was to be the most decisive battle of the first phase of the war. General Franco, head of the military rebels since 1 October 1936, ordered the concentration of all his forces to take the capital, with the Africa army in the vanguard, reinforced by squadrons of German and Italian aircraft.

The government was incapable of organising the defence of the capital effectively. On 6 November, during the first cabinet meeting attended by the CNT ministers, it was decided unanimously to transfer the government from Madrid to Valencia. This was an impetuous move, stealthily carried out, and no public explanation whatsoever

---

[17] Largo Caballero, *Mis recuerdos*, Ediciones Unidas, México, 1976, pp. 175–6; Manuel Azaña, 'El cuaderno de la Pobleta', annotation 20 May 1937, in *Memorias políticas y de guerra*, 4 vols., Crítica, Barcelona, 1981, vol. II, p. 43.

was given. To the public, it looked as if the government was fleeing and the people were being left to their fate. Just before the transfer, Largo Caballero ordered the setting up of a *Junta de Defensa* under General Miaja, which was to run things in a Madrid that was under siege from that day until 22 April 1937.

Largo Caballero also appointed Vicente Rojo, who had been promoted to Lieutenant Colonel a month previously, Chief of General Miaja's General Staff. It looked as if the rebel army would take Madrid in a matter of days, but despite the confusion and disorder that reigned at that time in Madrid, apparent also in the *sacas* and killing of prisoners, Franco's army failed in its objective. Rojo and Miaja, with the help of various officers who had remained loyal to the Republic, such as Lieutenant Colonel Fernández Urbano and Major Matallana, organised the defence with all the forces at their disposal, which included, for the first time in the war, the International Brigades. And arriving just in time was the Soviet military aid, by then paid for by the shipment of the gold reserves. The whole city, stirred up by the constant air-raids and bombardments from the rebel army, helped to stem the advance of the attackers. Many saw it as a decisive battle between international Fascism on one side, and Communism and democracy on the other. 'Madrid, the heart of Spain', wrote Rafael Alberti in 1936.

Women and children lay dead among the rubble, as may be seen from the wealth of documentary evidence testifying to those 'heroic feats'. Among the combatants who died was the anarchist leader Buenaventura Durruti, on 20 November, who had arrived with his column a few days previously. To die in a defenceless Madrid that his old comrades had abandoned: that was the final proof of his strength as against the weakness of those who had become involved in the game of politics. The hero was buried in Barcelona, two days later, in the biggest demonstration that the city had known during those tumultuous years of the Republic and war.

The Communist Party, with a decisive presence in the *Junta de Defensa*, grew markedly from then on. It had been a minor party in the elections of February 1936, although before the war it had managed to unite young socialists and Communists to form the *Juventudes Socialistas Unificadas* (JSU), and soon after the defeat of the rising in Barcelona, various Catalan socialist and Communist groups had set up the *Partit Socialista Unificat de Catalunya* (PSUC), an organisation that was soon to come into open conflict with the POUM and the anarchists for political control away from the front. However, its growth and reputation were linked to the presence of the International Brigades, Soviet aid and the order and discipline that its leaders managed to impose on the running of the war.

The militarisation of the militias, or the transformation of scattered armed groups into an army under a centralised military command, was one of Largo Caballero's principal objectives as soon as he came into office as Prime Minister and Minister of War. He created a new Central High Command, in which Vicente Rojo, an expert in military tactics, very quickly began to shine; he organised the fronts into four theatres of operations: the Centre, Aragon, the North and Andalusia; and he created the mixed brigades, which the militias were forced to join. The political side of running the war was in the hands of the new body of commissars set up on 16 October, 'a kind of workers' front in the army', as Santos Juliá puts it, because Largo initially shared out the responsibilities between socialists, Communists and UGT and CNT syndicalists.[18]

There was heated debate over militarisation in the libertarian movement. The setbacks suffered by the militias following the first two months of euphoria and the entry of the CNT into the government changed this attitude. 'When it comes to serving the revolution, we are the first to step forward', said *Solidaridad Obrera* on 23 December 1936, in an attempt to convince the movement that it should accept militarisation as 'a necessity imposed by the war'. As far as the CNT and FAI committees were concerned, militarisation was inevitable from the moment it became clear that the militias, that superior force known as 'the people in arms', were useless for a long-term war, and that the CNT's entry into the government implied supporting their transformation into an army. 'Union life is based on agreements at general assemblies; war, on command and obedience', declared Helmut Rudiger, the AIT delegate in Spain, neatly capturing the tone of these events.[19]

[18] Santos Juliá, 'El Frente Popular y la política de la República en guerra', pp. 137–8.
[19] Helmut Rudiger, *El anarcosindicalismo en la Revolución Española*, Comité Nacional de la CNT, Barcelona, 1938, p. 49.

The members of the 'Iron Column', who had for some time been airing their protests in their newspaper, *Línea de Fuego*, called a plenum of confederate and anarchist columns in Valencia on 5 February 1937. There they heard the two postures that were dividing the anarchist movement: the one that was for order and discipline, which maintained that this was war and precious principles had to be laid aside; and the one that accused the CNT leaders of 'showing too much concern for the war, and little for the revolution', of renouncing that 'bright, benevolent tomorrow' that would herald the victory of the armed people. 'Are we going to accept ... those tin-pot officers, manufactured wholesale in a couple of weeks in any old military college?'[20]

That was the last act in an argument that was already settled. In early 1937, most of the militias on the Aragon front, the scene of the latest acts of resistance, joined the new army. However, this militarisation did not mark the end of the struggle for the political and strategic control that had been raging in this zone since the summer of 1936. Confrontations between the 27th Division, led by the Communist Antonio Trueba, and the 25th, 26th and 28th Divisions, under the command of the anarchists Antonio Ortiz, Ricardo Sanz and Gregorio Jover, were frequent, reaching crisis point in August 1937 with the dissolution of the Council of Aragon and the break-up of the collectives. Somewhat more unsettled was the situation with the 29th Division, consisting of members of the POUM, under José Rovira, which was accused that spring of abandoning the front and 'aiding the Fascist plans'. Rovira was imprisoned and the division dissolved.

But avoiding militarisation in a sector away from the front in which the CNT still wielded almost absolute political influence was not very difficult – not even for those who felt that anti-militarism was not a renounceable principle, or for those who felt unfairly treated by this measure because it meant losing their areas of influence. There were desertions in various columns, such as the Durruti and Carod Columns, and some 400 men left the Iron Column when it was militarised in March 1937 and transformed into the 83rd Brigade. For

---

[20] *Acta del Pleno de Columnas Confederales y Anarquistas celebrado en Valencia el día 5 de febrero de 1937*, 63 pp., ed. 'Los Amigos de Durruti', CNT-FAI.

the situation to escalate from anti-militarist protests to desertions was something that caused concern to those in favour of discipline and was hard for them to accept. Their methods of persuasion failed, and there were no other ways, except armed confrontation, to halt this trend. Many of these deserters and dissidents brandished their arms in the streets of Barcelona in May 1937. And it was there that they finally realised that they were now on their own.

The reconstruction of central power was Largo Caballero's other major objective. The first step was the replacement of the 'spontaneous' power of the revolutionary committees by municipal councils, 'made up proportionally of all the union organisations and anti-Fascist parties'. The *Generalitat* of Catalonia was the first to implement this on 9 October 1936, and Largo Caballero's government did the same with a decree issued by the Interior Minister, the socialist Ángel Galarza, on 4 January 1937. The anarchist, Joaquín Ascaso, leader of the Council of Aragon, also implemented this order on 19 January, even though in practice it meant stripping the CNT of power in many towns in Aragon.

But although by the end of 1936 republican Spain was no longer a conglomeration of local authorities, the government in Valencia could not stop Catalonia and what was left of Euskadi from increasing their autonomy, or regional councils from becoming consolidated elsewhere. In Catalonia, the government of the *Generalitat* which had incorporated all the region's political forces on 26 September, thereby putting an end to the Central Committee of Anti-Fascist Militias, set up its own army, had full political and economic autonomy and, up to May 1937, exercised absolute control of the police and public order, in the hands of the anarchists Aurelio Fernández and Dionisio Eroles. There were regional councils in Asturias and Santander, but the one that stood out was the Council of Aragon, set up by anarchist columns on this front in October 1936, which, despite being legalised by Largo Caballero at the end of that year, had its own police organisation, requisitioned property, controlled the collectives' economy and administered justice. In the face of such defiance, the central authority dissolved it by decree, aided by the military, in August 1937.

The Basque Country, its area by now reduced, since mid-September 1936, to Vizcaya and a small part of Guipúzcoa and Álava, was a particularly unusual case. There was revolution and violence against the right-wingers in Guipúzcoa, sending some 500 people to their graves in less than two months, including the traditionalist Víctor Pradera and the *Renovación Española* leader, Jorge Satrústegui, but the *Junta de Defensa* of Vizcaya, with representation from all the political organisations, managed to bring the situation under control. Another difference was that in Bilbao the army never rose up, while in San Sebastián the violence began as soon as the rebellion was defeated. On 29 July, Colonel León Carrasco Amilibia, who had led the rising there, was taken from the regional council building, where he had been detained for a few hours, and was murdered alongside the railway track. One day later, at dawn, a group of militiamen went to the provincial gaol, where they killed fifty-three people, forty-one of whom were army officers.

On 1 October 1936, the Cortes of the Republic passed the Basque Statute, and the seven councillors of this small republican area chose José Antonio Aguirre, the leader of the PNV, as *lehendakari* (Prime Minister of the Basque government, literally 'first secretary'). Aguirre presided over a coalition cabinet, with a majority of nationalists but no anarchists, which in its eight months of existence, until the fall of Bilbao on 19 June 1937, set up, in the words of Santiago de Pablo, a 'quasi-sovereign State'. It created the army of operations in Euskadi, a constant cause of friction between the autonomous government and that of the Republic; a new police force, the *Ertzaña*; controlled the economy; decreed a wide range of social and welfare policies; and administered what de Pablo has defined as 'orderly and responsible' justice.[21] There was no revolution, and hardly any anticlerical violence – although twenty-eight priests were murdered during those eight months – and religious services and festivals were permitted. For this reason, it was called the 'Basque oasis', as compared to other places where the killing was rife, although it should be remembered that in the barely one year that it remained part of the Republic, there were 500 killings in Vizcaya and over half of these were the result of attacks on prisons and ships and convents that had been refurbished as gaols. The last of these attacks, on 4 January 1937, in reprisal for an air-raid on Bilbao, sent 244 people to their deaths – paradoxically, at a time

---

[21] Santiago de Pablo, 'La guerra civil en el País Vasco: ¿un conflicto diferente?', in Enrique Moradiellos (ed.), 'La guerra civil', *Ayer*, 50 (2003), pp. 126–9.

when this violence of mass *sacas* had died out in the rest of the republican territory.

Indeed, one of Largo Caballero's government's greatest achievements, particularly after the beginning of 1937, was that the 'legal' violence meted out by the popular tribunals finally replaced the 'hot-blooded' terror that characterised the early months of the war. There were various reasons for this. Firstly, this coalition government involved all organisations to defend responsibility and discipline. Nothing illustrates this better than the fact that it was an 'anarchist of action', García Oliver, who consolidated the popular tribunals and created work camps for the 'Fascist prisoners', instead of a shot in the back of the neck. Secondly, this control and discipline was to be seen in the municipal councils, whose formation was the result of deals between the various political organisations, and which replaced the early revolutionary and anti-Fascist committees, and in the militarisation and incorporation of the militias into the army of the Republic. With stronger political and military powers, and with the war centre stage, the revolutionary storm blew over, and the violence of the *sacas* and *paseos* was halted.

However, militarisation, control away from the front and the reconstruction of republican power were tackled amid heated debate between some of the political sectors that made up the government coalition. The Communists, who had been unsuccessfully pressing Largo Caballero since the autumn of 1936 to bring the PSOE and PCE together into one large Marxist party, as the young socialists and Communists had done, began to protest, both publicly and privately, against the ineffectiveness of the government, the fragmentation of politics into regional authorities and the progress of the war. Criticism was heightened after the fall of Málaga. On 8 February 1937, Franco's troops, supported by thirteen Italian battalions under General Roatta, took the city and initiated a brutal repression that was reminiscent of the 'hot-blooded terror' of the summer of 1936 in other regions of Andalusia.

The Communists, not to mention Manuel Azaña, wanted the CNT out of the government, and Largo Caballero, under pressure, had the idea of forming a 'trade union government', a true workers' alliance. Largo Caballero was afraid of the Communists, said André Marty, the Comintern representative and organiser of the International Brigades, to Georgi Dimitrov, Secretary-General of the Communist

International, in a report sent on 28 March 1937: 'Caballero does not want defeat, but he is afraid of victory. He is afraid of victory because victory is not possible without the active participation of the Communists. Victory means an even greater consolidation of the Communist Party'.[22]

The Communists held Largo Caballero responsible for the fall of Málaga. At the same time, the socialists sympathetic to Indalecio Prieto, who controlled the PSOE national committee and also wanted to oust the trade union organisations from the Executive, apprised Manuel Azaña in the middle of March of the need to replace Largo Caballero as Minister of War, but that he should stay on as Prime Minister. The Communists and Prieto's socialists began to come to an understanding with this common policy against trade union power, and 'this rapprochement culminated', according to Santos Juliá, in an agreement on 15 April, 'whereby both parties decided to set up liaison committees at all levels of their respective organisations', with the UGT left out in the cold.[23] This was the beginning of the struggle, settled very quickly as a result of the May crisis, between parties and trade unions.

May 1937

Barcelona provided the ideal setting for this confrontation. It was a city far from the front, the symbol of anarcho-syndicalist revolution, which many people believed belonged to the people. It had its own political characteristics: an autonomous government with notable leftist-republican influences, a powerful anarchist movement, a Communist party that controlled the UGT, and a tiny revolutionary party, the POUM, bitter enemies of the Communists. Its economy relied heavily on industrial production, the control of which was hotly contested by the revolutionary syndicalists, the UGT and the *Generalitat*. It also had a high population density, with tens of thousands of refugees. All this made for tension from various sides.

And there was no absence of arms, wielded by the police forces, militants from the various political organisations and the ex-militiamen

---

[22] Miralles, *Juan Negrín*, pp. 117–18.
[23] Santos Juliá, 'El Frente Popular y la política de la República en guerra', p. 142.

who had brought them back from the front. There were also too many revolutionary 'tourists', foreigners who could do nothing in their own countries, but for whom this revolution was still not enough. And then there were the agents provocateurs, of all hues, who had infiltrated into all factions, from the police to the POUM, said by García Oliver to be 'acting of their own accord', and who obviously had not created this volatile situation themselves, but who were the first to have the match ready to cause it to explode. In short, a stormy atmosphere reigned in wartime Barcelona, much stormier than in other cities in the republican zone. Even the Francoists tried to take the credit for lighting the fuse. General Wilhelm von Faupel, the German ambassador in rebel Spain, told his superiors that Franco claimed that 'thirteen' of his agents had started the disturbances in Barcelona.[24]

The first exchange of fire was heard on 3 May. That day, the *Ezquerra* leader, Artemi Aiguader, in charge of Security in the *Generalitat*, ordered Eusebio Rodríguez Salas, recently appointed Commissar-General of Public Order, to occupy the State telephone company building in the Plaza de Cataluña, which had been in the hands of the CNT since the 'glorious' events of July 1936. Three truckloads of assault guards were deployed. They surrounded the building. They were met by gunfire from some CNT militants who were inside. It was rumoured that an armed attack had been launched against the CNT, one of the symbols of power gained some months earlier in the fight against the military rebels. Armed anarchists arrived to help those inside. The fighting spread. Many workers left their posts. The barricades were once again seen in the streets. Behind them, against the forces of order, socialists and Communists, were former militiamen who had refused to join the new army, young libertarians, FAI anarchists who were no longer recognised by this organisation, and POUM militants.

By the morning of Tuesday 4 May, the situation was serious and a cause for great concern. On his own and caught in the crossfire, Manuel Azaña asked the government in Valencia to step in. As he saw it, the problem had 'two sides': 'one, the anarchist insurrection with all its serious consequences and deplorable effects', something which, although not at close hand, he had already experienced twice

[24] David T. Cattell, *Communism and the Spanish Civil War*, University of California Press, Berkeley and Los Angeles, 1955, pp. 146–7.

as Prime Minister in January 1932 and 1933; 'the other, the lack of freedom of the Head of State not only to travel freely, but also to carry out his duty'.[25] Largo Caballero called an urgent meeting of the government. They agreed to send a delegation made up of two CNT ministers, García Oliver and Federica Montseny, the secretary of this organisation's National Committee, Mariano R. Vázquez, and Hernández Zancajo, a man loyal to Largo in the Executive Committee of the UGT. Since words were not going to be enough, some 2,000 police, rising later to nearly 5,000, would also set out for Barcelona.

The members of the delegation spoke on the radio that same day, after meeting the representatives of the various political organisations in the *Generalitat*. They appealed for a ceasefire and an end to 'provocations', 'in the name of anti-Fascist unity, proletarian unity, and of those who had died in the struggle'. All those manning the barricades, those who had died that day, were 'brothers', García Oliver told them: guards, anarchists, socialists and republicans, all 'victims' of the anti-Fascist struggle. That night, a very different message was broadcast on the radio, asking for their 'comrades at the front … to be prepared to come to Barcelona when their aid was required'. And so the night passed, amidst disparate appeals and gunfire, and fairly heavy gunfire at that.[26]

There was no hope of an agreement yet. Nor did the situation improve over the next two days. By then it was known that there were several notable militants among the dead: Antonio Sesé, an ex-CNT member who was now secretary-general of the UGT in Catalonia; the Italian, Camilo Berneri, who had fought in the Ascaso Column and was a contributor to the anarchist newspaper *Guerra di Clase*; and Domingo Ascaso, brother of Francisco, one of the organisers of this column who had deserted when it was militarised and transformed into the 28th Division. On 5 May, 'a group of between 1,500 and 2,000 men', members of the former Red and Black Column, the 127th Brigade of the 28th Division, and the POUM, deserted the front and were arrested 1 kilometre from Lérida by air force troops under the command of Lieutenant Colonel Reyes. Here Reyes had a meeting with

[25] Azaña's impression in 'Telex messages between the President of the Republic in Barcelona and the Central Government in Valencia concerning the internal situation in the former city', 4–6 May 1937, Servicio Histórico Militar, cabinet 53, batch 461, file 1.
[26] García Oliver, *El eco de los pasos*, pp. 419–34.

Rovira, head of the POUM's 29th Division, García Vivancos, of the 25th Division, and an unidentified delegate from the regional committee of the CNT – 'apparently the leaders and organisers of the expedition'. They negotiated an agreement that the air force troops would be withdrawn in exchange for the deserters returning to the front. The day before, troops from the 25th Division, commanded by Saturnino Carod, deserted their posts and started out for Catalonia through the province of Teruel. They ran into forces sent by the Directorate-General of Security in Valencia to this area, which bordered the provinces of Castellón and Tarragona, and although it did not come to armed confrontation, they did, according to anarchist sources, break up machinery and equipment on some collective farms.[27]

Events were now beginning to become tainted with blood, with dozens of people killed and wounded in the streets. There were more fruitless appeals on the radio from Mariano R. Vázquez, Rafael Vidiella and Montseny. The government moved onto the offensive. It appointed General Sebastián Pozas as commander of the 4th Division, replacing General José Aranguren, and took over the services of Public Order in the *Generalitat*, which would now 'answer directly to the government of the Republic', under the command of Colonel Escobar. By the afternoon of 7 May, wrote Orwell, 'conditions were almost normal'.[28] The assault guards from Valencia, helped by PSUC militants, occupied the city and put down the last vestiges of resistance. The official casualty figures were 400 dead and 1,000 wounded.

That day there were disturbances and violent incidents in Aragon. The most serious of these occurred in Barbastro, where several armed groups, who were returning to the front after the meeting with Lieutenant Colonel Reyes, attacked a military barracks, taking away arms and munitions, and the prison, where they killed eight inmates. There was another attack on the barracks at Monte Julia, and some 500 armed men, 'many of whom were sure to have been expelled from the Madrid Front', committed 'all manner of excesses' in the district

---

[27] Data on the desertions (and other disturbances, mentioned later) come from the 'Report issued by the Legal Consultancy of the Aragon front by virtue of the telegraphed order from the senior general of the army of the East', Servicio Histórico Militar, cabinet 62, batch 788, file 1, a document signed on the Aragon front, in Sariñena (Huesca), on 15 May.

[28] George Orwell's account, *Homenaje a Cataluña*, Ariel, Barcelona, 1983, pp. 158–95.

of Binéfar. Apparently, among those taking part in these violent incidents were public order forces of the Council of Aragon, including one of its councillors, Evaristo Viñuales, in charge of Information and Propaganda, who, 'according to a reliable report, albeit not substantiated ... led a group of fifty armed men and occupied the frontier post at Benasque, disarming the carabineros stationed there'. There was more to come. On the same day, at El Grado, a town in Huesca, three UGT militants were found killed. According to the statement before the judge, the alleged murderers were members of the CNT. Five others had suffered the same fate two days earlier in Oliete, in the province of Teruel: two Communists, one UGT militant, one member of *Izquierda Republicana* and one 'right-winger'. Charges were brought against CNT members, some of them 'self-confessed Fascists' before 19 July, and the chairman of the municipal council, 'formerly a trainee priest'.[29]

With 'normality' restored, it was time to resolve what was likely to be a government crisis that had been looming since the fall of Málaga in February, a major setback for the Republic which caused the Communists to openly criticise the running of the war, for which Largo Caballero bore the principal political responsibility. In fact, 'normality' would never be restored, as things would never be the same again after these events. What had happened in Barcelona and on the Aragon front went beyond political confrontation between parties and trade unions, between the unions themselves and between the various tendencies within the same union organisation. This was something more than a confirmation of the now unassailable gulf that separated Communists and anarchists. The cracks were deeper and shook the very core of the republican camp, thus jeopardising any chance of it meeting its objectives. All this was the result of the basic problems that had remained unresolved since the beginning of the conflict, and which grew worse as time went by: military defeat after military defeat, in spite of the subjugation of the militias; the government's inability to organise food supplies on a fair basis to a people at war; and the constant divisions that prevented the joining of forces in the economic, political and social spheres.

---

[29] 'Informe que emite la Asesoría Jurídica del frente de Aragón en virtud de la orden telegráfica del general jefe del Ejército del Este', Servicio Histórico Militar, Madrid, cabinet 62, package 788, binder 1.

Surprisingly, the outcome of the political crisis was the matter of most concern to the libertarian leaders. In the Cabinet meeting held on 13 May, the two Communist ministers, Vicente Uribe and Jesús Hernández, called for Largo Caballero to resign as Minister of War, and for the POUM to be dissolved. The Prime Minister refused to accept the first condition and tried to shelve any resolution on the second until the full facts were known about who was responsible for the disturbances in Barcelona. The Communist ministers resigned from the Cabinet. The crisis continued. On 15 May, the CNT and UGT both issued communiqués expressing their common criteria in three basic points: they denied all responsibility for any of the possible causes of the crisis; they refused to collaborate with any government that did not have Largo Caballero as Prime Minister and Minister of War; and therefore they proposed 'a government built on the foundations of workers' organisations'.

On 16 May, Largo Caballero sent a letter to all the political forces, explaining his proposal for the structure of the new government. The UGT would occupy three ministries and he would be Prime Minister and Minister of National Defence, an amalgamation of the former Ministry of War and Ministry of the Navy and Air; the PSOE, PCE, IR and CNT would each have two ministries; *Unión Republicana*, one; and one representative of the *Partido Nacionalista Vasco* and another from *Esquerra Republicana* would occupy Ministries without Portfolio. The proposal received a favourable response from the UGT, UR and IR; it was rejected by the PCE, PSOE and the CNT, who refused 'to occupy the position of inferiority that they were being offered'. The following day, Manuel Azaña, who had hoped that others would tackle the crisis, even though he was the first to want to get rid of Largo Caballero, asked the socialist Juan Negrín to form a government from which the two trade union organisations were excluded. Party politics had got the better of the trade unions. 'A counter-revolutionary government has been formed', said *Solidaridad Obrera* in its editorial of 18 May.[30]

Despite this bombastic statement, the revolution/counter-revolution dilemma (if indeed one ever existed in these terms) had been resolved a long time before. Thus May 1937 did not represent the dividing

---

[30] All the information on the handling of the crisis and the letter from the CNT to Largo Caballero is in the Civil War Archive, Salamanca, file 39 for Bilbao.

line between two distinct stages of the civil war (libertarian social revolution and Communist reaction), the climax of the confrontation between those who wanted only revolution and those who wanted to win the war. As Helmut Rudiger was to say after these events, with accurate prophetic insight as it turned out, the debate over whether revolution was preferable to war, or vice versa, was futile: 'If we lose the war, we lose everything, and for the next half century or more there will be no further discussion about the issue of revolution'.[31]

However, what is beyond any doubt, even if we do not accept the usual portrayal of these events as the triumph of counter-revolution, is that some things did change after May 1937. The POUM was eliminated, Largo Caballero found himself isolated, and the anarcho-syndicalists were rapidly losing their political and armed power – no small development, considering the major roles they had played in this drama.

Juan Negrín

Largo Caballero was not the right man to impose unity in the republican agricultural sector and order away from the front, or to win the war. Such was the opinion of the republicans, the Communists and Prieto's socialists, who 'were sticking together', as José Giral said to Manuel Azaña, 'to facilitate any solution'. The Communists 'could no longer put up with Largo making random decisions without consulting the government'. The former trade union leader was 'in the pocket' of the CNT.[32]

With Largo out of the way, in isolation and without even the support of his own trade union, the question now was who was going to be prime minister. Azaña recovered the initiative and, as he wrote in his memoirs, the very parties that 'had elevated Largo and accepted the FAI' could now, months later, 'no longer put up with him, and they turned to me to solve the problem'. Parliament, the body with the power to solve this crisis, was not sitting. And Azaña made it quite clear in his meetings with the various political representatives – the socialists Cordero and Vidarte and the Communists Díaz and

[31] Helmut Rudiger, 'Materials for discussion concerning the Spanish situation, in the Plenary Session of the AIT of 11 June 1937', Civil War Archive, Salamanca, file 39 for Bilbao, p. 6.

[32] Miralles, *Juan Negrín*, p. 125.

Dolores Ibárruri – that he was not going to strip Largo Caballero of power 'on what might seem a mere whim'. It was the parties that had changed their minds, and policies, from 'praising' Largo Caballero to wanting him out of the way.[33]

Azaña decided to ask Juan Negrín to form a new government. 'The public might have expected it to be Prieto', but the President of the Republic felt that Prieto would be a better option in the three ministries, War, the Navy and Air, merged into a new Ministry of Defence. Furthermore, as prime minister, 'Prieto's mood swings, his "tantrums", might pose a problem'. This is why he preferred to make use of 'Negrín's unruffled energy'. Negrín 'was not unduly surprised by the assignment', although 'he did express some reservations, alleging that there were others who had a higher profile'. After consultations with the socialist executive, Negrín gave Azaña the list of the new government.[34]

As well as Prime Minister, Negrín would continue as Minister of Finance, a post he had occupied in the two previous governments under Largo Caballero. There were two other socialists: Indalecio Prieto in National Defence and Julián Zugazagoitia, the editor of *El Socialista*, and an ally of Prieto's, in the Interior Ministry. The Communist ministers were the same and occupied the same posts: Vicente Uribe in Agriculture and Jesús Hernández in Education, which now also included Health. José Giral, the first wartime Prime Minister of the Republic, took over the Foreign Ministry, which is what Azaña wanted, although the Communists and the UGT were pressing right up to the eleventh hour for Álvarez del Vayo to continue in this post. Bernardo Giner de los Ríos, the *Unión Republicana* leader who had served in all the wartime governments, stayed on in Communications, which now included Public Works. Jaime Aiguader, of *Ezquerra Republicana*, took over Labour and Social Welfare, and finally, Manuel de Irujo, of the PNV, replaced García Oliver in Justice. The eighteen ministries in Largo Caballero's government were reduced by half. It was a *Frente Popular* government, which had been received, according to Azaña, 'with great satisfaction. The people have breathed a sigh of relief'.[35]

---

[33] Azaña, 'El cuaderno de la pobleta', annotation 20 May, pp. 54–5.
[34] Ibid., pp. 55–6.
[35] Ibid., p. 56.

Negrín was to be the Republic's man until the end of the war. And he was not nominated by the Communists, as many have repeatedly claimed, in an attempt to show that Negrín, who sent the gold to Moscow, had sold out to Communism and the International. He was nominated by Azaña, who, as President of the Republic, was the person who had the power to do so, and he did it because Negrín possessed qualities besides his 'unruffled energy'. 'His effectiveness in the Finance Ministry of a country at war was no mean feat', writes Ricardo Miralles. Unlike Indalecio Prieto, he had no history of confrontations with the Communists and the CNT. But, according to Santos Juliá, the 'decisive reason' that Azaña chose Negrín was one of international politics. Almost from the beginning, Azaña believed that the Republic could not win the war and that the only possible exit strategy was international mediation. Negrín, not Largo Caballero, was the ideal man for brokering peace with outside help. He was an educated politician, who spoke several languages and had nothing of the revolutionary about him.[36]

Juan Negrín López was born in Las Palmas de Gran Canaria in 1892, to a wealthy and deeply religious family. He was an excellent student, and his father sent him to Germany, first to the University of Kiel, where he studied between 1906 and 1908, and then to the Institute of Physiology at the University of Leipzig. There he obtained his doctorate in 1912, and began a distinguished career as a physiologist, which continued in Madrid, from 1916 onwards, in the laboratory of general physiology at the *Residencia de Estudiantes*, under the tutelage of Santiago Ramón y Cajal. In 1922 he was appointed Professor of Physiology at the University of Madrid. When his marriage to María Brodksy Fidelman Mijailova, the daughter of a Ukrainian Jew, broke down, he lived with Feliciana López de Dom Pablo from the late 1920s up to his death in 1956.

He joined the PSOE in 1930, and soon afterwards, following the fall of Alfonso XIII and the coming of the Republic, he won a seat in the Constituent Cortes for the electoral district of Gran Canaria. During the years of the Republic, he was again elected in 1933 and 1936, and was a member of the Budget Commission and representative to the International Labour Organisation in Geneva. It was

---

[36] Miralles, *Juan Negrín*, p. 129; Santos Juliá, *Los socialistas en la política española, 1879–1982*, Taurus, Madrid, 1996, pp. 262–3.

also during this time that he became a personal friend and staunch defender of Indalecio Prieto.

Such was the man chosen by Azaña: physiologist, socialist, polyglot and an acknowledged expert in financial affairs. Some months previously he had organised the shipment of three-quarters of the Bank of Spain's gold reserves to the Soviet Union, and had reorganised the Corps of Carabineros, the police force that looked after the frontier posts and was responsible for collecting customs duties. He was not nearly so well known as Prieto or other socialists, but Azaña had every confidence in this 'still young', 'intelligent', 'educated' man, who seemed energetic, determined and courageous. 'Some people will think that the real Prime Minister will be Prieto. They are wrong ... that is not in Negrín's nature'.[37]

And what Azaña expected of the new Executive was 'a will to govern' and that it would put an end to the indiscipline and 'disarray' away from the front. The Republic's authority needed to be re-established in Catalonia, particularly with regard to public order.[38] That prompted Negrín's first move. His government took over the enforcement of public order that up to then had been the *Generalitat*'s responsibility, and on 11 August it dissolved the Council of Aragon and appointed the republican, José Ignacio Mantecón, Governor-General of this territory. Several hundred CNT members were imprisoned. The municipal councils controlled by libertarians were suppressed and replaced by 'executive committees' appointed 'by government order'. The new local power bodies, with the help of the security forces and the 11th Army Division under the command of Enrique Lister, destroyed the collective farms, confiscated all their assets and returned the land to their owners. The chairman of the council, Joaquín Ascaso, the cousin of Francisco Ascaso, who was killed in the fighting against the rebels in July 1936 in Barcelona, and of Domingo Ascaso, a mortal victim of the confrontations of May 1937 in the same city, was arrested in Valencia, on a charge of jewel theft. Soon afterwards he was released and began a nomadic existence, writing report after report to stave off his ostracism. In September 1938, the National Committee expelled him from the CNT.

[37] Azaña, 'El cuaderno de la pobleta', pp. 56–7.
[38] Ibid., p. 58.

The other matter pending since May 1937, what to do with the POUM, was resolved more swiftly and effectively. The Communist press in Aragon, published in Lérida, helped to fuel the atmosphere. On 14 May, the first edition of *La Vanguardia*, the mouthpiece of the regional committee of the PCE, called for the immediate dissolution of the POUM, 'Trotskyite provocateurs', 'an unconditional ally of the dissident *Junta* in Burgos'. There was no argument more categorical than to call someone a 'Fascist' at precisely the time when an 'anti-Fascist war' was being waged. What the Spanish Communists wanted, urged on by the Russian Consul-General in Barcelona, Vladimir Antonov-Ovsenko, was the destruction of this party of 'Trotskyite agents' and 'Fascist spies', who were, moreover, openly criticising the execution of former Bolsheviks carried out by Stalin in the Moscow trials.[39]

That was only the beginning. The 29th Division was once more accused of deserting the front, an accusation that the Communists had been making since February 1937, and on 16 June, José Rovira was arrested. Faced by protests from the anarchist leaders of the 25th, 26th and 28th Divisions, the Minister of Defence, Indalecio Prieto, ordered his release on 10 July. The 29th Division was disbanded and reorganised. As we know, the POUM militants ended their days being hunted down and tortured. A worse fate was to befall Andreu Nin – kidnap, 'disappearance' and murder. Despite the harsh tone of some of the accusations, the CNT, itself a target but ready to return to the government, limited itself to asking for 'legal proof' of the accusations and 'making available to the POUM' Benito Pabón, a syndicalist deputy who won a seat in February 1936 for Zaragoza, and Secretary-General of the Council of Aragon, who defended some of its militants in court.[40]

Andreu Nin, an anti-Stalinist and former secretary of Leon Trotsky in Moscow, had been Councillor for Justice in the *Generalitat* until mid-December 1936, when the POUM, then being goaded by the burgeoning PSUC, was separated from the Catalan government and politically ostracised. It was Nin who decreed the rules for setting up the popular tribunals, thus putting an end to the revolutionary

[39] Paul Preston, *La guerra civil española*, Debate, Barcelona, 2006, pp. 262–3; Casanova, *Anarchism, the Republic and Civil War in Spain*, p. 153.
[40] Casanova, *Anarchism, the Republic and Civil War in Spain*, p. 153.

committees and control patrols, although in the early days of the revolution he had supported the anticlerical violence, as had many others, because he believed that the 'bourgeois' Republic had not solved the 'problem' of the Church: in the end, it had been the workers and revolutionaries who had solved it as only they knew how, by 'attacking the roots', leaving no church standing and suppressing 'priests, churches and worship'. That was how he put it in an interview with *La Vanguardia* on 2 August 1936.

On 16 June 1937, at the same time as the POUM was being declared illegal, Andreu Nin, its political secretary, was arrested in Barcelona by the police, who transferred him to Madrid and thence to the prison at Alcalá de Henares. In spite of being guarded by members of the Special Brigade of the Directorate-General of Security, he was kidnapped on 21 June and murdered, no one knows when, by agents of the Soviet Secret Service in Spain, under the command of the General of the NKVD, Alexander Orlov. His body never appeared. Graffiti painted by his supporters with the question 'Where is Nin?' was answered by others with: 'In Burgos or Berlin'.

The scandal forced Negrín's government to do some juggling. Firstly, Julián Zugazagoitia, the Interior Minister, accused Soviet 'technicians' of the kidnap and the murder, and the Communist Colonel Antonio Ortega, Director-General of Security, was dismissed, accused of connivance with the Soviet agents, in spite of the fact that the PCE ministers defended their comrade 'with extraordinary passion'. But Negrín never provided a convincing explanation of the affair in response to requests from Manuel Azaña, and investigations were called off after Ortega was replaced by the socialist Gabriel Morón on 14 July. Prieto said it was Negrín who did not want the investigations to continue, possibly because it would have brought about a major government crisis, little more than a month after its formation, and because, as Gabriel Jackson states, he could not risk the delivery of Soviet arms over an internal affair that deep down he felt to be a minor matter.[41]

But minor it was not, because as well as Nin, other foreign Trotskyites were kidnapped and went missing, including the journalists Kurt

---

[41] Gabriel Jackson examines in detail everything that is known about Nin's disappearance and the subsequent investigations in *Juan Negrín. Médico, socialista y jefe del gobierno de la II República española*, Crítica, Barcelona, 2008, pp. 117–37; see also Miralles, *Juan Negrín*, pp. 144–6.

Landau and Mark Rein, and José Robles Pazos, a friend of the novelist John Dos Passos. The Nin affair caused friction between Negrín and Zugazagoitia and Irujo, the two ministers who were most anxious to clear up the matter, and it further deepened the distrust between the Communists and the rest of the political organisations fighting on the republican side, particularly the socialist left and the libertarian movement. The political violence in Catalonia and Aragon, which ended with the murders of various anarchists, Communists and POUM militants, plus the hundreds of deaths in the street violence in Barcelona in May 1937, were the clearest evidence yet that the Republic had a serious problem with its internal discord, a true stumbling block in any attempt to win the war.

Negrín wanted to win by fighting, with discipline away from the front and in the army, and organising a solid war industry, although the primary aim of his strategy was to bring about a radical change in the non-intervention policy, thereby obtaining the support of the western democratic powers. The war would be long and it could be won – so thought Negrín when he took office – and in the two years of his premiership he experienced moments of optimism, but others that were disastrous, moments that seemed to herald the final defeat.

On 19 June, barely a month after Negrín assumed office, the Italian forces and the Navarre Brigades took Bilbao. The Basque battalions disobeyed the order to withdraw to Santander and Asturias, and on 26 August they surrendered in Santoña to the troops of General Mario Roatta, the same troops that had marched victoriously into Málaga at the beginning of February and suffered a resounding defeat in Guadalajara in March. The same day, the Francoist forces entered Santander, despite the diversionary tactics prepared by Colonel Rojo on the Aragon front, around Belchite. The Francoist offensive, in which 60,000 men were employed, continued until the occupation of Gijón and Avilés on 21 October, and the fall of the entire territory of Asturias. All of a sudden, the Republic had lost the north, its important mineral resources and its industry. The Francoists, according to Paul Preston, 'already better off in terms of tanks and aeroplanes ... were now able to consolidate their military superiority through control of the production of iron ore'.[42]

---

[42] Preston, *La guerra civil española*, pp. 280–1.

The collapse of the northern front forced Negrín to accelerate the organisation of the war industry. 'The Catalan war industry will never surrender', he said to Azaña. On 31 October, he decided to move the government and the capital to Barcelona, in order to 'establish once and for all the government's authority in Catalonia and get the war industry running at full capacity'. This move relegated the government of the *Generalitat* to a secondary role, furthered control over the collectives and restricted any autonomy the trade unions still had in the running of businesses. In many cases, particularly in the metal sector, control and restrictions were translated into expropriation, which in practice meant the end of collectivisation and union power. Over the following months, the government of the Republic came to control the entire war industry in Catalonia, but it had taken them almost two years to do so.[43]

The progress of the war, despite these measures, gave very little cause for joy and even fewer strategic victories. An exception was the occupation of Teruel at the beginning of the harsh winter of 1938, the only provincial capital to fall to the Republic's army during the war, causing euphoria among the republican political authorities; they celebrated it with a large demonstration in Barcelona. But less than two months later, on 22 February, Franco's troops re-entered the city, and on 9 March they launched a general offensive on the Aragon front, which collapsed within three weeks. By the beginning of April, they had already conquered some parts of Catalonia, Lérida to the north of the River Ebro and Gandesa to the south. On 15 April, they had reached the coast, Vinaroz and Benicàssim, the setting for the famous picture of the two Carlist soldiers splashing about in the waters of the Mediterranean.

These defeats revealed the deep divide between those who believed the war could be continued, starting with Negrín, and those in favour of negotiating a surrender with Franco-British support, a notion which Manuel Azaña had supported all along. The problem at this stage of the war was that the Minister of Defence himself, Indalecio Prieto, shared the latter view, and this gave rise to the second great internal crisis in the republican camp, one year after the first one in May 1937. In fact, Prieto began to express his defeatist attitude after the fall of Bilbao, when he confessed to Zugazagoitia that, as well as

---

[43] Miralles, *Juan Negrín*, p. 150.

presenting his resignation to Negrín, which was not accepted, he had thought of committing suicide, 'and I had my pistol ready'. He told the President of the Republic at the end of June 1937 that, in view of the fact that he could not say that the war was going to be lost in public, 'all we can do is wait until everything collapses around us'. After the fall of Asturias in October, he once again tendered his resignation to Negrín, and once again it was refused.[44]

The war was lost, Prieto kept saying, during the days of the collapse of the Aragon front. The new ambassador for France in Barcelona, Eirik Labonne, asked Negrín on 27 March whether he understood what the Minister of Defence was saying. How were the French or British going to change their policy if even the Republic's Minister of Defence was not confident of winning the war? Two days later, Prieto presented the Cabinet with a devastating report on the situation. On the night of 29–30 March, Negrín decided to remove his intimate friend and collaborator from his post as Minister of Defence, because, as he wrote to him later while in exile, 'you, with your suggestive eloquence, your habitual pathos and the authority of your office completely demoralised our government colleagues'. Prieto, on the other hand, always believed that Negrín had got rid of him in response 'to demands from the Communist Party'.[45]

In the government that was formed on 6 April 1938, without Indalecio Prieto, Negrín took on the post of Minister of National Defence as well, and the two trade union organisations were once more represented, with Ramón González Peña, the UGT leader in the Asturias uprising, as Minister of Justice, and Segundo Blanco, of the CNT, who also came from Asturias and had defended the workers' alliance in 1934, as Education Minister. The latter replaced Jesús Hernández, and thus the PCE was left with just one member in the government, Vicente Uribe in Agriculture. The socialist Julio Álvarez del Vayo was once more Minister of Education, and as well as Aiguader and Giner de los Ríos, who continued in Labour and Communications, José Giral and Manuel de Irujo were once again Ministers without Portfolio, as was the case in the government formed by Largo Caballero on 4 November 1936. Another republican, Francisco Méndez Aspe, who had played an important role

---

[44] Preston, *La guerra civil española*, p. 280.
[45] Miralles, *Juan Negrín*, pp. 196–200.

in the first shipments of the gold reserves with Giral's government, replaced Negrín as Minister of Finance.

The UGT and CNT, which had long been requesting their return to the government, did so after signing a 'unity of action programme' in March. This was the famous 'workers' solution', the oft-aborted 'revolutionary workers' alliance', which finally came to fruition when the two trade union organisations were a shadow of their former selves, with the UGT broken and split and the CNT impotent. This impotence healed the wounds. While the two organisations had muscle, it was never going to be possible to bridge the gap between them or get them to respond favourably to the countless calls for unity that were made.

This 'War government', or government of 'national union', kicked off with a programme passed by the Cabinet on 30 April and made public, significantly, on 1 May, which everyone called Negrín's 'Thirteen-point Plan', a number chosen 'on purpose', according to Gabriel Jackson, 'in defiance of old superstitions'. Among other things, it called for the independence and territorial integrity of Spain; it claimed respect for private property and freedom of conscience and religion; and it proposed a general political amnesty to enable the rebuilding of Spain after the war was over.[46]

But the survival of the Republic after May 1938 depended not only on a good army and the resistance of the civilian population, but also on the abandonment of the non-intervention policy, something that was not to be, despite the diplomatic efforts that Negrín made during the middle months of that year. If France and the United Kingdom were not going to change their minds, it was suggested that at least they could put pressure on the Fascist powers to convince Franco to offer a negotiated settlement, an armistice that would prevent the 'reign of terror and bloody vengeance' that Negrín knew Franco would impose.[47]

There was still hope in the summer of 1938, with the beginning of the Battle of the Ebro and the granting of a loan of 60 million dollars from the Soviet Union, now that the gold reserves were about to run out. These hopes were frustrated, firstly on the international front, by the Munich Agreement at the end of September, whereby the United

---

[46] Jackson, *Juan Negrín*, pp. 252–8.
[47] Miralles, *Juan Negrín*, pp. 358–9.

Kingdom and France handed Czechoslovakia over to Hitler; and secondly on the domestic front, by the outcome of the Battle of the Ebro on 16 November, which ended with the Republic's army returning to the positions it had held on 24 July at the start of the battle. What made it worse was that the Republic suffered tens of thousands of casualties and a considerable loss of war materiel, which it could no longer use to defend Catalonia against the decisive Nationalist offensive. With the signing of the Munich Agreement, which saw the end of Czechoslovakia, the only democracy left standing in central and eastern Europe, the western democracies also wiped out the Spanish Republic. According to Helen Graham, this was because they showed their unshakeable commitment to appeasing the Fascist powers and undermined Negrín's strategy of resistance and that of the Spaniards who believed in him.[48]

And it was when the Republic was risking everything, putting up a military resistance until a war broke out in Europe or, at worst, continuing the struggle in order to maintain a position of strength and negotiate a surrender without reprisals, that internal discord reappeared, one of the curses that plagued the Republic throughout the war. Many republican and socialist leaders became demoralised and began to criticise Negrín's resistance strategy and his dependence on the Soviet Union and the PCE. Food shortages also wore down resistance, but the end of the Republic was speeded up by the coup mounted by Colonel Segismundo Casado, head of the army of the Centre, whose principal aim was to overthrow Negrín's government and negotiate a surrender with Franco. He obtained support from various officers and politicians, including Cipriano Mera, an anarchist who was always in favour of insurrection, and now commander of the 4th Army Corps, and Julián Besteiro, who had already held conversations with agents of Franco and the underground *Falange* in Madrid. On 5 March, the rebels formed the National Council of Defence. It was a military rebellion against the legitimate government, still in power, and as Azaña, surprised that Besteiro was involved, said, 'it repeated Franco's coup d'état and, what was worse, with the same pretext: the excessive preponderance or intolerable dominance of the Communists'.[49]

[48] Graham, *The Spanish Republic at War 1936–1939*, p. 383.
[49] Cipriano Rivas Cheriff, *Retrato de un desconocido. Vida de Manuel Azaña*, Grijalbo, Barcelona, 1979, p. 437.

Fighting was intense in Madrid for a few days, until 10 March, leaving around 2,000 dead. It was not hard for the rebels to squash any Communist resistance, amid their fatigue and general malaise. They trusted Franco's promise of clemency – a promise that Negrín and many others knew he would not keep, because the war waged by the July 1936 military rebels, with Franco at their head, was a war of extermination, and that meant destroying the roots of the enemy, so that it would take decades for them to lift their heads again. It is now time to take a look at the other camp, the rebel Spain of Franco and the crusade.

10 | 'Nationalist' Spain

Those who rose against the Republic did not have so much difficulty finding a single military and political leader. As of 1 October 1936, Francisco Franco was 'Head of Government of the Spanish State'. His military colleagues who put him there thought that this post would be temporary, that the war would soon be over with the conquest of Madrid and that then would be the time to think of the political framework of the new State. However, after various frustrated attempts to take the capital, Franco changed his military strategy, and what might have been a rapid seizure of power became a long, drawn-out war. He was also convinced, particularly after the arrival in Salamanca of his brother-in-law, Ramón Serrano Suñer, who had managed to escape from the 'red confinement' in Madrid in mid-February 1937, that all the political forces needed to be united in a single party.

'Head of Government of the Spanish State', *Caudillo*, *Generalísimo* of the Armed Forces, undisputed leader of the 'Movement', as the single party was known, Franco confirmed his absolute dominance with the creation, on 30 January 1938, of his first government, in which he carefully distributed the various ministries among officers, monarchists, Falangists and Carlists. The construction of this new State was accompanied by the physical elimination of the opposition, the destruction of all the symbols and policies of the Republic and the quest for an emphatic, unconditional victory, with no possibility of any mediation.

In this quest, Franco had the support and blessing of the Catholic Church. Bishops, priests and the rest of the Church began to look on Franco as someone sent by God to impose order in the 'earthly city', and Franco ended up believing that he did indeed have a special relationship with divine providence. Thus emerged Franco's Church, which identified with him, admired him as *Caudillo*, as someone sent by God to re-establish the consubstantiality of traditional Spanish culture with the Catholic faith.

Franco

Francisco Franco was born in El Ferrol on 4 December 1892, and was 43 years old at the time of the rising against the Republic. Almost all his military service had been in Africa, and this provided him with rapid promotions for his exploits in battle, and a good number of decorations and distinctions. He entered the Military Academy in Toledo in 1907, and despite passing out 251st of the 312 officers in his year, by 1915 he was a captain, and in February 1926, at the age of 33, he had risen to brigadier. Between 1920 and 1925, he served in the Spanish Foreign Legion, created in 1920 by José Millán Astray, with Franco joining as second-in-command. He was appointed Director of the Zaragoza Military Academy on 4 January 1928, where he served until it was closed down by the Second Republic; during the years of the Republic, he was military commander of La Coruña in 1932, general commander of the Balearic Isles in 1933 and 1934, Supreme Commander of the Spanish forces in Morocco at the beginning of 1935, Chief of General Staff from 17 May 1935 until February 1936, and General Commander of the Canary Islands from March until 18 July that year. He was promoted to major-general at the end of March 1934, on the recommendation of the then Minister of War, the radical Diego Hidalgo.

Franco was considered by his brother officers to be a well-trained and competent commander, but his path to the highest command was smoothed by the disappearance from the scene of some of his more qualified rivals for the position. General José Sanjurjo, who had to fly from Portugal to Spain to head the rising, died on 20 July when his small aircraft, piloted by the Falangist Juan Antonio Ansaldo, crashed near Lisbon. Generals Joaquín Fanjul and Manuel Goded had failed in their attempt to take Madrid and Barcelona, and they were arrested and shot a few days later. José Calvo Sotelo, the far-right monarchist leader, who maintained close contact with the plotters, had been murdered on 13 July, and José Antonio Primo de Rivera, the head of the *Falange*, was in prison in Alicante, another city in which the uprising had failed.

Gonzalo Queipo de Llano, who led the rising in Seville, was, like Franco, a major-general, although he had held this rank longer. The problem was that he had been a republican and plotted against monarchist governments, and thus could not be a reliable leader for all the rebel officers. That left Emilio Mola, who had prepared the plot and the rebellion as its director, although he was a lieutenant general, a lower rank than Franco. Potentially, however, he was a rival. His was the idea to set up the *Junta de Defensa Nacional de Burgos*, the first body to coordinate the military tactics of the rebels, and he had, with considerable help from the *Requeté*, been winning control of a large part of the northern zone of Spain, including almost the entire province of Guipúzcoa, since the beginning of September.

Franco played his cards with cleverness and ambition. He presented himself to the media and diplomats as the principal general of the rebels, and this is also what he told the Germans and Italians, so that a few days after the coup d'état, certain European Foreign Ministries were already referring to the rebels as 'Francoists'. He also commanded the best-trained troops of the Spanish army, the 47,000 soldiers of the Foreign Legion and the *Regulares Indígenas*, which he managed to transfer to the Peninsula thanks to the transport planes and bombers sent by Hitler and Mussolini. This, say the experts, was the decisive factor in placing Franco as the best candidate in the struggle for power: the control of the army of Africa and his swift transfer of these troops to the Peninsula, thereby ensuring that any aid from the Fascist powers would pass through his hands alone.

The advance of the professional troops of the Foreign Legion and the Arab mercenaries of the *Regulares* left its mark in Almendralejo, Mérida, Zafra and Badajoz. Franco was not unduly concerned about the lives of the reds. He would save Spain from Marxism, whatever the cost, shooting, if necessary, 'half of Spain'. The republican militias fled in terror from the advance of the Moors, as affirmed by John T. Whitaker, of the *New York Herald*, who accompanied General Yagüe around Extremadura and Toledo. In Talavera, which they occupied on 3 September, 'it seemed the killing would never end'. The victims were peasants and workers. According to Whitaker, all it took was to be in possession of a trade union card, to have been a freemason or to have voted for the Republic.[1]

---

[1] The idea that Franco played his cards astutely and with ambition is one of the main hypotheses of Paul Preston in his indispensable biography, *Franco: A Biography*, HarperCollins, London, 1993; see pp. 144–98 for what the author calls 'The making of a Generalísimo'.

Such was the prevailing situation in the early days in the territories occupied by the military rebels: the imposition of order against the forces that had mobilised the masses in favour of socialism and revolution; the forging of an authoritarian mentality as against liberalism, the parliamentary system of parties and free elections. It was also, as various authors such as Fusi, Preston and Moradiellos have pointed out, the application of 'a national-militaristic theory' originating in the personal experiences of the *Africanista* officers, 'a militaristic view of political life and public order that made the army a Praetorian institution virtually independent of civilian power'. This view was shared by many officers who had been born in the last two decades of the nineteenth century and had served in Morocco during the final years of the Restoration and the dictatorship of Primo de Rivera, such as Goded, Mola, José Enrique Varela, Juan Vigón, Juan Yagüe and Franco. The transformation of the coup d'état into a civil war produced a regime of terror, with mass executions, imprisonment and torture for thousands of men and women.[2]

The aim was for the new order to be constructed around the destruction of the adversary. The first task was to create a single military command and a centralised political apparatus. The Third Reich authorities who were negotiating with Franco the loan of war materiel had been pressing him since the end of August to take up the reins. Meanwhile, certain generals who were intensely loyal to Franco, including Kindelán, Orgaz and Millán Astray, as well as his brother Nicolás, formed, in the words of Preston, 'a kind of political campaign staff committed to ensuring that Franco became first Commander-in-Chief and then Chief of State'.[3] It was Alfredo Kindelán, the former head of Aviation with the Monarchy, who had asked to be released from the army with the Republic, who suggested that a meeting be held of the *Junta de Defensa Nacional* and other generals to choose a supreme chief.

The meeting took place on 21 September in a barrack hut of an aerodrome near Salamanca. It was chaired by General Miguel Cabanellas,

---

[2] Juan Pablo Fusi, *Franco. Autoritarismo y poder personal*, Taurus, Madrid, 1995, pp. 12–13; Enrique Moradiellos, *Francisco Franco. Crónica de un caudillo casi olvidado*, Biblioteca Nueva, Madrid, 2002, pp. 28–30.
[3] Preston, *Franco*, p. 177.

and among those present were Generals Franco, Mola, Queipo de Llano, Dávila and Saliquet. At lunch on the estate of Antonio Pérez Tabernero, a bull-breeder, all were in favour of naming a single command, except for Cabanellas, who advocated a junta such as the one already set up, over which he presided. And they all proposed naming Franco *Generalísimo*, except Cabanellas, who abstained, and later commented: 'You don't know what you've done, because you don't know him like I do – he served under me in the army of Africa as head of one of the columns under my command; and if you want to give him Spain now, he is going to believe it is his alone and will not let anyone replace him either during or after the war, until he is dead'.[4]

The same day, Franco decided to delay the advance on Madrid to relieve the Alcázar in Toledo, where republican forces had besieged a thousand civil guards and Falangists under the command of Colonel José Moscardó, who were holding the wives and children of known leftist militants hostage. On 27 September, legionnaires and *Regulares* entered Toledo and liquidated anyone who stood in their path, including the wounded in the hospital who were finished off in their beds, or the pregnant 'reds' who were taken out of the maternity wing and shot in the cemetery. The 659 names inscribed in the cemetery's registry of deaths between 1 and 7 October leave no room for doubt. It was a 'sacred revenge', wrote the Jesuit priest Alberto Risco in *La epopeya del Alcázar de Toledo* a little later: 'That was why, with the encouragement of God's vengeance on the tips of their machetes, they hunted down, destroyed and killed, without giving the fugitives time to reach the walls to take evasive action'.[5]

The capture of the Alcázar fuelled the legend of General Franco. Moscardó's famous utterance 'all quiet in the Alcázar', repeated to Franco and numerous journalists, two days after its liberation, was suitably propagated. Franco was the saviour of the besieged heroes, the symbol of an army prepared to win the war at any cost. On 1 October he was named 'Head of Government of the Spanish State', in the words of the decree drawn up by the monarchist José Yanguas Messía, a professor of international law. In the investiture ceremony,

[4] Quoted by his son Guillermo Cabanellas, *La guerra de los mil días. Nacimiento, vida y muerte de la II República española*, 2 vols., Grijalbo, Barcelona, 1973, vol. I, p. 652.
[5] Quoted in Isabelo Herreros, *Mitología de la Cruzada de Franco. El Alcázar de Toledo*, Vosa, Madrid, 1995, p. 75.

General Miguel Cabanellas, in the presence of diplomats from Italy, Germany and Portugal, handed over power on behalf of the *Junta de Defensa*, over which he had presided since 24 July, and which was dissolved to be replaced by a *Junta Técnica del Estado*, headed by General Fidel Dávila. Franco adopted the title of *Caudillo*, in an allusion to the medieval warrior lords. A warrior he had always been. A saint he had been since the day before, when the bishop of Salamanca, Enrique Pla y Deniel, published his pastoral letter, 'Las dos ciudades', in which he contrasted the heroism of the military rebels with the savagery of the Republic. This war was a crusade – a crusade blessed by the Church and led by Franco.

Franco had been 'a practising Catholic the whole of his life'. All the members of the *Junta Técnica del Estado* were noted for their 'religious beliefs', and were 'pious', but 'the one who stands out in this aspect is the *Generalísimo*'. Such was the view of Cardinal Isidro Gomá, the Primate of the Catholic Church in Spain, when he spoke about Franco for the first time to the Secretary of State for the Vatican, Cardinal Pacelli, later Pius XII, on 24 October 1936. Gomá had yet to meet Franco personally, but he already believed 'that he will be an exceptional collaborator in favour of the work of the Church from the high position he occupies'.[6]

Gomá sent Franco a telegram to congratulate him on his election as 'Head of Government of the Spanish State', and Franco answered him by saying that on taking on this post 'with all its responsibilities, I could receive no better help than the blessing of Your Eminence'. Franco asked him to pray to God that 'He enlighten me and give me sufficient strength for the immense task of creating a new Spain, the happy outcome of which is already ensured by the gracious collaboration that is so patriotically offered by Your Eminence, whose pastoral ring I kiss' – a veritable baring of the soul.[7]

Franco was anxious to hawk his religious piety at this time, and he had understood, as had the majority of his brothers-in-arms, how important it was to introduce religion into his public statements and

[6] 'Report by Cardinal Gomá to the State Secretariat. Third general report on the situation of Spain on the occasion of the civilian-military movement of July 1936', 24 October 1936, *Archivo Gomá. Documentos de la Guerra Civil. Julio–diciembre de 1936* (ed. José Andrés Gallego and Antón M. Pazos), 12 vols., CSIC, Madrid, 2001, vol. II, pp. 245–52.
[7] Ibid.

mingle with the 'people' in solemn religious acts. Once established as Head of State, says Paul Preston, his propagandists moulded an image of him as a 'great Catholic crusader' and his public religiosity notably intensified. From 4 October 1936 until his death on 20 November 1975, Franco had a personal chaplain, Father José María Bulart. He heard mass every day and, whenever he could, he joined his wife, Doña Carmen Polo y Martínez Valdés, for the evening rosary.[8] In short, the man was an 'exemplary Christian', a 'fine Catholic', said Gomá, 'who cannot imagine the Spanish State outside its traditional bounds of Catholicism at all levels'.[9]

Pla y Deniel lent him his palace in Salamanca for use as a centre of operations – 'headquarters', as it was known throughout Christian Spain. There, surrounded by the Moorish guard, he held court. Franco needed the support and blessing of the Catholic Church. He needed to be acknowledged by all the Catholics and respectable people of the world, with the Pope at the head. He needed the Church to wage a war of extermination and be seen as a saint. And he needed the Church to remain untroubled because he would know how to express his gratitude later. Gomá had already said as much to Cardinal Pacelli on 9 November 1936, after Franco had been supreme head for barely a month:

I have had a long talk with the Head of State ... My impressions are frankly favourable ... He intends to respect the freedom of the Church, promote the interests of the Catholic religion, to propose a Concordat with the Holy See, to see to the temporal needs of the Church and its ministers, to defend education and give it an openly Christian orientation at all levels.[10]

Despite the creation of this high political and military command, there were still some centres of autonomous power, at least until April 1937. From the start, Queipo de Llano acquired considerable popularity with his radio broadcasts. He issued numerous orders and decrees without informing the *Junta de Defensa*, and law-abiding

---

[8] Preston, *Franco*, p. 188.
[9] *Informe del Cardenal Gomá a Secretaría de Estado. Tercer informe general sobre la situación de España con motivo del movimiento cívico-militar de julio de 1936 (24 de octubre de 1936)*, in *Archivo Gomá*, pp. 242–52.
[10] 'Letter from Cardinal Gomá to Cardinal Pacelli', 9 November 1936, *Archivo Gomá*, pp. 289–93.

citizens were grateful to him for eradicating the revolutionary movement. However, beyond his lust for power or eccentricities, Queipo shared the basic ideas of the military dictatorship that was being exercised in the territory controlled by the rebels: 'Spain cannot be reconstructed until the entire political rabble is swept away', he declared in November 1936, when the cleansing was already well under way.[11]

This cleansing received a great deal of help from the Carlists and Falangists, the two elements of civilian mobilisation that had been aiding the rising from the beginning. The recruitment of thousands of Carlists in Navarre and Álava gave them greater political weight in the early months of the war. They set up a *Junta Central de Guerra*, presided over by the leader of the Communion, Fal Conde, divided into two sections, military and political, which exercised full power in Navarre. Anxious to have military control of this mobilisation, in December 1936 the Carlist leaders set up a Royal Military Academy for *requetés*, a measure that was totally incompatible with Franco's decision to incorporate the Carlist and Falangist militias into the regular army. Franco expressed to the Count of Rodezno, Fal Conde's rival for the leadership of the Communion, his 'displeasure', because, besides the 'Head of State', there was another power 'that was creating and regulating armies, and granting promotions'. He classed this as a 'crime of treason' and told him that Fal Conde would have to give up this venture. General Dávila, on behalf of Franco, gave Fal Conde forty-eight hours to leave Spain or face a court martial. Fal went to Portugal and Franco thus eliminated a potential competitor and clipped the wings of a group that was enjoying great success at mobilising followers at that time.[12]

Also spectacular was the growth of the *FE de las JONS* in the early months of the civil war, when a good many of its leaders – some of them released from gaol by the military rising – channelled their energies into recruiting new members who were flooding into the Fascist camp. It had been a small organisation before the elections of February 1936, although the defeat of the CEDA and the fascistisation of the right in subsequent months had swelled its membership by the eve of the coup d'état. Its radical thinking and paramilitary structure,

[11] Ian Gibson, *Queipo de Llano. Sevilla, verano de 1936,* Grijalbo, Barcelona, 1986, pp. 72, 224, 256.
[12] Preston, *Franco,* pp. 208–9.

as well as the loss of credibility of organisations such as the CEDA, which had decided to accept the legitimacy of the Republic, made it a pole of attraction when arms replaced politics. By October 1936, there were in excess of 36,000 Falangists on the fronts, together with over 22,000 Carlists and more than 6,000 members of other tendencies, such as the Alfonsines or the CEDA.

Now it had thousands of members, but it still lacked the solid direction of undisputed or charismatic leaders. José Antonio Primo de Rivera, the national leader, was in prison in Alicante with his brother Miguel. Onésimo Redondo had died on 24 July in Labajos, Segovia, in a gun battle with republican militias. Julio Ruiz de Alda and Fernando Primo de Rivera, José Antonio's younger brother, were murdered in August in the Modelo prison in Madrid. Two months later, after a *saca* from the Las Ventas prison, it was the turn of Ramiro Ledesma Ramos. Also in prison were Raimundo Fernández Cuesta, who was exchanged in October 1937, and Rafael Sánchez Mazas, who managed to escape a mass firing squad a little before the end of the war. As one of the backroom Falangist leaders, José Luna, the provincial head in Cáceres and an infantry captain, said: the *Falange* had gone from having 'a tiny body with a big head to a monstrous body with no head at all'.[13]

Falangist heads from the various sectors of rebel Spain met in Valladolid on 2 September 1936 and set up a provisional command junta, presided over by Manuel Hedilla, a man loyal to José Antonio, who was then busy training Falangist militias. The junta moved to Salamanca at the beginning of October, to be near Franco's headquarters. From there, various operations to rescue José Antonio were planned, directed by Agustín Aznar, head of the Falangist militias, but they all failed, and in any case, the venture was not one of Franco's priorities. Before he was shot in the prison yard in Alicante on 20 November, José Antonio wrote his will, naming as executors his friends Raimundo Fernández Cuesta and Ramón Serrano Suñer, and after managing to cross over into the Francoist zone, these two were to play a major role in the unified *Falange*.

News of the death of José Antonio, published in the republican and foreign press, was suppressed in rebel Spain. Franco used the

[13] Quoted in Javier Tusell, *Franco en la guerra civil. Una biografía política*, Tusquets, Barcelona, 1992, pp. 91–2.

cult of *el Ausente* (the absent one) in order to create a vacuum in the party's leadership and manipulate the *Falange* as a tool for the political mobilisation of the civilian population. One month later, on 20 December, Franco issued a decree placing the Falangist militias and those of the other organisations under the orders of the military authorities. All combat personnel, militarised and regular, were now under the authority of the *Generalísimo*. The autonomous centres of power began to disappear. The arrival of Serrano Suñer in Salamanca brought about the formation of a single political force, a mass movement that would be used to enable it to identify with its Fascist and Nazi allies.

Unification

By the end of 1936, all the political forces that backed the military uprising, once they had accepted the supreme command of Franco, were in favour of some kind of unification, although the problem lay in figuring out which force would predominate. In this aspect, everyone feared it would be the *Falange*. Such was the opinion of the Alfonsines, led by Antonio Goicochea, what was left of Gil Robles' CEDA, and particularly the Carlist sectors who supported the Prince Regent, Don Javier de Borbón-Parma, who was living in the south of France, and Manuel Fal Conde, in exile in Portugal. Franco was thinking of a party that would help him to gain even more power for himself. He was also being pressured in this direction by the Italian Fascists. In February 1937, an envoy sent by Mussolini, Roberto Farinacci, who used the highly radical and violent influence of the *Squadristi* to get himself appointed secretary of the Fascist party, urged Franco to create, 'with the political forces that have contributed combatants', a Spanish National Party, with a genuine Fascist and corporatist programme.[14]

Around the same time, Ramón Serrano Suñer arrived in Salamanca, after managing to escape from republican Madrid with the help of Doctor Gregorio Marañón. In 1933 and 1936, Serrano Suñer had been a CEDA deputy for Zaragoza, the city where he practised law. He was married to Carmen Polo's younger sister, Ramona or 'Zita' Polo, and had been a close friend of José Antonio since his time as a

---

[14] Ibid., p. 112.

student at the Universidad Central in Madrid. He arrived in Salamanca with his wife and children, traumatised by his captivity and by having seen his brothers José and Fernando killed for organising his escape. According to Joan Maria Thomàs, Serrano Suñer, an expert in administrative law, was the ideal person 'to lay the legal foundations of the New State', a task for which neither Nicolás Franco nor the rest of the *Generalísimo*'s collaborators were suited. 'It was Serrano Suñer who was finally to give specific shape to Franco's ideas for setting up a single-party regime'.[15]

Serrano Suñer explained to Franco that what he was running was a 'field State', with a barrack-room mentality, which needed to be replaced by a permanent political mechanism, a new State similar to those run by Fascist regimes. Serrano Suñer's plan consisted of creating a mass political movement based on the union of the *Falange* and the Traditionalist Carlist Communion, a venture in which Franco's brother, Nicolás, his right-hand man until Serrano Suñer's arrival, had had no success.

Franco first called Rodezno and other Navarran traditionalist leaders to tell them his decision: there would be no negotiations between the two groups, as this would smack of democratic party politics, and he would be the one to decree unification. He was more worried about the *Falange*, because it was a bigger party, with totalitarian aims, but since the death of José Antonio, its leaders had been locked in a power struggle: on the one hand there was Hedilla, closely supported by two fellow Cantabrians, the journalist Víctor de la Serna, son of the novelist Concha Espina, and Maximiano García Venero; and on the other, the militia chiefs Agustín Aznar and Sancho Dávila.

This power struggle developed into a bloody brawl between the two rival groups, a situation that was exploited by Serrano Suñer to silence any focus of resistance to unification. On 16 April 1937, friends and relations of José Antonio, the so-called *legitimistas*, dismissed Hedilla, who they feared wanted to take over the leadership of the *Falange*; they dissolved the provisional *Junta de Mando* that he presided over and appointed a triumvirate of Aznar, Dávila and José Moreno, the organisation's general administrator. Armed militiamen loyal to both camps converged on Salamanca.

[15] Joan Maria Thomàs, *Lo que fue la Falange*, Plaza & Janés, Barcelona, 1999, p. 145.

That same night, Hedilla, who had been led to believe by Franco that he had his full support, sent a group of men to the hotel where Sancho Dávila was staying, with the intention of arresting him, and in the ensuing struggle the head of the Santander militias, José María Alonso Goya, and one of Dávila's bodyguards, named Peral, were killed. The police arrested Dávila and Aznar for creating a disturbance in the rearguard, and Franco ordered the army to control any militiamen entering or leaving the city. By the morning of 17 April, all the centres of disturbance were under control. The following day, a National Council of the *Falange Española* elected Hedilla as national leader, but with one condition attached to his appointment, that it would be 'until José Antonio Primo de Rivera or Raimundo Fernández Cuesta returned to their posts'. Hedilla, who did not realise that he was being manipulated by Franco, immediately proposed 'the setting up of a commission to write a speech for the *Generalísimo* establishing the indispensable bases for the national-syndicalist State'. In other words, his intention was to tell Franco that the Falangist programme would be the guideline for the unified party and the New State.[16]

But Franco was in no mood for negotiation because his mind was made up. On 19 April, the unification decree was issued, with a long preamble and three points, drawn up by Serrano Suñer. *Falange Española* and the *Requeté* would combine under the leadership of Franco in a 'single national political unit', *Falange Española Tradicionalista y de las JONS*, 'a link between the State and society', in which the 'Catholic spirituality' of the *Requeté*, 'the traditional force', would be integrated into 'the new force', as had happened 'in other countries with a totalitarian regime'. All the other groups that had supported the rebel war effort, including the Alfonsines and the CEDA, were excluded.

In practice, this meant that the hierarchical structures of the Falangists and *Requeté* would disappear, because from that moment, the supreme chief was Franco. Hedilla would be reduced to a mere member of the Political Council; not only did he not accept this, pressurised as he was by the 'old guard' and the *legitimistas* close to Pilar Primo de Rivera, who accused him of 'betraying' José Antonio's *Falange*, but he also told his provincial bosses to obey his orders

---

[16] The process of unification is efficiently described in Thomàs, *Lo que fue la Falange*, pp. 146–221 and Tusell, *Franco en la guerra civil*, pp. 79–137.

alone. On 25 April, Hedilla was arrested, along with other dissident Falangists. Apparently, no less a personage than the German ambassador, von Faupel, had advised him to accept the post and even offered him an aircraft to take him to Germany.[17]

Two months later, Hedilla appeared before two summary courts martial. The prosecution had been prepared by the military legal adviser in Franco's headquarters, Lorenzo Martínez Fuste, and by the Civil Guard Major Lisardo Doval, the public order delegate for Salamanca and chief of the headquarters' police service, a crony of Franco's who had made a name for himself for his brutality in putting down the revolution in Asturias in October 1934. Hedilla was accused of 'supporting rebellion' and refusal to comply with the unification decree, and he was sentenced to death. In a letter that his mother delivered to Franco, Hedilla asked for 'mercy and magnanimity'. Pilar Primo de Rivera and Serrano Suñer also intervened for a reprieve, while von Faupel advised that 'in the current climate it is very dangerous to create martyrs'. Franco reprieved him, but he spent four years in gaol and, says Javier Tusell, 'Hedilla was to live the rest of his life in a situation of official ostracism, thinking about an independent *Falange* that would always remain an impossibility'.[18]

In view of the hold that Franco had on the situation, there was little chance of resistance, however angry the Carlists or the hardline sector of the *Falange*, grouped around the founder's sister, were about the way unification had come about. From the outset, it was a party dominated by Franco, thus leaving him without any political rivals. Antonio Goicochea dissolved *Renovación Española*, and Gil Robles, who enthusiastically accepted unification and gave instructions for *Acción Popular* to comply with the decree, saw no improvement in his situation. The Falangists never forgave him for his spell in the government of the Republic, and Franco had no intention of incorporating a representative of the old regime, especially as he had been his superior as Minister of War.

And if anyone still had any doubts as to Franco's position, barely a month and a half after unification, the only rival with any chance left was also eliminated. On 3 June 1937, the aircraft taking General Emilio Mola to inspect the front, at the height of the campaign to

---

[17] Thomàs, *Lo que fue la Falange*, p. 212.
[18] Tusell, *Franco en la guerra civil*, pp. 130–1, 301.

control the north, crashed near Alcocero, a small village in the province of Burgos. According to the official version, the plane crashed into a hill because of the fog, although there were rumours of sabotage and also that the aircraft, an Airspeed A.S. 6 Envoy manufactured in the United Kingdom, was shot down by friendly aircraft by mistake. The German ambassador, von Faupel, wrote shortly afterwards: 'There is no doubt that Franco feels relieved at General Mola's death'.[19]

Although Franco was the undisputed head, and the unification attempted to satisfy the various groups in the rebel camp, the *Falange*, according to Javier Tusell, came out of it well at the beginning, and its leaders held the most important posts in the administration and the party. Proof may be found in the appointment of the fifty members of the National Council of *FET y de las JONS* in October 1937. Half of them were Falangists, while the traditionalists accounted for a quarter of the total, five were monarchists and there were also eight officers, all of them close to Franco or, as was the case with Queipo de Llano, were difficult to dispense with at the time. The four councillors at the top of the list were Pilar Primo de Rivera, the Count of Rodezno, General Queipo de Llano and José María Pemán. At the beginning of December, Franco appointed the first secretary of the *FET y de las JONS*, a post that was given to Raimundo Fernández Cuesta, the most prominent of the old guard remaining, who had just arrived in the rebel zone after being exchanged for the republican Justino de Azcárate.[20]

However, other historians maintain that after the unification, most of the more radical Fascists, *legitimistas* or followers of Hedilla, were left, as Ismael Saz says, 'politically neutralised', or that the party became, in Preston's words, 'a machine for the distribution of patronage'.[21] There were some people, Pemán for one, who seemed not to take their posts seriously. 'I have been appointed a member of the *Falange Española Tradicionalista* National Council', he wrote, 'but I don't think the new post will be too burdensome: I imagine the Council will be a showpiece, in the style of the Fascist Great Council,

[19] Preston, *Franco*, p. 279.
[20] Tusell, *Franco en la guerra civil*, pp. 147–50.
[21] Ismael Saz's argument in 'Política en zona nacionalista: la configuración de un régimen', in Enrique Moradiellos (ed.), 'La guerra civil', *Ayer*, 50 (2003), pp. 79–83; Preston, *Franco*, p. 271.

which meets, for example, to declare war on Abyssinia after it has already been declared'.[22]

Pemán may have been a joker, yet he took very seriously his work in the Culture and Education Commission of the *Junta Técnica del Estado*, where he unleashed a brutal repression on teachers and began to undo all the republican educational reforms. It might well be that the National Council was of not much use, because Franco was said never to accept advice, but monarchists, Carlists and Falangists fought to occupy posts in city councils, provincial councils and local branches of the new party. *FET y de las JONS* attracted anyone, outside the former CEDA or Carlism, who subscribed to the idea of order and cleansing put into practice by the rebels since July 1936, and many of its members, according to Ángela Cenarro, found in these local or provincial institutions 'ample scope for feathering their nests'.[23]

The principal national delegations of the new party also went to ex-Falangists: the *Sección Femenina* to Pilar Primo de Rivera; Press and Propaganda to the Navarran priest, Fermín Yzurdiaga; *Auxilio Social*, the new name given to *Auxilio de Invierno*, to Mercedes Sanz Bachiller. And other leaders who had been imprisoned for the events of April 1937, such as Agustín Aznar and Sancho Dávila, were rehabilitated and promoted to important posts. No former leading figure of the *Falange*, with the exception of the odd Hedilla supporter, was left without a share of the cake. These figures included Dionisio Ridruejo, Alfonso García Valdecasas, José Antonio Giménez Arnau, Pedro Gamero del Castillo, Antonio Tovar and Julián Pemartín.

It took somewhat longer for this pet project of Serrano Suñer's, the creation of the new State, to take shape, although major progress was already being made during the war. The 'field State' gradually gave way to a bureaucracy that was more organised. In the summer of 1937, the monarchist general, Francisco Gómez Jordana, took over the presidency of the *Junta Técnica del Estado*, replacing another general, Fidel Dávila, who had been fairly ineffective during the months he had presided over this body, and whom the Falangists referred to as 'Don Fávila'. Gómez Jordana, Count of Jordana, deplored the chaos

---

[22] Tusell, *Franco en la guerra civil*, pp. 147–50.

[23] Ángela Cenarro, 'Instituciones y poder local en el Nuevo Estado', in Santos Juliá (ed.), *Historia de España de Menéndez Pidal. República y guerra civil*, 42 vols., Espasa Calpe, Madrid, 2004, vol. XL, pp. 332–4.

and 'shambles' that had been left and, together with Serrano Suñer, he tried to restore order to the administrative apparatus. They both believed that what rebel Spain needed was a proper government, not a *Junta Técnica*. And this is what they told Franco.

On 30 November 1938, Franco named his first government, based on suggestions from Serrano Suñer, if we are to believe what he himself claimed in his memoirs. As with all subsequent Francoist governments, the posts were carefully shared out between officers, Carlists, Falangists and monarchists – in other words, between all the sectors that joined forces to rise against the Republic in July 1936. Each sector controlled the area that it felt an affinity to: the military and public order ministries for the officers; the syndical and 'social' ministries for the Falangists; the financial ministries for technocrats, lawyers and engineers; and education and justice for Catholics, traditionalists or ex-members of *Acción Española*. Not once in thirty-seven years of Francoist governments did a woman occupy a ministry. And what the *Caudillo* always required, above any other merit, was loyalty to the 'command'.

Most experts agree that this first government represented a victory for Serrano Suñer, the Interior Minister, over Nicolás Franco, the representative of the poorly structured administration that had prevailed in the first year of the war. General Severiano Martínez Anido, now aged 75, well known for his violent repression of anarchism in the Barcelona of the 1920s, was named Minister of Public Order, although he died before the year was out and his duties were taken over by Serrano Suñer. Fidel Dávila, forever loyal to Franco, was appointed Minister of National Defence. The Ministry of Foreign Affairs went to another officer, Gómez Jordana, who was also appointed Deputy Prime Minister, having previously been a member of General Primo de Rivera's military advisory staff. Franco gave Justice to Tomás Domínguez de Arévalo, the Count of Rodezno, for his loyal work in the unification process. The young fascistised monarchist, Pedro Sainz Rodríguez, was given the Ministry of Education. An engineer, Alfonso Peña Boeuf, was appointed Minister of Public Works, and another engineer, Juan Antonio Suanzes, a close friend of Franco's, took over Industry and Trade. A member of the 'new guard', influenced by Italian Fascism, Pedro González Bueno, who was described by Rodezno as Serrano's 'lapdog', was given Syndical Organisation and Action. And an 'old guard', Raimundo Fernández

Cuesta, was rewarded with Agriculture. Finally, Andrés Amado, a member of *Acción Española* and a friend of Calvo Sotelo's, who had served under him as Director-General of the Treasury in Primo de Rivera's dictatorship, was appointed Minister of Finance.

As Franco said, the government would see to the 'national-syndicalist organisation of the State', although rather than construction, what it oversaw was the destruction of the legislation of the Republic, particularly in anything that had to do with the 'revision of lay legislation'. But above all, it was a government 'born for war and at war', and therefore, to win it outright, it took on Fascist overtones to keep to its commitment with the Axis powers.[24]

The principal political outcome of this new phase was the passing on 9 March 1938 of the *Fuero del Trabajo* (Labour Rights), a kind of mock Constitution based on the *Carta del lavoro* in Fascist Italy. The text stood for a compromise between Falangism, represented by Ridruejo, and Catholic traditionalism (the drafting of this part clearly being the work of Eduardo Aunós, of *Acción Española*); it struck a middle line between 'liberal capitalism and Marxist materialism', guaranteeing Spaniards 'the Fatherland, bread and justice in a military and devoutly religious style'.

Fascism and Catholicism: these were the two cornerstones of the New State that emerged as the war progressed. On the one hand, the Caudillo was exalted like the *Führer* or *il Duce*, with the straight-arm salute and blue shirts; on the other, rituals and religious displays made their appearance with processions, open-air masses and political-religious ceremonies in the medieval style. Rebel Spain became a territory particularly suitable for the 'harmonisation' of Fascism, of the 'modern authoritarian current', with 'glorious tradition'.[25] There was therefore to be a twofold process, running in parallel and simultaneously, says Juan Pablo Fusi, with 'the gradual Fascistisation of the State apparatus (and Spain's national political style) and the restoration of religious life'.[26]

For a time, Fascism and Catholicism were compatible, in declarations and daily life, in the projects that emerged within the rebel camp and in the form of government and way of life imposed by the

---

[24] Preston, *Franco*, pp. 295–8; Tusell, *Franco en la guerra civil*, pp. 228–46.
[25] Julián Casanova, *La Iglesia de Franco*, Crítica, Barcelona, 2005, pp. 332–5.
[26] Fusi, *Franco*, p. 76.

victors. Fascism was 'a vigorous protest against an absurd democracy and sterile liberalism', wrote Eloy Montero in 1939, in his book *Los estados modernos y la nueva España*. It was useless to oppose this 'torrent': 'as Catholics we could not oppose this movement known as Fascism, which was eminently national in nature; we had to accept it with love and follow it along traditional, Christian paths: the modern authoritarian current had to be harmonised with our glorious tradition, and thus a new State would emerge, free of outdated democratic and liberal traces, impregnated in our historic institutions'.[27]

The Jesuit, Constantino Bayle, wrote in the same vein at the height of the war, delighted by Fascism's call to overthrow parliamentarianism and universal suffrage, to wipe out parties and trade unions, to 'abominate' democracy, to 'crush' the 'poisoned Judaeo-Masonic seed'. If this was Fascism, then 'the Nacional Rising, Franco's government, the whole of Christian Spain' were Fascist.[28]

Another Jesuit priest, Félix G. Olmedo, perceived in 1938 an 'incredible similarity ... between the beginning of the reign of the Catholic Monarchs and now. The same religious sentiment, the same idea of Spanish-style Christian social justice ... even the same language and the same symbols and emblems of that time: Imperial Spain, the yoke, the arrows and the eagles'.[29]

The radicalisation that Fascism brought to counter-revolutionary projects and practices, its totalitarian potential, its ideological purity and exclusivity, and the experience of the war of attrition that had been waged by the military rebels since July 1936, was melded with the restoration of this historical parallel between Catholicism and the Spanish national identity. Catholicism was the perfect antidote to the lay Republic, separatism and revolutionary ideologies. It became the perfect hook for all those who joined the rebel camp, from the most hardline Fascists to those who had proclaimed themselves to be rightist republicans. And so, this civil war, caused by a coup d'état, became a religious crusade to save Christian civilisation, the protective cloak for the annihilation of the 'wicked Marxists' and the 'red rabble'.

27 Quoted in Alfonso Botti, *Cielo y dinero. El nacional-catolicismo en España (1881–1975)*, Alianza Editorial, Madrid, 1992, pp. 102–3.
28 Constantino Bayle, 'El espíritu de Falange Española ¿es católico?', *Razón y Fe*, 112 (1937), p. 326.
29 Félix G. Olmedo, *El sentido de la guerra española*, El Mensajero del Corazón de Jesús, Bilbao, 1938.

Victory with divine protection

The uprising was not undertaken in the name of religion. The military rebels were more concerned with other things: saving order, the Fatherland, casting out liberalism, republicanism, and the socialist and revolutionary ideologies that were serving to orientate large sectors of urban and rural workers. But from the outset, the Church and most Catholics lent all of their not inconsiderable support to this cause. And naturally, they did so to defend religion. But also to defend this order, this Fatherland that would liberate them from anticlericalism and restore all their privileges. The rebels did not have to ask the Church for its support, which it gladly offered; the Church had not wasted any time in coming to its decision. While some said they wanted order and others said they were defending the faith, they all recognised the benefits of the arrival of the sacred onto the scene.

The success of this religious mobilisation, this liturgy that attracted the masses in the dioceses of 'liberated' Spain, encouraged the army to adorn its speeches with references to God and religion, hitherto absent from the proclamations of the military coup and declarations in the days to follow. The rebels were convinced of the importance of the emotional link, as well as of the destruction and annihilation of the enemy, at a time when they knew what they did not want, but still lacked a clear political focus. The union between religion and patriotism reinforced national unity and legitimised the genocide that they had launched in that summer of 1936. One of the principal officers responsible for this killing, General Gonzalo Queipo de Llano, confessed to the archbishop of Seville, Eustaquio Ilundáin, during a mass rally presided over by the clergy, army officers and right-wing authorities: 'I believe that the priority for any good patriot is religion, because anyone who does not love God or his family is of no use to the Fatherland'.[30]

Mobilisation from below was accompanied by substantial rhetoric from above. The interpretation of the war as a crusade reached the Church hierarchy from the fronts and from the popular demonstrations of religious fervour all through rebel Spain. The Church authorities, safe in their episcopal palaces, understood this spirit of religious

---

[30] Juan Ortiz Villalba, *Sevilla 1936. Del golpe militar a la guerra civil*, Imprenta Vistalegre, Córdoba, 1997, pp. 170–1.

rebellion and imbued it with reason and legitimacy. They only spoke after others had acted, and this served to reinforce the justice of their cause even more, helping them to give the impression that they only made an appearance when the anticlerical and revolutionary violence left them no option. They had neither taken part in the rising nor encouraged anyone to go to war. But there they were, obliged to take a stand against the material and spiritual decadence that 'the sons of Cain' had left the Fatherland in. They knew that this was the best approach for a rapid legitimisation of the military rising – in other words, the right to rebellion – and the war that ensued.

The union between the sword and the cross, religion and the 'civilian-military movement', was a recurrent theme in all the pronouncements, circulars, letters and pastoral preaching issued by the bishops during August 1936. Before the end of that month, three bishops had already explicitly described the civil war as being a 'religious crusade'. The first to do so was Marcelino Olaechea, the bishop of Pamplona, on 23 August. Three days later it was Rigoberto Doménech, the archbishop of Zaragoza. And the archbishop of Santiago, Tomás Muniz Pablos, put it categorically on 31 August: the war against the enemies of Spain was 'certainly patriotic, very patriotic, but fundamentally a religious crusade, of the same type as the Crusades of the Middle Ages, because now, as then, the struggle is for the faith of Christ and the liberty of the people. It is God's will! *¡Santiago y cierra España!*' ('For Saint James, and close ranks, Spain!', a traditional Spanish battle-cry dating back to the ninth century).[31]

With this idea pervading Spanish ecclesiastical and traditionalist thought, and the fact that it had been revived in the battle against the French in the Peninsular War in the nineteenth century, it was inevitable that it would reappear in 1936 – 'ominous moments that will determine the destiny of religion and the Fatherland'.[32] General Emilio Mola, hardly one for theological musings, was one of the first officers to understand the benefits of bringing the sacred into the picture, and the advantages of setting forward higher principles to steer

[31] Alfonso Álvarez Bolado, *Para ganar la guerra, para ganar la paz. Iglesia y guerra civil: 1936–1939*, Universidad Pontificia de Comillas, Madrid, 1995, pp. 55–6.

[32] Javier Ugarte, *La nueva Covadonga insurgente. Orígenes sociales y culturales de la sublevación de 1936 en Navarra y el País Vasco*, Biblioteca Nueva, Madrid, 1998, p. 185.

a political and class conflict. This is what he said in a broadcast on Radio Castilla on 15 August 1936:

We are being asked ... what direction we are taking. The answer is simple and one that we have repeated many times. We are going to impose order, to give bread and jobs to all Spaniards and give everyone a fair deal. And then, on the ruins left behind by the *Frente Popular* – blood, mire and tears – we shall build a great, strong, powerful State that is set to be crowned by a Cross ... the symbol of our religion and our Faith, the only thing that has remained untouched among so much savagery that attempted to pollute the waters of our rivers with the glorious and valiant crimson of Spanish blood.[33]

Mola was speaking from Navarre, the land of the crusaders, from where the Carlists had come at the start of the rising to spill blood 'for God and for Spain'. Also in Navarre at the time, cloaked in this atmosphere of a crusade, was Cardinal Primate Isidro Gomá, who, in his room in the spa hotel of Belascoain, wrote the Pastoral Instruction of the bishops of Vitoria and Pamplona on the 'Basque–Communist collaboration', published on 6 August. It had been these two bishops, Mateo Múgica and Marcelino Olaechea, who had visited him to ask him to draw up a document 'declaring the inadmissibility or unlawfulness of Basque nationalism'.

He did so on the spot, so as to 'clear up any misunderstandings'. 'Behind the civilian-military movement in our country', he wrote, 'lies the traditional love of our sacrosanct religion'. He identified the 'enemy' that supported the republican cause in the Basque Country as 'a modern monster, Marxism or Communism, a seven-headed hydra, the synthesis of all heresies, diametrically opposed to Christianity in its religious, social and economic doctrine'. It was not acceptable 'to fragment the Catholic forces against the common enemy'; it was not acceptable that Catholic Basques, 'our children, devotees of the Church and followers of its doctrines', should have found common cause with the 'sworn bitter enemies of the Church'.

Far from achieving its objective, which was to get the Basque nationalists to change sides, this Pastoral Instruction managed to highlight even further the split between the ecclesiastical authorities in the

---

[33] Fernando Díaz-Plaja, *La guerra de España en sus documentos*, Plaza & Janés, Barcelona, 1973, p. 87.

dioceses of Pamplona and Vitoria, who had been staunch supporters
of the military rebels from the outset, and large sections of the Basque
population, who may have been Catholic and conservative, but who
opposed this Spain-centric authoritarianism that had been making
its threatening presence felt in Álava and Navarre after 18 July. This
was just the first symptom of a wound that would take a long time to
heal, with Basque priests shot by the military rebels, and many others
persecuted and imprisoned during Franco's dictatorship. Even Mateo
Múgica, by no means a nationalist, ended up being hounded by the
Junta de Defensa in Burgos, for 'being over-tolerant of the nationalist
priests, who are most to blame for this militant movement' and for
having turned the seminary in Vitoria into 'a school of nationalism'.

The officers were incensed over the 'nationalist struggle' and they
mistakenly put the blame on the bishop of Vitoria. The *Junta de
Defensa*, through the archbishop of Burgos, Manuel Alonso Castro,
asked Múgica to meet with them to study 'a suitable way to deal
with the nationalists'. The meeting did not take place, and the officers interpreted it as a refusal by Múgica to cooperate. General Fidel
Dávila told Cardinal Gomá that it would be 'advisable for the bishop
of Vitoria to take his leave from his diocese temporarily ... and withdraw voluntarily to somewhere near the French border'; otherwise the
Junta would have to 'take a unilateral decision that would go against
the Catholic sentiments of its members'. After various meetings and
diplomatic dealings, Mateo Múgica left Vitoria on 14 October 1936
and moved to Rome.[34]

About two weeks before that, on 30 September, Enrique Pla y Deniel
published 'Las dos ciudades', his pastoral letter in which he correlated
into a single doctrine all the postures and views that his 'brothers in
Christ' had been expressing over the previous two months. He provided
a defence of the right to rebellion for 'just' causes – the justification being
the Communist peril that was threatening Christian civilisation – and
he evoked Saint Augustine's 'two cities', the 'celestial' and the 'earthly',
to symbolise, in all its Manichean glory, the current conflict, describing

---

[34] The drafting of the Pastoral Instruction and the expulsion are explored in
Juan María Laboa, 'La Iglesia vasca', in Javier Tusell, Juan María Laboa,
Hilari Raguer *et al.*, 'La guerra civil', *Historia*, 16, 13 (1986), pp. 96–9. The
document, from which the quoted words are taken, is reproduced in Antonio
Montero Moreno, *Historia de la persecución religiosa en España, 1936–
1939*, BAC, Madrid, 1961, pp. 682–6.

all those who died in the name of religion as martyrs. But above all, he coined the sentences repeated by everyone, which went down in history as the official doctrine adopted by the Spanish bishops: 'It may look like a *civil war*; but it is, in fact, a *crusade*. It was an *uprising*, designed not to create unrest, but *to re-establish order*'.[35]

Priests and others in holy orders, particularly Jesuits and Dominicans, unblushingly sailed with the authoritarian and Fascist winds that were then blowing in many parts of Europe. There was no holding back the belligerent ardour of this clerical legion. The bishops 'gave free rein to their hearts' when they spoke, as Juan de Iturralde put it, inciting others to do the same, and the few who were reluctant to join in with this cleansing and extermination were punished and deported. Selflessness, discipline, obedience, submission to the hierarchy were the watchwords. The Church had to become militarised, wrote the well-known Jesuit, Francisco Peiró. But it needed to be an 'interior militarisation' that would not settle just for 'donning the blue shirt and taking part in a parade'. It was a rhetoric charged with impassioned patriotism, with 'it is God's will and the Fatherland demands it', with fervent support for a 'new national reconquest that is colouring with crimson hues of blood the dawn of a new Spain'. Spain, wrote the Benedictine Federico Armas, in *Ecos de Valvanera*, the magazine of the sanctuary of that name in La Rioja, 'must be Catholic, unified, great and free; it must be one in its faith, in its geography, in its history, and in its empire'.[36]

The crowning point of this union between the Catholic Church authorities and the military rebels came with the 'Collective letter of the Spanish bishops to bishops all over the world'. This text was in response to the reaction by some of the world's Catholic press and in certain Catholic circles in Europe to the bombing of Guernica on 26 April 1937, organised by the commander of the Condor Legion, Colonel Wolfram von Richthofen, following several consultations with the then Colonel Juan Vigón, Mola's Chief of General Staff.

---

[35] The pastoral letter is reproduced in Montero Moreno, *Historia de la persecución religiosa en España*, pp. 688–708.

[36] Francisco Peiró's article, 'Sentido religioso y militar de la vida' (1938), comes from José Ángel Tello, *Ideología y política. La Iglesia católica española, 1936–1959*, Pórtico, Zaragoza, 1984, p. 74; Federico Armas, *Ecos de Valvanera* (mouthpiece of the sanctuary and brotherhood written by the Benedictine monks of this sanctuary in La Rioja), January 1937, p. 5.

Guernica was a symbol of Basque identity and both Vigón and Mola were well aware of this. Monday 26 April was market day. Among inhabitants, refugees and peasants who went to the market that day in the former Basque capital, there were some 10,000 people. The city had no anti-aircraft defences. It was attacked in the middle of the afternoon for three hours by the Condor Legion and the Italian *Aviazione Legionaria*, under the command of General von Richthofen. The Basque government estimated a death toll of over 1,500 and said that a further thousand had been wounded in the air-raid, although the number of deaths, while not known for certain, was probably fewer than 500.

Franco's press and propaganda services denied at first that any bombing had taken place in Guernica. When this position became untenable, they blamed the destruction of Guernica on the Basques themselves, a lie maintained throughout the years of the dictatorship. But there were witnesses, including four journalists and a Basque priest, Alberto Onaindía. Two days after the attack, George Steer, the correspondent for *The Times*, published in that paper and in the *New York Times* an account of the massacre that would be read all over the world. Everyone now knew that Guernica had been destroyed by explosive and incendiary bombs. What certain historians, except the Francoist apologists, wrote later also made it quite clear: the idea originated in Mola's general staff and the Germans implemented it.[37] And thanks to Pablo Picasso, Guernica became a symbol of the horrors of war.

Explosive bombs raining down on a defenceless civilian population – the massacre seemed to confirm what a few Catholic intellectuals were already saying abroad: that Franco's Christian Spain was a hotbed of ruthless killing. Concerned about the repercussions that this news might have in certain European government circles, Franco personally summoned Cardinal Isidro Gomá to a meeting, which was held on 10 May 1937. According to Gomá's own account, Franco asked him to arrange for 'the Spanish bishops ... to publish a letter addressed to all the world's bishops, along with a request that it be published in the Catholic press, that would set the record straight, and coincidentally would be performing a patriotic act and revision

---

[37] As recounted by Preston, *Franco*, pp. 243–7.

of history, which would be of enormous benefit to the Catholic cause the world over'.[38]

Gomá hastily satisfied the *Caudillo*'s wishes. On 15 May, he sent a 'secret' letter to all the bishops, setting out his request. They all replied positively, except for the archbishop of Tarragona, Francesc Vidal i Barraquer, who was in Italy, having managed to escape from the anticlerical violence of the summer of 1936. In a letter that he sent to Gomá on 30 May, Vidal considered that a 'collective document' was not the most 'effective, opportune or tactful' way, and besides (and here he was clearly thinking of Franco), he was not happy 'to accept suggestions from people outside the hierarchy over purely Church matters' – in other words, the Church, instead of remaining outside 'party politics', was tarnished by the cause of the military rebels.

On 14 June 1937, Gomá sent the draft of the collective letter to all the bishops. After a few final touches, probably the work of Pla y Deniel and the bishop of Madrid-Alcalá, Leopoldo Eijo y Garay, the galley proofs were sent to the Holy See at the beginning of July. At the last moment, Mateo Múgica withdrew his signature, claiming that he had been away from his diocese for over eight months, 'with all the sad consequences deriving from such an abnormal situation'. It was not that he would not sign, but could not: 'I might have signed the Document if I had still been in my post, physically and personally, with all the guarantees of liberty and independence that are stipulated for the spiritual exercising of the ministry and episcopal duties'.[39]

The 'Collective Letter from the Spanish Bishops to the Bishops of the World' was dated 1 July 1937, but it was sent to the bishops three weeks later, with the request that they did not publicise it until it had begun to be published abroad. It was signed by forty-three bishops and five capitular vicars. Around this time, Gomá sent two copies to Franco, and he pointed out to him, as if Franco did not know, that it had been written 'so that the truth of what has been

---

[38] Cited in María Luisa Rodríguez Aisa, 'La carta del Episcopado', in Tusell, Laboa, Raguer *et al.*, 'La guerra civil', *Historia*, 16, 13 (1986), pp. 56–63.

[39] The groundwork and preparing of the Collective Letter has been related in detail by Hilari Raguer in *La espada y la cruz. La Iglesia, 1936–1939*, Bruguera, Barcelona, 1977, pp. 102–19. I have also based my account on the documented description by María Luisa Rodríguez Aisa, 'La carta del episcopado', in 'La guerra civil', *Historia*, 16, 13 (1986), pp. 56–63.

happening in Spain in recent years be known and, especially, what the National Movement means for our beloved Fatherland and for western civilisation'.[40]

From a doctrinal point of view, there was nothing new in this letter that had not already been said by bishops, priests and others in holy orders in the twelve months since the military rising. But the international impact was so great – it had been published immediately in French, Italian and English – that many people accepted permanently the Manichean and tendentious version transmitted by the Church of the 'armed plebiscite': that the National Movement personified the virtues of the best Christian tradition, and the republican government all the vices inherent in Russian Communism. As well as insisting on the lie that the 'military uprising' put a stop to a definite plan for a Communist revolution, and offering the typical statement in defence of order, peace and justice that reigned in the 'national' territory, the bishops included a matter of capital importance, which is still the official position of the Church hierarchy today: the Church was an 'innocent, peaceful, defenceless' victim and 'at risk from total extermination at the hands of communism'; it supported the cause that ensured the 'fundamental principles of society'. The Church was the 'benefactor of the people', not the 'aggressor'. The aggressors were the others, those who had caused this 'Communist', 'anti-Spanish' and 'anti-Christian' revolution, which had already accounted for the murder of over '300,000 of the lay population'.

The 'Collective Letter' was viewed favourably by some 900 bishops in thirty-two countries. 'We should congratulate ourselves that with this document we have helped to dispel any misunderstandings and put a good light on the events and ideas that are being aired with the current war in Spain', wrote Gomá to Pacelli on 12 October 1937.[41] This unreserved support for the rebel side served as a decisive argument for Catholics and people of order the world over. This was fundamentally because it was accompanied by a shameless silence regarding the destructive violence that the army had been practising since the first moment of the uprising. The letter demonised the enemy, who were only moved by the desire for religious persecution,

[40] Cited in María Luisa Rodríguez Aisa, 'La carta del Episcopado', in Tusell, Laboa, Raguer et al., 'La guerra civil', Historia, 16, 13 (1986), pp. 56–63.
[41] Ibid.

and decisively codified support for the war as a holy, just crusade against Communism's assault on the Fatherland and religion.

Franco and the Catholic Church emerged notably strengthened. The transformation of the war into a purely religious conflict, ignoring the political and social aspects, justified all the previous violence and gave Franco licence to carry on with the killing. The Church, the military rebels' travelling companion right from the start of the journey, now took its seat at the front of the train bound for victory. Javier Conde, then Director of Propaganda, informed the Jesuit Constantino Bayle, the editor of *Razón y Fe* and a confidant of Gomá's, of the satisfaction expressed by those in the Francoist political and military circles over this wonderful document: 'Please tell the Cardinal that I, an expert in these affairs, want to say the following: he has achieved more with the Collective Letter than all the rest of us with our efforts'.[42]

As the war progressed, Catholicism gained ground, helped by the bombs and rifles deployed against the forces of revolutionary atheism, which were forced to bend their knees before the victor. First in Málaga, and then in all the other republican cities, the entry of the Francoist troops was celebrated with the Te Deum and other Catholic rituals, which gave unity to all the reactionary forces. The bishops gave the Fascist salute at all the civilian-military ceremonies, blessed arms, rallied the troops and encouraged the persecution of the vanquished. The interpretation of the victories of Franco's army as the result of supernatural protection from Saint James, Saint Theresa and the Virgin of the Column was widely supported during the war, and was carried over into the years of the dictatorship.

The revitalisation of religion reached the farthest corners of the reconquered territory, with street names being changed, the restoration of public worship, the re-establishment of religious education in the schools and the return of the crucifix in public places. At the first meeting of Franco's first government, held on Thursday 3 February 1938, it was decided to 'revise' all the Second Republic's lay legislation, and thus one law after another was repealed by decree, from the Civil Marriages Act to the Religious Confessions and Congregations

---

[42] Álvarez Bolado, *Para ganar la guerra, para ganar la paz*, p. 159; the international repercussion of the 'Collective Letter' are examined on pp. 207–9.

Act, the Act passed in June 1933 that marked the climax of the alien-
ation between the Catholic Church and the Republic.

Cardinal Gomá, the primate of the Spanish Church, approved of
Franco's first government, containing as it did good Catholics such
as Tomás Domínguez Arévalo, the Count of Rodezno, as Minister of
Justice, and Pedro Sainz Rodríguez in Education. As soon as it was
formed, Gomá sent a report to Cardinal Pacelli, informing him of his
conviction that in Spain they were on the eve of 'a renovation of legislation concerning all aspects of Church affairs'.[43]

This 'renovation of legislation' was so swift that only a few months
later, on the last day of June 1938, José María Yanguas Messía gave
an assessment of his government's 'Catholicity' in his speech on presenting his credentials as ambassador to the Holy See:

It has already returned the crucifix and religious teaching to the schools,
it has repealed the Civil Marriages Act, it has suspended divorce, it has
restored the Company of Jesus into civil law, it has officially recognised the
identity of the Catholic Church as a perfect association, it has decreed its
civil and social effects, the sanctity of religious festivals, and has brought
an authentically Catholic and Spanish conception to Labour Rights.[44]

Steeped in this victorious atmosphere, the Spanish clergy did not
want to hear anything about pardon or mediation to end the war.
Franco and his brothers-in-arms had been making it quite clear
since the beginning of 1937 that they would not accept any mediation to end the war, 'just unconditional surrender'. All attempts to
end the war through a negotiated peace, fostered by Manuel Azaña,
the President of the Republic, and even looked upon favourably
by the Vatican in the spring of 1937, failed. Franco said as much
to Gomá in June 1937, so that he, by now a good friend of the
Generalísimo's, would inform the Holy See. He would not accept
a settlement, nor did he have to apologise for the alleged harshness
shown by the army to the enemy, 'because nobody has been condemned without going through the proper procedure as laid down
in the military code'.

[43] 'Report from the Primate to Cardinal Pacelli', 2 February 1938, in María
Luisa Rodríguez Aisa, *El cardenal Gomá y la guerra de España. Aspectos de
la gestión pública del Primado 1936–1939*, CSIC, Madrid, 1981, pp. 295–6.
[44] Quoted in Álvarez Bolado, *Para ganar la guerra, para ganar la paz*, p. 254.

One year later, Franco's attitude to a possible mediation was monotonously repeated: 'All those who want mediation, either consciously or unconsciously, are helping the reds and the covert enemies of Spain ... Our justice could not be more dispassionate or noble; its generosity is merely aimed at the defence of the highest interests of the Fatherland; no type of mediation could make it more benign'. On 18 October and at the beginning of November 1938, towards the end of the long drawn-out Battle of the Ebro, he offered more of the same to the Reuters correspondent: 'The outright decisive victory of our army is the only solution for Spain to survive ... and there can only be one outcome: the unconditional surrender of the enemy'.[45]

No mediation, no pardon. The only thing the officers talked about was a process of 'cleansing', as if Spain needed to be 'purged' of her 'sick bodies'. And a good many Church authorities, bishops, priests and others in holy orders, went even further in their defence of this hysteria. Mediation was 'inadmissible' and 'absurd', said Leopoldo Eijo Garay, bishop of the diocese of Madrid-Alcalá at the time, because 'to tolerate democratic liberalism, entirely Marxist in its nature, would be a betrayal of the martyrs'.[46]

There was no betrayal, because the victory of Franco's army was as unconditional and resounding as the Church had wanted. Christ was the victor. And with no hope of a negotiated peace, a 'graveyard peace' was imposed. And Franco's successful strategy of a war of attrition, the total destruction of the adversary, meant that he could now establish an enduring regime.

---

[45] Franco's declarations against mediation and reconciliation may be found in Álvarez Bolado, *Para ganar la guerra, para ganar la paz*, pp. 316–19.
[46] Ibid.

11 | *Battlefields and rearguard politics*

In the three months following the July 1936 uprising, the war was a struggle between armed militias, who lacked the basic elements of a conventional army, and a military power that concentrated all its resources in authority, discipline and the declaration of martial law, and that almost from the start was able to employ the services of the well-trained troops of the Africa army.

The Battle of Madrid, in November of that year, saw the arrival of a new form of waging war and transformed this group of militiamen into soldiers in a new army. After the failure of various attempts to take Madrid, between November 1936 and March 1937, Franco changed his strategy and chose to unleash a war of attrition, the gradual occupation of territory and total destruction of the republican army. His materiel and offensive superiority led him to the final victory two years later.

'Wars are lost in the rearguard', wrote General Vicente Rojo.[1] And this is what was happening to the Republic, where hunger created major conflicts as the war went on, and one defeat after another ended up demoralising large sectors of the population, who abandoned their commitment to the values and material interests they were fighting for. The air-raids by the Italians and Germans on Madrid, Valencia and Barcelona also helped Franco to win the war. The outcome of the horrors of this war leaves no room for doubt: before its defeat, the Republic had been slowly battered, with battles that left its troops decimated and brutal repression after Franco's army entered any city it captured.

From Madrid to the Ebro

By the middle of October 1936, the rebel troops, now well equipped with Italian artillery pieces and armoured vehicles, had occupied

---

[1] Quoted in José Andrés Rojo, *Vicente Rojo. Retrato de un general republicano*, Tusquets, Barcelona, 2006, p. 270.

most of the towns and villages around Madrid. The militiamen, cowed by the advance of the Africa army, withdrew to the capital, and they were joined there by hundreds of refugees fleeing from the occupied localities. Franco announced that he would take Madrid on 20 October, and General Mola is said to have arranged to meet the *Daily Express* correspondent in the Puerta del Sol for coffee. On 29 October, the first Soviet tanks and aircraft, sent by the Kremlin to counteract Italian and German aid, arrived in Madrid.

General José Enrique Varela, an *Africanista* and Carlist sympathiser, attacked with 25,000 men via the Casa de Campo and the University campus. General José Miaja, whom the Prime Minister, Largo Caballero, had left in charge of the *Junta de Defensa* of Madrid, and Lieutenant Colonel Vicente Rojo, Chief of General Staff for the defence of Madrid, had 20,000 men at their disposal. Nobody in the government, least of all Largo Caballero and Prieto, was confident that Madrid could resist the attack of the military rebels. On 8 November, the militiamen and the Moors were engaged in hand-to-hand combat on the university campus. Two weeks later, Franco and Varela had to call a halt to the attacks.

Franco, writes Julio Aróstegui, 'aimed too high with limited resources. Thirty thousand men could not conquer a city with over a million inhabitants determined to defend themselves'. Furthermore, Franco had put back the attack on Madrid in order to relieve the Alcázar in Toledo and that, which might have provided him with important political and propaganda advantages to attain power, gave more time for the republicans to organise their defence, take delivery of the first lot of Soviet aid and welcome the International Brigades. Vicente Rojo, however, in his book *Así fue la defensa de Madrid*, downplayed the role of these forces who had come from all over the world, and instead stressed the courage and bravery of thousands of anonymous citizens, angered by the destruction wrought by the rebel air-raids and because they felt that their freedom was under threat. It was a battle of resistance in which, in the republican camp, 'compliance with military duty, which began to prevail over any other type of duty', was seen for the first time in the war.[2]

---

[2] Ibid., pp. 102–4; Julio Aróstegui, 'La defensa de Madrid y el comienzo de la guerra larga', in Edward Malefakis (ed.), *La guerra de España (1936–1939)*, Taurus, Madrid, 1996, p. 151.

While the popular hero of the defence of Madrid might have been General José Miaja, who was seen all over the city attempting to raise the people's morale, the technical and military aspects were in the hands of Vicente Rojo, an officer who remained loyal to the Republic because he believed that such was his duty, and a few months later he became head of its army. He always defined himself as a 'Catholic, officer and patriot', and according to his grandson, José Andrés Rojo, he felt caught between the world of the *Africanista* officers who took part in the coup, with whom he did not feel identified, and that of the armed militiamen who defended the revolution and burnt churches. Between these two worlds, he took it upon himself to design a new strategy to organise an efficient force to confront the military rebels, and tried to establish the authority of professional officers like himself and the chain of command of this army.[3]

Vicente Rojo was born on 8 October 1894, in a small town in the region of Valencia, Fuente de la Higuera. He was two years younger than Franco and was not yet 42 when the war began. His father, an officer who had served six years in Cuba, died three months before he was born, and when he was 13 he lost his mother too. In order to continue with his studies, he was sent to a boarding school for orphans of infantry officers and he entered the Toledo Infantry Academy in June 1916. He left as a second lieutenant of the infantry, having come second in a class of 390 cadets.

In 1915, he served as a volunteer in Africa, was promoted to captain in 1918, and between 1922 and 1932 taught at the Academy in Toledo. He then went to the War College to obtain the Staff Diploma, and in June 1936, shortly after his promotion to major, he joined the Central Staff. After the chaos caused by the military uprising, Largo Caballero's first government reorganised the Central Staff and Rojo became number two there, under the immediate orders of Lieutenant Colonel Manuel Estrada. On 25 October 1936, Rojo was promoted to lieutenant colonel 'for his loyalty', a few days before Miaja received the order to appoint him Chief of General Staff for the defence of Madrid. He was made colonel 'for his war service' on 24 March 1937, and in May, Juan Negrín appointed him Chief of Central Staff of the

---

[3] Rojo, *Vicente Rojo*, p. 76.

Republic, a post he held until the end of the war. On 24 September that same year, he was promoted to general.

One of the biggest drawbacks in the Republic's army was the shortage of professional officers. Of the 16,000 officers in the army who were serving before the military uprising, only about 20 per cent stayed in the republican zone, and this, in the words of Gabriel Cardona, 'was totally inadequate for an army whose troop numbers increased five-fold in less than a year'. Very few of its officers had held high command before the war, and this shortcoming 'brought about the rapid promotion of officers who knew nothing about commanding large units'.

Thus, this improvisation of commands posed a serious problem, which intensified as one moved down the ranks, because most of the more junior officers were on the rebel side. Battalion and company commanders had to be appointed precipitately, and the army took in and commissioned the political heads of the militias and columns that were created in the days that followed the military uprising. In Cardona's opinion, 'while the republicans were on the defensive, these shortcomings were not so dramatic as when the major offensives started, in which a clear chain of command was required'.[4]

But it is worth pointing out that, as well as Rojo, there was a group of professional officers, including Juan Hernández Sarabia, Antonio Escobar, Francisco Llano de la Encomienda, José Fontán and Manuel Matallana, who remained loyal to the institutions of the Republic, yet they are now forgotten. In spite of the fact that many of them were the last to flee Spain, ultra-radical writers in exile, both anarchist and socialist, branded them as traitors, Francoists or mere Stalinist puppets. With the bitter taste of defeat, the Communists also joined in the chorus of invective, while they never warranted respect from the victors. On the one hand, there were officers, those who won the war, who are still remembered in the street names of many towns and cities in Spain, and there were others, those who lost, who today are complete unknowns.

The other group of commanders in the republican army came from the militias. They had had no military skills, although Enrique Lister

---

[4] Gabriel Cardona, 'Entre la revolución y la disciplina. Ensayo sobre la dimensión militar de la guerra civil', in Enrique Moradiellos (ed.), 'La guerra civil', *Ayer*, 50 (2003), pp. 41–51.

had received some training in the USSR and Manuel Tagüeña had risen through the ranks. The most rapid promotion was that of Juan Modesto, who had been a corporal in the Legion and, in the summer of 1937, was appointed the first commander of the 5th Army Corps, a shock unit in which the Communists played a major role. In addition, some of the anarchists who had been commanding columns since July 1936 joined the chain of command of the Republic's army, shelving their anti-military prejudices. Prime examples included Cipriano Mera, Gregorio Jover and Miguel García Vivancos.

At the beginning of 1937, the republican forces numbered almost 350,000 men, a figure very similar to that of Franco's army, although the latter boasted the priceless aid of almost 80,000 Italians in the *Corpo de Truppe Volontarie* (CTV), under the command of General Mario Roatta, and several thousand Germans, who, since November 1936, had been serving in the Condor Legion, as well as in anti-tank and artillery land units. In fact, it was the Italians who entered Málaga on 8 February 1937. Two days earlier, tens of thousands of people – men, women and children of all ages – had begun to swarm out of the city towards Almería, to escape the reprisals and pillaging of their subjugators. They were bombarded by aircraft and the warships *Cervera* and *Baleares*, and the road was littered with the dead and wounded, while many families lost their children in the flight. The unofficial death toll of what Doctor Norman Bethune called *The Crime on the Road, Málaga–Almería*, was over 3,000, but no reliable sources have been found to back that up. Numbers apart, we do have testimonies of one of the most tragic episodes of the civil war: 'the torment from Malaga to Almería, the ruthless crime' as Rafael Alberti wrote.[5]

Franco, meanwhile, had begun to prepare a new offensive against Madrid, via the Jarama valley, along the road from Madrid to Valencia. This operation was supposed to be completed with an attack by the Italian CTV troops from Sigüenza towards Guadalajara, to catch Madrid in a pincer movement. Over three weeks in February, from 6 February to the end of the month, both sides lost thousands of men, and although the Francoists managed to advance their front

---

[5] Antonio Nadal, *Guerra civil en Málaga*, Arguval, Málaga, 1984, pp. 190–1; cited in Encarnación Barranquero, *Málaga entre la guerra y la posguerra. El franquismo*, Arguval, Málaga, 1994, pp. 203–29.

a few kilometres, the Battle of the Jarama was fairly unproductive. A few days later, on 8 March, General Amerigo Coppi's motorised division began its attack, but it was surprised by a heavy snowstorm, and within a few days it suffered a crushing defeat, among other reasons because Franco failed to carry out his diversionary operation from the Jarama, and the republican troops, aided by the Garibaldi Battalion of the International Brigades and Soviet tanks, were able to concentrate all their efforts on halting the Italian advance.

The succession of failures to capture Madrid brought about a change in Franco's strategy, and from that moment on he opted for a long, drawn-out war of attrition to grind down the enemy. He said as much to Colonel Emilio Faldella, General Roatta's Chief of Staff, who was trying to convince him of the advantages of a *guerra celere* (lightning war): 'In a civil war, a systematic occupation of territory, accompanied by a necessary clean-up operation, is preferable to a rapid defeat of the enemy armies that will leave the country infested with adversaries'. And he said it again, in more detail, to Mussolini's ambassador, Roberto Talupo, on 4 April 1937:

We must carry out the necessarily slow task of redemption and pacification, without which the military occupation will be largely useless ... Nothing will make me give up this gradual programme. It will bring me less glory, but greater internal peace ... I will take the capital not an hour before it is necessary: first I must have the certainty of being able to found a regime.[6]

Franco held all the trumps to apply this military strategy. He had plenty of men, made possible by the continuance of the traditional system of recruitment and by the large number of Moroccan volunteers swelling the ranks of the Africa army. Since September 1936, he had two academies, in Burgos and Seville, to rapidly train university graduates as second lieutenants, and he also set up four establishments to train officers and NCOs. But above all, he had the confidence that the international prospect of German and Italian backing for his cause and the isolation of the Republic by the western democracies was not going to alter. Thus he had plenty of men and a guaranteed supply of materials.

[6] Paul Preston, *Franco: A Biography*, HarperCollins, London, 1993, pp. 222, 242.

The Nationalists now concentrated their attention on the industrial and mining areas of the north, which were cut off from the rest of the republican zone. General Mola wanted to conquer these areas and teach the Basques a lesson: 'I have decided to finish the war quickly in the north ... If submission is not immediate, I will raze Vizcaya, beginning with the industries of war'.[7] And the Germans thought that obtaining coal and steel from the north-west would help Hitler's aggressive rearmament programme. Mola began his campaign at the end of March with heavy bombing by the Condor Legion, designed to shatter the morale of the civilian population and destroy ground communication networks. First it was Durango, on 31 March, then Guernica on 26 April. On 19 June, 'the industrious city' of Bilbao was 'reintegrated into civilisation and order', in the words of the war dispatch of the occupiers for that day. And a few days later, on 1 July, in his inaugural speech, the new mayor of Bilbao, the Falangist José María de Areilza, warmly embraced the patriotic and bloodthirsty atmosphere of the moment:

Let us be clear about this: Bilbao has been conquered by force of arms. There have been no pacts or posthumous acknowledgements. Be in no doubt that here there are the victors and the vanquished. The winner has been a united, great and free Spain. We have seen the last of this fearsome sinister nightmare called Euskadi which was the result of socialism on the one hand and Vizcayan stupidity on the other: Vizcaya is once again part of Spain *through military conquest, pure and simple.*[8]

The united, great and free Spain spread later to Santander, and in October to the red zone of Asturias. With the fall of the industrial north, the balance of power began to tip clearly in favour of the Nationalists. Colonel Vicente Rojo, recently appointed Chief of General Staff of the Republic, organised a defensive strategy aimed at limiting the Nationalist advance as far as possible, given the material superiority of the enemy and the difficulties involved in consolidating a true republican army. This was the objective of the surprise diversionary offensives launched in Brunete, in July 1937, to halt the Nationalist advance on Santander; at Belchite, in August and

[7] Ibid., p. 239.
[8] Quoted in Gonzalo Redondo, *Historia de la Iglesia en España 1931–1939. La guerra civil 1936–1939*, 2 vols., Rialp, Madrid, 1993, vol. II, p. 288.

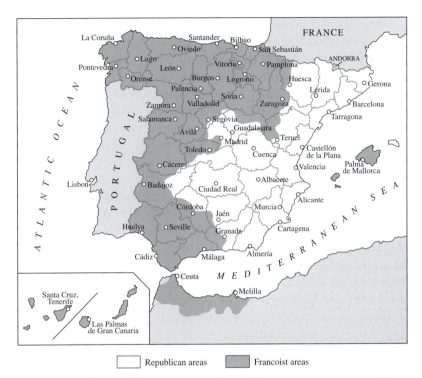

Map 2 Evolution of the war, September 1937

September, to slow down the conquest of Asturias; and in Teruel, in December 1937, to counteract the expected Nationalist attack on Madrid.

And indeed, now that he had occupied the north, Franco was planning to launch a new attack on Madrid, through Guadalajara, the same route that the Italians had taken unsuccessfully in March 1937. Vicente Rojo, who had been promoted to general at the end of September, decided to launch a preventive attack against Teruel. He deployed some 40,000 men there, with some of the divisions fighting on the Aragon front, the 11th, under Lister and the 25th under García Vivancos, as well as the Levante army, commanded by Colonel Juan Hernández Saravia. The attack, initiated by Lister on 15 December 1937, caught the limited Nationalist forces that were defending the city, under the command of Colonel Domingo Rey d'Harcourt, and counter-attacks by Generals Varela and Aranda were hampered by the extremely harsh weather conditions of those days.

On 7 January 1938, the republican troops broke through Rey d'Harcourt's defence, and he signed the surrender document, which he ended by requesting 'that the lives of civilian personnel be spared'. Teruel became the only provincial capital to be taken by the republicans throughout the war. As well as Rey d'Harcourt, the Augustine friar Anselmo Polanco, the bishop of Teruel, was arrested and they were taken, along with many other prisoners, to the San Miguel de los Reyes prison in Valencia and then moved to Barcelona, to the 'Depot for prisoners and escapees of 19 July', installed in the Servants of Mary convent in the Plaza Letamendi.

On 16 January 1939, a few days before Barcelona fell to Franco's troops, the prisoners were evacuated from the 'Depot' and taken to Santa Perpetua de Mogoda and thence to Ripoll. On its way to the border, the expedition suffered repeated Nationalist bombing. The members of this 'pilgrimage', made necessary by the Nationalist military advance, arrived on 31 January at Port de Molins. A week later, on 7 February, they were taken to the Can de Tretze ravine to be machine-gunned down. The decision was taken by Major Pedro Díaz, and the killers disobeyed the order given by General Rojo for the prisoners to be handed over to the republican air force to be taken to Madrid. Forty-two were executed. Their number included Bishop Polanco, Colonel Rey d'Harcourt and the vicar-general of the diocese of Teruel, Felipe Ripoll Morata. Colonel Barba, wounded in one of the Nationalist air-raids, escaped with his life as he was in hospital. The bodies of Bishop Polanco and Ripoll were later taken to Teruel. Rey d'Harcourt, however, was treated by his side as incompetent, responsible for the fall of Teruel, and so his remains did not deserve to be removed from that remote ravine near the French border. His family were not able to transfer his body to their private vault in Logroño until 1972.

Teruel was retaken on 22 February, by troops under the direction of General Juan Vigón, who deployed 100,000 men, including the Italian CTV. Thus ended one of the cruellest battles of the civil war, with 40,000 Nationalist and over 60,000 republican casualties. The two armies had the same number of troops mobilised at that time, almost 800,000 each, but the material superiority of the Nationalists was overwhelming. In just a few weeks, Teruel went from being the republicans' biggest victory, blown out of all proportion in their propaganda, to what Antony Beevor calls 'the biggest republican disaster in the whole war', because 'the Republic had set out to seize a city of no strategic value, which it could never have hoped to hold, all at a catastrophic cost in lives and equipment'.[9]

The disaster widened the breach between the Communists and Indalecio Prieto, the Minister of Defence, who became the butt of all their accusations, although General Vicente Rojo also began to be held responsible for the defeats in the reports that some of the Comintern delegates in Spain sent to Moscow. However, Rojo was quite adamant that little could be done with 'the lack of materiel, the poor morale of our units, their incomplete organisation, and the ineptitude or incompetence of many of the commanders'. As he wrote to Prieto in his report of 26 February 1938, a few days after the withdrawal of the troops from Teruel: 'So far, we have only an outline ... an embryonic organisation'. He also complained about the lack of discipline and how long it took to prepare the recruits that were joining the ranks. On the very morning of the fall of Teruel, Rojo presented his resignation to Prieto. Negrín, the Prime Minister, replied to him the following day that, with him, the army of the Republic was in good hands, that he did not know of anybody who 'comes near you for your professional skill, composure, clear vision ... precision and sense of organisation in your acts', and, as if that were not enough, 'above all these qualities', what he most admired about him was 'your human character'.[10]

Although Negrín was trying to repair the 'physical and moral damage' affecting Rojo after 'twenty months of constant stress' in his work, it is true to say that the state of the republican troops following the Teruel disaster was worrying, and this was borne out just a few days later in the full-scale push begun by the Nationalists through Aragon and Castellón to the coast. On 9 March, some 150,000 men, backed up by hundreds of artillery pieces and aircraft of the Condor Legion and the *Aviazione Legionaria*, began their advance through Aragon. On 10 March, they recaptured Belchite, which they had lost the previous summer; on 14 March, Alcañiz, having dropped several tonnes of bombs on the town a few days previously; and on 17 March, the Morocco Corps and the 1st Division entered Caspe, which had

[9] Antony Beevor, *The Battle for Spain: The Spanish Civil War 1936–1939*, Phoenix, London, 2007, p. 329.
[10] Rojo, *Vicente Rojo*, pp. 190–6.

been the headquarters of the Council of Aragon and was now that of the republican authority that replaced it, the Governor-General José Ignacio Mantecón. There then followed two simultaneous actions: one, to the south of the Ebro, with the capture of Gandesa, in the province of Tarragona, on 1 April; and the other, to the north of the river, which saw Yagüe take Fraga on 27 March and Lérida on 3 April. The campaign ended on 15 April on the Mediterranean coast. 'The victorious sword of Franco', said the Seville daily, *ABC*, the following day, 'has split the Spain still held by the reds into two'.

The report sent by the examining magistrate, General Carlos Masquelet, on 2 April, to the Minister of Defence on the 'collapse' of the Eastern front showed the situation in which the divisions of the Eastern army found themselves at that time:

The performance of our army left a great deal to be desired: incomplete units; unarmed units; artillery of poorer quality than ordered, particularly anti-aircraft guns; communications that were flawed or misused and with little protection, with the commanders unable to re-establish them promptly; rudimentary fortifications, with little tactical thought behind them and hardly any infantry working on them; shortage of transport, so useful these days for supplying and motorising the troops, providing them with mobility and flexibility and, above all, the vast discrepancy between our equipment and that of the enemy, in their favour.[11]

The republican troops and civilians withdrawing to Catalonia suffered endless bombing from the Savoia-Marchetti of the *Aviazione Legionaria*. According to a report by the Jesuits in Lérida, on 27 March, the fourth Sunday in Lent, 'some thirty bombers, totally unopposed, devoted themselves to pounding the city for several hours'. Tortosa, near the mouth of the Ebro, was reduced to rubble. In the bombing of Balaguer, on 6 April, over one hundred aircraft took part. However, the most violent air-raids of all occurred in Barcelona, far from the front, on 17 and 18 March, with over a thousand casualties. In some places like Lérida, the Nationalists later removed the lists in the Civil Registry that contained the names of the victims.

[11] 'El derrumbamiento del Frente del Este en marzo de 1938', report of the examining magistrate, 2 April 1938, Servicio Histórico Militar, armario 46, batch 768, file 1.

Split in two, beset by a serious economic crisis and with its morale shattered, the Republic was in torment. Indalecio Prieto, who made no secret of his defeatism, left ('driven out', as he put it) the government of the Republic, which he had served both in peace and in war. Outside Spain, things were no better: on 20 February, Anthony Eden, the only minister in Neville Chamberlain's government who had not openly expressed any antagonism towards the Republic, resigned as Foreign Secretary. On 16 April, his successor in the Foreign Office, Lord Halifax, signed an agreement with Italy in which, once again, the British turned a blind eye to the Fascist intervention in Franco's camp. In France, after a short-lived government led by the Socialist, Léon Blum, which lasted only thirty days, the radical Édouard Daladier took over in April, and in June he once more closed the border with Spain. Such was the harsh situation that the Republic found itself in, and the government began to reconstruct the army of the East with all the units that had withdrawn to Catalonia. It had to defend itself, resist and at least prevent a swift collapse that would almost certainly be accompanied by the likely unconditional victory of Franco, while all the time waiting for the international headwinds to change direction.

But Franco insisted on the idea of a long drawn-out war of attrition, in which he would conclusively crush the Republic. 'He had a vast army and could afford to be careless of his men's lives', writes Paul Preston. Instead of launching a swift attack against Barcelona, as it appears his colleagues had asked him to do, in view of the victorious Aragon campaign, Franco ordered Generals José Varela, Antonio Aranda and Rafael García Valiño to advance from Teruel to Castellón, which they took on 13 June.[12] The offensive against Valencia – the main objective of this campaign that was initiated a few days later – came up against an effective defensive response from the republicans. However, the Nationalist troops remained less than 50 kilometres from what had been the capital of the Republic for a year. Franco said that he would enter Valencia on 25 July, the feast day of Saint James the Apostle. And it was on that night, 24 to 25 July, that various units of the republican army, under the command of the Communist Juan Modesto, crossed the Ebro in rowing boats, following the plan outlined by General Rojo to relink the Levante with

---

[12] Preston, *Franco*, pp. 304–16.

Catalonia. Thus began the Battle of the Ebro, the longest and harshest of the whole war.

Almost all the commanders in this ad hoc army of the Ebro were Communists. The commander-in-chief was Lieutenant Colonel Juan Modesto, and on his staff were Enrique Lister, who commanded the 5th Army Corps, and Lieutenant Colonel Manuel Tagüeña, a physics and mathematics student who had begun the war in the ranks and ended up commanding the 15th Army Corps. General Rojo told them, according to Tagüeña in *Testimonio entre dos guerras*, 'that he would answer for any decision we might take on the opposite shore if we found ourselves cut off and in a difficult situation'.[13] They crossed the river in various locations, from Fayón in the north and Miravete in the south. The initial advance, as was normal in these republican actions, was considerable, but it was quickly halted, as was also normal. And Franco acted as he had done on previous occasions, in Brunete, Belchite and Teruel, and began to take back the ground lost.

At first, the battle looked like a tactical victory for the republicans, as they had halted the Nationalist offensive on Valencia, but almost throughout it was a defensive battle whose aim was to tire the adversary and force them to negotiate a victory that was less unconditional, rather than to defeat them, which was impossible. For nearly four months, until 16 November, 250,000 men fought. The Nationalists lost over 30,000 men (dead and wounded) and the republicans double that number, although leading military historians disagree over the exact number of dead, some citing 13,000 in total, spread almost equally between the two sides. The Republic had lost the best of its army and soon afterwards lost the whole of Catalonia. The Republic by now seemed to have been defeated, particularly because the Munich Pact, signed at the end of September, allowing Hitler to advance freely on Czechoslovakia, ruined Negrín's resistance and showed that the democracies had no intention of changing their policy of appeasement of the Fascist powers. On 7 November, Franco told the Vice-President of the United Press, James Miller, something that he had never tired of repeating throughout that year: 'There will be no negotiated peace. There will be no negotiated peace because the criminals and their victims cannot live side by side'.[14]

---

[13] Quoted in Rojo, *Vicente Rojo*, p. 218.
[14] Preston, *Franco*, p. 316.

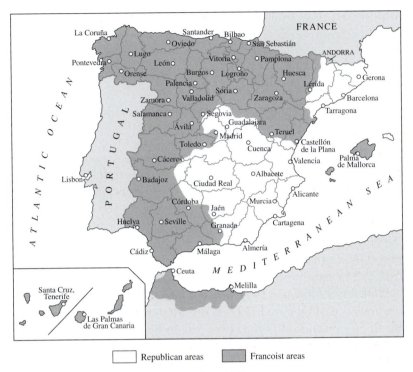

Map 3 Evolution of the war, November 1938

Rojo's opinion after the withdrawal from Teruel still held after the Battle of the Ebro: all they had was an 'outline' of an army, 'an embryonic organisation'. Policy and military strategy did not always coincide in the republican camp. And there was more conflict and disunity than in the Nationalist camp. The civil war in the republican camp began with a revolution and ended with a desperate attempt by Negrín to introduce a democratic and disciplined alternative that would bring about a change in French and British policy, and which many people, particularly anarchists and the socialist left, saw as a Communist dictatorship, because of the Republic's dependence on the Soviet Union for military equipment and for the rise of Communist militants in the republican army.

The military rebels, despite the disparity of their forces, never had any problems of that type. Aid from the Fascist powers was more readily available, and the military authorities, under the sole command of Franco, controlled the home front with an iron glove. Those who shared their values were happily experiencing the renaissance of a new Spain, because their army always won its battles, so loss of morale was out of the question. For those who did not support them, a savage violence awaited them, implemented from the very day of the uprising, a violence that did not cease until many years after the end of the war.

Opposing worlds

In some of the cities where the uprising had been defeated, the war seemed far away for months. Away from the front, their inhabitants made the most of the revolutionary celebrations, the enthusiasm for the destruction of order and its symbols, and they knew nothing of the harshness of the trenches or the bombings. This enthusiastic atmosphere, with armed people in the streets, the requisitioning of luxury cars and houses belonging to aristocrats and the middle classes, the abundance of food, can be seen in the press cuttings, testimonies and documents that we have from that time. It may be seen in the image of the luxury restaurant of the Hotel Ritz in Barcelona occupied by the working classes. The dispossessed were eating where only the well-to-do had eaten before – an image that summed up the reversal of order. It could be seen in Málaga, Valencia and the Madrid of the first few weeks. But Barcelona would always be the clearest example of this earthly paradise.[15]

To George Orwell, who had recently arrived in Barcelona, this exterior aspect of the city, even in December 1936, seemed to him to be 'something startling and overwhelming: it was the first time that I had ever been in a town where the working class was in the saddle'. The buildings were adorned with red and black flags; the churches looted; the shops and cafés collectivised. 'Waiters and shop-walkers looked you in the face and treated you as an equal. Servile and even ceremonial forms of speech had temporarily disappeared'. '*Tú*' was used instead of '*usted*', and '*¡salud!*' replaced '*¡adiós!*' The loudspeakers 'were bellowing' revolutionary songs. Apparently, 'the wealthy

---

[15] The image in the Hotel Ritz may be seen in the anarchist documentary 'Barcelona trabaja para el frente', included in *La guerra filmada*, a series of documentaries presented by Julián Casanova on TVE (the State-financed television service in Spain), edited by the Filmoteca Nacional-Ministerio de Cultura, Madrid, 2009.

classes had ceased to exist': there were no 'well-dressed' people. Overalls, or 'rough working-class clothes' had replaced middle-class outfits. But things were not as they appeared: 'I did not realize that great numbers of well-to-do bourgeois were simply lying low and disguising themselves as proletarians for the time being'.[16]

So the bourgeois in Barcelona were in disguise, forced to wear working-class clothes if they wanted to stay alive. And the same went for the bourgeois and landowners in Madrid in the weeks following the uprising. People like José Félix, the protagonist of *Madrid de corte a checa*, by Agustín de Foxá, who 'had taken off his tie and went around open-necked ... because the middle classes of Madrid, backed into a corner, spent their days next to the stove or the heating boiler, burning photographs and receipts from *Renovación* or *Acción Popular*'.[17]

Armed militias went out of the cities to the front, 'hunting for Fascists', and in this scenario women played a leading role. The revolution and the anti-Fascist war generated a new climate and a fresh image of women, which could be seen in the propaganda and war slogans, and this transformed the way in which they were usually portrayed. The image of women as 'perfect wives' and 'angels of the household' gave way, in the revolutionary fervour of the first few weeks, to the figure of the militiawoman, portrayed graphically in numerous posters as an attractive woman in blue overalls, rifle on her shoulder, striding out to the front to hunt the enemy.

During those early days, the image of the militiawoman, an active and warlike heroine, strong and brave, became the symbol of Spanish mobilisation against Fascism. While the rejection of the 'middle-class outfit' was for men a sign of political identification, as Orwell had observed, for women, according to Mary Nash, wearing trousers or overalls took on a deeper significance, since women had never before adopted this male costume, which challenged the traditional female appearance. But the militiawomen who dressed like men, thus displaying their claim for equality, were in a small minority, CNT affiliates, sisters or wives of militants, and were not representative of the female population. Most working-class women rejected this form of dress. And it hardly needs to be said that it found little favour among

---

[16] George Orwell, *Homenaje a Cataluña*, Ariel, Barcelona, 1983, pp. 2–4.

[17] Agustín de Foxá, *Madrid de corte a checa*, Planeta, Barcelona, 1993, p. 288. (Original edition published by La Ciudadela, Madrid, 1938.)

men either. War was something very serious and should not be confused with a carnival, said, among others, the *Diari oficial del Comité Antifeixista i de Salut Pública de Badalona* on 3 October 1936.

In fact, this aggressive image of the woman as part of the revolutionary spirit of adventure that was current in the summer of 1936 quickly disappeared, to be replaced by the slogan 'men to the front, women on the home front', more in keeping with the roles assigned to both sexes in the war effort: the former occupied with combat duties in the trenches, and the latter giving aid and support on the home front. After the upheaval of revolution, the exaltation of motherhood and the right of mothers to defend their children against the brutality of Fascism made for a much more powerful form of female mobilisation. Starting in September 1936, with Largo Caballero as Prime Minister, a new policy was implemented which required women to return from the front. By the end of the year, posters and propaganda displaying militiawomen had disappeared. By the beginning of 1937, these heroines in blue overalls were history. As far as we know, no women's organisation, not even the anarchist *Mujeres Libres*, publicly protested against the decisions, taken by men, to force the women to give up armed combat. All these organisations, concludes Mary Nash, in what has been the most comprehensive study on this matter, saw the integration of the female labour force into production on the home front 'as an essential ingredient for winning the war'.[18]

Despite the platitudes and propaganda, it was unlikely that relations between the sexes could change much in such a short time, particularly in the rural world. In the words of Pilar Vivancos, daughter of a smallholder from the town of Beceite, in Teruel, and partner of the anarchist leader of the militia and later of the 25th Division, Miguel García Vivancos, 'the question of women's liberation was not addressed by the revolutionary process', and in the self-styled libertarian Aragon, 'a woman's place was in the kitchen or the fields'.[19] Women, as confirmed by the documents available, did not take part in the management committees of political and trade union organisations. This also went for the municipal councils, the bodies of local

---

[18] Mary Nash, *Defying Male Civilization: Women in the Spanish Civil War*, Arden Press, Denver, CO, 1995, pp. 52, 101–21.

[19] Quoted in Ronald Fraser, *Recuérdalo tú y recuérdalo a otros. Historia oral de la guerra civil española*, 2 vols., Crítica, Barcelona, 1979, vol. I, p. 402.

power dominated by the CNT until August 1937. And with regard to the equality of opportunities of the working woman, the gender factor was still a major element of distinction, as borne out by the minimum wage set by the anarchist Miguel Chueca, of the Labour Department of the Council of Aragon: ten pesetas for men and six for women.

The militants of the anarchist organisation *Mujeres Libres*, whose membership included the notable figures of Lucía Sánchez Saornil, Mercedes Comaposada and Amparo Poch y Gascón, the only ones who tried to correct this contradiction between ideas and practice, never managed to achieve recognition as an autonomous branch of the libertarian movement, an objective which, on the other hand, had been attained by the *Juventudes Libertarias* when this organisation was set up in 1932. Despite their efforts and aspirations, the traditional relationship between men and women, like many other aspects of day-to-day life, was maintained with very few changes within the context of the revolutionary experience. To be more precise, the opportunities presented in the early days of revolutionary fervour, which had served to enhance the image of the militiawoman as a heroine and symbol of the mobilisation of the Spanish people against Fascism, were closed off as the struggle for power, the reconstruction of order and the war neutralised the most radical aspects of popular power.

After the early days of euphoria, many workers in Catalonia felt distanced from revolution and collectivisation. They were supposed to bring improvements in social and labour conditions. They might have done at the beginning. But a few months later, seeing that this was collectivisation in time of war, the opposite occurred: hours were increased, wages could not match galloping inflation, and the shortage of food supplies meant that the daily struggle to obtain them became a fundamental obsession. The inhabitants of Barcelona had to adapt to exceptional circumstances: supply problems as a result of price rises in consumer goods, a fall in real wages, the use of inferior-quality materials and the sudden appearance of the black market. And in a city whose industries had hitherto included the manufacture of machinery, textiles and chemicals, they now had to set up a war industry. In fact, the whole of Catalonia was a society that was being overwhelmed with refugees fleeing from territory overrun by Franco's army.

As the war went on, there were more and more people denouncing the inefficiency of the supply system and protests against the appearance of the black market. Many of these complaints and accusations were lodged by women, who raided food shops and town halls to ask for bread and war rations for their families. It is obvious that these protests should never be divorced from the exceptional conditions dictated by the war and the influx of refugees that Catalonia experienced. But they also highlight the contrast between the lives of luxury and plenty of certain sectors of the population linked to the new power base, and the shortage of staple products suffered by most of the civilian population.

Following the loss of Aragon, in March 1938, agricultural production fell and hunger and pessimism increased among a rapidly rising population that saw the prosperity promised by the revolution receding at the same rate as it was experiencing a deterioration in its welfare. The revolution was no longer the be-all and end-all, the devastating force that had overrun the old order. It disappeared from the agenda of the CNT, and indeed from its philosophy. The movement was entering its death throes. Every day there was less and less territory to defend. These difficult months were too much for some anarchist newspapers, and one by one they folded. This hardship also affected *Solidaridad Obrera*, which had lived its golden age in the early months of the revolution. In May 1937, newsprint became increasingly scarce, and the censors showed no mercy on the newspaper that had epitomised the power of the CNT.

And if people were being ground down by the war in Barcelona, things were not much better in Madrid, where conditions were extremely harsh in the autumn and winter of 1936. There also, the women demonstrated publicly in protest against the shortage of food supplies. The workers 'were going hungry' and 'mothers demanded milk for their children', wrote Palmiro Togliatti, the delegate of the Communist International in Spain. The bread ration fell sharply at the front and behind the lines. In Madrid, bread rationing went down from the 230 grams per day per inhabitant before the war, to 100 grams at the end of 1938. As a result of all this, said a report from the Central-South Army Group on 19 November 1938, the troops' attitude was that '*the war is drawing to a close* … That is what is being talked about at the front and behind the lines, in soldiers' letters from the front, in gatherings, in the streets, and places of entertainment'. Support for Negrín and his resistance strategy was fading fast.[20]

Fifth columnists, deserters working in Madrid, Valencia and Barcelona for the Nationalists, began to crawl out from under their stones. To put a brake on these activities, on 16 August 1937, Negrín's government had set up the Military Investigation Service, charged with tracking down espionage, treason and defeatism, although in fact it ended up by also hunting POUM militants and anarchists, and created a system of repression that gave rise to protests, censure and even more division on the republican home front. The fifth column in Madrid, which had been collaborating throughout the war with international espionage, in networks connected with the embassies, went as far as negotiating with Colonel Casado the surrender of Madrid in March 1939. Rojo was right: wars were also lost on the home front.

In Nationalist Spain, on the other hand, there were no food shortages. From the outset, the military rebels controlled the major agricultural production areas. The predominance of military over civilian rule was clear from the beginning, with a united military leadership which, in the words of Pablo Martín Aceña, 'ordered that all economic activities be steered towards the war effort. In contrast to the indiscipline caused by the revolution, in the Nationalist zone production was subject to an unwavering discipline'. And in contrast to the monetary chaos in the republican zone, with a large number of coins and promissory notes in circulation, the 'Nationalist' peseta suffered a limited depreciation and there were no serious disruptions to supplies. The external aid from Italy and Germany and the major international companies' preference for Franco's cause were also a basic factor in maintaining unity, morale and faith in victory.[21]

While the anarchists and socialists were requisitioning and collectivising lands, one of the first measures taken by the *Junta de Defensa Nacional*, set up in Burgos on 24 July 1936, and its successor, the *Junta Técnica del Estado*, was to dismantle the Republic's legislation and the activities of the *Instituto de Reforma Agraria* (IRA). Wherever possible, beginning with Andalusia, lands were returned to

---

[20] The two reports are in Ricardo Miralles, *Juan Negrín. La República en guerra*, Temas de Hoy, Madrid, 2003, pp. 297–8.

[21] Pablo Martín Aceña, 'La economía española de los años treinta', in Santos Juliá (ed.), *Historia de España de Menéndez Pidal. República y guerra civil*, 42 vols., Espasa Calpe, Madrid, 2004, vol. XL, p. 403.

their former owners. In 1938, the Minister of Agriculture in Franco's first government, the Falangist Raimundo Fernández Cuesta, set up the *Servicio Nacional de Reforma Económica y Social de la Tierra* (National Land Economic and Social Reform Service), but the owners had not expected to recover their lands 'legitimately', and the violent counter-revolution of officers, landowners, *señoritos* and Falangists had already taken their revenge on thousands of peasants in Extremadura and Andalusia.

There were others, however, who managed to flee and take refuge in the mountains of Andalusia, Asturias, León and Galicia. They were the *huidos* (fugitives), many of whom formed the core of subsequent guerrilla activity, because they knew that they would never be able to return, and that if they were captured, harsh repression awaited them. But those who took to the mountains soon after the military rising did so, in the words of Secundino Serrano, 'without any planning ahead, their first objective being to save their lives'.[22]

And this was the start of the Nationalist repression of those suspected of collaborating against them, which intensified from the end of 1937 onwards, especially after the conquest of Asturias, where thousands fled and at least 200 were killed in the early confrontations with the Nationalist armed forces. The reprisals were brutal in Cáceres on Christmas Day 1937. Two days before, the military authorities had discovered a plot, so they said, headed by Máximo Calvo Cano, a Communist leader and mayor of Cadalso, who had fled to the republican zone after the military rising, in which he aimed to seize Cáceres and turn the city 'into a Marxist centre of terror and devastation'. Máximo Calvo was discovered by a security guard near Almoharín. According to the official version, he was disguised as a beggar when he was gunned down. His guerrilla comrades said that, surrounded by the Civil Guard, he shot himself with his own rifle.

The military chief of the province, Ricardo Rada Peral, ordered the execution of over 200 people who had been in contact with the guerrilla leader, whose names appeared in the papers found in his clothes. Whether there was a plot or not, a totally different matter was the twenty-five men who were picked to be murdered on Christmas Day. Among their number was Antonio Canales, a socialist and mayor of

[22] Secundino Serrano, *Maquis. Historia de la guerrilla antifranquista*, Temas de Hoy, Madrid, 2001, p. 34.

Cáceres for most of the time of the Republic. He had been arrested on 21 July 1936 and sentenced to death by a court martial on 9 August the following year. Most of those who fell with him were railway employees working at Arroyo-Malpartida station. They were buried in a mass grave. Before he died, Canales asked to see Elías Serradilla, the parish priest of Santa María. When he slumped before the firing squad, he had on his person 'a small crucifix, a medal of the Virgin of the Mountains, photographs of his family and a notebook containing the dates of birth of his children'.

The executioners were rewarded, decorated, blessed and commended before the images of virgins and saints. Ricardo Rada, the military governor of Cáceres responsible for this Christmas massacre, was named an honorary citizen of the city at a plenary session of the city council. Many months previously, in September 1936, Civil Guard Lieutenant Pascual Sánchez, who had, with his machine pistol, delivered the coup de grâce to dozens of people lying face down in the square in the town of Baena, in Córdoba, was presented with the Military Medal in front of an image of Jesus the Nazarene, and an altar was erected in the very place where he had caused so much blood to flow. After this divine punishment, charitable souls suggested building orphanages, such as the one in Puente Genil, so that at least the children of the reds, 'who not long before were raising a clenched fist and insulting any religious person who went by', would receive the 'Christian education' that their parents had rejected.[23]

The re-establishment of religious education was one of the distinguishing features of the Nationalist home front. Heavy symbolism was also to be seen in the many ceremonies involving the 'replacement' and 'return' of crucifixes in schools after the beginning of the 1936–37 school year. The abolition of republican legislation went hand in hand with the restoration of a traditional Spain, with children as witnesses. The ritual and the celebrants took many forms. In Tarazona, the same person who had removed the crucifixes five years earlier, 'much to

---

[23] The information on Cáceres comes from Manuel Veiga López, *Fusilamiento en Navidad. Antonio Canales, tiempo de República*, Editorial Regional de Extremadura, Mérida, 1993, pp. 238–66 and Julián Chaves Palacios, *La represión en la provincia de Cáceres durante la guerra civil (1936–1939)*, Universidad de Extremadura, Cáceres, 1995, pp. 246–93; the information on Córdoba is in Francisco Moreno Gómez, *La guerra civil en Córdoba (1936–1939)*, Alpuerto, Madrid, 1985, p. 235.

his and his parents' chagrin', was charged with replacing them on 30 August 1936. In La Coruña, it was the civil governor who gave the order on 13 August. And in Zaragoza, the order came from the rector of the university. In most cases, mayors and priests ran the ceremonies, while bishops usually delivered the speeches.[24]

Crucifixes, Sacred Hearts of Jesus, Virgins of the Column and pre-republican flags – the restoration of traditional symbols won many adherents and was enthusiastically greeted. Republican, anarchist, socialist and secular symbols all caved in under the drive of the military and religion. In Pamplona, one of the first things the Carlists did after the uprising was to shatter the plaques containing the names of notable socialists and republicans in the streets and squares. Old habits of popular religious life were restored. Religious feast days returned to the official calendar, and others of a 'national' character began to be celebrated, which were maintained during Franco's dictatorship, until his death.

The bishop of Salamanca, Enrique Pla y Deniel, in his pastoral letter 'Los delitos del pensamiento y los falsos ídolos intelectuales' ('The crimes of thought and false intellectual idols'), published in that province's Ecclesiastical Gazette on 20 May 1938, asked for 'the expurgation of libraries, particularly public and school libraries, into which so much flawed and poisonous material has been introduced in recent years'.[25] It was very important, as the Ecclesiastical Gazette of the Archdiocese of Burgos maintained a few months earlier, to instil religious discipline in children, 'as tomorrow they will be the spouses, parents and heads of the family'.[26]

It was not all religion, however, on the Nationalist home front. And to escape the old concept of charity and assistance, and to give expression to the Falangist dreams of 'social justice', the struggle against 'hunger, cold and misery' in the middle of a war, October 1936 saw the setting up of *Auxilio de Invierno* (Winter Assistance), later to become the *Delegación Nacional de Auxilio Social* (National Social Assistance Delegation) in May 1937. It was

[24] The significance of all these acts of replacing crucifixes is explored in Alfonso Álvarez Bolado, *Para ganar la guerra, para ganar la paz. Iglesia y guerra civil: 1936–1939*, Universidad Pontificia de Comillas, Madrid, 1995, pp. 47–50.
[25] Ibid., p. 292.
[26] *Boletín Eclesiástico del Arzobispado de Burgos*, 16 April 1938.

the brainchild of Mercedes Sanz Bachiller, the widow of Onésimo Redondo, and Javier Martínez de Bedoya, an old student colleague of Onésimo's, who, after spending some time in Nazi Germany, returned to Spain in June 1936, and in the autumn of that year suggested to Sanz Bachiller, at that time provincial head of the *Sección Femenina* in Valladolid, that they set up something similar to the Nazi *Winterhilfe*, to collect donations and distribute food and warm clothing to the most needy. In less than a year, according to Ángela Cenarro, they turned it 'into an institution at the service of the demographic policy of the Nationalist "New State", defending motherhood, with the setting up of a charity to protect mothers and their children: "We need strong, fecund mothers to give us plenty of healthy children to fulfil the desire for supremacy of the youth that has died in war".'[27]

And thus, with strong, fertile mothers and healthy, educated children, with hundreds of schoolteachers murdered and the destruction of books – 'the worst drug of all!', in the words of Gonzalo Calamita, rector of the University of Zaragoza – dawned 'with gladdening light a new golden age for the glory of Christianity, Civilisation and Spain'. So wrote Modesto Díez del Corral, Chairman of the *Comisión Depuradora del Magisterio* (Commission to Purge the Teaching Profession) in the province of Burgos, and it was no mere dream. He and many others were convinced of success if priests, civil guards, mayors and all others with 'total ideological solvency' identified with this 'way of thinking' and offered 'their full valuable cooperation'.[28] An era of opulence was also predicted by the Zaragoza Catholic daily, *El Noticiero*, on 9 March 1938, as republican and collectivist Aragon was collapsing under the advance of Franco's troops. Children would sing patriotic anthems, learn about the lives of heroes and saints, and look upon the portrait of the *Caudillo* while they were being nurtured by the Gospels. Just over a year later, all this came to pass in the New Spain, united now under the all-conquering sword of Franco.

---

[27] Ángela Cenarro (quoting Martínez de Bedoya), *La sonrisa de Falange. Auxilio social en la guerra civil y en la posguerra*, Crítica, Barcelona, 2006, pp. 1–13.

[28] Gonzalo Calamita, quoted in Ángela Cenarro, *Cruzados y camisas azules. Los orígenes del franquismo en Aragón, 1936–1945*, Prensas Universitarias de Zaragoza, 1997, p. 239; Circular de la Comisión Depuradora del Magisterio de Burgos, 23 December 1936.

The end

The end of the Republic had been a foregone conclusion since the Munich Pact and the outcome of the Battle of the Ebro, but its last three months were particularly painful. The whole of Catalonia fell to Franco's troops in barely a month, in the midst of patriotic and religious fervour. They entered Tarragona in the middle of January 1939 and Barcelona on 26 January. Three days later, on Sunday 29 January, a multitudinous open-air mass was celebrated in the Plaza de Cataluña, presided over by General Juan Yagüe. The official entry into Barcelona was led by the troops of the army of Navarre, under General José Solchaga Zala. In the words of the British military attaché in Burgos, 'the Navarrans marched at the head, not because they had fought better, but because they were the ones that felt the most burning hatred' for Catalonia and the Catalans.[29]

'The city's bleak period of slavery was over', concluded Francisco Lacruz in his account of 'revolution and terror' in Barcelona. Such had been the transgression of its inhabitants that the scene offered by the city to its liberators was 'Dantesque': 'hunger, suffering and terror had turned it into a city populated by the living dead, hallucinatory beings, ghosts'. The inhabitants left behind came out to acclaim the victors, 'starving and haggard', drawing on their last ounce of strength. 'They had suffered the terrible years of the reds, years which cannot be measured, years which seem like centuries or infinity'.

This was a far cry from the earthly paradise that George Orwell had portrayed. It was a 'gigantic midden' over which 'sovietism' had passed 'like a millenary horror'. It was imperative to sate the hunger of the starving, recover the 'will to live' and 'the industrious, tenacious and enduring energy of this great Spanish city with its glorious history', and to punish all those responsible for the 'red dictatorship'.[30]

As Michael Richards has pointed out recently, the occupation of Catalonia 'was viewed in pathological terms'. Víctor Ruiz Albéniz (*El Tebib Arrumi*), a doctor and friend of Franco's from the war in

---

[29] Quoted in Michael Richards, *Un tiempo de silencio. La guerra civil y la cultura de la represión en la España de Franco, 1936–1945*, Crítica, Barcelona, 1999, p. 46. (Originally published in English: *A Time of Silence*, Cambridge University Press, New York, 1998.)

[30] Francisco Lacruz, *El alzamiento, la revolución y el terror en Barcelona*, Barcelona, 1943, pp. 264–5.

Morocco, recommended, in the *Heraldo de Aragón* of 4 February 1939, a 'biblical chastisement (Sodom and Gomorrah) ... to purge the red city, the seat of anarchism and separatism ... as the only way to extirpate those two cancers by ruthless cauterisation'. And Ramón Serrano Suñer, the Interior Minister of the first Nationalist government formed on 30 January 1938, also knew how to treat this 'secessionist virus', the illness that was Catalan nationalism. 'Today we have Catalonia at the tip of our bayonets', he said to the *Noticiero Universal* on 24 February 1939. 'The question of material supremacy will soon be resolved. I am sure that the moral incorporation of Catalonia into Spain will come about as quickly as its military incorporation'.[31]

The republican troops withdrew in a rabble to the French border. According to Manuel Azaña's description, 'the horde just kept on growing to immeasurable proportions. A crazed mob jammed the roads, and spilled onto shortcuts looking for the frontier. It was one solid mass of humanity stretching 15 kilometres along the road. Some women had miscarriages at the roadside. There were children who died from the cold or were trampled to death'.[32] Large numbers of people were killed or injured by bombing and machine-gun fire from Nationalist aircraft.

The retribution against red Catalonia rekindled the 'hot-blooded' terror, with on-the-spot firing squads without trial. Between the total occupation of Catalonia and the final victory of Franco's army, there were fifty days of an orgy of anti-Catalan reprisal, in the form of beatings, acts of humiliation against women, looting and destruction of libraries, and killings of those whose 'hands were stained with blood' and who could not escape. British diplomats, in an assessment made two years later, thought that the 'treatment received by the Catalans is worse than that suffered by the victims of the Gestapo and the OVRA' (Italian secret police).[33]

With the fall of Barcelona and the total conquest of Catalonia, the Republic was in its death throes. The United Kingdom and France finally recognised Franco's government on 27 February 1939. Manuel Azaña, who had crossed over into France three weeks previously,

[31] Richards, *Un tiempo de silencio*, p. 45.
[32] Manuel Azaña, 'Carta a Ángel Osorio', in *Obras completas*, 7 vols., ed. Juan Marichal, Oasis, México, 1967, vol. III, p. 539.
[33] Richards, *Un tiempo de silencio*, p. 229, n. 151.

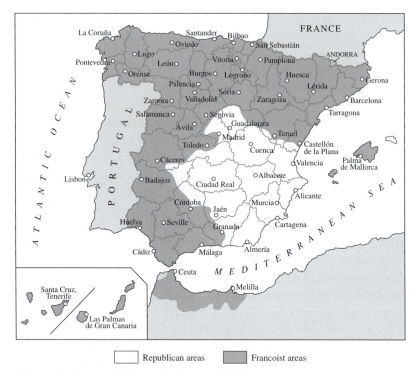

| | Republican areas | | Francoist areas |

Map 4 Evolution of the war, February 1939

resigned as President of the Republic. A few days later, a coup by Colonel Segismundo Casado made things worse.

Madrid, the anti-Fascist city of resistance, the seat of the *Junta Delegada de Defensa*, had gradually become, according to Ángel Bahamonde and Javier Cervera, the passive city and, above all, the city of the fifth column, which, since 1938, used 'the tactic of infiltration into the apparatuses of republican power so that it could maintain a presence there and, over the long term, control their nerve centres'. Hunger, the black market and loss of morale were rife towards the end of 1938. The accumulated tensions were as big as, or even bigger than that which had led to the bloody May of 1937 in Barcelona, and they had not emerged earlier because of 'the physical proximity of the enemy' and the 'pressing need to hold on'.[34]

---

[34] Ángel Bahamonde and Javier Cervera, *Así terminó la guerra de España*, Marcial Pons, Madrid, 2000, pp. 247–56.

Casado's coup was not only the culmination of a political conflict, but also 'the rebellion of the officers' against the republican government, whose legitimacy they no longer recognised. It was also the embodiment of the idea that 'it would be easier to settle the war through an understanding between officers'. It heralded a desperate, costly, fratricidal struggle in this moribund Republic, with offshoots in other parts of the central zone and Cartagena, which achieved not an 'honourable peace', but an unconditional surrender, something which Franco, the officers, the civil authorities and the Catholic Church never tired of announcing – in other words, the annihilation of the republican regime and its supporters.[35]

Still to come was the drama of Alicante. Some 15,000 people, including senior officers, republican politicians, combatants and civilians, had been crowding together in the port since 29 March. At dawn the following day, Italian troops of the Vittorio Division, commanded by General Gaetano Gambara, arrived in the city before most of this assemblage was able to board French and British ships. Many of those captured were executed on the spot. Other preferred to kill themselves before becoming victims of Nationalist repression.

'Today, with the red army captured and disarmed, our victorious troops have achieved their final military objectives. The war is over', said the last official report issued by Franco's GHQ on 1 April 1939, read by the broadcaster and actor, Fernando Fernández de Córdoba.

Catholicism and the Fatherland had united, liberated by the redeeming power of the cross. The war had been necessary and inevitable because 'Spain could not be saved by conventional means', wrote Leopoldo Eijo y Garay, bishop of Madrid, in his pastoral letter 'La hora presente', issued on 28 March, the day of the 'liberation' of the capital. It was 'the moment for settling mankind's account with the political philosophy of the French Revolution'.[36]

A few hours after announcing that the red army had been captured and disarmed, the *Generalísimo* received a telegram from Pius XII, the former Cardinal Pacelli, who had been elected Pope on 2 March that year, after the unexpected death of his predecessor Pius XI on 10 February: 'With heart uplifted to the Lord, we sincerely give thanks,

---

[35] Ibid., pp. 349–404.
[36] Quoted in Redondo, *Historia de la Iglesia en España*, pp. 603–5.

along with Your Excellency, for this long-desired Catholic victory in Spain'.

And it did not take long for Cardinal Isidro Gomá to join in the chorus of congratulations. Writing from Pamplona on 3 April, he reminded Franco 'how keen I was to support your endeavours from the start; how I collaborated with my limited strength in my capacity as Prelate of the Church; you have always been in my prayers and those of my priests'.

For this reason, Gomá felt he had 'special legitimate cause to share your joy in these moments of definitive triumph'. Spain and its Church might have sunk without trace, and yet God, 'who has found Your Excellency to be a worthy instrument to carry out His favourable plans for our dear Fatherland', had ensured that this would not happen. God and the Fatherland would recompense the 'glorious Spanish army' and 'particularly' Franco for 'the mighty effort you must have put in to culminate this massive endeavour'. And He would pay them 'with the love of the people' and 'a long life to carry on the work you did during the war in peacetime'.[37]

The war had lasted almost a thousand days, leaving long-lasting scars on Spanish society. The total number of dead, according to historians, was nearly 600,000, of which 100,000 deaths were due to the repression unleashed by the military rebels, and 55,000 due to the violence in the republican zone. Half a million people were crowded in prisons and concentration camps.

The Spanish Civil War was the first of the wars in the twentieth century in which aviation was used in a premeditated fashion in bombing raids behind the lines. Italian S-81s and S-79s, German He-111s and Russian *Katiuskas* turned Spain into a testing ground for the major world war that was on the horizon. Madrid, Durango, Guernica, Alcañiz, Lérida, Barcelona, Valencia, Alicante and Cartagena were among the cities whose defenceless populations became military targets. According to the study by Josep María Solé i Sabaté and Joan Villarroya, bombing by the Nationalist, Italian and German planes accounted for over 11,000 lives, over 2,500 of which were in Barcelona, while deaths caused by republican and Soviet aircraft, if we accept the figures given by the winners themselves, numbered 1,088 up to May 1938. The intervention of Italian and German air

---

[37] Ibid., pp. 607–8.

power was a decisive factor in hastening the Nationalist victory. The majority of bombing raids had as their sole objective to punish and spread panic among the population, and many of them occurred in Catalan and Levantine cities from the end of 1938, when the war was as good as won.[38]

The exodus of the defeated population also left its mark. 'The withdrawal', as this great exile of 1939 was known, saw some 450,000 refugees fleeing to France in the first three months of that year, of whom 170,000 were women, children and the elderly. Some 200,000 returned in the following months, to continue their living hell in the Nationalist dictatorship gaols.

Many Spaniards viewed the war as a horror from the outset; others felt that they were in the wrong zone and tried to escape. There were distinguished figures of the Republic who took no part in the war, such as Alejandro Lerroux or Niceto Alcalá Zamora, dismissed as President of the Republic in April 1936, who was on a cruise in northern Europe when the military uprising occurred. He learnt about it in Reykjavik, from where he went to Paris and Buenos Aires, where he died in 1949. There was also the so-called 'third Spain', intellectuals who were able to 'abstain from the war', as Salvador de Madariaga said of himself. But the war caught most of the Spanish population, millions of them, and forced them to take sides – although some would suffer more than others – and saw the beginning of a period of violence without precedent in the history of Spain, however much some historians see this war as a logical consequence of a Spanish ancestral tendency to kill each other.

From April 1939 onwards, Spain experienced the peace of Franco, the consequences of the war and of those that caused it. Spain was left divided between victors and vanquished. From before the ending of the war, the churches were filled with plaques commemorating those who had 'fallen in the service of God and the Fatherland'. On the other hand, thousands of Spaniards killed by the violence initiated by the military rebels in July 1936 did not have even an insignificant tombstone to remember them by, and their families are still searching for their remains today. The reformist project of the Republic and all that this type of government meant was swept away and the dust

[38] Josep Maria Solí i Sabaté and Joan Villarroya, *España en llamas. La guerra civil desde el aire*, Temas de Hoy, Madrid, 2003, pp. 9–10, 313–16.

scattered over the tombs of thousands of Spaniards; and the workers' movement and its ideas were systematically wiped out, in a process that was more violent and long-lasting than that suffered by
any of the other European movements opposed to Fascism. This was
the 'surgical operation on the social body of Spain', so vehemently
demanded by the military rebels, the land-owning classes and the
Catholic Church.

Epilogue: Why did the Republic lose the war?

'Italy and Germany did a great deal for Spain in 1936 ... Without the aid of both countries, there would be no Franco today', said Adolf Hitler to Galeazzo Ciano, the Italian Minister of Foreign Affairs and son-in-law of Benito Mussolini, in September 1940.[1] It is an opinion that sums up perfectly what many contemporaries believed then, and studies have confirmed decades later: that the German and Italian intervention had been decisive in the defeat of the Republic or the victory of the rebel officers who rose against it July 1936.

Some historians, however, believe that the international intervention was not so decisive, and that the causes are to be found in the characteristics of the two armies – Franco's was better – and in their policies, which is usually summed up as the 'unity' of the national zone and republican 'discord'. Political, military and international causes would thus summarise the essence of complex explanations that would answer the simple question as to why the Republic lost the war.

The international situation 'determined' the course and outcome of the civil war. That is the conclusion of Enrique Moradiellos when he assesses all that he and other researchers, including Ángel Viñas, Robert Whealey, Paul Preston, Walther L. Bernecker, Gerald Howson and Pablo Martín Aceña, have written on this subject. Without the aid of Hitler and Mussolini, 'it is very hard to believe that Franco could have won his absolute and unconditional victory', and 'had it not been for the suffocating embargo imposed by non-intervention and the resulting inhibition shown by the western democracies, it is very unlikely that the Republic would have suffered an internal cave-in and such a total and merciless military defeat'.[2]

[1] Quoted in Walther L. Bernecker, *Guerra en España 1936–1939*, Síntesis, Madrid, 1996, p. 45.
[2] Enrique Moradiellos, *El reñidero de Europa. Las dimensiones internacionales de la guerra civil española*, Península, Barcelona, pp. 61–2.

The Republic was not short of money or weaponry. In fact, the Republic spent a similar amount of money in losing the war as Franco did in winning it – some 600 million dollars on each side – but the war materiel it acquired using Bank of Spain gold reserves was inferior, both in quantity and in quality, to that which the Fascist powers supplied to the military rebels. And the most important aspect is that they received this aid constantly, while the Soviet aid depended, among other factors, on the entente between Moscow and the western democratic powers. Thus, at the end of 1937 and in 1938, shipments were either interrupted or blocked at the French border. The expansionist policies of the Fascist powers and 'appeasement', defended by the United Kingdom and supported by France, played a major role in the development and outcome of the Spanish Civil War.

Anthony Beevor gives less importance to the foreign intervention and much more to the strategy followed by the Republic's High Command and the 'disastrous conduct of the war' by the Communist commanders and their Soviet advisers. Beevor feels that Hitler's decision to send Junkers 52 transport planes to help the army of Africa to cross the straits of Gibraltar was not decisive, because it would have happened sooner or later, in view of 'the incompetence and lack of initiative of the republican fleet' during the revolutionary chaos of the early weeks. And it was not the Fascist and Nazi intervention that gave Franco victory in the end, although he does believe that it 'cut short' the war considerably in his favour, above all because of the Condor Legion's actions in the rapid conquest of the north, enabling the rebels to 'concentrate their forces in the centre of Spain', and because of its 'devastating effectiveness' to counter the major republican offensives of the second half of 1937 and 1938.

For Beevor, an expert in some of the great battles of the Second World War, it was not so much a case of Franco winning the war, as the senior republican officers losing it – a theory that supports what

Authors and works previously cited are: Ángel Viñas, *Franco, Hitler y el estallido de la guerra civil*, Alianza Editorial, Madrid, 2001; Robert Whealey, *Hitler and Spain: The Nazi Role in the Spanish Civil War, 1936–1939*, University Press of Kentucky, Lexington, 1989; Paul Preston, *La guerra civil española*, Debate, Barcelona, 2006; Bernecker, *Guerra en España*; Gerald Howson, *Armas para España. La historia no contada de la guerra civil española*, Península, Barcelona, 2000; and Pablo Martín Aceña, *El oro de Moscú y el oro de Berlín*, Taurus, Madrid, 2001.

certain Francoist historians, such as Ramón Salas Larrazábal, had held in the last few years of the dictatorship. Against the war machinery of the military rebels, the republican High Command and its Soviet advisers insisted on launching 'conventional offensives which gradually destroyed the Republic's army and resistance'. These were normally implemented for 'propaganda reasons', and at first they had a 'surprise factor', but as the republicans did not maintain their attacks, the Nationalists would manage to 'redeploy' their troops and the Condor Legion. Once the initial impetus was lost, the republican High Command did not withdraw its forces 'because of the grossly exaggerated propaganda claims that had been made when announcing the offensive'. And so, with defeat after defeat, morale among the troops and on the home front lay shattered. With the Battle of the Ebro, the last time that they applied this orthodox tactic of a general offensive, the military power of the Republic 'was exhausted' and there was nothing left that it could do. The solution, according to Beevor, would have been to combine, from the outset, a defensive conventional war and guerrilla action with short, lightning attacks, but this strategy was impossible because 'political propaganda' needed 'prestige operations'.[3]

Other experts, such as Gabriel Cardona, maintain that the rebels won the war because from the very first shot they had an army, and all they had to do was to 'expand their military resources', while the Republic had to organise one 'practically from scratch'. On one side there were the militias and the whole interminable discussion over whether a regular army should be set up; and on the other, the highly trained troops of Morocco. It is hardly surprising that, under Franco's command, they managed 'to arrive unbeaten to the edge of Madrid'. When Negrín, with Rojo advising him, embarked upon military reorganisation, he found himself with too many insurmountable problems, particularly 'the poor quality of many of the middle and junior command'. An army in action, adds Cardona, 'needs guaranteed supplies and the support of a solid rearguard'. Because the arms came to republican Spain by sea and depended on the policies of

---

[3] Antony Beevor, *La guerra civil española*, pp. 676–80; the discipline of Franco's army and the indiscipline of the republican army are also emphasised by this author, on pp. 82–3, 193–5. One of the best-documented works by a Francoist historian is Ramón Salas Larrazábal, *Historia del Ejército Popular de la República*, 4 vols., Editora Nacional, Madrid, 1973.

Stalin, naval monitoring by the Non-Intervention Committee and the vagaries of French politics as to whether to allow the shipments to go through or not, 'there were constant ups and downs in the supply line, and they could find themselves without arms or munitions at the most vital or critical moment'. Furthermore, the rearguard had enough on its plate, what with hunger, air-raids and military defeats.[4]

However, Michael Seidman believes that the rearguard could have done much more and that this was where, in fact, the Republic lost the war. His categorical conclusion is that the Republic was incapable of retaining the 'commitment and devotion' of the urban population who at first defended it. Nor could it raise enthusiasm among the rural population, including the collectivists, who did not agree with price control. The initial activism and militancy gradually faded, and commitment turned into unwillingness to sacrifice their own self-interests, and the 'struggle for basic survival'. Many citizens of the Republic were more concerned with their *patria chica*, their homes and families, than with 'larger entities, such as the State and the nation'.[5]

This emphasis on the personal aspect without doubt adds to the general vision of the war, but it cannot be set apart from the international rivalries, foreign aid received, the availability of a better army and the political disputes that characterise democracies, or those attempting to achieve this status, as against authoritarian ideas and practices.

After the First World War and the triumph of the revolution in Russia, no civil war could be said to be solely 'internal' any more. When the Spanish Civil War began, the democratic powers were trying at all costs to 'appease' the Fascist powers, especially Nazi Germany, instead of opposing those who were really threatening the balance of power. The Republic found itself, therefore, at an enormous disadvantage in having to wage war on some military rebels, who, from the outset, were the beneficiaries of this international situation that was so favourable to their interests. Dictatorships dominated by

---

[4] Gabriel Cardona, 'Entre la revolución y la disciplina. Ensayo sobre la dimensión militar de la guerra civil', in Enrique Moradiellos (ed.), 'La guerra civil', *Ayer*, 50 (2003), pp. 41–51. Cardona's detailed research into these themes may be found in his book, *Historia militar de una guerra civil*, Flor del Viento, Barcelona, 2006.

[5] Michael Seidman, *A ras del suelo. Historia social de la República durante la guerra civil*, Alianza Editorial, Madrid, 2003, pp. 26, 232, 349–55. (Originally published in English: *Republic of Egos: A Social History of the Spanish Civil War*, University of Wisconsin Press, Madison, 2002.)

authoritarian governments of a single man and a single party were at that time replacing democracy in many countries of Europe, and except for the Soviet Union, all these dictatorships were based on the ideas of order and authority of the extreme right. Six of the most solid democracies on the continent were invaded by the Nazis during the year after the civil war ended. Consequently, Spain was no exception, nor the only country in which the ideas of order and extreme Nationalism replaced those of democracy and revolution.

The two sides in Spain were so different from the point of view of ideas, of how they wanted to organise the State and society, and they were so committed to the objectives that led them to take up arms, that it was hard to come to an agreement. And the international context did not allow for negotiations either. Thus, the war ended with the crushing victory of the Nationalists, a victory that, from that moment onwards, was linked to all types of atrocity and violation of human rights. This exterminating violence had little in common with the repression and censorship used by the monarchist regime of Alfonso XIII or the dictatorship of Primo de Rivera. The dictatorships that emerged in Europe in the 1930s, in Germany, Austria or Spain, had to face mass opposition movements, and to contain them they needed to implement new instruments of terror. It was no longer enough to ban political parties, impose censorship or deny people their individual rights. A group of murderers had seized power. And the brutal reality that resulted from their decisions was killings, torture and concentration camps. The victory of Franco was also a victory for Hitler and Mussolini. And the defeat of the Republic was also a defeat for the democracies.

Why did the military rebels win the war? They had the best-trained troops in the Spanish army, economic power and the Catholic Church on their side, and with them, the winds of international sympathy blew their way. This was Spain as portrayed in the poster by Juan Antonio Morales, *Los Nacionales*, published by the republican government's Under-Secretary for Propaganda: a general, a bishop and a capitalist, with a swastika, a vulture and colonial troops in the background. They could not lose.

Glossary

Caciquismo: A word derived from 'cacique', the name denoting an Indian chief in the Spanish Empire. In the nineteenth century, and up to the Republic, it referred to the common organisation of social and political control, whereby the cacique controlled the elections and handed out favours to his political cronies.

Comités: In the towns and cities where the military uprising was unsuccessful or the military rebels were defeated, the workers' unions and parties set up *comités* under different categories (e.g. revolutionary, popular, war), whose task was to organise armed resistance and the new revolutionary order.

Nationalists: The name by which the officers who rose up in July 1936 defined themselves and by which General Franco's camp, opposing the republican or 'red' camp, came to be known.

Paseo (a walk): A euphemism for murder in the early months of the civil war, particularly in the summer of 1936. *Dar el paseo* (to take a walk) meant to seize the victim, murder him and leave him in a ditch, well, mineshaft or common grave.

Pronunciamiento: An official declaration by a group of army officers stating their opposition to the current government. This might develop into a coup d'état if it gains enough support from the rest of the army.

Rojos: Term used by the Nationalists to denote the enemy, whether they were republican, socialist, Communist or anarchist. As the Nationalists took more cities during the war, the term was used disrespectfully to denote all those on the republican side, in 'red' Spain, human beings with no right to live.

Saca (removal): Term used in the civil war to denote the operation of removing prisoners from gaol to murder them in the countryside, usually at night. There were *sacas* on both home fronts, but most occurred in November 1936 in the Madrid gaols, from where tens of thousands of officers and right-wingers were 'removed' and taken to Paracuellos del Jarama to be murdered.

Appendix 1: Leading figures

Azaña, Manuel (1880–1940): Intellectual, writer and main republican leader in the 1930s, Minister of War, Prime Minister (1931–33 and February–April 1936) and President of the Republic from May 1933. Crossed into France when the defeat of the Republic was imminent; resigned and died in Montauban in November 1940.

Franco, Francisco (1892–1975): An army general, he plotted and rose against the Republic and on 1 October 1936, his brother officers designated him head of the three branches of the armed forces, *Generalísimo*, and principal leader of Nationalist Spain against the Republic. He won the war and became dictator of Spain until his death on 20 November 1975.

Gil Robles, José María (1898–1980): Lawyer, Catholic politician and founder of the CEDA. An advocate of a corporative and authoritarian State, he was the Republic's Minister of War in 1935; he supported the military coup of 1936 and, once the war had started, Franco's cause, although from Portugal and without taking active part in the war.

Largo Caballero, Francisco (1869–1946): Principal leader of the Partido Socialista Obrero Español and its trade union organisation UGT, he was Minister of Labour (1931–1933) and wartime President of the Republic between September 1936 and May 1937.

Lerroux, Alejandro (1864–1949): Republican leader, he was part of the republican–socialist coalition which took power in April 1931, but broke with this coalition in December of that year, and was Prime Minister during 1934 and 1935, together with the non-republican rightist party CEDA. He took no part in the civil war.

Martínez Barrio, Diego (1883–1962): A republican leader, Prime Minister after the dismissal of Azaña in September 1933, he was Speaker of the Cortes in the spring of 1936 and throughout the civil war.

Mola, Emilio (1887–1937): An army general and principal organiser of the July 1936 uprising, which he coordinated under the alias of *El Director*. He accepted Franco as leader and died in a plane accident in June 1937.

Montseny, Federica (1905–1994): An anarchist leader, she was Minister of Health in Largo Caballero's government, between November 1936 and May 1937, thus becoming the first female minister in Spain's history.

Negrín, Juan (1892–1956): A socialist leader, distinguished Professor of Physiology in the University of Madrid, having studied in Leipzig, Germany. Leader of the republican government from May 1937 onwards, he preached discipline and order on the home front and resistance to the end.

'Pasionaria', Dolores Ibárruri (1895–1989): A Communist leader, she became famous during the civil war for her speeches defending the Republic and for her slogan *No pasarán*, when Franco's troops were trying to take Madrid in the autumn of 1936.

Serrano Suñer, Ramón (1901–2003): Leader of the Catholic right during the Republic, he managed to escape from prison in Madrid at the beginning of 1937 and became the principal champion of Fascism in the zone ruled by Francisco Franco, his brother-in-law. It was he who was responsible for organising a single party, *FET y de las JONS*, founded in April 1937.

Appendix 2: Political parties and organisations

Acción Española: A fundamentalist monarchist group, inspired by *Acción Francesa*.

Acción Nacional (Popular): A Catholic right organisation, founded after the proclamation of the Republic to defend 'Religion, Family, Order, Labour and Ownership'. It changed its name to *Acción Popular* in April 1932 and was the forerunner of the CEDA.

Acción Republicana: A left-wing republican group founded by Manuel Azaña in the 1920s, one of the Republic's governing parties during its first two years. In April 1934, it merged with other republican parties to form *Izquierda Republicana* (IR).

Comunión Tradicionalista: Carlist organisation, monarchist defenders of the Carlist wing, as opposed to the Bourbon supporters, at the time represented by Alfonso XIII.

Confederación Española de Derechas Autónomas (CEDA): A Catholic party set up in February 1933, led by José María Gil Robles. It was the first grass-roots right-wing party in the history of contemporary Spain, and its aim was to defend 'Christian civilisation' and fight republican legislation.

Confederación Nacional del Trabajo (CNT): A syndical organisation with anarchist influences, set up in 1910, which stood for direct action and anti-politicism, and which took firm root in the 1930s, particularly in Catalonia.

Esquerra Republicana de Catalunya: Republican left-wing party in Catalonia, led by Francesc Macià and then by Lluís Companys, who led the governments of the *Generalitat* after the granting of the Statute of Autonomy to Catalonia in September 1932.

Falange Española (y JONS; y Tradicionalista): A Fascist organisation founded by José Antonio Primo de Rivera, son of the military dictator, in October 1933. It merged with the JONS at the beginning of 1934 and was the single Francoist party from April 1937, with the name of FET-JONS.

Federación Anarquista Ibérica (FAI): Anarchist organisation set up in 1927 to safeguard the purity of the anarchist ideas of the CNT.

JAP: Youth wing of *Acción Popular*, radicalised during the Second Republic, which practised the cult of leadership (Gil Robles), mobilising young people with Fascist demonstrations.

Juntas de Ofensiva Nacional Sindicalista (JONS): Fascist organisation founded in October 1931 by Ramiro Ledesma Ramos and Onésimo Redondo, later merging with *Falange Española*.

Partido Comunista de España (PCE): Founded at the beginning of the 1920s, arising from a split with the PSOE, it was a minor party during the Republic, but began to have considerable influence in the republican zone during the civil war, as a consequence of the Soviet intervention.

Partido Nacionalista Vasco (PNV): A moderate nationalist party which claimed a Statute of Autonomy for the Basque Country, and which remained loyal to the Republic during the civil war.

Partido Obrero de Unificación Marxista (POUM): A Marxist organisation, set up in 1935, which fought Stalinism and was dissolved and persecuted following the events of 1937 in Barcelona. Its leader, Andreu Nin, was assassinated by agents of the Soviet secret services.

Partido Radical Republicano (PRR): The main republican party in Spain, set up at the beginning of the twentieth century by Alejandro Lerroux. It broke with the coalition of left-wing republicans and socialists in December 1931 and governed with the Catholic right in the second biennium of the Republic. It disappeared from the political scene a few months before the coup d'état of July 1936, following corruption scandals.

Partido Socialista Obrero Español (PSOE): Founded by Pablo Iglesias in 1879, it played a major political role during the Republic and the civil war. Its leader was Francisco Largo Caballero.

Partit Socialista Unificat de Catalunya (PSUC): A Communist party set up at the beginning of the civil war, which dominated the home front in Catalonia from May 1937.

Renovación Española (RE): A monarchist group formed by right-wing politicians who left *Acción Popular* to defend a new, Catholic and corporative State. Its leader was José Calvo Sotelo, assassinated a few days before the military coup of July 1936.

Unión General de Trabajadores (UGT): A syndical organisation, dependent on the PSOE, set up in 1888, and led in the 1930s by Francisco Largo Caballero. Its largest section during the 1930s was the *Federación Nacional de Trabajadores de la Tierra* (National Federation of Land Workers).

Index